Good Food from
Morocco

Also by Paula Wolfert

Mediterranean Food
The Cooking of South-West France

Good Food from Morocco

PAULA WOLFERT

Drawings by Sidonie Coryn

Concerning the spices of Arabia let no more be said. The whole country is scented with them, and exhales an odour marvellously sweet

– Herodotus

JOHN MURRAY

To Bill Bayer

This revised edition first published 1989
by John Murray (Publishers) Ltd
50 Albemarle Street
London W1X 4BD

This book was first published as *Couscous and Other Good Food from Morocco* in the United States
of America by Harper & Row Publishers, Inc. 1973, 1987

British Library Cataloguing in Publication Data
Wolfert, Paula
Good food fromMorocco.
1. Food: Moroccan dishes—Recipes
I. Good food from Morocco. Title
641.5964

ISBN (cased) 0 7195 4601 X
(paperback) 0 7195

Printed and Bound in Great Britain by
Butler & Tanner Ltd, Frome and London

Contents

Illustrations

Preface

THE MOMENT the Yugoslav freighter touched at Casablanca in 1959 I boarded a bus and rushed to Marrakesh, in search of the adventurous and exotic life. I felt immediately that I belonged in this country, and have never forgotten that feeling – I am still enchanted by all things Moroccan.

I lived in Morocco two years, then went on to Paris, where I spent eight years plotting ways to return.

Morocco is the only place I know where there is nothing that I do not love: the music, the great Berber city of Marrakesh, the long sandy coast, Tangier. I love the oases of the pre-Sahara, Fez in the early morning, the *souks* of the *bled* (countryside), the landscape that changes every hundred kilometres, and the Moroccans themselves, whose simplicity and hospitality always touch me and fill me, whenever I am away from them, with nostalgia and a deep longing to return.

And then, too, I love the food. For me it is one of the world's great cuisines, but one that is, unfortunately, hardly known outside North Africa. Even in Paris, what passes for Moroccan food is very disappointing. For these reasons I finally decided, after years of cooking Moroccan dishes, to write a cookery book and reveal all I knew.

But as I began to work, I realized how little that was – there were so many mysteries, so many variations, so many good cooks I could never meet. Soon I changed my mind about writing a definitive work – that seemed an absurd and pretentious task for a foreigner – and, besides, I knew it would take a lifetime to complete.

So this book is not a comprehensive study of Moroccan cookery: rather it is about the 'good food' of Morocco, the Moroccan food I like the best. My criteria for including recipes changed, too: it was no longer a question of finding a recipe for every Moroccan dish, but of finding or developing a good recipe for every dish that I felt tasted good.

Many people have helped on this adventure. I owe my greatest thanks to Consul General Abdeslam Jaidi and his

American wife, Janet, and to his mother, Khadija Jaidi, in whose Moroccan kitchen I learned so much.

I also want to thank many others who contributed to this book:

Khadija and Mehdi Bennouna of Tetuán and Rabat; Taleb Jouarhri of Fez; Touria Serraj of the Morrocan Ministry of Tourism; Majoubi and Miriam Ahardan of Oulmes and Rabat; Jaffa El Glaoui of Marrakesh; Abdelaziz Lairini of Tangier; Hadj Mohammed Liludi of Rabat; Fama El Khatib of Tetuán; Alqoh M'hamed, caid of Itzer; Paul Bowles, the writer and the American best versed in Moroccan things; Abouchita Hajouji of Fez; Zohra Lahlimi Alami of Safi; Lydia Weiller of Tangier and New York; James Skelton of Marrakesh; the Minister of Tourism, His Excellency Abderrahmen El Kouhen; Taïeb Amara, Pasha of Safi; M. Ben Gabrit, Pasha of Chaouen; Aziza Benchekroun of Tetuán; Abdelhakim El Bahid, caid of Tineghir; Alan Lapidus of New York; John Hopkins of Marrakesh; Frances McCullough, my editor at Harper & Row; H. Lemdeghri Alaoui, Pasha of Essaouira; Omar Kadir, Mina Kallamni, Rakia Nadi, Corinna Scariot, Fatima ben Lahsen Riffi, Fatima Drissiya – all equally fine cooks; my mother, Frieda Harris, who helped test many recipes; and my husband Bill Bayer, who tasted everything, travelled with me in Morocco and shared my excitement in its making.

Important Notes
to the Cook

A MOROCCAN cookbook written for people outside North Africa by definition alone must be a form of adaptation. Though I have painstakingly tried to reproduce the authentic flavours of Morocco in these recipes, it has been difficult in some instances to give more than a glimmer of their original tastes, due to the special Moroccan methods of cooking. The cooks I met had no food processors or other electrical equipment. Onions were grated, parsley pounded. I have altered these methods to fit into the western kitchen and its capabilities, using high oven temperatures to replace glazing under hot coals, cooking times allowing just enough time for tenderer European meat and poultry, to cook to perfection (i.e., 'falling off the bones' or meat that separates easily from the bone). Where a special pot or implement is required I have described it. I assume the obvious kitchen knives, forks, wooden spoons, and so on, will be at hand when you start to cook.

A note about pronunciation: I have not included a guide because words differ, sometimes dramatically from region to region. I have chosen the most widely used pronunciation and given a *phonetic* transcription. I beg those who may ever be embarrassed by mispronouncing a Moroccan dish to accept my apologies.

CHAPTER 1

Moroccan Food

THERE ARE PEOPLE, alas, who do not like Moroccan food. More than a century ago one Edmondo de Amicis had 'a dreadful experience' in Tangier. He wrote: 'The Arab dishes, objects of our intense curiosity, began to circulate. I tasted the first with simple faith. Great Heaven! My first impulse was to attack the cook.'

I have met people who have tasted *couscous* at some '*couscous* joint' in Paris and were unimpressed, or who ordered a 'Moroccan speciality' at a Moroccan hotel and were served a *tagine* (a stew) consisting mainly of grease. At the Parisian '*couscous* joint' they were undoubtedly served the Algerian version of that great dish, undeniably robust but about as delicate as a fiery curry. And the friends who suffered at the Moroccan hotel endured an infuriating and disgraceful situation: with less than half a dozen exceptions there is no fine Moroccan restaurant in Morocco; in fact, in the gastronomic capital of Fez it is nearly impossible to find a restaurant that serves even half-way decent Moroccan food.

But those fortunate ones who have dined at a Moroccan home, or attended a Moroccan *diffa* (banquet), know what the others have missed. Moroccan food is great, by any definition of that word. It may be last of the great 'undiscovered' cuisines – a situation I hope this book will remedy.

There are at least four Moroccan dishes (and probably many more) that can be compared, without exaggeration, to such great and unique specialities as the sukiyaki of Japan, Peking duck, bouillabaisse, and paella Valenciana.

First there is *couscous*, the Moroccan national dish, which has been called one of the dozen greatest dishes in the world. I have included here recipes for seventeen versions of Moroccan *couscous* and descriptions of many more. Imagine a platter piled high with fine, light, tender, delicate grains of wheat flour that have been steamed over the broth of a delicately and exotically spiced chicken or lamb and vegetable stew. The grains are served along with the vegetables and meat, and doused with its delicious gravy.

1

Imagine, too, *bisteeya*, (sometimes called *bistayla* or *pastilla*) or *bstilla* or *bastella*, the most sophisticated and elaborate Moroccan dish, a combination of incredibly tasty flavours representing the culmination of all the foreign influences that have found their synthesis in Moroccan culture. *Bisteeya* is a huge pie of the finest, thinnest, flakiest pastry in the world, filled with three layers – spicy pieces of pigeon or chicken, lemony eggs cooked in a savoury onion sauce, and toasted and sweetened almonds – and then dusted on top with cinnamon and sugar.

And then there is *mechoui*, the Berber version of roasted lamb. The entire animal is roasted on a spit after the meat has been rubbed with garlic and ground cumin. When cooked the lamb is fully crisped on the outside, and so tender inside that you can eat it easily with your fingers – which is the way Moroccans eat.

Or take *djej emshmel*, (also called *meshmel* and *emsharmel*, depending on the region), one of the four versions of the famous Moroccan chicken, lemon, and olive *tagine*. The chickens are slowly simmered with soft, luscious olives and tart, preserved lemons in a silken sauce seasoned with saffron, cumin, ginger, and paprika. Like *mechoui*, the final result is meat that can easily be eaten with the fingers.

I could go on, could describe the delights of shad (alose) stuffed with dates; spiced balls of minced lamb simmered in a seasoned tomato sauce in which, at the last minute, eggs have been poached; *djej mefenned*, braised chicken covered, at the very end, with a delicate coating of eggs; a rich stew of lamb, prunes, and sesame seeds that looks, when served, like a starry night; chickens and squabs stuffed with *couscous* grains and honey and nuts; Moroccan brochettes; the infinite graces and refreshing tastes of Moroccan salads; 'gazelles' horns', crescent-shaped pastries filled with cinnamon-flavoured almond paste; and *m'hanncha* (also known as 'the snake'), a sublime coil of stuffed and browned pastry. The list is endless, I have described only the beginning. What about fresh green barley sprouts grilled with wild herbs and served with cold buttermilk? What about fish simmered with tomatoes and green peppers on a bed of celery or fennel stalks? What about the rich *harira* soup of chick-peas, vegetables, lemon, eggs and myriad spices? What about courgettes and tomatoes stuffed with delicately spiced minced meats? All these are part of the extraordinary Moroccan cuisine, and there are many more.

The Prerequisites for a Great Cuisine

To my mind four things are necessary before a nation can develop a great cuisine. The first is an abundance of fine ingredients – a rich land. The second is a variety of cultural influences: the history of the nation, including its domination by foreign powers, and the culinary secrets it has brought back from its own imperialist adventures. Third, a great civilization – if a country has not had its day in the sun, its cuisine will probably not be great; great food and a great civilization go together. Last, the existence of a refined palace life – without royal kitchens, without a Versailles or a Forbidden City of Peking, without, in short, the demands of a cultivated court – the imaginations of a nation's cooks will not be challenged.

Morocco, fortunately, is blessed with all four. In its ever-changing landscape and geographical situation are riches that rival those of France. Situated in the north-west corner of Africa, only a few miles across the straits from Europe, with a Mediterranean coast and an Atlantic coast, with green fertile agricultural belts, five mountain ranges, and encompassing areas of desert, Morocco has every type of environment except tropical jungle. In this small but highly variegated space some of the finest raw ingredients may be found. There are the mint, olives, and quinces of Meknes; the oranges and lemons of Fez and Agadir; the pomegranates of Marrakesh; the almonds, lamb, and *za'atar* of the Souss; the dates of Erfoud; the shad of the Sebou River; rosebuds from the Valley of Dades; walnuts, chestnuts, from the Rif; Barbary figs, also known as prickly pears, from the region of Casablanca; the honey of Tagoundaft; the barley of the Dra; the cherries of Sefrou; the melons of the Doukkala; the fish caught by the men of Essaouira; the seafood collected by the men of Safi; and the spices that for thousands of years have been brought to this country, first by Phoenicians, then by Senegalese traders and caravans that crossed North Africa from Arabia, the Sudan, and the Middle East. It is all there – Morocco is, literally, a land of milk and honey.

3

As for cultural influences, there have been an enormous number. The indigenous culture is Berber, and Berbers still constitute a good 80 per cent of the people. (Berbers are not Arabs; ethnically they are Hamites with a suspected Nordic strain (according to C. G. Seligman, in *Races of Africa*) but they embrace Islam, and it is in fact this common religion that holds the country together.)

In 683 Morocco was invaded by Arabs in what the painter-writer Brion Gysin has so aptly called 'The Damascus Thrust.' An Arabian conqueror named Ogba ben Nafi reached Morocco in that year, and his invasion was followed by other waves of Arabs bringing the religion of Islam and the cultural influence of Arabia and the Middle East.

The Arabs, as everyone knows, went on to conquer Spain. Their Spanish empire, known as the Andaluz, founded in AD 711, produced a great and delicate culture, less strong in terms of military might than the kingdom of Morocco, but perhaps more graceful, excelling in such refinements as the art of courtly love and magnificent architectural feats. (Some of the greatest buildings in Morocco, the Koutoubia Mosque in Marrakesh, for example, were designed by Andalusian architects.) For centuries there was cultural exchange between Morocco and Muslim Spain; their reciprocal influences were perhaps as great as the original influence of their Arabian invaders.

Each of the great dynasties of Morocco – the Almoravides, the Almohades, the Merinides, the Saadians, and the Ala-ouites – included, at one time or another, kings whose power went far beyond the borders of present-day Morocco. Idriss II, the son of an Arabian shrif, founded Fez in the ninth century, and for hundreds of years that city was known as a centre of Arab culture. The Almoravides, whose king Yusuf ibn-Tashfin (1061–1106) founded the city of Marrakesh, possessed an empire that encompassed half of Spain, more than half of Algeria, and extended as far south as Senegal. The Saadians were powerful as far south as Timbuktu, and Moulay Ismail (1672–1727), the man who built Meknes, was highly regarded by Louis XIV, with whom he exchanged many letters, including pleas that *Le Roi Soleil* convert to Islam.

Morocco, on account of the invasions of Arabs and the exterior adventures of Moorish kings, was strongly influenced by Middle Eastern culture and the culture of the Andaluz. The Arabs learned culinary secrets from the Persians and brought them to Morocco; from Senegal and other lands south of the Sahara came caravans of spices. North African conquest did not penetrate Moroccan territory, their cultural influence was felt within its borders.

From a culinary point of view these cultural influences can be seen quite well in the three gastronomic centres of the land. In the Berber city of Marrakesh the food is basically Berber, with a Senegalese and African influence. In the Arab city of Fez the cuisine shows the influence of the Andaluz. And in the Andalusian city of Tetuán the Spanish influence is strongest, with some Ottoman traces. Portuguese influence may be found in the cuisine of the Portuguese settlement cities on the Atlantic coast, and here Essaouira, a city of white buildings and blue shutters, became the home of a large Jewish population who worked out their own variations on the national cuisine. The Moroccans picked up tea-drinking from the British traders; and the French, from the forty-four years (1912–1956) of their protectorate, left behind some Gallic touches. There are indeed an enormous number of outside influences – the African spice meets the Andalusian chick-pea, the Saharan date confronts Middle Eastern pastry, Berber butter competes with Spanish oil – and then all merge to become Moroccan food.

The greatness of Moroccan culture? This nation had its day when its influence radiated thousands of miles from Fez, a city that was pre-eminent in theology, astronomy, medicine, mathematics, and metallurgy when Europe was deep in the Middle Ages. Fez was an Athens, a city of enormous vitality and refinement, and Moroccan knowledge of agriculture and irrigation (Marrakesh is basically a huge grove of palms, an enormous man-made oasis) made Spain flourish. In fact, after the fall of Granada and the final explusion of the Moslems from Spain in 1492, Spanish agriculture began to suffer a reversal.

The high culture of Fez was developed in parallel with the rich folk culture that had strong Berber origins: that mad charge of horsemen known as the *fantasia*; Berber trance-dancing; the great Berber pilgrimages (*moussems*), which are today important tourist attractions; folk music and poetry; and the basic cuisine of the mountains and plains.

This cuisine would certainly be worthy of attention even at its present level, but, as developed in the kitchens of the royal palaces of Fez, Meknes, Marrakesh, and Rabat (the four Royal cities), it reached summits of perfection. The Moroccan dynasties always originated in powerful warlike tribes, whose leaders, as soon as they obtained power, were quickly refined. Thus the Saadians, who came from the pre-Saharan Valley of the Dra, were transformed from primitive tribesmen into regal monarchs, their tombs in Marrakesh being among the most lavishly decorated in all Morocco. (The garden of these tombs, by the way, is filled with a glorious aroma, the result of high, thick hedges of rosemary.) In the same way, in our own time Thami el Glaoui, whose power rivalled and sometimes exceeded the power of the sultan, was transformed from a feudal warlord of the High Atlas stronghold of Telouet, into the pasha of Marrakesh; friend of Winston Churchill, he dealt with premiers and presidents of France, and moved, in the latter half of his long, ruthless, and now generally discredited life, in the most civilised and refined international circles.

These monarchs and lords, as soon as they learned to entertain in regal style, began to make great demands upon their chefs to produce some of the great cosmopolitan specialities of Morocco. A case in point is *bisteeya*, which had humble origins in a simple Berber dish of chicken cooked with saffron and butter. It was combined with the primitive Arab pastry called *trid*, enhanced when later Arabs brought the fine art of Persian pastry making to Morocco, and was further embellished with Andalusian ideas until it became the *bisteeya* we know today.

People still speak with awe of the food served in the king's house. One hears rumours of 'mounds of pigeons' each differently stuffed, flowing to diners on golden platters and then being whisked away, only to be replaced by equally luxurious foods. Meknes, a royal city conceived like Versailles as a place devoted to court life, was where much of modern Moroccan cooking reached its final form.

Moroccan Cooking – A Shared Heritage

Unlike her American or French counterpart, a young Moroccan girl, recently married, cannot go to a bookshop and find a text that will teach her how to cook. This cuisine has not been codified; there is no Moroccan culinary establishment, no Moroccan equivalent of the Cordon Bleu. The cuisine developed in the kitchens of the palaces is found throughout the land in less luxurious forms.

It is not surprising that nearly all Moroccan cooks are women, for cooking is considered a woman's work, and a Moroccan wife spends much of her time preparing food. The cooking knowledge that is passed from mother to daughter, mother-in-law to daughter-in-law, is also shared in another way. When a family feasts, the female relatives and neighbours will come and help with the work. This constant cross-fertilisation, this sharing of culinary knowledge, has kept the culinary art alive in a country where the number of literate people is extremely low. A person who cannot read or write, who cannot note things down or find knowledge in books, must develop their memory to an extraordinary degree.

The Philosophy of Abundance

Arab hospitality is legendary – an embarrassment of riches, total satisfaction, abundance as an end in itself and as a point of pride for the host. At a Moroccan *diffa* (banquet) so much food is served that you can't imagine who is expected to eat it. Dish after dish is offered, each piled high. After a few bites, if there are many courses – and at a grand *diffa* there can easily be as many as a dozen – these platters will be whisked away. To puritans like us this may all seem vulgar, ostentatious, showy, and chauvinistic. To Moroccans it is the essential requisite of a feast.

At my first few *diffas* I worried about these barely touched, high-piled platters going to waste. Later I learned the truth, that not a speck of them would be wasted, for the kitchen was filled with people – women, children, relatives, servants – all of whom would finish off every crumb.

Moroccans have large, healthy appetites; perhaps it takes them longer to achieve that state of total satisfaction which they call *shaban*. The fact that after an entrée of *bisteeya* or an array of salads, or both, a *mechoui*, a succession of *tagines* (chicken, lamb, and fish), and an enormous platter of *couscous*, there still remains a dessert of fruits and nuts to be devoured and then some glasses of mint tea to be drunks strikes many foreigners as decadently lavish. But even in a poor house such an abundance of culinary riches can be presented when the occasion warrants, because the vegetables vastly outweigh the meat in *tagines*; the sauce is always what counts, and the lack of expensive ingredients goes unnoticed.

Nineteenth-century foreign travellers to Morocco have described some incredible dinners. Walter Harris, a correspondent for *The Times* around the turn of the century, wrote of a dinner in Marrakesh at which he was served with seventy-seven different dishes (he selected only fifteen to try). A certain Dr Leared, who wrote a book entitled *A Visit to the Court of Marocco* [*sic*], told of a dinner given by the Prime Minister at which he was served thirty dishes of meat and poultry, twelve salads, and thirty-two sweet-meats.

Here is an extremely verbose description from a nineteenth-century book about Moroccan cuisine that may give some notion of the Moroccan sense of culinary abundance. It is from George D. Cowan, and L. N. Johnston, *Moorish Lotus Leaves* (London, 1883). These same writers, whose love of the literary flourish often exceeds my desire to read their prose, describe *couscous* thus: 'The mere sound of the syllables is musical, with a sweet sibilance, suggestive of two kisses united to the coo of the turtle-dove and the note of the cuckoo.'

> Now the Moorish paradise is a glutton's dream. Its soil, of whitest wheaten flour, is irrigated by rivulets of milk and wine and honey. The musical branches of the immeasurable tuba tree, which adorns the celestial palace-garden of the Prophet of Islam, are laden with exquisite fruits, and ready-dressed banquets of thrice a hundred courses, in golden dishes, such as the Slave of the Lamp served up to Aladdin. In short the haven of the Moor is an elysium wrought out of a pastry-cook's shop and a harem where the existence of the blessed will be one eternal 'guzzling-bee,' somewhat similar to Sydney Smith's description of the future state of beatified epicures – 'the eating of *pâtés de foie gras* to the sound of trumpets.' No wonder therefore that the Moor's *summum bonum* here and hereafter is repose and abundance.

Moroccan hospitality is notorious for its flourishes and sweet suffusion, well conveyed in this nineteenth-century dinner invitation quoted in Budgett Meakin's *The Moors* (London, 1902).

To my gracious master, my respected lord.... This evening, please God, when the King of the army of stars, the sun of the worlds, will turn towards the realm of shades and place his foot in the stirrup of speed, thou art besought to lighten us with the dazzling rays of thy face, rivalled only by the sun. Thy arrival, like a spring breeze, will dissapate the dark night of solitude and isolation.

After sending out an invitation like that the host was virtually obliged to serve a great succession of exquisite courses.

I have noted that the Moroccan banquet bears a curious and striking resemblance to the Chinese. First, the dining process is communal – many people crowd around a circular table and serve themselves from central dishes. In China the last dish before dessert is always rice; in Morocco it is *couscous*, another and perhaps more fanciful grain. In both countries the number of courses can be high, and it is a point of pride for the host to offer his guests as many different things as he can. Each cuisine plays games with its diners' palates, playing off salty against sweet against spicy, and varying the textures of successively offered dishes so that the diner will experience a full range of culinary pleasures. Each also ends its meals with what is basically a ceremony of tea.

There is another resemblance in the actual cooking process, discussed more fully in Chapter 6; the pastry for *bisteeya*, called *warka*, is made precisely the same as the dough for Chinese spring rolls – a method of pastry-making unique to these two regions of the world. But the two cuisines differ in their basic ways of preparing food. The key to the preparation of a Moroccan *tagine* (stew) with its spices and accompanying vegetables and fruits is long, slow simmering in a shallow, glazed earthenware pot. In the city of Tetuán there is a saying that food should be cooked until it is 'standing in the sauce'. The great amount of spices naturally gives Moroccan food a piquant flavour, but not, usually, a spicy-hot one. Your tongue and lips will not be burned, as they would be by the hotter types of Chinese food, such as Szechuan, or those from India or Korea.

An old book on Andalusian cooking describes this process so well that it might well be describing the Moroccan *tagine*-simmering method itself:

The philosophy of the Spanish [i.e. Moroccan] cuisine is strictly oriental – it is the stew or pilaf. The *prima materia* on which the artist is to operate is quite secondary; scarcity of wood and ignorance of coal prevent roasting; accordingly *sauce* is everything; this may be defined to be unctuous, rich, savory, and highly spiced.... (Richard Ford, *Handbook for Travellers in Spain*, London, 1845.)

How to Eat Moroccan Food

With the exception of *couscous* (which is *sometimes* eaten with a spoon) Moroccans eat with the first three fingers of their right hands. This is in the tradition of the Arabs, who always, before they dine, go through an elaborate hand-washing process. At a Moroccan dinner a servant or a young member of the family assists each diner by holding a basin beneath his hands, pouring water over them, and then offering him a towel from an extended arm.

Bread is very important in Moroccan dining, both as food and as an implement for grasping hold of meat or vegetables, swirling them in the gravy of a *tagine*, and then transporting them to the mouth. Moroccan bread, being highly absorbent, is also ideal for sopping up the savoury juices.

Bryan Clarke, in his book *Berber Village*, describes the folklore of eating with the fingers: 'To eat with one finger is a sign of hatred; to eat with two shows pride; to eat with three accords with the Prophet; to eat with four or five is a sign of gluttony.'

Though *couscous* is occasionally eaten with a spoon, any self-respecting Moroccan will eat his national dish with his fingers – a difficult process for an unschooled foreign visitor. A nineteenth-century travel writer described this process miraculously well:

> With the points of the fingers of the right hand a portion of grains is drawn towards the side of the dish. It is fingered as the keys of a pianoforte till it gathers together; it is then taken up into the hand, shaken, pressed till it adheres, moulded till it becomes a ball; tossed up and worked till it is perfect, and then shot by the thumb, like a marble, into the open mouth. (David Urquhart, *Pillars of Hercules*, London, 1848.)

However, such delicacy has not always been observed. A very old book entitled *Account of Barbary*, published in 1713, contains the following passage:

> When he (the Sultan) is intent upon a piece of work, or eager to have it finished, he won't allow himself to go to his meals, but orders some of his

eunuchs or negroes to bring him a dish of kuscoussoo [*couscous*], which he sits down and eats after a brutish manner; for as soon as he has rolled up the sleeves of his shirt, he thrusts his arms into the dish up to his elbows, and bringing a handful from the bottom he fills his mouth, and then throws the rest into the dish again, and so on till he is satisfied.

A Moroccan meal is best eaten in a traditional dining room, which also doubles for receptions. The walls are lined with luxuriously cushioned divans and a circular table is set up in a corner. After the meal, for the serving and drinking of mint tea, the diners will spread out and lounge on the divans so they can stretch their legs.

Some Moroccan families cover their table with a piece of opaque plastic and simply throw bones and other inedible bits on to the table. Afterwards the servants simply roll up this plastic sheet – bones, garbage, and all – and carry it away.

All of this may sound barbaric – no pun intended on the word Berber, from which the word 'barbarian' originally comes – but it is actually an extremely sensible way to eat, ranking with Chinese chopsticks and Indian hands and fingers, and opposed to the decadence of using all sorts of silver utensils. I find that Moroccan food always tastes better when eaten Moroccan style – the contact between fingers and a hot *tagine*, fingers and a crisp *bisteeya*, fingers and a tender *mechoui*, always adds to the pleasure – and I urge everyone to eat a Moroccan dinner this way. It is sensible, too, in that there will be far fewer dishes to wash, since the cooking vessels (earthenware *tagine slaouis*) double as serving platters and communal plates.

I also urge everyone to make Moroccan bread. It is not at all difficult (see page 44), enhances Moroccan food enormously, and makes eating with the fingers a pleasure.

Moroccan Regional Specialities

Moroccan food is more or less homogeneous; the country is unified, and its cuisine is distinct, even from the other two countries of the Maghreb, Algeria and Tunisia. But, like all countries with great cuisines, Morocco has its regional specialities.

The three great gastronomic capitals, Fez, Tetuán and Marrakesh, have developed their own variations of particular

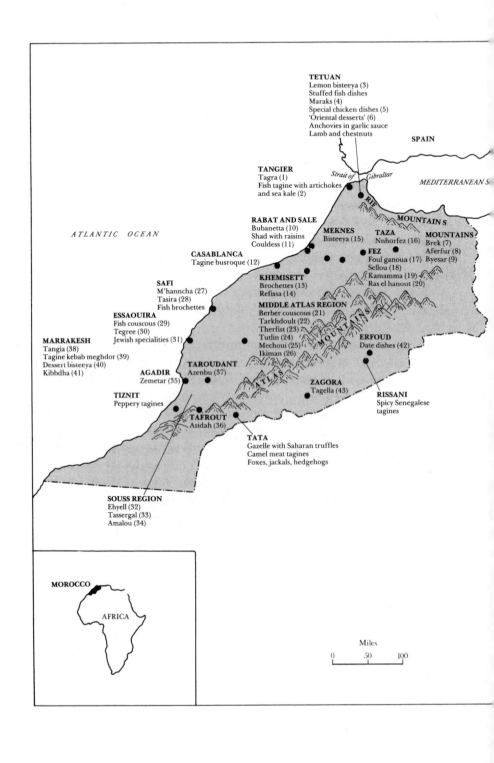

TETUAN
Lemon bisteeya (3)
Stuffed fish dishes
Maraks (4)
Special chicken dishes (5)
'Oriental desserts' (6)
Anchovies in garlic sauce
Lamb and chestnuts

SPAIN

Strait of Gibraltar

MEDITERRANEAN S

TANGIER
Tagra (1)
Fish tagine with artichokes
and sea kale (2)

ATLANTIC OCEAN

RIF MOUNTAINS

RABAT AND SALE
Bubanetta (10)
Shad with raisins
Couldess (11)

MEKNES
Bisteeya (15)

TAZA
Nnhorfez (16)

MOUNTAINS
Brek (7)
Aferfur (8)
Byesar (9)

CASABLANCA
Tagine busroque (12)

FEZ
Foul ganoua (17)
Sellou (18)

Kamamma (19)
Ras el hanout (20)

SAFI
M'hanncha (27)
Tasira (28)
Fish brochettes

KHEMISETT
Brochettes (13)
Refissa (14)

MIDDLE ATLAS REGION
Berber couscous (21)
Tarkhdoult (22)
Therfist (23)
Tutlin (24)
Mechoui (25)
Ikiman (26)

ATLAS MOUNTAINS

ERFOUD
Date dishes (42)

ESSAOUIRA
Fish couscous (29)
Tegree (30)
Jewish specialities (31)

MARRAKESH
Tangia (38)
Tagine kebab meghdor (39)
Dessert bisteeya (40)
Kibbdha (41)

AGADIR
Zemetar (35)

TAROUDANT
Azenbu (37)

ZAGORA
Tagella (43)

RISSANI
Spicy Senegalese
tagines

TIZNIT
Peppery tagines

TAFROUT
Asidah (36)

TATA
Gazelle with Saharan truffles
Camel meat tagines
Foxes, jackals, hedgehogs

SOUSS REGION
Ehyell (32)
Tassergal (33)
Amalou (34)

MOROCCO

AFRICA

Miles
0   50   100

1. Tagra, a dish of fish, tomatoes, and paprika oil.
2. Fish tagine with artichokes and sea kale, a wild herb found near Tangier.
3. Lemon bisteeya (see recipe page 87.)
4. Maraks, vegetable tagines (see recipes pages 71-75.)
5. Special chicken dishes-that is, chicken stuffed with celery and onions; chicken stuffed with bakoola (a wild herb); chicken with quinces, honey, ambergris, aga wood, and so on. (See page 150 for a list of fifty Tetuanese chicken dishes.)
6. 'Oriental desserts,' which show a Turkish influence; Ktaif, mulhalabya, taba, and so on (see recipes pages 235-236.)
7. Brek, the Riffian word for the North African brik. (See recipe page 100.)
8. Aferfur, a couscous made with sorgo.
9. Byesar, a soupy puree of favas eaten with green onions.
10. Bubanetta, a sausage made of innards.
11. Couldess, a form of dried salted lamb.
12. Tagine busroque, a tagine of mussels.
13. Brochettes of Khemisett. The economy of this town seems to depend upon the sale of brochettes to travellers on the Rabat-Meknes-Fez road. The main street is nothing but one brochette stand after another.
14. Refissa, a Berber tagine of biscuits soaked in bouillon with onions, salt, and pepper.
15. Bisteeya is served every where in Morocco, but the bisteeya of Meknes is as highly regarded as that of its rival, Fez.
16. Nnhorfez, a tagine of turnips.
17. Foul ganoua, a dish of Guinean lentils.
18. Sellou, a special dessert served at weddings, made of flour, grilled sesame seeds, fried almonds, and smen.
19. Kamamma, a tagine of lamb or chicken with layers of onions and tomatoes.
20. The ras el hanout of Fez is quite famous, and may be purchased there in brut form.
21. Berber couscous made with barley. (See recipe page 128.)
22. Tarkhdoult, a bisteeya of meat made by Berbers.
23. Therfist, Berber unleavened bread.
24. Tutlin, a Berber version of liver brochettes covered with sheep's caul and served with salt.
25. Mechoui, Berber-style roasted lamb. (Served throughout Morocco, but best at a Berber moussem, or pilgrimage.)
26. Ikiman, a form of cooked wheat.
27. M'hanncha, a coiled pastry stuffed with almond paste and prepared with a glazed honey coating.
28. Tasira, a dish of conger eel, raisins, onions, and cinnamon.
29. Fish couscous, also called baddaz bil hut.
30. Tegree, a dish of dried and spiced mussels.
31. Jewish specialities, among the many of which are sweet meatballs served with couscous, and braewats stuffed with fish.
32. Ehyell, a tiny bird unique to the Souss, served with raisins and onions and said to be delicious.
33. Tassergal, an especially delicious bluefish caught off this coast, which in season people come from far away to eat.
34. Amalou, a great speciality of the Souss, made with honey, almonds, and the oil extracted from the nuts of the argan tree after they have been expectorated by goats.
35. Zemetar, made of wheat germ, honey and argan oil, and served as a cereal.
36. Asidah, a kind of corn porridge.
37. Azenbu, a special Berber couscous of barley shoots grilled with wild herbs then steamed and buttered. Traditionally accompanied by a glass of cold buttermilk.
38. Tangia, a lamb stew, made with garlic and cumin and lots of oil. (There is a story in Marrakesh about a man who made tangia by mixing pieces of lamb with the meat of hedgehog. He sent it to a community oven to bake, and when he came to fetch it it wasn't there. The baker claimed innocence but the man was angry and took him before the caid. The baker could not explain why there was no tagine in his oven until it came out during the hearing that the man had mixed his lamb with hedgehog. 'Ah ha,' said the baker to the caid, 'that explains everything. The lamb and the hedgehog obviously started a fight, broke the pot and escaped.' The caid forgave the baker, and the man who had dared to mix these irreconcilable meats went home hungry.)
39. Tagine kebab meghdor, a delicious Marrakesh speciality in which previously grilled lamb is stewed in a spiced butter sauce. (See recipe page 191.)
40. Dessert bisteeya. (See recipe page 260.)
41. Kibbdha, a liver salad. (See recipe page 70.)
42. There are more than thirty varieties of dates grown in the oasis of Erfoud. Needless to say, the people of Erfoud have many ways of serving them.
43. Tagella, the bread eaten by the Tuaregs, cooked on hot stones.

dishes, as well as some dishes that are special and unique. And considering its modest size, Essaouira must also be thought of as a great city of food, as, to a lesser degree, should Tangier, Safi, and Rabat. But it is in the regions of Morocco – the Rif Mountains of the north; the Middle Atlas area, which is totally Berber; the Souss in the south-west; and the pre-Sahara – that one finds the most spectacular differences and inventions in food.

I have not included recipes for all the regional specialities indicated on the map on pages 12–13, but have listed them anyway for the culinary adventurer or adventuress who may travel to some of these places and find an opportunity to eat them. One opportunity, accessible to all, may occur on a Berber *moussem*; foreign visitors are welcome at many of these pilgrimages (including the famous *moussem* of Imilchil), and if you should get to one you will be able to eat some marvellous food in the tents.

The pre-Sahara and the outlying oases are a little harder to get to than Fez or Marrakesh, but they are among the most fascinating places in Morocco, and anyone who has the chance should visit them. In the farthest reaches, wandering Arab tribesmen not only eat camel, but also gazelle and hedgehogs, jackals and desert foxes, which they serve with simple, flat loaves of bread made from Indian millet, wheat, or barley. In some parts of Morocco there is even a bread made with locusts.

The people of the Souss are hard working, and they have huge appetites. There is a tree that grows only in their area, the argan, that produces a nut from which a delicious oil is extracted and then used in various foods. The 'hamburger' of the Souss is *asidah*, a pyramid of maize flour mush served in a wide, shallow wooden dish with a knob of fresh butter on top. Here, too, you may have a chance to eat the famous bluefish, or the tiny, delicious bird called the *ehyell*.

Kimia

Finally, a word about one of the most mysterious things in Morocco a – land, by the way, that according to many of its inhabitants is inhabited by numerous spirits and supernatural powers – a kind of magic called *kimia*. *Kimia*, according to those who know, is the power to multiply food. Thus a person with *kimia* can live on very little; if a man has some *couscous* and *kimia* he can presumably multiply his *couscous* into as much of that grain as he will need in his lifetime, and even into everything else he needs to eat. If you have *kimia*, you must not call attention to your poverty or else your power of multiplication may be lost. *Kimia* is something very personal, something that lies between the person who has it and the universe.

CHAPTER 2

The Souks

I FIND modern supermarkets seductive – everything is in its place, well-lighted and under one roof, the prices are clearly marked, and I can do my shopping in a few minutes. But I am not seduced, for I miss the chaos of Moroccan *souks*, the endless haggling, the crush of people, the freshly harvested goods so lovingly displayed, the squawks of live poultry, the spice stalls choked with fabulous seasonings and all sorts of dried insects and rare barks alleged to have magical properties.

The Moroccan word *souk* literally means 'market,' a place where anything is bought and sold. In cities there is an old, walled *medina*, the section devoted to market stalls is called the *souiqua*. Here, if you have lived in the city for a while, you will know exactly where to make the best deal on a belt, a barrel of olives, a chair, or a screwdriver.

In Fez, for instance, where the *medina* is perhaps the world's most complicated maze, each street seems to have its own trade, and only a born-and-bred Fassi can find his way about. Every time I've gone into the *medina* of Fez in search of some cooking utensil or some special spice, I've lost my way, had an adventure, and somehow emerged more or less intact, usually with the item I originally wanted to buy, plus, always, many things more.

In Marrakesh, too – where, on the other hand, the maze is less complicated – I've never failed to see something, some inexplicable bit of street action or some inscrutable sight, that has kept me puzzled for days. In these great cities the Moroccans have a life style that is endlessly fascinating, and often very difficult to penetrate and understand.

The country *souks* are marvellous, too, and on one trip I was struck again by the honesty of the Berber people. I drove with Madame Jaidi, who had kindly consented to let me work in the kitchen of her traditional Moroccan home, to the little *souk* of Tiflet in the Middle Atlas in search of some thick country honey. It was a hot day, we were both tired, and since the *souk* was built on a hillside we asked a young Berber man if he would help us. We explained what we wanted, he said he knew a good place to buy, we gave him money, and he disappeared into the crowd. I wandered around, and then, after an hour, when he failed to reappear and we were all set to drive away, he came running down the hill carrying a can of honey and our precise change. Why had it taken him an hour? Because, he explained, that was how long it took him to negotiate a good price. The honey, of course, was delicious, as country food usually is.

In the oasis of Goulimine there is a *souk* devoted entirely to camels. I once spent a morning there watching the furious trading on a flat piece of beige, stony earth, where the camels looked more sure of themselves than the young men who waited in line to consult a medicine man. The haggling over the camels was ferocious, but the medical interviews were grave, with much sympathetic nodding of the head and the inevitable finale, when the medicine man dispensed, no matter what the ailment, a pink packet of French aspirins. I didn't buy a camel, of course, but that may have been the one time I visited a *souk* and returned empty-handed.

Everything Moroccan that I own is combined in my mind with the story of how I bought it, including my favourite rug, which I bought for ten dollars in the town of Chichaoua, where it looked like a flame against the countryside, the people's clothing, the tents, and everything else. In Morocco shopping is an intricate process in which the pleasure and the adventure are forever part of your memory.

Shopping is a crucial matter when it comes to preparing good food, too. Though an absolutely delicious chicken with lemons and olives should, ideally, be made with Moroccan olives, preserved Moroccan *doqq* (a fragrant lemon especially amenable to salt preservation) and Moroccan chickens raised in the Moroccan style and butchered the Moroccan way, it is still possible to make a sublime version of this dish with materials that are available elsewhere. The trick, of course, is to shop carefully, to buy always for quality, to use organically grown vegetables if possible, and to settle for nothing less than the finest spices.

That is what this chapter is about: turning the markets of your town into *souks*, searching out the best purveyors of meat, vegetables, spices and fish, buying carefully and selectively so that you can make delicious Moroccan food. Any of the special ingredients you need for my recipes can be bought from ethnic shops. Do take the trouble – a Moroccan dish may have a totally different flavour if a crucial aromatic is left out. But in the end most of my recipes do not involve the purchase of exotic materials. Moroccan food is basically made of humble things: lamb shins and chickens, tomatoes and parsley, butter and olives. But they must be well bought, and thus these notes on spices, herbs and aromatics, fragrant waters, olives, oil, butter, eggs, honey, *couscous*, chick-peas, and utensils, with some recipes thrown in for the preparation of some of the basic components – such things as preserved lemons, *smen*, *ras el hanout*, hot *harissa* sauce and 'coriander water.'

———— ••• ————

SPICES, HERBS, AND AROMATICS

Wandering among the spice stalls in a great city like Fez, seeing myriad spices displayed in huge bags, small boxes, and glass jars with cork stoppers, the visitor is struck by the idea that the Moroccans have fallen in love with every spice in the world. In fact, this love of spices is in the tradition of their ancestors, who brought with them, on their great sweep across North Africa from Arabia, a sophisticated knowledge of their use in perfumes and medicines, for the enhancement of food, and as currency for trade. Since biblical times spices have been a symbol of luxurious living in the Middle East, and the earliest practitioners of the spice trade – the ancient Phoenicians, who were among the first foreigners to visit Morocco – began something that the Arabs have embellished and made into a way of life. The caravans that crossed the desert, and brought aromatics to people who treasured them like gold, became one of the economic pillars of the Arabian empire. The Moors taught the Spaniards the value of spices, and thus disposed them to finance the spice-seeking voyages of Christopher Columbus.

There is a widespread misapprehension about spices – the idea that they are used by people in poor nations to cover up the bad taste of decomposing food. The corollary of this belief is that 'pure' foods like grilled steak represent some sort of cultural and culinary advance. In fact this is not true at all: spices are used in countries in Morocco and India not to cover up but to *enhance* the taste of food. Cooks in these countries have a deep understanding of how spices should be used. Displaying none of our fearful calculation with measuring spoons and scales, they toss them into food with an apparent abandon that reflects a precise awareness of how far they can go without overwhelming a dish. While we are sometimes in awe of spices and use them conservatively, they are lavish with them and yet never push them too far.

Spices cannot help a tomato that has the texture of cardboard, or resuscitate rotten meat, or do much to improve the taste of a chicken so fattened by hormones that it has lost all traces of flavour. Spices can be used to *stretch* the taste of foods, to push them to a certain point without destroying or breaking up their individual flavours.

——— •• ———

THE TEN IMPORTANT SPICES

In Moroccan cooking there are ten important spices that are used over and over again; they appear frequently in recipes, and the prospective cook should always have them on hand: cinnamon, cumin, saffron, turmeric, ginger, black pepper, cayenne, paprika, aniseed, and sesame seeds.

CINNAMON: There are two kinds, Ceylon cinnamon (*Cinnamomum zeylanicum*), called *dar el cini* in Morocco, which is light tan and delicate; and cassia cinnamon (*Cinnamomum lauri*), called *karju* in Morocco, which has a stronger taste than the Sri Lankan variety and a little less delicacy of flavour. Cinnamon is used frequently in Moroccan food, as a final dusting in a Berber *harira* soup, in salads, *bisteeya*, *kdras*, *couscous* dishes, and desserts.

CUMIN (*Cuminum cyminum*), called *kamoon* in Morocco. This is one of the indispensable spices. Used frequently in fish and chicken dishes, brochettes, and *mechoui*, it is a most important component for minced meat dishes (*kefta*). Cumin seeds smell like old hay, but when they are ground in a mortar the released aroma is sensational. They are grown all along the North African coast and also in Mexico, where the taste is the same but the aroma is different.

SAFFRON (*Crocus sativus*), called *zafrane* in Morocco. A very small amount of saffron can totally change the aroma and colour of a dish, and, happily, only a small amount is ever needed, since saffron is the most expensive spice. To harvest one ounce you need to raise more than five thousand crocus flowers, each of which supplies only three tiny stigmas. The collection of the crocus stigmas was once a speciality of Moroccan Jews.

Saffron threads should be brittle before being pulverised, or else some of their potency will be lost and too bitter a taste imparted. To make them brittle, place them on a plate set over a pan of boiling water or dry in a warm oven. After ten minutes or so, pulverise them in a mortar. A pinch or two is all that will be needed. Some Moroccan recipes call for 'saffron water.' To make saffron water soak $\frac{1}{4}$ teaspoon pulverised saffron threads in a few tablespoons of *hot* water. Saffron water will keep about a week in a refrigerator if covered. If a recipe calls for a pinch of pulverised saffron you can use 2 tablespoons of saffron water instead.

TURMERIC (*Curcuma longa*), called *quekoum* in Morocco. Turmeric comes from the root of a tropical plant of the ginger family, and has a clean, bitter taste. In Moroccan cooking it is sometimes mixed with saffron for reasons of taste and economy. The soup called Harira (page 49) always contains a spoonful.

GINGER (*Zingiber officinale*), called *skinjbir* in Morocco. Ginger has a sweet, peppery flavour and is often used in Moroccan cooking, especially (along with black pepper) in *tagines* and all dishes with a *makalli* sauce.

BLACK PEPPER (*Piper nigrum*), known in Morocco as *elbezar*. This spice, so familiar and so good, is always added early in the cooking of Moroccan food so its coarse taste has time to mellow.

CAYENNE (*Capsicum frutescens*), known as *felfla soudaniya* in Morocco. This yellow-orange coloured spice is used mostly in southern Morocco, where many dishes reflect Senegalese influence.

PAPRIKA (*Capsicum annuum*), known in Morocco as *felfla hlouwa*. Though Hungarian paprikas are the best in the world, Spanish paprika is quite good and the most commonly used variety in Morocco. It appears in Moroccan salads, vegetable *tagines*, *kefta*, virtually all the tomato dishes (except the ones that use cinnamon and honey), and in the indispensable fish marinade known as Charmoula (page 142). Brown paprika is the poorest quality, but one cannot trust bright red purely on sight, since it has often been coloured with

20

cochenille. The only way to check the quality of paprika is to open up a jar and smell and taste it.

A paprika mixture called *felfla harra* (sharp and aromatic peppers), made up of equal parts of sharp paprika, cayenne, and ground long peppers, is used in some fish dishes, dishes that feature lentils, and in *khboz bishemar*, which I call Marrakesh 'Pizza' (page 46).

Paprika doesn't keep well, so I suggest you buy it in small amounts, and store it in a screw-top jar in a dark, cool place.

ANISEED (*Pimpinella anisum*), known in Morocco as *nafaa* or *habbt hlawa*. There are many types, but the best is the green aniseed from Spain, which has a strong, warm flavour. Aniseed is fragrant and tastes like liquorice; it is used in Moroccan bread, and some preparations of fish.

SESAME SEEDS (*Sesamum indicum*), known in Morocco as *jinjelan*. Sesame seeds are cultivated in Morocco and also in the Far East as the source of an important oil. They are used in Moroccan bread and desserts, and when toasted they are a popular garnish for chicken and lamb *tagines*.

———— •••• ————

NINE SECONDARY AROMATICS

These flavourings – allspice, caraway, cloves, coriander seeds, gum arabic, fenugreek, liquorice, honey dates, and orris root – are used much less frequently than the ten important spices, and need not be kept on hand unless you choose to make the one or two recipes in which some of them appear. Others are described here simply as curiosities.

ALLSPICE (*Pimenta officinalis*), called *noioura* in Morocco. This reddish-brown berry, with its special taste that combines the flavours of cloves, nutmeg, and cinnamon, is sometimes used in chicken dishes, in old recipes for *couscous*, in some varieties of *kefta*, and in a *bisteeya* made in Fez.

CARAWAY (*Carum carvi*), called *karwiya* in Morocco. Caraway grows in great abundance in the Rehamma Plain between Casablanca and Marrakesh. It is not used very often, but appears with garlic in Harissa Sauce (page 26), and in the famous dish called *boubbouche*, where it joins twelve or fifteen other aromatics in good quantity.

CLOVES (*Eugenia caryophyllata*), called *oud el nouar* in Morocco. Rarely used in Morocco, though it appears in some *couscous* recipes more than a century old.

CORIANDER SEEDS (*Coriandrum sativum*), called *kosbur* in Morocco and not to be confused with the herb, green coriander, which grows from these seeds, has a different taste, and is used frequently in Morocco. Coriander seeds are used very infrequently, but when they are it is with great vigour – for example in *mechoui* (Roasted Lamb, page 188), when they are rubbed with garlic and cumin into the lamb flesh, and in the preserved meat called Khelea (page 37).

GUM ARABIC (*Acacia arabica*), known as *mska* in Morocco. This has a strong scent and I love it, especially in almond paste, where I think it can make a decisive difference. It is most popular in Marrakesh pastries and as a flavouring for water; it also turns up in an unusual recipe for scrambled eggs (page 49).

FENUGREEK (*Trigonella foenum-graecum*), known as *helbah* in Morocco. It grows in Morocco and is used by the Berbers in the flat bread called *therfist*. Fenugreek has no taste unless heated, and then it tastes a little like burnt sugar and smells a little like celery. It is very difficult to pound into powder, but is favoured anyway by Berbers, who believe this spice makes women pleasingly plump – which is the way they like them.

LIQUORICE (*Glycyrrhiza glabra*), called *arksous* in Morocco. Used in the famous snail dish, *boubbouche*, and also in a recipe for squid.

HONEY DATES (*Rhamnus zizphys*), called *nabka* in Morocco. This reddish, shiny, sweet-tasting fruit-seasoning is found in central Morocco, and occasionally turns up in a lamb *tagine*.

ORRIS ROOT (*Iris germanica*), called *amber el door* in Morocco. When these off-white rhizomes are roasted they taste a little like coffee, and when they are sucked they sweeten the breath.

——— •••• ———

Ras el Hanout

Ras el hanout, which means, literally, 'top of the shop', seems to fascinate everyone, foreigners and Moroccans alike. It is a very old mixture of many spices, sometimes ten, sometimes nineteen, sometimes twenty-six; Moroccans have told me of a *ras el hanout* that contained more than a hundred ingredients.

It is incorrect to think of *ras el hanout* as curry powder by another name. It lacks the abundance of fenugreek, coriander seeds, mustard seeds, poppy seeds, and cumin of commercial curry. Though theoretically almost anything is permissible in *ras el hanout* – even dried garlic and saffron – obviously some mixtures are better than others. The aphrodisiacs (Spanish fly, ash berries, and monk's pepper) that appear in most formulae seem to be the reason why the mere mention of this mixture will put a gleam into a Moroccan cook's eye.

Ras el hanout is used in Moroccan game dishes; in *mrouzia* (Lamb Tagine with Raisins, Almonds, and Honey, page 231), a sweet lamb dish; in various rice and *couscous* stuffings; and even in some recipes for *bisteeya*. I bought a packet in the Attarine quarter of Fez, where it is sold in *brut* form, and, after a long analysis, a friend in New York who is a spice importer and I came up with the list of ingredients, printed on page 271.

With a Moroccan girl who lives in New York, I worked out a formula for *ras el hanout* that obviously lacks some of the rare Moroccan items like cubebe peppers and the aphrodisiacs. Nevertheless, it's a pretty good approximation.

Try to make it yourself if you want; your blender will undoubtedly survive all these nuts, sticks, barks, and seeds, but the aroma will linger on – *ras el hanout* is *strong*. (Follow with a separate grinding of cane sugar and your blender will be clear and clean).

4 whole nutmegs	1 tablespoon white peppercorns
10 rosebuds	2 pieces galingale
12 cinnamon sticks	2 tablespoons whole ginger root
12 blades mace	6 cloves
1 teaspoon aniseed	24 allspice berries
8 pieces turmeric	20 white or green cardamom
2 small pieces orris root	pods
2 dried cayenne peppers	4 wild (black) cardamom pods
$\frac{1}{2}$ teaspoon lavender	

A rather simple recipe for *ras el hanout* – although far less thrilling to make or use – can be made with the following formula (buying in ounces from a spice merchant and grinding at home):

Makes about 2½ tablespoons

1 teaspoon cumin seeds
1 teaspoon ground ginger
1¼ teaspoons coriander seeds
1½ teaspoons black peppercorns
¼ teaspoon cayenne pepper

4 whole cloves
6 allspice berries
6 blades cinnamon (about 1½ teaspoons ground cinnamon)

Combine the spices in an electric spice grinder or blender. Sieve and bottle carefully to preserve the freshness.

Ras el hanout can also be bought ready-made in some specialist shops.

──────── •∙• ────────

HERBS

There are nine important herbs in Moroccan cooking: onions, garlic, parsley, green coriander, basil, marjoram, grey verbena, mint, and *za'atar*.

ONIONS (*Allium cepa*), called *sla* in Morocco. Most commonly used in Moroccan cookery, and the one I recommend, is the Spanish onion. Onions are used in great quantity in these recipes, so I recommend that you buy the biggest ones you can find and save yourself a lot of unnecessary peeling.

Sweet red onions are used with tomatoes in Moroccan salads, and their fat spring onions, are delicious in chicken *tagines*.

GARLIC (*Allium sativum*), called *tourma* in Morocco. Moroccan garlic cloves are smaller than ours and pink, but they should not be confused with red garlic, which is milky and chewable. Quite surprisingly garlic is often used in honeyed dishes, where it helps to balance out the flavours.

PARSLEY (*Petroselinum crispum*), called *madnouss* in Morocco. Moroccans use the flat-leaved Italian variety, which is a little milder than ours. You may be surprised at the large amounts – sometimes several cupfuls – that go into *tagines*, but in the end the flavours balance out and the dishes become vitamin-rich.

GREEN CORIANDER (*Coriandrum sativum*), called *kosbour* in Morocco. Coriander is readily available in city ethnic shops and is also easy to grow. You'll need plenty of it, as it is one of the most important Moroccan herbs and is what gives many *tagines* their special flavour.

If you find a regular supply of coriander a problem, I suggest three different ways of preserving it.

1 Keep it in the refrigerator in an air-tight plastic container (1 week to 10 days).

2 Clean it, chop it, salt it and freeze it. Many people do this and then scoop out a piece whenever they need some for a recipe. My own experience is that, despite freezing, coriander stored this way sometimes rots.

3 Make 'coriander water' – and I think this method is the best. 'Coriander water' will work in all the recipes in this book that call for green coriander except the salads, where the coriander leaves *must* be fresh. To make 'coriander water' cut off and discard half the stalks. Wash the leaves well and chop them coarsely. In a blender purée 3 handfuls of tightly packed leaves with cold water. Place in an ice tray and freeze into cubes. When frozen, separate the cubes and pack in a plastic bag. Each cube of 'coriander water' or 'coriander ice' is equivalent to 2 tablespoons of chopped green coriander.

BASIL (*Ocimum basilicum*), called *hboq* in Morocco. Not used in cooking, but I've been told it is used in Moroccan tea. In his books about spices John Parry tells of the superstition that a person will be bitten by scorpions on the same day that he has eaten basil. I find this fascinating, since Moroccan families keep a few pots of basil in their houses to ward off insects.

MARJORAM (*Origanum majorana*), called *mrdeddouch* in Morocco. This is a very common herb in Middle Eastern cooking, but the Moroccans use it less frequently than the Greeks or Syrians. It is found in some recipes for *kefta*, in the snail dish called *boubbouche*, and most often in tea. It is also used as a cure for bronchitis, in a drink of hot milk and sugar.

GREY VERBENA (*Lippia citriodore*), called *louisa* in Morocco. It is used by Moroccans in tea, which it gives a slightly bittersweet taste. Also said to have medicinal qualities.

MINT (*Mentha viridis*), called *nana* in Morocco. This, of course, is

25

the foundation for Moroccan mint sea. Spearmint is best, but any good, fresh, bunch of mint will do. The purple-tinged stalks are considered best.

ZA'ATAR (*Origanum cyriacum*). *Za'atar* is a sort of hybrid of thyme-marjoram–oregano. Use any of these three commonly available herbs or mix them and substitute for *za'atar* when called for in a recipe. Do not confuse it with the mixture of thyme and sumac that is sold as *za'atar* in some Middle Eastern markets.

——— •••• ———

FRAGRANT WATERS

The Moroccans use both orange-flower water and rosewater in cakes, confections, certain *tagines*, and salads, and also for perfuming themselves after dining. You can buy both in Middle Eastern food shops, imported from either Lebanon or France. (I prefer the French water – it is cheaper and more aromatic).

In Morocco, of course, the fragrant waters are often homemade. Arabs invented the process of distilling, and their *alambic* or *quettara* stills are basically the same as the distilling apparatus found in a modern chemical laboratory.

Orange-flower water, called *zhaar* in Morocco, is usually made from the flowers of the Bergamot orange tree, and rosewater, called *ma ward*, is made from rosebuds collected in the Valley of Dades and sold in the *souks* by the kilo from enormous baskets. It takes seven pounds of rosebuds or orange blossom to make a gallon of fragrant water.

Both fragrant waters are used throughout Morocco, but there seems to be a preference for rosewater in Marrakesh and for orange-flower water in Fez.

Harissa Sauce

This popular sauce is served along with many salads, mixed with olives, and, when thinned with a little oil and lemon juice, is sometimes used to flavour brochettes and *couscous*.

You can buy tinned *harissa* paste imported from Tunisia, or substitute the Indonesian spice paste called *sambal oelek*. Or, if you want, you can make your own. When refrigerated, *harissa* keeps 2 to 3 months. It is also available in powdered form.

30 g (1 oz) dried red chilli peppers	salt to taste
1 clove garlic	olive oil

Cover the peppers with hot water and soak for 1 hour, then drain and cut into small pieces. Place in the mortar or spice mill and pound or grind to a purée with the garlic. Sprinkle with a little salt, then spoon into the jar and cover with a layer of olive oil. Cover tightly and refrigerate.

Preserved Lemons

Preserved lemons, sold loose in the *souks*, are one of the indispensable ingredients of Moroccan cooking, used in fragrant lamb and vegetable *tagines*, recipes for chicken with lemons and olives, and salads. Their unique pickled taste and special silken texture cannot be duplicated with fresh lemon or lime juice, despite what some food writers have said. In Morocco they are made with a mixture of fragrant-skinned *doqq* and tart *boussera* lemons.

Moroccan Jews have a slightly different procedure for pickling, which involves the use of olive oil, but this recipe, which includes optional herbs (in the manner of Safi), will produce a true Moroccan preserved-lemon taste.

The important thing in preserving lemons is to be certain they are completely covered with salted lemon juice. With my recipe you can use the lemon juice over and over again. (As a matter of fact, I keep a jar of used pickling juice in the kitchen, and when I make Bloody Marys or salad dressings and have half a lemon left over, I toss it into the jar and let it marinate with the rest.) Use wooden utensils to remove lemons as needed.

Sometimes you will see a sort of lacy, white substance clinging to preserved lemons in their jar; it is perfectly harmless, but should be rinsed off for aesthetic reasons just before the lemons are used. Preserved lemons are rinsed, in any case, to rid them of their salty taste. Cook with both pulps and rind, if desired.

To make preserved lemons:

5 lemons
70g (2½oz) salt, more if desired

Optional Safi mixture:
1 cinnamon stick
3 cloves

5 to 6 coriander seeds
3 to 4 black peppercorns
1 bay leaf
freshly squeezed lemon juice, if
   necessary

1 If you wish to soften the peel, soak the lemons in lukewarm water for 3 days, changing the water daily.

2 Quarter the lemons from the top to within 1cm (½″) of the bottom, sprinkle salt on the exposed flesh, then reshape the fruit.

3 Place 1 tablespoon salt on the bottom of a preserving jar. Pack in the lemons and push them down, adding more salt, and the optional spices, between layers. Press the lemons down to release their juices and to make room for the remaining lemons. (If the juice released from the squashed fruit does not cover them, add freshly squeezed lemon juice – *not* chemically produced lemon juice and *not* water. According to the late Michael Field, the way to extract the maximum amount of juice from a lemon is to boil it in water for 2 or 3 minutes and allow it to cool before squeezing.) Leave some air space before sealing the jar.

4 Let the lemons mature in a warm place, for 30 days, shaking the jar each day to distribute the salt and juice.

To use, rinse the lemons as needed under running water, removing and discarding the pulp, if desired – and there is no need to refrigerate after opening though a layer of olive oil will keep them fresh. Preserved lemons will keep up to a year, and the pickling juice can be used two or three times over the course of a year.

———— ••• ————

Aziza Benchekroun's Five-Day Preserved Lemons

If you run out of preserved lemons, or decide at a few days' notice to cook a chicken, lamb, or fish dish with lemons and olives and need preserved lemons in a hurry, you can use this quick five-day method taught to me by a Moroccan diplomat's wife. Lemons preserved in this way will not keep, but are perfectly acceptable in an emergency.

With a razor blade, make 8 fine 4 cm (2″) vertical incisions around the peel of each lemon to be used. (Do not cut deeper than the membrane that protects the pulp.) Place the incised lemons in a stainless-steel saucepan with plenty of salt and water and cover and boil until the peel becomes very soft. Place in a clean jar, cover with cooled cooking liquor, and leave to pickle for approximately 5 days.

——— •• ———

OLIVES

There are stalls that sell nothing but olives – olives of every flavour, size, quality, and colour. An olive's colour depends upon the moment in the ripening cycle that it is picked. As it ripens on the tree it turns from pale green to green-tan to tan-violet to violet-red to deep winy red to reddish black and finally to coal black. After that it loses its glistening appearance and begins to shrivel in the sun.

A freshly picked olive is inedible; it must be pickled or cured, and the way this is done will determine whether it is tart, bitter, salty, lemony or sweet. There are other variables that affect its final flavour – the size of its stone, its shape, its meatiness, and the conditions of the soil and the climate.

Basically, three types of olives are used in Moroccan cooking: unripened green, cracked or whole olives for salads and such dishes as *meslalla*, where they literally 'smother' the chicken (or lamb or fish); ripe 'midway' olives ranging in hue from green-tan through violet and winy red, used in chicken or lamb *tagines* with lemon and olives and similar fish *tagines*; and salt-cured, shrivelled black olives used in Moroccan salads.

GREEN, CRACKED OLIVES: One type of green olive used in the 'smothering' dishes is so unripe when the olives are picked that they must be soaked in a strong brine to draw out their bitterness. In Morocco these olives are then cracked with a rock hard enough to open the flesh but not enough to break the stone. After seven changes of salted brine the bitterness seeps out and a sharp, tangy taste develops inside. Then lemon juice is added to improve the flavour.

Green, cracked olives bottled in brine are readily available. To use them in Moroccan cooking you must wash, drain, and boil them at least three times to get rid of excessive bitterness. To use them in salads you must also stone them and then marinate them for a few hours in a sauce that contains lemon juice, a clove or two of slightly crushed garlic, some chopped fresh herbs (parsley and green coriander), paprika and cumin in a ratio of 2 to 1, cayenne, and salt to taste. I can't give a precise recipe because the amounts depend on the type of olive. Use a small olive.

RIPE OR 'MIDWAY' OLIVES: These can be green, but the best ones are tan, russet, violet, or deep purple. I particularly recommend Italian Gaetas and Greek Kalamatas, and I have had excellent luck with Greek Royal-Victorias, which are a little more pungent. You can even use the enormous brown Alfonsos from Spain, but I suggest you stay clear of Italian colossals and Spanish and American ripe green olives – though excellent for eating, they just don't seem to work in Moroccan *tagines*.

You don't have to do anything to these ripe olives except rinse them before adding them to the pot. If you buy them in bulk from barrels, drain them and then store in a solution of the juice of 3 lemons, 225ml (scant $\frac{1}{2}$ pint) olive oil, a little salt, and sufficient water to cover for 2 kg ($4\frac{1}{2}$ lbs) olives. I am advised by fastidious Moroccans that under no circumstances should you reach into this brine; they claim that fingers will spoil the brine and that the olives must be removed with a spoon.

CURED BLACK OLIVES: These are readily available, and as a matter of fact the salt-cured, shrivelled olives sold under the house name of a famous Italian food packager are actually from Morocco. In the olive stalls you often find these olives either partially coated or totally covered with the hot relish called *harissa*.

———— •••• ————

OIL

Many Moroccans cook their *tagines* with amounts of oil that are unacceptable to other tastes. I have reduced the quantities of oil to acceptable limits, but leaving enough so that the *tagines* will properly bind. For those who cannot take oil at all it can be reduced further or the *tagine* can be skimmed before serving.

There are some dishes (with tomatoes and other vegetables) in which all liquid is cooked away until only oil is left in the pan. This procedure follows a principle of Moroccan cooking: the vegetables, having been thoroughly stewed, are allowed, in the final minutes, to fry, producing a firmer texture and a crisper taste.

Salad, vegetable, or peanut (arachide) oil is used mainly for cooking, and olive oil for cold dishes such as salads. One of the best oils is home-made by Berbers, who extract it from unripened green olives. When scented with wild thyme this green olive oil is exquisite.

A hundred years ago a particular method of cooking with oil was widely prevalent, but it is now confined to a few pigeon and game bird dishes. The bird, often fully stuffed, is plunged into a pot of terrifically hot oil, searing it instantly and sealing the juices inside. The pot is removed from the fire and allowed to cool, and then cooking continues at a simmer. The oil itself – with a few spoonfuls of water and more butter and some spices – becomes the sauce!

In the Souss region (the south-west), the people often cook with an oil extracted from the nuts of the argan tree, (*Argania sideroxylon*) a plant unique to that region and famous for its attractiveness to goats, who literally climb up into its branches. Argan oil can be mixed with almond paste and honey (fresh walnut oil may be the closest available substitute) to make a delicious almond butter called *amalou*, or kneaded with grilled wheat germ and honey to make a breakfast gruel called *zematar*.

———— •• ————

Amalou

225 g (½lb) blanched almonds
salad oil
8 tablespoons French walnut oil

½ teaspoon salt
4 tablespoons thick honey

An adaptation for the Moroccan *amalou* can be made with fine French walnut oil.

Brown the almonds in a little hot salad oil. Drain and pulverise them in a blender with the walnut oil and the salt. When the mixture is smooth and creamy, spoon the honey into a blender jar and continue blending for 20 seconds. Pour the *amalou* into a stoneware jar and store in a cool place. *Amalou* is spread on Moroccan bread or fried breads.

———— •••• ————

MILK PRODUCTS

Zebda, Leben, Smen
(*Country-Fresh Butter, Buttermilk, and Preserved Butter*)

Moroccan *zebda* (a kind of fresh country butter) is extremely pungent, but should not be confused with the even more potent *smen* (a form of preserved butter that is prepared like the Indian butter-oil called *ghee*), or the rancid butter called *boudra*.

Zebda is made by leaving fresh milk in an earthenware jug for two or three days and allowing it to 'turn' naturally. It is then poured into an earthenware churn called a *khabia*, which though never washed is kept very clean and only used for this purpose. The naturally cultured milk is churned until the butter particles separate out and the liquid turns to buttermilk (*leben*). In southern Morocco the churning is done inside a goatskin bag slung between trees. A woman swings it until she hears splashing sounds inside that tell her that the butter has separated from the milk. *Zebda* is used for cooking, and also to make the infamous *smen*.

Leben, or buttermilk, is much appreciated by Moroccan Berbers, who use it as a thirst-quencher, and often down it with a plate of cold barley *couscous* or broad beans buttered with *zebda*. Since commercial buttermilk (which *is* different) isn't at all bad, I recommend that you serve it with these Berber dishes.

As for *smen*, it was the *bête noire* of the early travel writers, particularly the British, who time and again referred to it as 'rancid' 'foul-smelling,' and so on, and told harrowing tales of how they were forced, at the risk of appearing rude, to eat it for breakfast with their Moroccan hosts. Unfortunately its terrible reputation has continued to this day, and at its very mention some people will retch and indicate their repulsion with all sorts of sour exclamations and expressions.

My first experience with *smen* came on one of my earliest trips to the pre-Saharan area. Taking the road south from Tiznit we turned off onto a trail in search of Targhist, one of the most beautiful and least known of the Moroccan oases. We finally stumbled into town with two flat tyres, and though there was no garage some people found a boy who knew how to fix bicycle tyres and he patched us up. We met a man who worked in Ifni and who spoke Spanish, and he and his wife invited us to join them and their ten children for lunch. On the table was a giant slab of *smen* that had been made with strange wild herbs gathered from the surrounding desert. I thought it was one of the most delicious things I had ever tasted.

I have since learned to make *smen* with unsalted fresh butter and easily obtainable herbs; it can be used for cooking, and gives a marvellous flavour to *couscous*:

———— •●• ————

Herbed Smen

salt	marjoram, and thyme
4 tablespoons oregano or a combination of oregano,	450 g (1 lb) very fresh unsalted butter

1 Boil a small handful of salt and the oregano leaves in 900 ml (1½ pints) water. Strain into a shallow bowl and allow to cool.

2 When the blackened 'oregano water' has cooled to the point where it will no longer melt butter, add the butter, cut up into pieces, and knead until it has the consistency of mashed potatoes, pressing the mixture again and again against the bottom of the bowl so that every bit has been thoroughly washed. Drain the butter and then squeeze to extract excess water. Knead into a ball, place in a sterile glass container, and cover tightly.

3 Keep the container in a cool place (not the refrigerator) for at least 30 days before using. Once it has been opened, store in the refrigerator, where it will keep for 1 to 2 months longer.

In Safi I have tasted *smen* made by washing the butter with water containing cinnamon, ground coriander seeds, and other pickling spices. Of course in the *bled*, or countryside, one finds some extremely potent *smens*. Some Berbers cook it, salt it, and bury it in the ground in earthenware jugs for a year, after which it comes up tasting something like Gorgonzola cheese. The rich people of Fez (the Fassis) are the keepers of legendary quantities of *smen*, stored away in secret caches in the cellars of their magnificent homes, and brought out on rare occasions in all its pungent, dark-brown glory, to be sniffed by honoured guests.

Here is another recipe for *smen*, no doubt not to be compared to what may be found in the basements of the Fassis, but nevertheless Moroccan in flavour, nutty on account of the cooking of the butter, and more practical than the herbal *smen* because it will keep much longer.

Cooked and Salted Butter
(Smen)

It is traditional to add a small spoonful of this to soups, and to mix a few tablespoons with *couscous* grains before serving. It is also excellent in *kdras*.

450 g (1 lb) unsalted butter, cut
up

1 tablespoon coarse salt

1 Melt the butter over moderate heat, stirring frequently to avoid colouring it. Bring to a boil, lower the heat and simmer, undisturbed, for 45 minutes, or until the butter is clear and the solids on the bottom are light brown.
2 Spoon the clear liquid into a cheesecloth-lined strainer, and to keep the *smen* from turning rancid, repeat the straining; the *smen* must be absolutely clear. Discard the milk solids in the saucepan.
3 Stir in the salt, then pour the liquid butter into a sterile glass container, cover, and store in a cool place or in the refrigerator.
Note: This will keep a long time, six months or longer.

Moroccan 'Yogurt'
(Raipe)

Raipe is a type of sweetened junket or 'yogurt' in which the milk thickens and 'firms up' on account of a most unusual ingredient: the hairy centres, or 'chokes,' of wild Moroccan artichokes. Unfortunately these wild artichokes, called *coques* (*Cynara humilis*) by the Moroccans, are not available here, but if you get to Morocco and find ten or so of them you should not hesitate to let the chokes dry in the sun, bring them home, and make *raipe* – it's simple to prepare and absolutely delicious.

10 *coques* or wild artichokes
1.8 litre (3 pints) fresh milk
6 tablespoons granulated sugar,

more or less, to taste
4–8 tablespoons orange-flower
water to taste

1 Break off the outer leaves of the *coques* and trim carefully – they are very spiky. Remove the base and set the chokes aside. (If desired, let the chokes dry in the sun for a few days, then crumble them and pack them in a cheesecloth bag.)

2 Heat the milk, with the sugar, to lukewarm.

3 Pound the hairy chokes to a pulp in a mortar. Wrap the pulp in cheesecloth and swirl around in the lukewarm milk, then gently squeeze the bag to extract all the brown juice. Remove and discard the bag, and stir the orange-flower water into the milk. Cover and leave in a warm place for 1 to 1½ hours, until set. Serve cool or chilled in cups.

——— •••• ———

EGGS

In country *souks* one finds fresh eggs packed in reed baskets, each one nestled in a bit of straw. When a Moroccan buys an egg he holds it up to the light: if it is translucent he knows that it is absolutely fresh.

Eggs are sold hard-boiled on the streets. The hungry stroller shells them, then dips them in a mixture of salt and ground cumin.

Often a Moroccan will dip a hard-boiled egg into saffron-tinted water, slice it, and then fry the slices as for one Fez version of *tafaya* (lamb cooked with spices, almonds, and decorated with saffron-coloured eggs). Sometimes he will hard-boil eggs all night in a meat and bean casserole, as in the Jewish speciality called Sefrina (page 217); this long simmering turns the whites to a soft brown and gives the yolks a creamy texture.

In Morocco eggs are often treated differently than they are here. For example, we try very hard to keep our eggs from curdling, but curdled eggs are ideal for the most famous Moroccan dish, *bisteeya*. They are deliberately beaten with lemon juice to encourage curds when boiled; otherwise they become stringy and leathery inside the pastry. Other dishes that require curdled eggs are *briouats* (page 99) (eggs, onions, and lemon wrapped in pastry leaves and then fried) and *masquid bil beid* (pieces of chicken set within layers of curdled eggs and a spicy sauce).

36

One of the best family dishes in Moroccan cuisine is a preparation of eggs poached in a spicy tomato sauce with *kefta* (meatballs), or in a buttery onion sauce with cubed lamb.

Every country has its own versions of the omelette, and all the Mediterranean countries have a method of cooking eggs in a frying-pan with potatoes and onions or other vegetables. Among such dishes the Moroccan *khboz bil beid* is a *ne plus ultra*: it is made with potatoes, parsley, cumin, paprika, and cubes of bread and is garnished with olives and preserved lemon. At the other end of the scale I hear there is an omelette filled with bits of locust!

Eggs are often used to glaze stuffed vegetables, and one of the great *tours de force* of the Moroccan kitchen is *djej mefenned* (Chicken Braised and Browned and Coated with Eggs, page 172).

———— •••• ————

MOROCCAN PRESERVED MEAT (KHELEA)

Khelea, a preserved beef that bears a close resemblance to the *confits* of south-west France, is usually prepared in Moroccan homes during the summer months, when the sun shines brilliantly all day. The meat is salted, spiced with ground cumin and coriander seeds, rubbed with garlic, and then dried in the sun – sometimes by hanging it from the clothes line!

Meat being turned into *khelea* is left to dry in the sun for six days, and is brought inside each night so that nocturnal dampness will not cause mould. Once it has dried and the spices have penetrated fully, it is cooked in boiling olive oil mixed with lamb or beef fat and plenty of water. It is then removed to an earthenware container, while the oil continues to boil until all the water has evaporated. The remaining grease is used to cover the meat and seal it off from the air.

A well-to-do family might purchase up to 100 pounds of meat at a time to make a year's supply of *khelea*. Moroccans unable to afford such a huge outlay can buy it tinned in the *souks* – or, for that matter, in Arab stores elsewhere.

Khelea can be used in *couscous* in place of meat or poultry, in Rghaif (page 101), in certain *tagines*, and in a highly spiced dish that also contains dried beans and pumpkin. Because *khelea* is preserved, it is often taken on forays into the Sahara, where its spicy flavour warms up the diner on chilly desert nights – though it leaves *me* cold.

If you wish, you can prepare *khelea* in an 'instant' version:

'Instant' Khelea

450 g (1 lb) beef topside	3 tablespoons chopped garlic
4 tablespoons ground cumin	3 tablespoons salt
4 tablespoons ground coriander seeds	115 g (4 oz) beef fat
	Salad oil to cover

Rub the beef with the ground cumin, ground coriander seed, chopped garlic, and salt. Melt the beef fat in 250 ml (scant $\frac{1}{2}$ pint) water over high heat. When the water has evaporated, put in the spiced beef and enough oil to completely cover the meat. Cook it slowly, covered, for 1 to 2 hours. Drain the meat and cool the fat. Place the meat in a clean enamelled or glass mixing bowl and strain the fat over it.

Note: This 'instant' form of *khelea* should keep for 2 to 3 days in a cool place.

———— •••• ————

HONEY

The best Moroccan honey comes from Melilla (in the north) and Tagoundaft (in the Souss). Both honeys are thick and aromatic, sometimes crystallised, and are marvellous in the desserts, glazed dishes, poultry stuffings, and *tagines* where honey is an important ingredient. As substitutes, Spanish rosemary honey is very good, and Mount Hymettus honey from Greece, with its strong thyme flavour, is particularly recommended. If you cannot get any of these I suggest, as a last resort, the orange-flower honeys available everywhere; these impart the correct amount of sweetening, although they lack a good, strong, herbal flavour.

———— •••• ————

COUSCOUS GRAIN

You can buy packaged *couscous* grains in some supermarkets and at nearly all organic food stores and gourmet shops. The best-tasting *couscous*, however, is sold loose, and can be obtained in health food stores. In an airtight container *couscous* grains can be kept for years.

Unfortunately neither the *rough*-grained semolina flour (*smeeda*) used to make the *couscous seffa* nor the very large hand-rolled grains called *mhammsa* are yet widely available. You really shouldn't follow the directions or recipes on a *couscous* package – the directions are poorly expressed, the recipes are second-rate, and if you follow them you will not have the lightest, tenderest *couscous*.

Beware the packages of 'precooked' or 'instant' *couscous*. Some are very poor. If the wording on the package indicates that it is imported and can be cooked 'the traditional way' as well as 'instantly,' then it will probably be all right.

——— ••• ———

CHICK-PEAS

There is an interesting theory, developed by Richard Ford, nine-teenth-century travel writer and historian, and supported by Arnold Toynbee, that both the Spaniards and the Berbers are Punic people. Ford finds partial proof in their mutual fondness for the chick-pea, and he points out that the Punic love of chick-peas so pleased the Roman playwright Plautus (*c.* 200 B.C.) that he introduced a chick-pea-eating character speaking Punic, which is comparable to Shakespeare's use of a toasted-cheese-eating Welshman speaking Welsh.

Be that as it may, the chick-pea is popular throughout the Middle East, especially in the form of *hummous*, and in Morocco it appears over and over again in couscous dishes and *tagines*. As for peeling chick-peas, it is not necessary, but I recommend you do it for aethetic reasons, especially if you use chick-peas that are canned. (In Morocco dried chick-peas are soaked in water, in sunlight, then drained and rubbed against the sides of a reed basket to facilitate the removal of their skins. You can peel them easily by cooking the dried chick-peas separately for an hour and then plunging them into cold water; rub them lightly between your fingers – the skins will come off and rise to the surface.) In all these recipes I have left open the option of using dried or canned chick-peas. The choice is yours, but my own preference is for the dried ones, even though they must be soaked the night before preparing the dish.

——— •••• ———

KITCHEN EQUIPMENT

There are rows and rows of market stalls devoted to pots and pans, earthenware *tagines slaouis* (shallow dishes with conical tops), knives, *couscoussiers*, brass mortars and pestles, and all the other pieces of equipment used to make Moroccan food. A friend who is a great authority on food tells me that he always visits a hardware shop and a cooking equipment shop as soon as he arrives in a country; between the two, he says, one can understand a nation's culture.

Despite the great array of equipment for sale in the *souks*, I am constantly amazed by the small number of utensils found in a Moroccan restaurant kitchen or even a well-to-do home. There will always be a *couscoussiere*, a few copper *taouas* (casseroles), a pan for frying almonds or fish, knives and earthenware bottles for keeping spices, a simple brazier for charcoal, and a two-burner stove. One rarely sees an oven; in one restaurant I visited, if a *tagine* was to be baked or 'gratinéed', an earthenware dish heaped with burning charcoal was placed on top. For extensive baking, a servant or a child is dispatched to a neighbourhood communal oven.

Naturally, this kind of simplicity is more practical in a country where labour is cheap and there are many hands to do the things that we do with the help of gadgets. Nevertheless, it suggests to me the elegant simplicity of Moroccan cooking; with the exception of a few dishes (*bisteeya*, *trid*, and so on), it is accessible to nearly anyone who wishes to try it, and that cannot be said of French haute cuisine or Viennese pastry.

Another thing that I noticed about Moroccan cooks is their total lack of reliance on any sort of measuring equipment except their noses and eyes. I watched one Moroccan cook time and time again hack off lamb into perfect five-ounce portions (confirmed on my scale) and add amounts of ginger with a wave of her hand that were always accurate to the quarter teaspoon. (I discovered this when we repeated *bisteeya* – the amounts were the same to a fraction.) This kind of consistency comes from years of cooking experience, plus years of observation when she was a little girl. But every good Moroccan cook has this kind of measuring instinct – as do most good cooks almost everywhere in the world.

You will need very little new equipment to cook Moroccan food: a *couscoussier*, of course (a wise investment, since it can be used for steaming all sorts of things – though, if you like, you can substitute a pot and a snug-fitting colander, or use a steamer); perhaps a heavy brass mortar and pestle for pounding (not wood, since garlic and saffron will soon leave their traces); and a few shallow serving casseroles for *tagines* (earthenware, if possible, especially for fish). Enamelled cast-iron or tin-lined copper pots will do nicely – though you may have to transfer the food to serving platters, since these pots are rarely shallow enough for dining with the hands *à la Marocaine*.

If you go to Morocco you can buy the real thing, earthenware or copper *couscoussiers*, beautiful, four-handled brass mortars (*mehraz*), and glazed earthenware *tagine slaouis*, with their marvellous conical hats.

If you become a real Moroccan enthusiast like me, you can then buy all sorts of esoteric cookware: a *gsaa*, the wooden or earthenware basin used for kneading dough for bread, *rghaifs*, and pastry; a *gdra dil trid*, a domelike utensil of earthenware used for stretching dough to make the pastry leaves for *trid*; a *tobsil*, a large, round, tin-covered copper pan to be placed over charcoal or boiling water when you make the *warka* for *bisteeya* (page 81); a *tbicka*, a large basket with a conical hat used for storing bread and serving *tagines*; the *m'ghazel* skewers, made of silver in Fez, for *kefta* and brochettes; a Moroccan teapot, tea glasses, and tea trays; copper, silver, and brass serving trays; and implements for pouring perfumed water over the hands after eating. And then, if you are really dedicated, you can go the Valley of Ammeln in the Anti-Atlas and find a special kind of unglazed earthenware pot that I first heard about from Paul Bowles. It looks like a pumpkin with a handle at the top; if you tap it lightly near a small air hole it cracks around the circumference, making a perforated line. Tapping along this line you end up with a perfectly matched top and bottom that fit together and will seal in the juices when you cook *tagines*.

CHAPTER 3

Bread

*Manage with bread and butter until
God sends the honey.*

– Moroccan Proverb

IN NORTH AFRICA bread is sacred, and is treated with respect. If you see a piece lying on the ground, you pick it up and kiss it and put it some place where it will not be dirtied. A woman who wishes her bread to impart that special kind of God-given luck called *baraka* will send the first three leaves of the unleavened *therfist* to a Koranic scholar. And there is a tale in Morocco of a Negro woman imprisoned in the moon because she defiled a loaf.

The round, heavy-textured, spicy bread of Morocco is quite different from the flat, hollow discs that pass for 'Arab bread' elsewhere. Chewy, soft-crusted Moroccan bread is highly absorbent, ideal for dipping into the savory sauces of *tagines* and as a kind of 'fork' for conveying food when eating with one's hands. Because it is left to rise only once it is extremely easy to make, and is well worth the trouble if you are planning to serve Moroccan food.

The custom at a Moroccan dinner is that only one person distributes the wedges cut from the round loaves; otherwise, there will be a quarrel at the table.

In most Moroccan homes bread is still prepared every morning, kneaded in a large, unglazed red clay pan called a *gsaa* and then sent to the community oven on the heads of children wearing padded caps. The loaves of each family are identified with a wooden stamp, and the bread is returned as soon as it is baked.

To my mind the best bread in Morocco is made with such coarse grains as whole wheat or barley mixed with unbleached flour. But whenever a visitor (and especially a foreigner) is coming to the house, many Moroccans unfortunately feel that it is 'finer' to prepare their bread with refined white flour, and the result is, predictably, bland.

Moroccan women knead bending over the *gsaa* while pushing and folding a long roll of dough back and forth until it gains maximum elasticity. The best-tasting breads are the ones most thoroughly kneaded – the yeast is evenly distributed and the bread is protein-rich: my image of bread making in Morocco is concentrated around the memory of myself on my knees kneading in tune to the recorded songs of the great Egyptian singer Oum Kaltsoum.

Besides the classic Moroccan breads called *kisra* or *khboz* there is a Marrakesh speciality called *khboz bishemar* (very similar to the pastry called *rghaif* and which I call Marrakesh 'Pizza' [page 46]); *therfist*, an unleavened bread that is prepared in sheets, which are often spread with a foamy mixture of fenugreek and water reputed to make Berber women plump; and a kind of bread made by the 'blue people' (Tuaregs) of the Sahara, baked on hot sand and called *tagella*.

When Tuaregs share bread with a stranger they sanctify the occasion by saying: 'By bread and salt we are united.'

Moroccan Bread
(Kisra or Khboz)

For two 15 cm (6″) loaves

1 8 g ($\frac{1}{4}$ oz) package active dry yeast
1 teaspoon granulated sugar
500 g (18 oz) unbleached flour

150 g ($5\frac{1}{4}$ oz) whole-wheat flour
2 teaspoons salt
8 tablespoons lukewarm milk
1 teaspoon sesame seeds
1 tablespoon aniseed
maize flour

1 Soften the yeast in 1 tablespoon sugared lukewarm water; Let stand 2 minutes, then stir and set in a warm place until the yeast is bubbly and doubles in volume. Meanwhile, mix the flours with the salt in a large mixing bowl.
2 Stir the bubbling yeast into the flour, then add the milk and enough lukewarm water to form a stiff dough. (Since flours differ in their ability to absorb moisture, no precise amount can be given.) Turn the dough out on a lightly floured board and knead hard with clenched fists, adding water if necessary. To knead, push the dough outward. (It will take anywhere from 10 to 15 minutes to knead this dough thoroughly and achieve a smooth, elastic consistency. If using

an electric beater with a dough hook, knead 7 to 8 minutes at slow speed.) During the final part of the kneading, add the spices. After the dough has been thoroughly kneaded, form into two balls and let stand 5 minutes on the board.

3 Light grease a mixing bowl. Transfer the first ball of dough to the greased bowl and form into a cone shape by grasping the dough with one hand and rotating it aginst the sides of the bowl, held by the other hand. Turn out onto a baking sheet that has been sprinkled with maize flour. Flatten the cone with the palm of the hand to form a flattened disc about 12·5 cm (5″) in diameter with a slightly raised centre. Repeat with the second ball of dough. Cover loosely with a damp towel and let rise about 2 hours in a warm place. (To see if the bread has fully risen, poke your finger gently into the dough – the bread is ready for baking if the dough does not spring back.)

4 Preheat the oven to 200° C/400° F/Gas 6.

5 Using a fork, prick the bread around the sides three or four times and place on the centre shelf of the oven. Bake for 12 minutes, then lower the heat to 150° C/300° F/Gas 2 and bake 30 to 40 minutes more. When done, the bread will sound hollow when tapped on the bottom. Remove and let cool. Cut in wedges just before serving.

Note: A variation, *Khboz Mikla* is made as follows: A flattened circle of the dough is cooked, over an open fire, on a dry earthenware griddle called a *mikla* until browned on both sides. To my mind this is absolutely delicious with fresh butter and crystallised honey.

Holiday Bread

This is a family recipe from Essaouira.

For one 30 cm (12″) round loaf or two 15 cm (6″) loaves

8 g ($\frac{1}{4}$ oz) active dry yeast
unsalted butter, melted and cooled
40 g (1$\frac{1}{2}$ oz) granulated sugar
225 ml (scant $\frac{1}{2}$ pint) lukewarm milk or 170 ml ($\frac{1}{4}$ pint) lukewarm milk plus 4

tablespoons lukewarm buttermilk
600 g (21 oz) unbleached flour
2 teaspoons salt
1 tablespoon orange-flower water
1$\frac{1}{2}$ teaspoons aniseed
1$\frac{1}{2}$ teaspoons sesame seeds
maize flour

1 Prepare the yeast as directed in step 1 in the previous receipe, then add the cooled melted butter, sugar, milk, and enough lukewarm water to the flour and salt to make a stiff dough. Knead well. During the final kneading add the orange-flower water and spices.
2 Form and bake as directed in steps 3 to 5 in the previous recipe.

Marrakesh 'Pizza' (Khboz Bishemar)

It may seem odd to stuff bread with fat and spices, but the idea is extremely ingenious: the fat runs out through holes pricked in the dough, becomes the medium in which the bread is fried, and leaves behind its flavour and an array of spices and herbs that make it taste strikingly like pizza crust.

For four people

8 g ($\frac{1}{4}$ oz) active dry yeast
115 g ($\frac{1}{4}$ lb) mutton or beef suet
3 tablespoons chopped parsley
4 tablespoons finely chopped onion
$\frac{1}{4}$ heaped teaspoon ground cumin

1 dried red chili pepper
1 heaped teaspoon paprika
280 g (10 oz) unbleached flour
1 teaspoon salt
4 teaspoons unsalted butter, melted

46

1 Sprinkle the yeast over 4 tablespoons lukewarm water. Stir to dissolve and let stand in a warm place for 10 minutes, or until the yeast has become bubbly and doubled in volume.

2 Meanwhile, make the filling. Chop or mince the suet; pound the parsley, onion, and spices in a mortar or chop finely to a paste. Mix with the suet and set aside.

3 Mix the flour with the salt and make a well in the centre. Pour in the bubbling yeast and enough lukewarm water to form a ball of dough. (Add more water if the dough seems hard to handle.) Knead well until smooth and elastic, about 20 minutes. Separate the ball of dough into 4 equal parts.

4 Lightly flour a board. Begin patting the first ball of dough down to a disc shape, stretching and flattening it to make a rectangle approximately 20 cm (8") × 35 cm (14"). Spread one quarter of the filling in the centre. Fold the right and then the left side of the dough over the filling. Press down on this 'package' and begin flattening and stretching it (with the filling inside) until it is the same size as before. Repeat the folding, this time right side over centre and left side under. Repeat with the remaining 3 balls of dough. Set aside, covered, in a warm place for 45 minutes.

5 Heat the griddle. Prick the 'packages' with a fork six or seven times on both sides. Place on the griddle – they will begin to fry in the fat released from their fillings. Fry the packages 10 minutes on each side, until crisp. Dot each package with a teaspoonful of melted butter before serving.

———— •••• ————

CHAPTER 4

Soups

IN MOROCCO soup is usually a supper dish, heavy and well spiced, nourishing and rich. I have known people who lived on nothing but *harira* soup while visiting Morocco.

Harira, of course, is famous as the food eaten at sundown each day during the fasting month of Ramadan. But Moroccans eat it throughout the year, and also a lighter version called *chorba*, which is not thickened with yeast or flour or eggs and which is particularly good in summer.

Harira karouiya (Caraway-Flavoured Soup, page 52) is a fortifying curiosity usually served with lamb's head. Then there are the various 'medicinal' soups – a peppery concoction of garlic, saffron, thyme, and peppermint recommended for women who are about to give birth, and a soup of lightly toasted aniseed, ground in a mortar and cooked in boiling water with whole-wheat flour, pepper, salt, and butter, which is said to relieve a sore back or a cold. Thyme is added if the cold is complicated by a sore throat, and the anise has an additional effect – it will prevent nightmares and ensure a comfortable sleep.

——— ••• ———

HARIRA AND RAMADAN

The holy month of Ramadan is one of the most striking features of the Arab world. This ninth month of the Muslim year is called 'the month of fasting,' and not a bite of food or a drop of water is consumed between sunrise and sunset, which is announced, when it comes, by the report of a cannon.

At the moment of sunset, Moroccans sit down to the traditional Ramadan 'breakfast': *harira* soup, dates, *mahalkra* or *shebbakia* (Honey Cake, page 249), and coffee or milk. *Harira* is peppery and lemony, rich with vegetables and meat, and thickened with *tedouira* – a mixture of yeast or flour and water. It is always reddened with tomatoes, and sometimes enriched with beaten eggs.

I have heard that the beaten eggs are often omitted at the royal palace in favour of a more luxurious triumph of the Moroccan kitchen: in silver egg-cups sit eggshells, their tops removed, filled with eggs that have been softly scrambled with gum arabic, saffron, cumin, and salt. The diners imbibe this mixture like shots of whisky directly from the shells, for instant nourishment and while waiting for their *harira* to cool down.

Harira I

This is a city version.

For 6–8 people

2 large onions, chopped
1 large handful chopped parsley
1 tablespoon finely chopped
  celery leaves
1 teaspoon freshly ground black
  pepper
1 teaspoon turmeric
1 tablespoon *smen* (page 35) or
  tablespoons fresh butter
$\frac{1}{2}$ teaspoon ground cinnamon
225 g ($\frac{1}{2}$ lb) shoulder of lamb, in
  1 cm ($\frac{1}{2}''$) cubes
wings, backs and giblets of 1
  chicken
8 tablespoons dried lentils

2 tablespoons green coriander
  leaves
salt to taste
2 pounds red, ripe tomatoes,
  peeled and seeded (see page
  58), then puréed (1
  tablespoon tomato paste or
  more is optional for less than
  perfect tomatoes)
8 tablespoons fine soup noodles
3 tablespoons semolina or plain
  flour mixed with 8
  tablespoons water
lemon wedges

1 In a large soup pot, cook the onion, parsley, celery leaves, pepper, and turmeric in the *smen* for about 3 to 4 minutes, stirring, then add the cinnamon, lamb and chicken. Cook slowly, turning the mixture over and over until golden but not browned (about 15 to 20 minutes).
2 Meanwhile, pick over and wash the lentils. In a mortar pound the green coriander leaves with a little salt into a paste or purée the leaves in an electric blender with a spoonful of water. Add the lentils, coriander paste, and puréed tomatoes to the pot. Cook 15 minutes over low heat, then pour in 1·35 litres ($2\frac{1}{2}$ pints) water and cook until the lentils are soft and the soup is well blended.
3 Five minutes before serving, salt the soup and add the noodles.

Bring to a boil and cook for 2 minutes, then stir in the flour-water mixture. Cook 3 minutes longer, stirring continuously to avoid any flour nuggets forming. Serve at once with lemon wedges.

Note: In Marrakesh the *tedouira*, or flour-water mixture, used to thicken *harira* is prepared a day in advance so that the flour will ferment slightly and impart a musky flavour to the soup.

Harira II

A marvellous version from the *bled* (countryside), thickened with lemony eggs.

For 8 people

8 tablespoons dried chick-peas
450 g (1 lb) lamb, trimmed and
   cut into 1 cm ($\frac{1}{2}$") cubes
1 teaspoon turmeric
pinch of pulverised saffron
1 teaspoon freshly ground black
   pepper
1 teaspoon ground cinnamon
($\frac{1}{4}$ oz) teaspoon ground ginger
   (optional)
1 tablespoon *smen* (page 35) or
   2 tablespoons unsalted
   butter
100 g (3$\frac{1}{2}$ oz) chopped celery
   leaves and stalks

2 medium yellow onions
4 tablespoons chopped parsley
900 g (2 lbs) tomatoes, peeled,
   seeded and chopped (see
   page 58)
salt
125 g (4$\frac{1}{2}$ oz) dried lentils
8 small white onions
4 tablespoons fine soup noodles
   (optional)
2 eggs beaten with the juice of $\frac{1}{2}$
   lemon
lemon slices and cinnamon for
   garnish

1 Soak the chick-peas in water overnight. Drain and skin if desired.
2 Put the lamb, spices, *smen*, celery, chopped onion, and parsley in a soup pot and cook, stirring, over moderately low heat for 5 minutes. Then add the tomatoes and continue cooking 10 to 15 minutes longer. Salt lightly.
3 Meanwhile, wash the lentils in a sieve under running water until the water runs clear. Add the lentils to the pot with water. Bring to the boil, then lower the heat and simmer, partially covered, for 1$\frac{1}{2}$ hours.
4 Add the small white onions and continue cooking the soup 30 minutes.

5 Five minutes before serving add the soup noodles. When they are tender, pour the egg and lemon juice mixture into the simmering soup and turn off the heat immediately. Stir rapidly to form long egg strands. Taste for seasoning and serve with lemon slices and a light dusting of ground cinnamon.

Soup of Chick-peas
(Chorba Bil Hamus)

This is an excellent soup to serve before *diej mahammer* (Chicken Braised and Browned, page 171) or *djej mefenned* (Chicken Braised and Browned and Coated with Eggs, page 172).

Though chick-peas must be skinned (see page 161) if they are going into a chicken *tagine*, the process is optional for soup.

For 10 people

300 g (12 oz) chick-peas or 1
   575 g (20 oz) tin cooked
   chick-peas
1 lamb shin
wings, backs, and giblets of 2
   chickens
$\frac{1}{2}$ cup chopped parsley
salt
$\frac{1}{4}$ teaspoon freshly ground black
   pepper

2 pinches pulverised saffron
$\frac{1}{4}$ oz teaspoon turmeric
$\frac{1}{4}$ oz teaspoon ground ginger
3 tablespoons grated onion
3 tablespoons salad oil
1 tablespoon tomato purée
1 cup peeled, cubed potatoes
4 tablespoons lemon juice

1 The night before, soak the chick-peas in plenty of water.
2 The next day, drain the chick-peas and place in a casserole with the lamb, chicken, parsley, salt to taste, spices, onion, and oil. Cover with 1·8 litres (3 pints) water and bring to a boil. Reduce the heat, cover, and simmer 2 hours, after 1 hour adding the tomato purée.
3 After 2 hours remove the lamb and cut into dice. Return to the soup, along with the diced potatoes, and simmer another 30 minutes. Add the lemon juice, taste for salt, and serve.

Caraway-Flavoured Soup
(Harira Karouiya)

This fortifying soup, traditionally served with a lamb's head, is recommended by my Moroccan friends as fare suitable for a 'tired voyager'. Though I personally find it something less than sublime, I offer it here as a curiosity. When flavoured with sugar and a little orange-flower water, though, its curds make an excellent stuffing for *briouats* (page 99).

For 6–8 people

3·3 litres (5¾ pints) fresh milk
8 tablespoons lemon juice
1 heaped tablespoon caraway
   seeds
1 teaspoon thyme

7 to 8 sprigs fresh mint
150 g (5¼ oz) flour
Salt
40 g (1½ oz) granulated sugar

1 Heat the milk in a large enamelled cast-iron casserole. Add the lemon juice and bring to a boil. Stir quickly until curds have formed, then remove from the heat. Line the colander with a piece of cheesecloth. Set a colander over a large bowl and pour in the curds and milk. Holding the ends of the cloth together, let the curds drain well. Pour the milk back into the casserole.

2 Pound the caraway seeds, with the thyme, in a mortar. Sprinkle with water and wrap in another piece of cheesecloth. Add the mint sprigs and cheesecloth bag of caraway and thyme to the milk. Bring to a boil.

3 Mix the flour with 450 ml (scant pint) water and slowly add to the boiling milk, stirring constantly to avoid lumping. When smooth add a *handful* of curds broken into small pieces. Cook 5 minutes then let cool. Remove and discard the mint and the cheesecloth filled with aromatics.

4 Cut the remaining curds into dice and place in a soup tureen. Reheat the soup, add salt to taste and sugar, and pour over the curds. Serve hot.

CHAPTER 5

Salads and Vegetables

THERE ARE people who come to the *souks* of Morocco to buy silver and gold, caftans and rugs, or who like to wander through the streets of the carpenters, the tailors, the coppersmiths, or the cloth merchants. My favourite *souks* are the markets of fruit and vegetables – the ones in the countryside, where everything is young and tender and fresh, and the endless produce stalls of the great cities.

I love to roam the market of Tangier, where I can feast my eyes on tapering turnips, sweet green peppers, young carrots with their leafy tops, baby aubergines, knobbly Jerusalem artichokes, and long red radishes. Here I can caress luscious, vine-ripened tomatoes, young and fat spring onions, fine-stalked celery, huge cauliflowers, pale pink heads of garlic, and all manner of greens and gourds. I can run my fingers through beans of all kinds, and then press them lightly against oranges, clementines, fresh apricots, red and greenage plums, pink grapefruits, and many kinds of Moroccan grapes. These fruits and vegetables are always lovingly displayed; in the great urban markets one finds row after row of fresh produce, whole rows of stalls that sell nothing but greens. To move among these things, amid a swirl of people buying and selling, bargaining and bustling, is for me one of the great pleasures of life.

Vegetables were not a traditional part of the cuisine of the southern Berber peoples; for them there was little more than pumpkin and gourds, turnips, onions, nuts, and fruit. It is still customary in the south to start a guest off with a plate of dates and a bowl of milk, just as in the *bled* the first offering is usually some kind of biscuit served with honey and *smen*. But around Fez and along the coastal areas vegetables have always been popular. Here one finds the great agricultural districts of the country, the Sais Plain and the Sebou Valley, the Chaouia area stretching from Rabat to Casablanca, and the great gardens of the southern Atlantic coast that culminate in the famous orange groves of Agadir.

In the heartland, around Fez and Meknes, and down this

fruit- and vegetable-laden coast, one eats the salads of Morocco. These are not salads in the sense that of that word here – not mixtures of greens doused with dressings. Moroccan salads are more like Italian antipasti – dishes of spiced or sweetened, cooked or raw vegetables served at the beginning of a meal to inspire the appetite and refresh the palate.

The glories of these dishes are their unexpected contrasts and combinations of tastes – such things as courgettes flavoured with *za'atar*; orange sections, black olives, and garlic; carrots with orange-blossom water; and, by extension, meat dishes such as brains with herbs and spices; and salads of cubed liver. They are all delightful and delicious, gems that sparkle in the crown of a great national cuisine. Sometimes they are placed on the table at the beginning of a meal and left there throughout; other times they are whisked off upon the arrival of the first *tagine*. Either way, the memory of their superb flavours stays with the diner, who is rarely served with less than four different types.

——— •••• ———

AUBERGINE SALADS

Aubergine are used to make a Moroccan version of *ratatouille*, and, when cooked with small chili peppers, a dish closely related to the Tunisian *chatchouka*. One aubergine salad (Zeilook, opposite) is made of fried slices of the vegetable, seasoned with cumin and paprika, mashed to a purée, then fried again until rich and firm. In another (Aubergine Salad, Rabat Style, page 56), the vegetable is first grilled over charcoal and the pulp is fried until it condenses into a thick black jam. Both salads are delicious, and both keep well for many days.

Aubergines need to be salted before frying to rid them of their bitter juices; then they should be rinsed, squeezed, and dried on kitchen paper. Try to fry them in olive oil; vegetable dishes served cold taste better that way.

Aubergine Salad
(Zeilook)

You can play around with this recipe, using whatever you happen to have on hand. For example, you can add two or three courgettes, sliced, and fry them with the aubergine, or three or four sweet green peppers, which have been grilled, peeled, and diced with the tomatoes. Or you can simply execute the recipe as written below.

For 4 people as a single dish

900 g (2 lbs) aubergine
salt
olive oil for frying
3 red, ripe, tomatoes, peeled, seeded, and chopped
2 to 3 cloves garlic, peeled and chopped

scant $\frac{1}{2}$ teaspoon ground cumin
1 teaspoon sweet paprika
1 tablespoon freshly chopped green coriander (optional)
3 tablespoons lemon juice, or to taste

1 Remove 3 vertical strips of skin from each aubergine, leaving each striped, then cut into 1 cm ($\frac{1}{2}''$) thick slices. Salt them and leave to drain in a colander for 30 minutes. Rinse well, squeeze gently, and pat the slices dry with kitchen paper.
2 Heat a good quantity of oil in a frying pan and fry the aubergine slices until brown on both sides, removing them when done with a perforated spatula. Reserve the oil in the pan. Mash the aubergine with the tomatoes, garlic, spices, and coriander.
3 Fry the purée in the oil in the pan until all the liquid evaporates and there is only oil and vegetable left. Stirring the purée often to avoid scorching, continue frying 15 minutes. Pour off the oil and season with lemon juice to taste. Taste for salt. Serve warm or cool.

Note: This salad can be kept 3 to 4 days covered in a cool place.

Aubergine Salad, Rabat Style

The aubergine is traditionally grilled over a charcoal brazier; for convenience in this recipe, it is baked in the oven.

For 4 people

1 aubergine of 450 g (1 lb)	$\frac{1}{2}$ teaspoon paprika
1 clove garlic, peeled and sliced	$\frac{1}{2}$ teaspoon ground cumin
2 tablespoons chopped parsley	2 tablespoons olive oil
2 sprigs green coriander, chopped (optional)	1 to 2 tablespoons lemon juice
	salt

1 Stud the whole aubergine with garlic slivers, using a paring knife to 'drill' holes. Bake the aubergine in a 200°C/400°F/Gas 6 oven until very soft (it will seem as if it has collapsed; the skin will be black and blistery). Remove from the oven to cool.

2 When cool enough to handle, rub the skin off the aubergine and squeeze the pulp to release the bitter juices or scoop out the pulp with a wooden spoon and let drain in a sieve. Discard the bitter liquid.

3 Mash or push the aubergine pulp and garlic slices through a food mill. (Avoid the temptation to use a blender – it destroys the character of the dish.)

4 Add the chopped herbs and spices and mix well. Fry in the oil over moderate heat, turning the aubergine often with the perforated spatula until all the liquid has evaporated and the aubergine has been reduced to a thick black jam. (This turning and frying will take about 15 to 20 minutes.) Sprinkle with lemon juice, taste for salt, and readjust the seasoning to taste. Serve warm or slightly cooled. (You may want to decorate this salad with cherry tomatoes).

———— ••• ————

GREEN PEPPER AND TOMATO SALADS

There is no question that the green pepper and tomato salads of Morocco encompass the same spectrum of seasonings as the *gazpacho* of Spain. In fact, there is a fascinating historical connection between the two series of dishes. *Gazpacho* in Arabic means 'soaked bread.' The Spaniards first learned of *gazpacho* from the Moors, who made it of garlic, bread, olive oil, lemon juice, salt, and water. Just after the Moors left Spain, Columbus returned from America with tomatoes and peppers, and these two vegetables became the mainstays of the new *gazpachos* that the Spaniards developed. From Spain these two new vegetables came to Morocco to be used in, among other things, Moroccan salads. Thus, a culinary idea exported from Morocco to Spain was changed there by the addition of newly discovered ingredients, which were then in turn reimported into Morocco, where they found their way into a unique variety of dishes.

When making these dishes try to buy the plumpest, reddest, ripest tomatoes you can find, and be sure your green peppers are sweet. (Nibble on the tip of each one before using it.) The peppers are prepared by grilling them over charcoal or over a gas flame, but you can bake them in the oven if you prefer. Then they must be peeled, and cored.

Tomato and Green Pepper Salad, Fez Style

Exquisite!

For 4–6 people

3 sweet green peppers
4 large red, ripe tomatoes
1 clove garlic, peeled and
   crushed
pinch of sweet paprika
$\frac{1}{4}$ teaspoon ground cumin

2 tablespoons olive or salad oil
1 tablespoon lemon juice
$\frac{1}{2}$ teaspoon salt
$\frac{1}{4}$ teaspoon freshly ground black
   pepper
$\frac{1}{4}$ preserved lemon (see page 27)

57

1 To prepare the peppers, grill them over a gas flame, turning them until the skins are completely blackened, or bake them as follows: Preheat the oven to 230°C/450°F/Gas 8; wash the peppers, drain, and arrange on an ungreased baking-sheet; bake for 10 minutes, then turn over carefully and continue to bake for 10 minutes more, or until the skins are black and blistered.

2 Place the blackened peppers in a plastic bag or under a towel and set aside to cool. (This enables the skin to separate from the flesh.) Remove the peppers when cool, core, seed, and slip off their skins. Scrape off any extra seeds. Cut the pepper flesh into small pieces and set aside.

3 To prepare the tomatoes, bring 500 ml (scant pint) water to a boil; drop in the tomatoes and boil for 15 seconds. Remove the tomatoes and cut out the stem with a sharp paring knife. Peel off their skins, then slice each tomato in half crosswise and squeeze gently to remove the seeds. Cut the tomato flesh into small pieces.

4 Mix the tomatoes and peppers in a glass serving dish, then add all the remaining vegetables except the preserved lemon. Mix well to blend the spices with the vegetables. Rinse the preserved lemon under running water and cut away the pulp. Cut the peel into cubes and sprinkle over the salad. Serve cool.

Tomato and Hot Green Pepper Salad, Essaouira Style

This is hotter than the Fez recipe.

4 large, ripe tomatoes, peeled, seeded, and cubed

4 sweet green peppers, grilled or baked, cored, seeded and diced (see above)

1 cucumber, peeled, centre core removed, and diced, or 3 celery ribs, diced

1 tablespoon or more chopped chili peppers, cored and seeded

salt and black pepper

1 tablespoon lemon juice

2 to 3 tablespoons olive or salad oil

2 tablespoons chopped parsley

$\frac{1}{4}$ teaspoon ground cumin (optional)

2 cloves garlic, peeled and chopped (optional)

Combine all the ingredients in a mixing bowl and blend gently. Refrigerate at least 1 hour before serving.

Hot Chili Relish, Rabat style

Fry 6 hot green chili peppers in salad oil, then cool them under a towel; when they are cool, skin them and mix with a little lemon juice and salt. Serve whole.

Sweet Green Pepper Relish, Fez Style

Mix 6 grilled peeled, cored, and chopped sweet green peppers (see page 58) with 2 tablespoons lemon juice, a few tablespoons olive oil, and granulated sugar to taste.

Pickled Sweet Green Peppers (Filfil Mrakad), Tetuán Style

Split and clean 900 g (2 lbs) sweet green peppers. Trim off the stems, then fill the pepper cavities with salt. Pile the peppers into a large sterile jar, add 1 head peeled garlic cloves, and pour in 600 ml (1 pint) mild vinegar, 500 ml (scant pint) olive oil, and enough water to cover the peppers. Close tightly and store in a warm place 10 days.

Note: After opening store in a cool place. Use a fork to remove the peppers.

———— ••• ————

Sliced Tomato and Onion Salad

For 4–6 people

6 to 8 red, ripe tomatoes, peeled
(see page 58) and sliced
crosswise
½ Spanish onion or 1 sweet red
onion, sliced into thin rings
4 tablespoons olive oil
1 tablespoon vinegar

1 clove garlic, peeled and
crushed
salt and freshly ground black
pepper
chopped parsley
pinch of cumin (optional)
pinch of paprika (optional)

Combine the tomato and onion slices. Make a sauce with the remaining ingredients and pour over the tomatoes and onion.

Cooked Tomatoes and Sweet Green Pepper Salad

This is a rich and satisfying salad – sixteen, beautiful, red, ripe, plump tomatoes reduced to a delicious purée. (It takes a lot of attention to avoid burning the mixture during the final fifteen minutes.) In Essaouira the cooks add some hot green chili peppers and chopped parsley, but I generally leave them out.

In Tetuán this salad is used as a fish stuffing. The fish is baked under a layer of sliced tomatoes, onions, and lemons, with chopped olives and chopped preserved lemon peel scattered on top. Paprika-flavoured oil, salt, a little water, and 45 minutes baking in a 200°C/400°F/Gas 6 oven produces a marvellous dish.

For 6 people

16 red, ripe tomatoes (about
2 kg (4 lbs)), peeled, seeded,
and chopped (see page 58)
olive oil for frying
9 sweet green peppers, grilled,
cored, seeded, and chopped
(see page 58)

2 cloves garlic, peeled and
chopped
1 teaspoon paprika (optional)
salt and cayenne to taste

Fry the tomatoes in a small amount of oil, mashing and turning them with a spoon as they cook down. When they are very thick add the chopped green peppers, garlic, optional paprika, and some salt and cayenne to taste. Continue to reduce the mixture until all the liquid has evaporated and it starts to fry in the released oil. (At this moment you must give the dish your full attention, turning the tomatoes and peppers over and over in the pan to avoid scorching.) When everything is very thick and has reduced to about 340 ml ($\frac{2}{3}$ pint), remove from the heat and drain. Serve cool.

————— •••• —————

OTHER VEGETABLE SALADS

Carrot Salad

For 4 people

450 g (1 lb) carrots
1 clove garlic
$\frac{1}{8}$ teaspoon ground cinnamon
$\frac{1}{2}$ teaspoon ground cumin
$\frac{1}{2}$ teaspoon sweet paprika
pinch of cayenne (optional)

juice of 1 lemon
$\frac{1}{8}$ teaspoon granulated sugar
salt to taste
olive oil
chopped parsley

1 Wash and peel the carrots. Boil whole in water with the garlic until barely tender. Drain. Discard the garlic and dice or slice the carrots.
2 Combine the spices with the lemon juice, sugar, and salt and pour over the carrots. Chill. Sprinkle with oil and chopped parsley just before serving.

Sweet Carrot Salad

To prepare the same dish in a much sweeter but equally delicious variation, change the proportions as follows:

For 450 g (1 pound) carrots, use $5\frac{1}{2}$ tablespoons lemon juice, 3 heaped tablespoons granulated sugar, $\frac{1}{2}$ teaspoon ground cinnamon, 3 tablespoons chopped parsley, $\frac{1}{4}$ scant teaspoon ground cumin, and $\frac{1}{4}$ teaspoon paprika. Boil the carrots as in the preceding recipe. Mix all the other ingredients, add a pinch of salt, and pour over the carrots. Serve cool.

Grated Carrot Salad

For 4–6 people

7 large carrots, scraped and grated
4 tablespoons granulated sugar

4 tablespoons lemon juice
orange-flower water
pinch of salt

Mix the carrots with the sugar, lemon juice, orange-flower water, and salt. Marinate 1 hour before serving.

Beetroot Salad I

For 2 people

450 g (1 lb) beetroots
1 tablespoon granulated sugar
juice of 1 lemon
1 tablespoon olive oil

large pinch of cinnamon
1 tablespoon chopped parsley
salt to taste

Wash the beetroots well, being carefully not to break their skins. Cut off the tops, leaving a stalk of about 3.5 cm ($1\frac{1}{2}''$). Boil covered until tender. Allow the water to cool, then slip off the skins, trim off the tops and cut into bite-sized pieces. Mix the remaining ingredients and pour over the beetroots. Let marinate for 1 hour before serving.

Beetroot Salad II

Prepare as described above, but add 1 teaspoon orange-flower water, $\frac{1}{8}$ teaspoon cumin, a pinch of paprika, and a little water to the sauce.

Cucumber Salad

For 4 people

2 cucumbers, peeled, seeded
   and grated
1 tablespoon granulated sugar
1 teaspoon vinegar
1 tablespoon olive, salad, or
   peanut oil

$\frac{1}{4}$ teaspoon salt
$\frac{1}{8}$ teaspoon *za'atar*; or marjoram,
   thyme, or oregano; or a
   mixture of two or three
handful of cured black olives.

Drain off excess liquid from the cucumbers, then combine with the sugar, vinegar, oil, and salt. Crush the *za'atar* (or the substitute herbs) between your fingertips and sprinkle over the cucumbers. Mix well with two forks, then chill. Decorate with the olives just before serving.

——— •••• ———

Mixed Herb Salad I

In Morocco this dish is made with greens called *bakoola*, which are found growing wild in the fields. *Bakoola* tastes something like a cross between rocket leaves (arugula) and watercress, with a hint of sorrel, and there is no real equivalent for it here. I have experimented with sorrel and dandelion leaves and reasonably successfully with watercress. However, I have had the best luck with rocket, and I recommend it for this exquisite salad. In Morocco this same salad is also prepared with purslane.

For 2 small helpings

450 g (1 lb) rocket leaves and stalks (arugula) or purslane
1 handful parsley sprigs
small bunch of green coriander
1 or 2 large cloves garlic, peeled
salt

3 tablespoons olive oil
$\frac{1}{4}$ teaspoon paprika
cayenne to taste
lemon juice to taste
$\frac{1}{4}$ preserved lemon (see page 27); optional black olives

1 Wash the rocket leaves under running water. Drain and chop roughly. Fill the bottom of a *couscoussier* with water and bring to a boil. Fasten on the perforated top, add the rocket leaves and steam, covered for 15 minutes. Remove from the heat and allow to cool, uncovered. When cool enough to handle, squeeze out as much moisture as possible.
2 Wash, dry, chop, and pound the parsley, coriander, garlic, and $\frac{1}{4}$ teaspoon salt to a paste in a mortar.
3 Heat the oil in a frying pan and add the herb paste. Cook 2 to 3 minutes without burning, then add the rocket leaves and sauté slowly until all the liquid has evaporated, turning the mixture often to avoid burning. Chop the mixture fine and blend in salt, paprika, and cayenne to taste. Cool.
4 Just before serving, sprinkle with lemon juice and adjust seasoning. Rinse the preserved lemon peel and remove the pulp, then slice the peel into slivers. Put the salad in a serving dish with slivered peel and/or black olives. Serve cool.

Mixed Herb Salad II

A mixture of many salad leaves and greens makes an excellent dish to serve either warm or cooled. Use large handfuls of whatever is available: rocket, purslane, sorrel, lambs' lettuce, Swiss chard, sea kale, watercress, rampion, mustard greens, spinach, dandelion greens, or even celery leaves.

For 6 people

900 g (2 lbs) salad plants, including stalks
1 or 2 small dried red chili peppers
salt
10 to 12 cloves garlic
1 large handful parsley, chopped
1 handful green coriander, chopped

salad oil
115 g (4 oz) cured black olives
2 teaspoons paprika
2 teaspoons ground cumin
juice of 2 lemons
lemon wedges

1 Wash the greenery under running water. Drain and cut small. Fill the bottom of a *couscoussier* with water and bring to a boil. Fasten on the perforated top, add the greens, and steam, covered, for 30 minutes. Remove from the heat and allow to cool, uncovered. When cool enough to handle, squeeze out as much moisture as possible.

2 Pound the chili pepper in a mortar with 1 teaspoon salt and the garlic. Gradually add the chopped parsley and coriander and continue pounding until it becomes a paste.

3 Heat 3 tablespoons oil in a large casserole and slowly cook the olives with the paprika and cumin 2 to 3 minutes. Add the herb paste and the lemon juice, cook, and cover 5 minutes. Pour in 8 tablespoons oil, add the greens and cook together, stirring frequently, for 20 minutes, or until all the moisture has evaporated and the mixture is very thick. Salt to taste. Serve with lemon wedges.

Note: This is also very good with an extra dribble of Harissa Sauce (page 26).

——— •••• ———

ORANGE SALADS

Moroccan oranges make marvellous, clean-tasting salads, and superbly refreshing deserts.

Orange, Lettuce, and Walnut Salad
(Shlada Bellecheen)

For 6 people

1 head cos lettuce
3 navel or temple oranges
2 tablespoons lemon juice
2 tablespoons granulated sugar
pinch of salt

cinnamon
1 tablespoon orange-flower
   water
30 g (1 oz) chopped walnuts

1 Wash the lettuce and section into leaves, discarding the tough outer ones. Drain and wrap in a dish towel to dry. Store in the refrigerator until needed.

2 Peel the oranges and remove all the outside membranes, using a small serrated knife and employing a seesaw motion. Section the oranges by cutting away all the membranes from the orange flesh. As you work, lift out each section and place in a small mixing bowl. Squeeze the juice from the remainder of the orange over the sections to keep them moist. Cover and keep chilled.

3 Make a dressing by mixing the lemon juice, sugar, salt, $\frac{1}{2}$ teaspoon cinnamon, orange-flower water, and 2 tablespoons of the orange juice. Blend well, then taste – the dressing should be sweet.

4 Just before serving, shred the lettuce and arrange in a glass serving dish. Pour the dressing over and toss. Make a design around the edges with overlapping sections of orange, then sprinkle the salad with the chopped walnuts and dust with cinnamon. Serve immediately.

Orange and Chopped Date Salad

Prepare as in the recipe above, using 90 g (3 oz) chopped dates and almonds in place of the chopped walnuts.

Orange Salad with Rosewater

Oranges, rosewater, and cinnamon make an outstanding combination. The orange sections are arranged in a pattern of overlapping circles, and the rosewater is spooned on top. This salad also makes an excellent dessert.

For 6 people

6 navel or temple oranges	2 tablespoons icing sugar
$1\frac{1}{2}$ teaspoons rosewater	cinnamon

Peel and section the oranges as described on page 66. Arrange the sections in a pattern of overlapping circles in the serving dish, then sprinkle with the perfumed water, sugar, and $\frac{1}{4}$ teaspoon cinnamon. Taste for desired sweetness and adjust as necessary. Chill until ready to serve. Just before serving, dust with more cinnamon.

Note: Orange-flower water can be substituted for the rosewater.

Orange and Radish Salad

For 4–6 people

2 to 3 bunches long or round
   red radishes
2 tablespoons granulated sugar
juice of 1 lemon
1 tablespoon orange-flower
   water

salt
2 navel oranges
cinnamon

1 Wash and trim the radishes. Place in a blender and 'grate' by turning the machine on and off. *Do not purée.* Remove and drain off the excess liquid. Place in the serving dish and sprinkle with the sugar, lemon juice, perfumed water, and salt to taste. Toss lightly and chill.

2 Peel and section the oranges as described on page 66. (Save the juice for some other dish.) Just before serving, mix the orange sections with the grated radishes. Dust lightly with cinnamon and serve at once.

Orange and Black Olive Salad

For 4–6 people

3 navel or temple oranges
170 g (6 oz) ripe black olives,
   stoned
2 tablespoons olive oil
2 cloves garlic, chopped
   (optional)
$\frac{1}{2}$ teaspoon paprika

cayenne to taste
$\frac{1}{2}$ teaspoon salt
pinch or two of granulated
   sugar
pinch of cumin
2 tablespoons chopped parsley

Peel and section the oranges as described on page 66. Arrange the olives and oranges attractively in the serving dish. Make a dressing of the olive oil and remaining ingredients, pour over the olives and oranges, and serve at once.

Note: In some Moroccan homes 4 large preserved or fresh lemons are used in place of the fresh oranges.

Orange and Grated Carrot Salad

For 4–6 people

450 g (1 lb) carrots
1 navel orange
1 teaspoon cinnamon
2 to 3 tablespoons lemon juice

1 tablespoon granulated sugar
1 teaspoon orange-flower water
pinch of salt

Clean and grate the carrots. Peel and section the oranges as described on page 66, reserving the juice. Mix the leftover orange juice with the remaining ingredients. Stir in the carrots and orange sections, then chill. Before serving, drain partially.

—— •• ——

MEAT SALADS

Though these dishes are not built around vegetables, they are nevertheless treated as salads and served as part of a Moroccan 'antipasto'.

Brain Salad I
(Mohk)

Mohk, presented here in two slightly different versions, makes an excellent first course when teamed with a mixed herb salad, a salad of tomatoes and green peppers, and one of grated carrots or radishes. The contrasting textures and flavours make an interesting start to a Moroccan feast.

For 4–6 people

450 g (1 lb) lamb or veal brains
2 tablespoons freshly chopped
  green coriander
2 tablespoons freshly chopped
  parsley
$\frac{1}{2}$ teaspoon cumin
1 teaspoon paprika

2 to 3 cloves garlic, peeled and
  cut up
4 tablespoons olive or salad oil
3 tablespoons lemon juice
1 preserved lemon, rinsed and
  diced
salt to taste

1 Wash the brains under running water, removing the membranes and as much blood as possible. Soak the brains in salted water to cover for 1 to 2 hours, changing the water three times. Place the rinsed brains in a casserole with the herbs, spices, garlic, and oil. Pour 300 ml ($\frac{1}{2}$ pint) water over and bring to a boil. Reduce the heat, partially cover the pan, and simmer 30 minutes.

2 Add the lemon juice. Then, without removing the brains from the casserole, mash them into small pieces with the back of a wooden spoon. Continue simmering another 30 minutes, stirring often.

3 Ten minutes before the dish is finished add the diced preserved lemon. Taste for salt, and readjust the seasoning. Cool before serving.

Brain Salad II
(Mohk)

Follow the instructions for the preceding recipe precisely, substituting 1 small tomato, peeled, seeded and cubed, for the preserved lemon and adding a pinch or two of cayenne pepper along with the spices.

Cubed Liver Salad
(Kibbdha)

For 4 people

450 g (1 lb) thick slices of
  calves', lambs', or ox liver
1 clove garlic, peeled and
  crushed
1$\frac{1}{2}$ heaped teaspoons sweet
  paprika
1 teaspoon salt

cumin
2 tablespoons chopped parsley
  and green coriander
8 tablespoons lemon juice
flour, preferably semolina flour
salad oil for frying

1 Wash the liver and marinate in a mixture of the garlic, paprika, salt, $\frac{3}{4}$ teaspoon cumin, half the mixed herbs, and half the lemon juice for 1 hour, or longer.

2 Drain the liver well, reserving the marinade. Dust with semolina flour (preferred by Moroccans because they say it 'holds on to the food' best when frying) and fry in 1 cm ($\frac{1}{2}$") of hot oil for 5 minutes,

turning each piece over with the spatula when browned. Drain the liver and pour off all but 3 or 4 tablespoons of the oil. Cut the liver into 1 cm ($\frac{1}{2}''$) cubes and return to the pan to refry for about 1 minute, tossing the cubes so they brown on all sides.

3 Pour in the marinade and 8 tablespoons water and bring to a boil. Stir and cook down for 1 minute. Pour in the remaining lemon juice and herbs. Stir once or twice and cook 1 minute longer. Remove from the heat and dust with a little cumin. Put in a serving dish and serve at room temperature.

———— ••• ————

OTHER VEGETABLE DISHES

Besides the salads there are a number of other Moroccan vegetable dishes worthy of note. Among these are the all-vegetable *tagines*, called *maraks*, of Tetuán, where they are usually served after an array of salads.

One of the more interesting of these *maraks* is *marak silk* (Tagine of Swiss Chard, page 72) – not to everybody's taste – simmered down with onions, spices, and herbs, and thickened with rice. *Marak matisha bil melokhias* (Tagine of Okra and Tomatoes, page 73) might normally be considered a 'salad' but in Tetuán this savoury combination of tomatoes adorned with a 'necklace' of young okra is treated as if it were an entrée. There are other *maraks* built around such things as cabbage (known as a '*marak* of rags') and cauliflowerets flavoured with cumin and paprika, and there is one *marak* made with pumpkin, raisins, white beans, and bastourma (*khelea*) cooked with a whiff of cinnamon and sugar.

I have included a recipe for the famous Berber vegetable dish known as *byesar* (Purée of Dried Broad Beans, page 73), which in Tangier is made with dried split peas, and finally, a recipe for a Moroccan Jewish dish, Aubergine Stuffed with Brains (page 75), from the town of Sefrou.

Tagine of Swiss Chard
(Marak Silk)

In Tetuán this dish is often accompanied by boiled lentils.

For 4 people

900 g (2 lbs) finely chopped
   stalks and leaves of Swiss
   chard (about 4 bunches)
2 medium onions, chopped
4 tablespoons chopped green
   coriander

4 tablespoons salad oil
1 teaspoon sweet paprika
salt and freshly ground black
   pepper
40 g (1½ oz) raw rice

Place the chopped Swiss chard in a large casserole with the onion, coriander, oil, paprika, salt, pepper, and 4 tablespoons water. Cook, covered, for 30 minutes. Add the rice and continue cooking until all the liquid has gone and the mixture has become a thick sauce slightly filmed with oil, about 20 minutes. (The lid of your casserole must be tight-fitting so that the rice will cook in the water released by the vegetables.) If you are afraid the rice will burn, stir it from time to time and add water by the spoonful, if necessary, or bake the dish in the oven. Serve warm.

——— •••• ———

Tagine of Okra and Tomatoes
(Marak Matisha Bil Melokhias)

In Tetuán the cooks who make this dish want to be able to stir the tomato sauce without breaking the okra that is poaching inside. As always, Moroccan ingenuity has found a way: the okra is strung together with needle and thread into a long 'necklace'; when the cook wants to stir the sauce she pulls up the 'necklace', stirs, and then drops the okra back in to continue its poaching.

For 5–6 people

225 g ($\frac{1}{2}$ lb) fresh okra
2 kg ($4\frac{1}{2}$ lbs) fresh red, ripe,
   tomatoes, peeled, seeded,
   and chopped (see page 54)
2 tablespoons chopped parsley

$1\frac{1}{2}$ teaspoons sweet paprika
1 teaspoon chopped garlic
salt
3 tablespoons vegetable oil

1 Wash, top, and tail the okra and string together with thread into a 'necklace'.
2 Over high heat, cook the tomatoes with the parsley, paprika, garlic, salt, and oil, mashing down the tomatoes as they cook. After 10 minutes lower the heat to moderate, add the okra and begin to poach it in the sauce. From time to time lift up the 'necklace' to stir. After the okra is tender, remove and keep warm. Continue to reduce the tomatoes until all the water is evaporated and the oil is released. Fry the tomatoes in this released oil, stirring continuously to avoid scorching. Gently pull out the thread, then place the okra in the serving dish. Pour the sauce over, and serve hot or lukewarm.

Purée of Dried Broad Beans
(Byesar)

Byesar is the North African cousin of the famous Middle Eastern *hummous* made of chick-peas. It is a dish for the lovers of olive oil, a soupy mixture best eaten with Arab bread. First you sprinkle some mixed spices (see below) on your bread, then dip it into the *byesar* and scoop the purée into your mouth. The dish is so popular among

73

Berbers that Madame Guinaudeau, in her book on Fez cooking, was able to record the following conversation:

> A gentleman from Fez to a Berber mountaineer: 'What would you do if you were the sultan?'
> The mountaineer's reply: 'I would eat *byesar* every day.'

In Tangier *byesar* is made with split green peas and spring onions, and in some parts of the country it is cooked with cabbage and flavoured with paprika, cumin, garlic, and salt.

The best *byesar* is laced with olive oil made from green, *unripe* olives.

For 4–6 people

225 g ($\frac{1}{2}$ lb) dried broad beans
3 cloves garlic, peeled
1 teaspoon cumin seeds
best quality olive oil

salt
$\frac{1}{4}$ teaspoon *za'atar* or thyme,
   marjoram, or oregano

1 The night before, soak the dried broad beans in 3 to 4 times their volume of cold water. Discard any beans that float.
2 The following day, drain, skin, and cover with fresh water. Cook gently, with the garlic and cumin seeds, until the beans are tender (about 2 hours, depending upon the age and quality of the beans). Drain.
3 Purée the beans in a food mill or an electric blender. Stir in enough olive oil, and a little water, to give the purée a soupy consistency. Sprinkle with salt to taste and beat well. Heat just before serving with a little more olive oil and a sprinkling of crushed *za'atar*. Serve with Arab bread and a bowl of 'mixed spices' (ground cumin, cayenne, and salt).

Aubergine Stuffed with Brains

For 4–6 people

225 g ($\frac{1}{2}$ lb) lamb, calves', or
    beef brains
340 g ($\frac{3}{4}$ lb) small aubergines
salt
4 tablespoons salad oil

2 red, ripe tomatoes
2 cloves whole garlic, peeled
freshly ground black pepper
1 tablespoon chopped parsley
3 eggs

1 Soak the brains in salted water to cover for 1 to 2 hours, changing the water at least three times. Remove the membranes and any traces of blood.

2 Remove the aubergine stems. With a thin-bladed paring knife, remove 1 cm ($\frac{1}{2}''$) vertical strips from each aubergine, leaving them striped. Halve lengthwise and scoop out the centre pulp, carefully leaving a 5 mm ($\frac{1}{4}''$)-thick wall of flesh in each shell. Cube the pulp.

3 Sprinkle each half shell and the cubed aubergine with salt and let drain at least 30 minutes in a colander. Squeeze gently, then rinse well under running water. Pat dry with kitchen paper.

4 Heat the oil in a frying pan and fry the shells, on both sides, over low heat until soft. Remove and drain. Set aside all but 1 tablespoon of the oil. (Since aubergines tend to soak up oil, you may need to add the reserved oil later.)

5 Peel and cube the tomatoes (see page 58). Place in a colander and press lightly to drain. Sauté the tomatoes and aubergine cubes in the 1 tablespoon oil with the garlic, salt and pepper to taste, and chopped parsley. Cook a few minutes so that the flavours blend, then place the mixture in a bowl. Discard the garlic cloves.

6 In a saucepan simmer the brains in salted water for about 10 minutes. Drain and cut into small cubes. Add to the tomato-aubergine mixture and mash together.

7 Preheat the oven to 180°C/350°F/Gas 4.

8 Stuff the aubergine shells with the brain-tomato-aubergine mixture. Place the shells in a lightly oiled ovenproof serving dish, packing them tightly so they don't fall over. Beat the eggs to a froth and pour over the stuffed aubergine. Sprinkle with salt and pepper and bake for 30 minutes. Serve directly from the dish or loosen the sides of the firmly set eggs and then turn out on to a serving dish. Cut into long slices and serve warm or at room temperature.

CHAPTER 6

Savoury Pastries

BISTEEYA is so intricate and so grand, so lavish and so rich, that its extravagance always reminds me of *The Arabian Nights*. The traditional *bisteeya* of Fez is an enormous, flaky pigeon pie never less than fifty centimetres (twenty inches) in diameter. Beneath a perfectly crisped pastry top covered with cinnamon and sugar are layers of shredded squab or chicken, two dozen eggs curdled in a lemony and spiced onion sauce, and sweetened almonds. The whole is enclosed – top, bottom, and sides – in miraculous, tissue-thin pastry leaves called *warka*.

The concept of pastry enveloping meat mixed with spices and nuts was brought to Morocco from the Middle East sometime after the first wave of Arabs swept across North Africa. The paper-thin leaves came from Persia with the third wave of invaders, and, quite possibly, the Persians learned how to make them from the same Chinese who taught them the secrets of ice cream and sherbets. Moroccan *warka* (called *maslouqua* in Tunisia and *dioul* in Algeria) is made precisely the same way as Chinese spring-roll skins. Though many people confuse this type of pastry with Greek phyllo dough and Hungarian strudel leaves (both of which, by the way, will make an adequate *bisteeya*) the *warka*-spring-roll skin type is found only in China and North Africa.

The third wave of Arab invaders had been exposed to Persian culture, and the pastry leaves they brought with them were eventually adapted in one form or another by nearly all the countries of the Mediterranean. As Waverly Root wrote in *The Food of Italy*:

> You could draw a map of the limits of Moslem invasion by plotting the places where, during the Middle Ages, their fine flaky pastry became established. It is the *pastilla* [*sic*] of Morocco; the rustic *tourtière* and the aristocratic *millefeuille* of France (where they got as far as Poitiers); the *Strudel* of Central Europe (where they reached the Adriatic and threatened Vienna); and in Italy the *millefoglie* of Sicily and the *sfogliatelle* of Naples.

The process of making *warka* (which I shall explain later in great detail) is in principle quite simple: a soft, elastic, spongy mass of well-beaten flour and water is pressed lightly against a hot, flat pan; it is immediately removed, leaving a thin film of pastry to be lifted off. In the Middle East a similar type of pastry (the Turkish *cadaif*) is made by pushing the dough through a sieve onto the hot metal pan; this, too, is immediately removed and the result, instead of being a thin, flat leaf, is a finely spun type of pastry that resembles shredded wheat.

I wondered for a long time if this process was the original and basic way of pastry making; whether France, Italy, Hungary, and Greece developed their own pastry-making methods later on. When I discovered the striking similarity between *warka* and the ancient Chinese process for making spring-roll skins, I became convinced that this, indeed, is the case.

Bisteeya is a totally Moroccan delight; it is not found anywhere else in the world. For me everything great in Moroccan culture (the influence of the Arabs and the Spanish Muslims, and the indigenous culture of the Berbers) is represented in this extravagant dish. Many authorities believe *bisteeya* was totally created in Andalusia, where the music, architecture, and literature of the Moors flourished so brilliantly, and they seem to base this theory on the similarity of the word *bisteeya* to the Spanish word *pasteles*, which means 'pastry confections.'

I resisted this theory for many reasons, chief among them the fact that there is no trace of *bisteeya* in Spain today, and it seemed inconceivable to me that so great a recipe would totally vanish, not leaving behind even some variant form. I had my own ideas about the origins of *bisteeya*, and became enormously excited one day when I found my first bit of evidence in an old book. I was working in the great private library devoted to Berber culture in the Rabat home of Mr Majoubi Ahardan, formerly the Moroccan Minister of Defence and a great Berber leader. Suddenly, as I was glancing through Laoust's *Mots et Choses Berbères Dialetes de Maroc* (1920), I came across the Berber word *bestila*, which I learned was the name for chicken cooked in butter and saffron, the base layer of the three-layered *bisteeya* pie.

Clearly the Andalusian theory, which was based on the chance similarity between the words *bisteeya* and *pasteles*, was now in doubt, for the Berber word *bestila* not only had an even more similar sound, but had an actual connection in meaning.

With this as my starting-point, I began to reconstruct the history of this fabulous dish.

First there was the Berber *bestila*, the chicken cooked in butter and saffron. Then the first wave of Arab invaders arrived bringing the Arabian *trid*, which was said to have been the Prophet's favourite food. *Trid* is a primitive form of pastry made by stretching dough over a hot surface. In Morocco it was merged with the Berber *bestila*: the chicken cooked with butter and saffron was placed between layers of *trid*, making a dish similar to the *trid* served in Morocco today, and that is sometimes called 'poor man's *bisteeya*.' Finally, the third wave of invaders arrived with the Persian method for making *warka*. This finer pastry was substituted for the *trid*, the chicken cooked with butter and saffron remained inside, and over the years the lemony eggs of Tetuán and sweetened almond layers of the Souss were added until the final glory of the dish was achieved.

I dispute the Andalusian theory on another count. Andalusian cooking is not based on butter at all, but is totally a cuisine of oil. In fact, up to two hundred years ago the only butter to be found in Spain was sold in pharmacies as a kind of ointment. But the Berber cooking of most of Morocco is based on butter, though oil is used for frying. And, too, there is the fact that, despite the existence of a perfectly acceptable Spanish puff pastry called *hojaldres*, made with lard, Spanish pastry is markedly inferior to Moroccan. In Tetuán, the city of refugees from Moorish Spain, where the cuisine of Moorish Andalusia still survives, one finds that the pastries (aside from the traditional Moroccan ones) are based more on the Middle Eastern models than on anything even vaguely Spanish.

But enough of history – the dish is the thing, and what a thing it is! Besides the great and classic *bisteeya* of Fez there are numerous variations, though I have observed that Moroccans are so chauvinistic about the *bisteeyas* of their mothers and hometowns that they are shocked when I tell them the dish is prepared differently elsewhere. In the Middle Atlas there is a *bisteeya* called *tarkhdoult*, made with minced beef or lamb and cinnamon and eggs – unfortunately overloaded with *smen*. In Tetuán the *bisteeya* is made with lemon-flavoured onion sauce and chicken and eggs, but without the sweetened almonds and without sugar. There is an amusing story about a Tetuanese lady who never left her native city until, in her old age, she had occasion to visit Fez. When she returned to Tetuán she told everyone what the Fassis had done. 'They are so ashamed of their *bisteeya*,' she said, 'that they hide their mistakes with a layer of sugar!'

In Rabat there is a *bisteeya* served both as a first course and as a dessert: the *warka* leaves surround rice enriched with almond milk and perfumed with orange-flower water. And, finally, there is *keneffa* (Sweet Bisteeya with Milk and Almonds, page 264), of Marrakesh, a dessert version in which a sort of custard of milk and orange-flower water is poured between casually arranged layers of fried and crisped *warka* leaves.

There are other regional variations, of course, including special *bisteeyas* served in Meknes and Essaouira. I even read of one, in John Gunther's *Inside Africa*, served at a banquet given by the late Pasha el Glaoui of Marrakesh, that, according to Gunther, contained such things as mussels and brains. I wonder about that, but in Morocco anything is possible, and it occurs to me that the pasha might have ordered the invention of a new *bisteeya* merely for the purpose of flabbergasting an American guest.

The other savoury pastries – *briks*, *briouats* and *trid* – are less dramatic but unusual and delicious.

—————— •• ——————

PASTRY LEAVES

Bisteeya can be made perfectly well with commercially bought Hungarian strudel leaves, Greek phyllo dough, and even Chinese spring-roll skins, with some reservations, but if you want to make it absolutely authentic you should learn to make *warka*.

The major things to remember when using these substitute ingredients are (1) the leaves tend to dry out quickly and must be doused with butter, and (2) the *bisteeya* is baked in the oven rather than fried, as is the usual case with *warka*.

The relative proportions for a 30 cm (12″) *bisteeya*: approximately forty 20 cm (8″) *warka* leaves (for a full-sized Moroccan *bisteeya* of 60 cm (25″) the *warka* would be double this in size) equals 225 g ($\frac{1}{2}$ lb) to 340 g (12 oz) phyllo or strudel leaves.

STRUDEL: Packages of strudel leaves are easily obtainable at ethnic shops and bakeries. Their great advantage is that they can be frozen or kept refrigerated for at least 1 week. While *warka* leaves are paper-thin and slightly crisp, strudel leaves are soft, so strudel leaves used in the inner part of the *bisteeya* must be crisped in a slow oven before inserting in the pie. (The outside of the pie will anyway become crisp during the final baking.) Strudel leaves are very strong, and as a result are useful when making *briouats* (page 99).

PHYLLO: These pastry leaves are sold at nearly every Greek and Middle Eastern food store. They are made almost exactly like strudel, but since they are stretched a little differently they are thinner and more fragile. I have made excellent *bisteeyas* with phyllo, handling the dough the same way I handle strudel, crisping the leaves for inner layers in a slow oven before use.

CHINESE SPRING-ROLL SKINS: Obtainable at Chinese grocery stores. Though these skins are created the same way as *warka*, they are made with wheat starch instead of semolina flour or plain flour, and as a result they do not bake or reheat well and tend to become leathery and tough rather quickly. I do not particularly recommend them for *bisteeya*, but they are perhaps the next best thing for Briouats and Briks (page 99). As with *warka*, any pastry made with spring-roll skins is better fried than baked.

WARKA: As we have seen, this is the authentic Moroccan pastry. The next few pages show the process.

——— •••• ———

WARKA

Where I lived in Tangier, there was a famous cook named Mina who prepared *bisteeya* for a living – she was enormously fat and her bulk, as far as Moroccans are concerned, gave testimony to her culinary skill. Mina was always busy, cooking for every important wedding, birth, and party in town. One time, when she was hired by a friend to make two enormous *bisteeyas*, I asked if I could watch her, but she adamantly refused, doubtless on the grounds that no *nasrani* had a right to know her secrets.

I must confess that, though I did not find it difficult to make good *bisteeya*, I was always in awe of the process of making *warka* leaves, and so I usually bought mine, as do many Moroccan cooks, from women who specialised in making them. Finally I decided that this was ridiculous, that I was a perfectly good cook, and despite the rebuffs of Mina, and a line I had read in a cookery book that said, in effect, that no one could learn to make *warka* who was not brought up in a Moroccan home, I resolved to decipher the mysteries of this pastry.

My first attempts were farcical: among the descriptions I received from those who had witnessed the inscrutable process was that the dough was 'thrown' or 'flung' at the heated pan, an instruction I dutifully obeyed to the detriment of my clothes, my hair, and my entire kitchen, which was soon covered with dabs of 'flung' dough.

The dough, of course, is not 'flung' or 'thrown' but is gently tapped against the pan. I soon worked this out, but still I continued to fail, until I learned the method properly from Madame Jaidi in Rabat. She explained to me something that no cookery writer had bothered to mention: that the first five or so *warka* leaves rarely succeed, and that to give up after that, just as the pan has become properly 'seasoned,' is to give up before real *warka*-making begins.

To make 40 20 cm (8") *warka* leaves (enough to make a 30 cm (12") *bisteeya*):

1 It is best to do the kneading on the floor, with a big, shallow wash-basin in front of you (henceforth to be referred to as the *gsaa*) and a bowl of warm, lightly salted water at your side. Dump 560 g (20 oz) hard-wheat flour (or semolina, bread, or strudel flour, or a mixture of semolina and plain flour) into the *gsaa*. Work in the warm water, enough to make a softish bread dough. Knead and fold the dough back on to itself, at the same time adding water to the *gsaa*, spreading the dough *over* the water and then punching down with your fists, making squishy noises as the water is worked in. (The dough will begin to look like a sponge.) Pick the dough up, turn it over, and rub it with the heel of the hand, as you do a *fraisage* in French pastry-making.

2 Keeping your hands wet, beat the dough for 1 or 2 minutes against the *gsaa*, up and down, until it begins to perform like a yo-yo. Then break off a bit of dough, dip it in the water, fold it back into the remaining mass, and then punch down and knead again. Repeat this step three or four times during the next 5 to 10 minutes, building

elasticity by lifting the dough with the sway of the hand until you are lifting it about 12 inches above the *gsaa*. Then let the dough 'rest' a few hours in a warm place, under a film of 2 tablespoons of warm water and a towel. After a 3-hour 'rest' you can start to make *warka*, or you can refrigerate the dough and make *warka* the next day.

3 In Morocco, charcoal is heated in a brazier (*kanoun*) and then covered with a flat pan called a *tobsil del warka*, which has an inner lining of copper and a top surface of tin. To duplicate this, boil water in a shallow, sauté pan covered with a large, upside-down cake tin or large, smooth-bottomed frying pan.

4 Wrap a nugget of unsalted butter in cheesecloth and set it next to the pan. Rub the *tobsil* with a little butter and immediately wipe it off with a clean towel.

5 Try out the dough: wet your hands and then, twisting with the wrist as you would twist a baton, twist off a small amount of dough about the size of an apricot. Start flipping this piece in your palm, moving your whole arm back and forth until the dough becomes a sphere that bounces away from your hand and then immediately springs back. (If the dough does not become a ball it is not yet ready; replace the small piece of dough, wait 10 or 15 minutes, and then try again.)

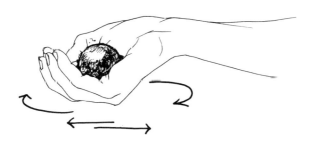

6 Turn your palm upside down, still moving it gently, and begin, *gently* to tap the dough sphere agains the hot *tobsil*, about 1½ inches from the edge. Make several soft slow taps to form a large circle of pastry. (Each time the dough touches the hot pan it should leave a thin, circular film of pastry.) Tap eight or nine times, so as to make a pastry leaf, and then tap against any places where there are holes and where the separate dabs have not joined well.

7 Allow the pastry leaf to dry slightly around its edges and then carefully lift it up, picking at the edges with your fingernails to loosen it from the pan. You will be able to peel it off after lifting approximately one-third of the leaf. If you are working alone, you may have trouble because your hands will be occupied, one keeping the *tobsil* steady and the other holding onto the sphere of dough, which should be kept in motion. In this case set the sphere down, quickly dip your hand in water, and then peel off the leaf.

Miscellaneous Notes on Making Warka

1 As I've said, your first five or six leaves will probably not succeed. Do not give up.

2 It is important to remember that, when you tap the *tobsil* with the dough, the dough does not really leave your hand; because of the very gentle downward motion of your hand the spherical mass stretches to touch the pan and then snaps back into your inverted palm. If you do this properly, not too fast, you will never lose control of the dough.

3 If you use a spatula to peel off the pastry, the leaf will tear.

4 Because the first five or six leaves will not succeed, you need a method for scraping off your mistakes. If the pastry sticks to the pan rub it with a little butter; then rub off the failed leaf with kitchen paper.

5 As you accumulate leaves, set them on top of one another and cover them with a clean towel. *Do not let them dry out.* They will keep 1 or 2 days wrapped in foil. If any of your leaves have thick spots, turn these over and let them dry for half a minute or so before piling them on top of the rest.

6 If the *tobsil* is too hot, the *warka* leaves will stick to the pan, and you may not be able to get your nails under their edges to peel them off.

7 If the dough skids off the pan, you haven't properly wiped off the butter.

8 Every time you pick up the *warka* dough, wet your hands. But do *not* add any water to the dough itself.

9 A *warka* leaf is cooked on only one side, unless it is excessively thick. A finished leaf should be slightly crisp.

10 Making *warka* is a labour of love. It may take you as long as 3 hours to make 40 leaves. If you are not up to this much effort, make your *bisteeya* with strudel or phyllo dough – you will still obtain a good result.

11 *Warka* must never be baked, always fried.

—————— •••• ——————

BISTEEYA

Note that *bisteeya* is made either with pigeons (squabs) or chicken; I do not recommend poussins – they are too dry. In Morocco the poultry inside a *bisteeya* is often left unboned, and the bones usually end up strewn all over the table. However, I can think of no earthly reason why the bones should not be removed before the poultry is placed inside the pie.

Bisteeya is customarily served as a first course, and should be hot to the fingertips. To eat it Moroccan style, plunge into the burning pastry with the thumb and first two fingers of your right hand and tear out a piece as large or as delicate as you want. You will burn your fingers, of course, but you will have a lot of fun and the pain will be justified by the taste.

Note that the sugar and cinnamon design on the top is always abstract; it is definitely *not* traditional to stencil on pictures of animals or other recognisable motifs – Muslim practice forbids it. Lattice designs of crisscrossed ground cinnamon always look good.

For 12 people – as one course in
   a Moroccan dinner

6 squab pigeons, or 2.25 kg
   (5 lbs) chicken legs and
   thighs
5 cloves garlic (approximately),
   peeled
salt
1 large bunch chopped parsley,
   mixed with a little chopped
   fresh green coriander
1 Spanish onion, grated
pinch of pulverised saffron
$\frac{1}{4}$ teaspoon turmeric
1 rounded teaspoon freshly
   ground black pepper
1 rounded teaspoon ground
   ginger

3 cinnamon sticks
225 g (8 oz) butter
4 tablespoons salad oil
1 pound whole, blanched
   almonds
icing sugar
ground cinnamon
4 tablespoons lemon juice
10 eggs
225 g ($\frac{1}{2}$ lb) to 340 g ($\frac{3}{4}$ lb) phyllo
   pastry or strudel leaves, or
   40 *warka* leaves
   (approximately)

1 Wash the poultry well and remove as much fat as possible. Crush the garlic and make a paste of it with 2 tablespoons salt. Rub the poultry with the paste, then rinse well and drain. Put the squabs or

chickens in a large casserole with the giblets, herbs, onion, spices, half the butter, a little salt, and 750 ml (1⅓ pints) water. Bring to the boil, then lower the heat, cover, and simmer for 1 hour.

2 Meanwhile, heat the vegetable oil in the frying pan and brown the almonds lightly. Drain on kitchen paper. When cool, crush them with a rolling pin until coarsely ground, or run them through a nut grinder. Combine the almonds with 115 g (4 oz) icing sugar and 2 teaspoons ground cinnamon. Set aside.

3 Remove the poultry, giblets, cinnamon sticks, and any loose bones from the casserole and set aside. By boiling rapidly, uncovered, reduce the sauce in the casserole to approximately 500 ml (scant pint), then add the lemon juice. Beat the eggs until frothy, then pour into the simmering sauce and stir continuously until the eggs cook and congeal. (They should become curdy, stiff, and dry.) Taste for salt and set aside.

4 Remove all the bones from the squabs or chickens. Shred the poultry into 3.75 cm (1½″) pieces and chop giblets coarsely.

5 Heat the remaining butter. When the foam subsides, clarify it by pouring off the clear liquid butter into a small bowl and discarding the milky solids. *Up to this point the dish can be prepared in advance, even the day before.*

6 Preheat the oven 220°C/425°F/Gas 7.

7 Unroll the pastry leaves, keeping them under a damp towel to prevent them from drying out. Brush some of the clarified butter over the bottom and sides of a 30 cm (12″) shallow cake tin, then cover the bottom of the tin with a pastry leaf. Arrange 6 more leaves so that they half cover the bottom of the tin and half hang over the sides. (The entire bottom of the tin should be covered.) Brush the extended leaves with butter so they do not dry out. (If you are using *warka*, arrange about 15 to 18 leaves around the bottom and sides; there is no need to butter the extended leaves.)

8 Fold 4 leaves in half and bake in the oven for 30 seconds, or until crisp but not too browned, or fry the leaves in an oiled frying pan. (This is unnecessary if using *warka*).

9 Place chunks of poultry or giblets around the inner edge of the tin then work toward the centre so that the pastry is covered with a layer of shredded poultry. Cover this layer with the well-drained egg mixture from step 3, and the four baked or fried pastry leaves (or *warka* leaves).

10 Sprinkle the almond-sugar mixture over the pastry. Cover with all but 2 of the remaining pastry leaves, brushing each very lightly with butter.

11 Fold the overlapping leaves in over the top to cover the pie. Brush lightly with butter. Put the remaining 2 leaves over the top, lightly buttering each, and fold these neatly under the pie (like tucking in sheets). Brush the entire pie again with butter and pour any remaining butter around the edge. (Use the same procedure for *warka*.)

12 Bake the pie in the oven until the top pastry leaves are golden brown, about 20 minutes. Shake the pan to loosen the pie and run a spatula around the edges. If necessary, tilt the pan to pour off excess butter (which could be kept on one side). Invert the pie on to a large, buttered baking-sheet. Brush the pie with the reserved butter and return to the oven to continue baking another 10 to 15 minutes, or until golden brown. (You *can* bake the pie made with *warka* leaves, but it is more traditional to gently fry the pie over low heat until golden brown on both sides.)

13 Remove the *bisteeya* from the oven. Tilt to pour off any excess butter. Put a serving plate over the pie and, holding it firmly, invert. (The traditional upper filling is always the almond layer) Dot the top of the pie with a little icing sugar and run crisscrossing lines of cinnamon over the top. *Serve very hot.*

VARIATION:

To make a superior – but more expensive – *bisteeya*, proceed as directed above, but double the quantity of almonds. Partially drain the browned almonds and run through a mincer, then knead with sugar and cinnamon (to taste) to form an oily paste. Roll the paste into 2.5 cm (1″) nuggets. Arrange the nuggets over the baked pastry leaves and proceed as directed in step 10.

91

Bisteeya, Tetuán Style

This is the *bisteeya* known to the old lady from Tetuán who was shocked at the Fez version. In the north the people prefer the dish more sharp than sweet.

Note that you have the option of adding a small amount of preserved lemons – an addition I highly recommend if you have them on hand, but one that is not absolutely necessary.

This dish will work out best if you perform steps 1 to 4 inclusive on the morning of the day the *bisteeya* is to be served: the better the eggs are drained, the better the *bisteeya* will be – crispy on the outside and moist within.

For 12 people as a course in a
    Moroccan dinner

2 kg (4¼ lbs) chicken parts, with
    giblets
5 cloves garlic (approximately),
    peeled
salt
2 medium onions, grated
2 good pinches pulverised
    saffron
¼ teaspoon turmeric
½ teaspoon freshly ground black
    pepper

½ teaspoon ground ginger
2 large cinnamon sticks
300 g (10½ oz) unsalted butter
2 large Spanish onions,
    quartered and thinly sliced
    lengthwise
1½ handfuls parsley, chopped
8 tablespoons lemon juice
8 to 10 eggs, well beaten
1½ preserved lemons (optional)
225 g (½ lb) to 340 g (¾ lb) phyllo
    pastry or strudel leaves or 40
    warka leaves (page 81)
ground cinnamon

1 Prepare the poultry with the garlic and salt as described on page 87.

2 Place the rinsed and drained poultry in a large heavy casserole with giblets, grated onion, 1 pinch of the saffron, the spices, and half the butter. Pour in 360 ml (⅔ pint) water. Add salt to taste and bring to the boil. Reduce the heat and simmer for 1 hour, covered.

3 Remove the chicken, giblets, cinnamon sticks, and any loose bones from the casserole. By boiling rapidly, uncovered, reduce the sauce to about 225 ml (scant half pint). Add the sliced onions, parsley, more pinches of pepper and saffron, and a few tablespoons water. Cook uncovered, stirring often, until the onions are soft and reduced to a thick mass.

4 Add the lemon juice and eggs and continue cooking until the eggs

become curdy and dry. Transfer this mixture to a colander set over a bowl and let drain all day if possible. Reserve the liquid.

5 Shred the chicken into chunks and discard all the bones.

6 Rinse the preserved lemons and discard the pulp. Dice the peel and set aside.

7 Heat the remaining butter. When the foam subsides, pour off the clear liquid into a small bowl, leaving the milky solids. [Up to this point the recipe can be prepared in advance.]

8 Preheat the oven to 220°C/425°F/Gas 7.

9 Unroll the pastry leaves and place them under a damp towel to prevent them from drying out. Cover the bottom of a 30 cm (12″) shallow cake tin with half the pastry leaves, overlapping as directed in step 7 of the previous recipe. Every few layers of pastry should be moistened with 2 tablespoons of the lemon-egg liquid (in place of the melted butter used in the previous recipe).

10 Place chunks of chicken and giblets around the inner edges of the tin and then work toward the centre so that pastry is covered with a layer of poultry. Cover this layer with one of onions and eggs. Sprinkle with the preserved lemon peel and about $\frac{1}{4}$ teaspoon ground cinnamon.

11 Cover with the remaining pastry leaves, brushing the remaining lemon-egg liquid on each, but without using more than 3 table-spoons. Fold the leaves as directed in step 11 of the previous recipe. Dribble the clarified butter over the top and sides of the pie.

12 Bake as directed in steps in 12 and 13 of the previous recipe and serve at once, with a mild dusting of ground cinnamon.

Bisteeya Filled with Almond-Flavoured Rice
(Bisteeya Bil Roz)

This is an adaptation of a dish in which rice, simmered in almond milk and perfumed with orange-flower water, becomes the filling for a *bisteeya* pie. Unfortunately, strudel leaves and phyllo dough cannot stand a great deal of weight and moisture, so I have had to reduce some of the rich creaminess of the filling. If you want to try the original recipe, follow the instructions for *Roz bil hleeb* (Moroccan Rice Pudding, page 261), partially drain, and make this *bisteeya* with the stronger *warka* leaves. Moroccans serve this dish as a first course, but it can also be used as a dessert. Thanks to the blender, we do not have to pound the almonds by hand in a brass mortar – a long, arduous procedure in a Moroccan kitchen.

For 6 people

3 tablespoons whole, blanched almonds
3.3 litres ($5\frac{3}{4}$ pints) milk
icing sugar
$\frac{1}{4}$ teaspoon almond extract
1 large cinnamon stick
150 g ($5\frac{1}{4}$ oz) washed raw rice (small or medium grain)
salt to taste

unsalted butter
1 to 2 tablespoons orange-flower water
225 g ($\frac{1}{2}$ lb) to 340 g ($\frac{3}{4}$ lb) phyllo pastry or strudel leaves, or 35 to 40 *warka* leaves (page 81)
1 egg
powdered cinnamon

1 Coarsely chop the almonds, then liquify in the blender with 8 tablespoons very hot water. Strain into a mixing bowl, pushing down with the back of the wooden spoon to extract as much liquid as possible. Return the almond pulp to the blender and add another 8 tablespoons very hot water. Repeat and discard the pulp.

2 Bring 500 ml (scant pint) of the milk to a boil. Add the almond milk, 100 g ($3\frac{1}{2}$ oz) icing sugar, the almond extract, cinnamon stick, rice, salt, and 2 tablespoons of butter. Return to the boil, stir once, partially cover, and let simmer over low heat for 45 minutes, or until all the liquid is absorbed.

3 Slowly, in 4 successive additions, stir in the remaining milk, stirring well and adding more *only* after the rice has completely absorbed the previous amount. Be careful not to scorch the rice; it should be creamy, soft, and very thick. Remove cinnamon stick. Stir in the orange-flower water and more icing sugar, to taste. Set aside, with one or two dabs of butter on top to prevent a skin from forming. Let cool. (This makes about 560 ml (1 pint) filling.)

4 Preheat the oven to 220°C/425°F/Gas 7.

5 In the small saucepan, melt a little unsalted butter.

6 If using strudel or phyllo pastry, butter a 20 cm (10″) shallow cake tin and in it arrange half the pastry leaves, one on top of the other so that they overlap the edges, quickly brushing melted butter between every other layer. (If you are using *warka*, see note below.)

7 Spread out the rice in one even layer over the pastry base, then cover with the remaining leaves, brushing melted butter in between. Fold the overlapping leaves up and cover with the last leaf, as

directed in step 11 on page 90. Brush the top and sides with butter.
8 Beat the egg with a little water and cinnamon and paint the top of the pastry. Bake 10 minutes, or until golden brown, then invert as directed in step 12 on page 90. Continue baking until golden brown. Finally, invert on to the serving plate and decorate the top with icing sugar and crisscrossing lines of powdered cinnamon.

Note: If you are using *warka*, scantily brush in between the layers with melted butter and, preferably, fry the pastry over gentle heat until golden on both sides.

170 g (6 oz) whole blanched almonds browned in oil and crushed with a rolling pin, mixed with some cinnamon and icing sugar, can be spread over the rice before covering and baking.

Packets of Almond-Flavoured Rice (Klandt)

Klandt is a delightful variation on *bisteeya bil roz*, tiny tea-cakes that are also served as a first course in Morocco. In Marrakesh the rice is simply steamed and then mixed with butter, raisins, and grilled chopped almonds before being wrapped in the pastry leaves.

Makes 24 *klandt*

Same as for *Bisteeya bil roz* (previous recipe), but substituting 8 phyllo or strudel leaves or 24 Chinese spring-roll skins, or *warka* leaves (page 81) and increasing the amount of melted butter to 8 tablespoons (less for spring-roll skin or *warka*)

plus
flour and water paste
salad oil for frying (for spring-roll skins or *warka*)

1 Follow steps 1, 2, and 3 on page 94.
2 Roll out the first pastry leaf or spring-roll skin. (Brush phyllo or strudel pastry with a little melted butter.) Cut into 3 sections lengthwise. Place about 2 tablespoons rice filled about 2.5 cm (1″) from the bottom of each strip. Fold the sides lengthwise over the

filling. Fold the bottom over, and roll up like a rug. Fasten the last inch of pastry with flour and water paste.

3 Fry in oil until golden brown on both sides. (If using phyllo or strudel dough, bake in a 190°C/375°F/Gas 5 oven for about 35 minutes, turning them over halfway through. Brush the tops with butter for a golden crust.)

4 Dust with icing sugar and cinnamon before serving. Serve hot or warm.

Trid

Trid, the 'poor man's *bisteeya*,' is said to have been the Prophet's favourite dish. I have to admit that *trid* is difficult and time consuming to prepare, and though I have found it delicious, I have not found it quite so delicious as *bisteeya*, which is easier to make. I include it here mainly as a curiosity, and because if you read the recipe you will see that *trid* is clearly a primitive form of the great pigeon pie.

Trid is served at Moroccan feast, sometimes even with the same filling as *bisteeya*, or with a *tagine* of chicken, ginger, pepper, and preserved lemons. In Fez the crêpes are left whole, and in Safi they are torn into small pieces.

For 10–12 people as a course in
    a Moroccan dinner

900 g (2 lbs) plain flour
salad oil
1 whole chicken of 2 kg (4¼ lbs), cleaned
5 cloves garlic (approximately)
1 Spanish onion, grated
½ teaspoon freshly ground black pepper

2 7.5 cm (3″) cinnamon sticks
½ teaspoon powdered ginger
1 teaspoon whole black peppercorns
2 to 3 pinches pulverised saffron
115 g (4 oz) unsalted butter
10 sprigs of green coriander, tied together with a thread

1 Prepare the dough for 60 pastry leaves by combining the flour with enough lightly salted lukewarm water to make a dough. Knead 5 minutes, then add 4 tablespoons vegetable oil by spoonfuls, kneading well before adding more. Knead the dough 15 to 20 minutes, until it is very elastic and smooth. (You can use an electric beater with a dough hook to do the job in 10 minutes.) Separate the dough

into 3 equal parts, coat with more oil and cover with a cloth. Set aside for 1 hour.

2 Make a paste of the garlic and 2 tablespoons salt and prepare the chicken as directed on page 87.

3 Place the rinsed, drained chicken in a heavy casserole with the onion, $1\frac{1}{2}$ teaspoons salt, the spices, butter, coriander, and 1.35 litres ($2\frac{1}{2}$ pints) water. Bring to the boil, then reduce the heat, cover, and simmer 1 hour. Remove the chicken and, by boiling rapidly, uncovered, reduce the sauce to a thick gravy of about 390 ml ($\frac{3}{4}$ pint). Return the chicken to the sauce and keep warm.

4 After 1 hour place one of the three balls of dough on your marble worktop and flatten by stretching and rubbing outward with the palms of your hands. Knead and roll the dough until smooth. Repeat with the other two balls.

5 Rub the work surface sparingly with oil. Twist the first ball of dough in half and start to work it as follows: press and rub the dough in your hands, forming a cylinder, make a small circle with your thumb and forefinger, push the cylinder through, and twist off small balls the size of a prune. Repeat until you have popped 10 'prunes' through your thumb and forefinger. Repeat with remaining half and the other two balls. Then flatten each piece into a 7.5 cm (3″) disc by tapping with oily fingers.

6 Invert a large frying pan or cake tin over a saucepan of boiling water, or set a *gdra del trid* (a glazen earthen dome) over hot coals. Oil your fingers and start tapping and stretching the first pastry disc until you obtain a paper-thin circle approximately 20 cm (8″) in diameter. Lightly oil the bottom of the pan or *gdra* and put the first leaf on to dry; turn after 30 seconds. Meanwhile, stretch and oil the next leaf. Place the second leaf directly on top of the drying first leaf, wait a second or two and then flip over so that the second leaf will start to dry, too. Continue in this manner until 10 flattened discs or leaves are piled together, cooking and drying on the pan bottom or *gdra*. Fold the pile loosely in half and then loosely in half again so that the ends will have a chance to dry. Remove and keep warm while continuing with the next batch. Continue until 6 sets of dried leaves have been prepared.

7 Preheat the oven 180°C/350°F/Gas 4.

8 Reheat the chicken and cut into serving pieces, removing any loose bones. Separate each leaf of pastry, tearing off and discarding any raw ends. Place one-third of the leaves, in two layers, on the

serving dish. Dribble a few tablespoons of the sauce over the leaves. Cover with the second third of leaves, arrange the pieces of chicken in the middle and spoon the remaining sauce over. Bake 10 minutes and serve.

Note: In some parts of Morocco sugar and cinnamon and a bowl of cold milk are served with *trid*.

BRIOUATS AND BRIKS

Briouats are small pastry envelopes stuffed with such things as rice pudding, *kefta* (cinnamon-flavoured minced meat), brains, minced fish and spices, spicy sausage, and the fillings normally used in Bisteeya (page 87), without the almonds, or Bisteeya, Tetuán Style (page 92). A platter piled high with *briouats* on the buffet table is a handsome sight.

A variation on *briouats* is the *brik*. Though most people associate *briks* with Tunisia, where they are extremely popular and sold on the street, they are also prepared in Morocco, in the Rif Mountains. A *brik* is basically just another kind of filled pastry, but it must be served like a soufflé – immediately.

Briouats Filled with Eggs, Chicken, and Lemons

Makes 40 *Briouats*

Same ingredients as for
  Bisteeya, Tetuán Style (page
  92) but using half the
  specified amounts with the
  exception of the pastry leaves
  (use 225 g ($\frac{1}{2}$ lb) phyllo
  dough, or strudel leaves, or
  40 *wakra* leaves) or spring-roll
  skins.

1 Follow steps 1 to 4 on page 92.
2 Shred the chicken finely and combine with the egg-and-onion mixture. Fold in the diced, preserved lemon peel and $\frac{1}{4}$ teaspoon ground cinnamon.
3 To make the *briouats*, spread a pastry leaf in front of you, keeping the other leaves under a clean cloth. Cut phyllo or strudel leaves vertically into three equal parts. Fold in three lengthwise. (Leave 17.5 cm (7″) spring-roll skins or *warka* leaves whole.) Brush with oil or melted butter. Place approximately 1 tablespoon filling on each piece, 2.5 cm (1″) from the bottom. Fold the left-hand corner over the filling so as to make a triangle. Fold the triangle straight up, then

fold upward to the left and continue folding as you would a flag until you reach the end and have a triangular *briouat*. Tuck in any loose ends and brush the *briouats* with butter or oil. Keep covered in the refrigerator until you are ready to bake.

4 Preheat the oven to 180°C/350°F/Gas 4.

5 Bake until golden, then turn to bake on the other side. The *briouats* will be done in approximately 20 minutes. (If you are using spring-roll skins or *warka*, fry in plenty of oil until golden on both sides.) Serve warm, with a sprinkling of powdered cinnamon.

Tunisian Briks

In Tunisia almost anything may end up inside a *brik* – tuna fish and anchovies are especially popular. In Morocco *briks* are nearly always filled with an egg, some salt and pepper, a pinch of Harissa Sauce (page 26), and a little sprinkling of ground cumin or chopped green coriander.

If you do not feel like making *warka*, the best pastry for *briks* is Chinese spring-roll skins. All you do is spread out the leaf, break a raw egg onto one half, add the flavourings, fold the leaf diagonally and then 'glue' the edges with a little frothy egg white. The *brik* is then deep fried in hot oil, turned over when brown and fried some more, and then drained on kitchen paper. The *brik* should be devoured immediately. To eat it, grasp it by its corners, being careful not to let any egg run down your face.

This recipe is basically Tunisian, and therefore, strictly speaking, it does not belong in this book. But I included it anyway, because it is North African in spirit, and utterly delicious and unique.

For 4 people as a snack

30 g (1 oz) unsalted butter
1 small onion, finely chopped
115 g (4 oz) canned tuna,
  drained and mashed
1 to 2 tablespoons chopped
  parsley
salt and black pepper
a few capers, drained, rinsed,
  and mashed

1 to 2 tablespoons grated
  Parmesan cheese
4 Chinese spring-roll skins or
  warka leaves (page 81)
4 medium or small eggs
1 egg white, lightly beaten, or
  flour and water paste
salad oil for frying
lemon

1 Melt the butter in a small frying pan and cook the onion over very gentle heat until soft but not browned. Add the tuna, parsley, salt and pepper to taste, capers, and cheese. Mix well and separate into 4 equal parts.

2 Spread out the pastry leaves. Place one quarter of the filling on one half of each leaf. Break an egg over each portion of filling. Fold each pastry leaf over to form a half circle or triangle, glue the edges with beaten egg white or flour and water paste. Fold each rim over 1 cm ($\frac{1}{2}''$) for a firmer rim, being careful not to break the egg yolk.

3 Put oil to a depth of 2.5 cm (1") in a large frying pan and heat until hot (but not smoking). Slide the *briks*, one at a time, into the frying pan. Spoon hot oil over top while frying. When the underside is nicely browned, turn and continue frying. Remove and drain. Serve at once, with lemon wedges.

Note: An electric frying pan set up wherever you are serving the *briks* works perfectly for cooking and serving.

———— •• ————

RGHAIF

Rghaif is to Moroccans what *madeleines* were to Marcel Proust – a dish that opens up all sorts of sweet memories of childhood and home. Many exiled Moroccans have told me that from time to time they feel an inexplicable longing for *rghaif*.

In 1968 my son Nicholas (he was then six) visited the mountain village of Joujouka to witness the annual celebration of the 'rites of Pan.' (The music of Joujouka was recorded by the late Brian Jones, of The Rolling Stones, with fascinating album notes by Brion Gysin.) When Nicholas returned he was full of stories of a man dressed in animal skins who danced with a fiery branch. But the thing he remembered best was being awakened in the morning by haunting flute music and being fed what he called 'an airy pancake.' He begged me to make it for him, but it took me quite a while to figure out that the 'airy pancake' he liked so much was actually a type of *rghaif*.

101

Rghaif is a primitive form of pastry, sometimes served with honey and butter for breakfast, sometimes coated with icing sugar, sometimes stuffed with almonds, or, best of all to a Moroccan, stuffed with spicy preserved meat, *khelea*. It bears a certain resemblance to the much finer French *pâte feuilletée*, in which firm butter is folded into pastry in complicated ways to build up many fine, thin butter layers, or 'flakes.' Actually *rghaif* is made with either oil or melted butter, which is spread over dough that is only folded in three twice. I should mention that for me *rghaif* can be very good if served hot, but quite ordinary and tough when cold.

Miklee

Miklee is the kind of *rghaif* served most often for breakfast. If the dough is properly worked, these airy pancakes can be quite good.

Makes 18 *miklee*

4 g ($\frac{1}{8}$ oz) active dry yeast
1 teaspoon granulated sugar
500 g (17 oz) flour
   (approximately), preferably
   bread or strudel flour

1$\frac{1}{2}$ teaspoons salt
salad oil
2 tablespoons unsalted butter
60 g (2 oz) honey

1 Sprinkle the yeast over 4 tablespoons sugared lukewarm water. Stir to dissolve and set in a warm place for 10 minutes, until bubbly.
2 Mix the flour with the salt and make a well in the centre. Pour in the bubbling yeast and enough lukewarm water to make a soft ball of dough. Knead the dough well, adding more water if kneading becomes difficult. (The dough, at first, should be sticky and soft, but after a good 20 minutes of kneading it should become highly elastic and smooth. If you have an electric beater with a dough hook attachment, set it on slow speed and knead about 10 minutes.)
3 Lightly grease your hands, the working space, and the dough with oil. With thumb and forefinger, squeeze off small balls of dough about the size of large prunes. Coat each ball with oil. Take the first ball and pat down to a disc shape. Flatten with the oiled palms and fingers of both hands, stretching the disc as you flatten it. If you have kneaded the dough well (until it is very elastic), it will practically

slide outwards. Avoid tearing the dough as it becomes paper-thin, and try to keep it consistently thin.

4 Stretch out the dough to a paper-thin rectangle 25 cm (10") × 22.5cm (9"), then coat with oil. Fold the ends of rectangles so they meet in the centre. Turn halfway and fold again. Pat down slightly with oiled fingers. Set aside and repeat with the other balls of dough.

5 Fill a frying pan to a depth of 2cm ($\frac{3}{4}$") with oil and heat. Press the 'package' out a bit and slip it into the pan. Fry the first package in oil until it puffs and its bottom becomes golden brown. Spoon a little hot oil over the top, then turn it over and continue frying for 1 minute. Transfer to kitchen paper to drain. Serve warm, with butter and honey.

Almond Miklee

Follow the previous recipe and fold an almond paste nugget inside the package.

Mtsimen

In this version of *rghaif*, dough is prepared as for Miklee (previous recipe) then the paper-thin disc is folded in half and then in half again, so that you end up with a shape like a wedge of pie. It is then fried on a lightly greased griddle (called a *mikla*), and when it browns (like a crêpe) it is served with honey and butter or butter and jam.

Meelowi

For this dish the *rghaif* pastry (prepared as for Miklee, page 102) is folded differently but fried the same as Mtsimen (previous recipe). A piece of dough is squeezed into a long cigar shape. With oiled fingers and palms it is then flattened on a pastry board until it is a long, flat, thin strip. One end, which is flattened very thin, is rolled up the length of the pastry, a procedure like rolling up a rug, except that as you roll you keep stretching the unrolled part. When you are finished you flatten the whole thing into a round pancake and then fry it on the griddle. It is very good hot, with butter and honey.

Azut Cadi

This form of *rghaif* is the most difficult to execute well. The dough (prepared as for Miklee, page 102) is worked into a thin thread. Whilst it is worked and being stretched, the completed portion is kept wrapped around a finger. When the thread is completed it is left for 20 minutes, then is flattened and fried in a small amount of oil. After frying it is pressed down, which loosens the pastry and makes it look like a plate of spaghetti. It is served with butter and dark country honey.

——— •••• ———

CHAPTER 7

Couscous

A THOUSAND tiny pellets of grain, light, separate, and tender, doused with a *tagine*, arranged into a pyramid, and then served upon a platter at the end of a meal – that is *couscous*, the Moroccan national dish.

The *couscous* concept is simple and it is brilliant. Take a container with a perforated bottom, fill it with grain, and place it above a bubbling stew; the steam from the stew will swell the grains and at the same time flavour them. When served together – the grain and the stew – the result is extraordinary; with the possible exception of *bisteeya*, *couscous* is the crowning achievement of Moroccan cuisine.

The word *couscous* actually has two meanings: the complete dish and the granules of semolina with which it is usually made. But *couscous* can also be made with other grains – barley, corn, millet, sorgum, green wheat, green barley shoots or sprouts, even crushed acorns and bread crumbs. These things become *couscous* when they are steamed above a boiling *tagine* in the top half of a *couscoussier*.

The derivation of the word *couscous* is obscure. Some believe it is onomatopoeic, a verbal approximation of the hissing sound as steam is forced through the holes into the grain. There are other theories, too, but the one fact that no one denies is that the dish itself is Berber.

Though everyone knows what you mean when you say you want *couscous*, they usually call it by other words. Most Moroccans say *seksu*; some Berbers can it *sikuk*; in the Souss region they say *sksu*; it is *sexsu* in the Rif Mountains, *utsu* in Figuig near the Algerian border, *ta'am* in Algeria, and *kouski* in Tunisia. And then there are variants beyond the Maghreb: in Trapani, in Sicily, where it is served with fish stews, they call it *cuscusu*; in Senegal, where it is substantially the same as in Morocco, it is *keskes*; and, strangest of all, it turns up in Brazil, where there are at least three types made with stone-ground maize meal, rice, or tapioca, served with such things as shrimps, sardines, and chicken, all called *cuscuz*. (It probably reached Brazil via Portuguese slave ships carrying West Africans, who had learned it from Senegalese traders, who had learned it, in turn, from Berbers.)

Originally the Berbers served *couscous* with preserved butter and downed it with a cup of milk. They called this preparation *sikuk*, and in the Middle Atlas, little by little, they began to elaborate upon it, adding chick-peas, and then, as agriculture and husbandry developed, pumpkins and gourds, other vegetables, then chicken, finally meat. Today there are nearly as many varieties of *couscous* as there are cooks: the dish can be a simple and pure Berber type, or an elaborate and spectacular extravaganza such as those allegedly served in palaces, great pyramids of semolina concealing mounds of pigeons, each stuffed in turn with *couscous* and other mysterious things.

In Morocco *couscous* is traditionally served for Friday lunch, or when it is warranted by a special occasion – or, of course, whenever anyone feels like eating it. It is so much a part of life that it is always served at feasts honouring weddings, births, and circumcisions, and when someone dies it is prepared by friends and neighbours, then placed in the home of the bereaved to be handed out to the poor during the mourning period. *Couscous* is the central image in a famous Moroccan proverb about the virtues of almsgiving:

> A handful of *couscous* [given in charity] is better than Mecca and all its dust.

As for wedding feasts, the Moroccan author, Ahmed Sefriou, in his charming book on the great Berber pilgrimage of Imilchil, tells how a bride of the Ait Hiddous tribe will use her silver brooch to separate grains, apportioning *couscous* between her husband's family and her own. By sharing the *couscous* in this way she symbolises the 'sharing of happiness.'

In Morocco *couscous* is rarely served at the evening meal; also – and many people don't realise this – it is not considered a main course. At a Moroccan *diffa* it is served at the end of a string of courses, to finally and fully satiate the hunger of the guests, and, in this sense, it is similar to the bowl of rice offered at the end of a Chinese banquet. No guest must go home hungry – the basic premise behind Arab hospitality – and, although this idea is often carried to the point of absurdity when, after being offered course after course, the possibility of going home hungry is out of the question, still satiation is symbolised by the appearance of a mound of *couscous*, highly flavoured, laden with vegetables and meats, served at the end so that the guest will achieve *shaban* (total satisfaction) and know that his host has held back nothing that would give him pleasure.

Moroccan *couscous* is different from the *couscous* served in Paris. French *couscous* is derived from the Algerian variation: the vegetables, the meat, the broth, and the grain are served to the diner on separate plates. Algerian *couscous* is good, strong in taste, and often flavoured with sausage, but it lacks the subtleties of the Moroccan types, whose spices are delicately blended, whose broth is pure ambrosia, and whose variations are infinite and sublime. Tunisian *couscous* is spicy and robust, and the recipes with seafood and fish are excellent and have found some Moroccan admirers. But really no country – Algeria, Tunisia, France, Sicily, Brazil, or Senegal – can begin to approach the exalted heights of Moroccan *seksu*.

In parts of Morocco, for example, you can find *couscous* that is both spicy and sweet at the same time, the two contradictory tastes interacting and tantalising the tongue. There is spicy *couscous* in which chili peppers and ground pepper is the pre-dominating note, or the great classic sweet *couscous* of Fez, in which onions, raisins, chick-peas, and lamb are served together in perfect harmony. One can prepare Moroccan *couscous* in the Berber style, with chicken, turnips, and creamy milk or as a dessert with dates, cinnamon, and sugar. There is *couscous* with fish, wild turnips, and fennel stalks, as prepared in the coastal town of Essaouira; *couscous* with a lamb's head, broad beans, and carrots, as served on the day after the Festival of the Sacrifice of the Lamb (Aid el Kebir); or *couscous* with lamb, chicken, and seven vegetables in a great and spectacular modern variation. There are *couscous* dishes in the styles of Rabat, Marrakesh, Tangier, Tetuán, and other cities and regions, all of them so delicious that it is impossible to choose a favourite because the last one eaten always seems the best.

———— ••• ————

HOW TO COOK COUSCOUS

In 1711 a Monsieur Mouette visited Fez and wrote the following description of the making of *couscous*:

> They take a great Wooden Bowl, or Earthen Pan, before them, with a Porringer full of Flower [flour]; and another of Fair Water; a Sieve; and a Spoon. Then they put two or three Handfulls of the Flower into the Bowl, and pour three or four Spoonfulls of Water on it, which they work well with their Fingers, every now and then sprinkling it with Water, till it all runs into little Lumps like small Pease, and this they call Couscousou. As it rolls up they take it out of the Bowl and put it into the Sieve to separate the Flower that may remain loose; and there are some Women so expert at making it, that it is no bigger than Hail shot, which is the best. In the meanwhile they boil a great deal of good Meat, as Pullets, Beef, and Mutton, in a Pot that is not above a Span open at the Mouth, and so narrow at the bottom that it may sink two Inches within the Mouth of the other, the bottom whereof is full of holes like a Cullender. Into this last Pot they put the Couscousou over the other Pot the Meat boyls in, when it is almost Ready, leaving it so about three quarters of an Hour, close cover'd with a Napkin, and a wet Cloth with a little Flower, being wrapped about the Mouth of the other Pot, that no Steam may come out that way, but all ascend to pierce the Couscousou. When ready they turn it out into a Dish. and stir it about, that it may not cling together, but lie loose in Grains: Then they Butter it, and lastly pour on the Broth and all the Meat.

One hundred fifty years later, in 1873, Amelia Perrier published her almost identical description of the *couscous*-making process in a book entitled *A Winter in Morocco*. The making of *couscous* is an age-old process that has changed little through the centuries; in fact, a non-technical description of *couscous*-making would read more or less the same today.

But please don't follow the instructions on *couscous* packages or those that come with *couscoussiers*; they're often confusing or short-handed, and they can be extremely frustrating.

Couscous cooking looks difficult, but actually it's easy once you understand the technique of handling *couscous* grains. If you follow these steps, and use them when indicated in the *couscous* recipes that follow, your grains will always be perfect: soft, light, separate, not lumpy, not sticky, not heavy, even though swelled by steam and cold water.

108

Equipment

The basic piece of equipment you need is a *couscoussier*. The lower part, the pot that holds the bubbling stew, is called the *tanjra* or the *gdra*; the upper part with the perforated bottom that holds the grains is called the *kakas*. Berber *couscoussiers* are made of unglazed earthenware, and the bourgeois Fassis use copper *couscous* lined with tin. But the aluminium ones are good, even though they sometimes come with a top, which is unnecessary, since *couscous* is steamed without a cover.

The only other thing you need is a substitute for the Moroccan *gsaa*, a large shallow basin of earthenware or wood in which the *couscous* is worked and where it dries. I have found that a large roasting tin, with sides at least 3·75 cm (1½″) high, is ideal. I've used baking sheets, but sometimes when I've circulated grains too much they've ended up on the floor.

Handling Couscous Grains

These are the master instructions for handling *couscous*, to be followed when indicated in the recipes. Though they look complicated, the principle behind them is very simple: all the wetting, drying, raking, aerating, and steaming of semolina grains is done with the purpose of swelling them with as much water as possible without allowing

109

them to become lumpy or soggy. But you must be careful: the smaller and fresher the *couscous* grain, the less water is needed.

1 *First washing and drying of couscous*: Wash the *couscous* in a large, shallow pan by pouring water over the grain in a ratio of 3 parts water to 1 part grain. Stir quickly with the hand and then drain off excess water through a sieve. Return the *couscous* grains to the pan, smooth them out, and leave them to swell for between 10 and 20 minutes. After roughly 10 minutes, begin, with cupped, wet hands, to work the grains by lifting up handfuls of grain, rubbing them gently and letting them fall back into the pan. This process should break up any lumps that may have formed. Then rake the *couscous* with your fingers to circulate it and help the grains to swell.

Note: Freshly rolled *couscous* is simply dampened and immediately steamed as directed in step 2.

2 *First steaming of the couscous:* Dampen a strip of cheesecloth, dust it with flour, and twist into a strip the length of the circumference of the rim of the bottom part of the *couscoussier*. Use this to seal the perforated top or colander on top of the pot. Check all sides for effective sealing: the top and bottom should fit snugly, so that steam rises only through the holes. *The perforated top should not touch the broth below.* Slowly dribble one-quarter of the swollen *couscous* grains into the steamer, allowing them to form a soft mound. Steam 5 minutes and gently add the remaining *couscous*. When all the grains are in the steamer, lower heat to moderate and steam 20 minutes. *Do not cover the couscous while it steams.*

3 *Second drying of the couscous:* Remove the top part of the *couscoussier* (or the colander). Dump the *couscous* into the large, shallow pan and spread out with a wooden spoon. Sprinkle a glass of cold water and 1 teaspoon salt over the grains. Separate and break up lump by lifting and stirring the grains gently. Oil your hands lightly and rework the grains – this helps to keep each grain separate. (Some people oil the grain *before* steaming, but this results in a tougher texture.) Smooth the *couscous* out and allow it to dry for at least 10 minutes. If the *couscous* feels too dry, then add more water by gradual stages, raking the *couscous* well before each addition. If you are preparing *couscous* in advance, at this point let it dry and cover it with a damp cloth. It can wait many hours. (*Very important note:* If the stew in the bottom of the *couscous* is fully cooked and well seasoned and the sauce reduced to the proper amount prior to the final steaming of *couscous* grains, you should transfer the stew and sauce to a separate saucepan, keeping it warm, and perform the final steaming over boiling water.)

4 If you want to serve right away, allow the *couscous* to dry for 10 minutes, then pile it back into the *couscoussier* top, being sure to reseal the two containers with cheesecloth, for its final steaming of 20 minutes. If you have prepared steps 1–3 in advance, 30 minutes before serving break up lumps of *couscous* by working the grains lightly between your wet fingers. Steam the *couscous* in the *couscoussier* top for 20 minutes, as previously directed.

Note: Each time you place the top or colander over the pot, use cheesecloth to reseal the top two containers.

————— •••• —————

COUSCOUS RECIPES

Pumpkin Couscous

This is a superb lamb *couscous* and makes a brilliant follow-up to *djej mechoui* (Roasted Chicken, page 170). I like the fact that it is both ultra-refined and rustic at the same time: ultra-refined because its relatively few ingredients suggest a great purity of gastronomic think-ing, and rustic because the inclusion of pumpkin is reminiscent of the earliest vegetable *couscous* preparations of the Berbers.

For 6–8 as part of a Moroccan
  dinner

6 oz (2 oz) dried chick-peas or
  300 g (10 oz) tin cooked
  chick-peas
680 g (1½ lbs) *couscous*
680 g (1½ lbs) lamb neck, cut
  into 5 pieces
4 to 5 large Spanish onions
1½ to 2 teaspoons freshly ground
  black pepper to taste

1 tablespoon salt
1 teaspoon ground ginger
2 pinches pulverised saffron
½ teaspoon powdered turmeric
225 g (8 oz) unsalted butter
450 g (1 lb) carrots
680 g (1½ lbs) pumpkin
4 tablespoons granulated sugar
225 g (8 oz) black raisins

1 Cover the dried chick-peas with water and soak overnight.
2 The next day, drain the chick-peas and cook in fresh water 1 hour. Drain, cool, and remove the skins by submerging them in a bowl of cold water and gently rubbing them between the fingers. The skins will rise to the top of the water – discard them. (If using tinned chick-peas, peel them and set aside.)
3 Prepare the *couscous* by following step 1 (first washing and drying of the *couscous* in the master instructions (page 110).
4 To prepare the broth, place the lamb in the bottom of a *couscoussier*. Quarter and slice the onions lengthwise. Add to the lamb, along with the salt, spices, half the butter, 1·8 litres (3 pints) water, and the drained chick-peas. (Tinned chick-peas should not be added until 30 minutes before serving.) Bring to the boil, then reduce the heat, cover, and simmer 1 hour.
5 Meanwhile, prepare the vegetables: scrape the carrots, halve

113

lengthwise, and cut into 6 cm (2½″) lengths. Peel and core the pumpkin, then cut into 5 cm (2″) chunks.

6 Follow steps 2 and 3 (first steaming and second drying of *couscous*) in the master instructions (page 111).

7 Add the carrots, sugar, and raisins to the broth. Continue cooking 30 minutes. [Up to this point the dish can be prepared in advance.]

8 Thirty minutes before serving, add the pumpkin and the drained peeled tinned chick-peas (if using them) to the broth. Bring to a boil, reseal the two containers with cheesecloth, and steam the *couscous* another 20 minutes.

9 Dump the *couscous* onto a large serving dish and toss with the remaining butter, using a fork to smooth out any lumps. Spread out and form a well in the centre. With a perforated spoon lift out pieces of meat (discarding loose bones). Cut the meat into small pieces and place in the well. Cover with the vegetables. Taste the broth for seasoning and readjust. Strain the broth over the *couscous* and vegetables and serve at once.

Note: Some people sprinkle a little cinnamon over the vegetables just before serving.

Omar's Couscous

This is not a classical Moroccan *couscous*, but a combination of some of the best ideas in many *couscous* recipes, plus a Tunisian touch – a peppery *harissa* sauce. My friend Omar Kadir invented this dish when we were trying to decide whether to serve a *couscous slaoui* or a modern Fez *couscous* at a large dinner party. The result was excellent – a vegetable *couscous* of lamb, raisins, onions, and almonds, sweet and spicy at the same time.

For 6–8 as part of a Moroccan dinner

60 g (2 oz) dried chick-peas or 300 g (10 oz) tin cooked chick-peas
11 medium yellow onions
680 g (1½ lbs) to 1 kg (2¼ lbs) lamb neck or shoulder, cut into 5 cm (2″) chunks
2 pinches pulverised saffron
¼ teaspoon turmeric
freshly ground black pepper
ground cinnamon
5 carrots
4 small courgettes

4 tomatoes or a 225 g (8 oz) tin peeled tomatoes
680 g (1½ lbs) *couscous*
100 g (3½ oz) black raisins
½ teaspoon ground ginger
60 g (2 oz) granulated sugar
4 to 5 sprigs parsley and 2 to 3 sprigs of green coriander, tied together
salad oil for frying
60 g (2 oz) whole, blanched almonds

1 Soak the dried chick-peas overnight.
2 The next day, drain the chick-peas, cover with fresh cold water, and cook, covered for 1 hour. Drain, cool, and remove the skins by submerging the chick-peas in a bowl of cold water and gently rubbing them between the fingers. The skins will rise to the top of the water. Discard them and set the well-rinsed chick-peas aside. (If you are using tinned chick-peas, peel them and set them aside.)
3 To prepare the broth, quarter three of the onions and place in the bottom of a *couscoussier* with the lamb, water, half the saffron and turmeric, 5 tablespoons butter, 1 tablespoon salt, 1 teaspoon pepper, and ½ teaspoon ground cinnamon. Bring to the boil, then reduce the heat, cover, and simmer for 1 hour over moderately high heat.
4 Meanwhile, perpare the vegetables: scrape the carrots and clean the courgettes; halve both lengthwise and cut into 5 cm (2″) lengths.

Peel, seed, and chop the tomatoes (see page 58). Cut the remaining onions into 5 mm ($\frac{1}{4}''$) thick 'quarter moons.' Set the vegetables aside in piles.

5 To prepare the *couscous* follow step 1 (first washing and drying of *couscous*) in the master instructions (page 110).

6 Begin the preparation of the glazed topping. After the lamb has been cooking for 1 hour, transfer 450 ml (scant pint) of the simmering lamb broth to a saucepan. Add the raisins to the broth, along with the onion 'quarter moons,' remaining saffron and turmeric, ground ginger, sugar, 3 tablespoons of the butter, $1\frac{1}{2}$ teaspoons cinnamon, salt, and freshly ground black pepper to taste. Cook, covered for 1 hour, then remove cover and continue cooking until liquid has evaporated and the onions have a glazed appearance (about 30 minutes). Set aside, uncovered.

7 While the glazed topping mixture is cooking, add the tomatoes, the drained chick-peas (do not add tinned chick-peas until 30 minutes before serving), herbs, and, if necessary, more water to the bottom of the *couscoussier*. Then follow steps 2 and 3 (first steaming and second drying of *couscous*) in the master instructions (page 111). Add the carrots to the lamb broth. Continue cooking the broth for 30 minutes. [Up to this point the dish can be prepared in advance.]

8 *Thirty minutes before serving*, with wet hands break up the lumps of *couscous* by working the grains lightly between your fingers. Add the courgettes (and drained and peeled tinned chick-peas if using them) to the lamb broth. Bring to a boil, reseal the two containers with cheesecloth, and steam the *couscous* another 20 minutes.

9 Reheat the glazed onions and raisins. Heat the oil in a frying pan and fry the almonds until golden brown. Drain and set aside.

10 Dump the *couscous* onto the serving dish and toss with the remaining butter. Use a fork to smooth out any lumps. Spread out and form a well in the centre. Place two ladlefuls of drained lamb and vegetables in the well. Cover the lamb and vegetables with the glazed onions and raisins and dust with ground cinnamon. Decorate with the almonds, then moisten the grain with strained broth. Serve with extra lamb and vegetables in an accompanying tureen and Red Pepper Sauce (see below) in a small bowl on the side.

Note: The *couscous* may be tossed with 2 tablespoons *smen* (Cooked and Salted Butter, page 35) instead of the remaining butter.

116

Red Pepper Sauce
(Harissa)

Makes 225 ml (scant ½ pint)

225 ml (scant ½ pint) lamb broth
from the *couscous* pot
1 teaspoon Harissa Sauce (page
26) or *sambal oelek*
1 tablespoon lemon juice

1 to 2 tablespoons olive oil
pinches of cumin to taste
sprinkling of freshly chopped
parsley and green coriander

Combine all the ingredients in a small saucepan over high heat. Beat
well and pour into a small serving bowl. Serve at once.

Couscous with Seven Vegetables in the Fez Manner

Fez is one of the great gastronomic centres of Morocco, and there
are many people who think the best food is to be found in Fassi
homes. The traditional Fez *couscous* is made with chick-peas, raisins,
and onions; the modern Fez variation employs seven vegetables
(onions, pumpkin, courgettes, turnips, chili peppers. carrots, and
tomatoes), two kinds of meat (chicken and lamb), and both sweetness
(raisins) and spiciness (harissa). This assemblage is rich and glorious,
and if you want you can even add other things: cabbage (early in
the cooking), peeled baby aubergines and broad beans (30 minutes
before serving), or even potatoes (which should be cooked separately
with the pumpkin). However, in Fez the number 7 is considered
lucky, and it is probably best to keep the vegetables down to that
number.

According to Robert Landry, in his *Les soleils de la cuisine*, it is
extremely chic to serve a Moroccan *couscous* with seven-year-old *smen*,
seven vegetables, and seven spices. (I have yet to taste seven-year-old
smen (though one-year-old *smen* is fairly common). As for seven spices,
the only recipe I have found is one noted down by the great English
travel writer, Budgett Meakin, in his book *The Moors*, published in

1902. He describes a *couscous* flavoured with pepper, ginger, nutmeg, corinander seeds, allspice, turmeric, and saffron.)

For 6–8 people, as part of a
   Moroccan dinner

120 g (4 oz) dried chick-peas or 600 g (20 oz) tin of cooked chick-peas
680 g (1½ lb) *couscous*
2 lamb shins or 900 g (2 lbs) stewing beef, trimmed
2 sets chicken wings and backs
2 tablespoons salad oil and 10 tablespoons unsalted butter)
2 tablespoons salt
1 tablespoon freshly ground black pepper
pinch of pulverised saffron
½ teaspoon powdered turmeric

2 medium yellow onions, quartered
2 cinnamon sticks (optional)
1 small bunch of herbs (green coriander and parsley sprigs tied together with a thread)
4 to 5 red, ripe tomatoes, peeled, seeded and quartered
450 g (1 lb) carrots
450 g (1 lb) turnips
450 g (1 lb) courgettes
225 g (½ lb) pumpkin
1 fresh chili pepper (optional)
a handful of black raisins

1 Soak the dried chick-peas overnight.

2 The next day, drain the chick-peas, cover with fresh, cold water, and cook, covered, for 1 hour. Drain, cool, and remove the skins by submerging the chick-peas in a bowl of cold water and gently rubbing them between the fingers. The skins will rise to the top of the water. Discard them and set the peeled chick-peas aside. (If you are using tinned chick-peas, peel them and set them aside.)

3 To prepare the *couscous*, follow step 1 (first washing and drying of *couscous*) in the master instructions (page 110).

4 To prepare the broth, place the trimmed meat and chicken in the bottom of the *couscoussier* with half the butter (or the oil and the butter), the salt, pepper, saffron, turmeric, the quartered onions, the cinnamon sticks, herbs, and quartered tomatoes. Cover and cook gently over low heat for 10 minutes, giving the pan a swirl from time to time. Then add 2·8 litres (5 pints) to 3·6 litres (6½ pints) of water and the drained chick-peas (do not add tinned chick-peas until 30 minutes before serving) and bring to the boil. Simmer for 1 hour, covered.

5 Meanwhile, prepare the vegetables: scrape the carrots and turnips and cut them into 3·75 cm (1½″) lengths. Cut the courgettes into quarters. Peel and cut up the pumpkin.

6 Follow steps 2 and 3 (first steaming and second drying of the *couscous* in the master instructions (page 111). Add the carrots and turnips to the lamb broth. Continue cooking the broth for 30 minutes more. (The broth has now cooked for 2 hours, so add more water if necessary.) Cut the meat into chunks, discarding the bones. [Up to this point the dish can be prepared in advance.]

7 Thirty minutes before serving time, cook the pumpkin, in a separate pan, in lamb broth-flavoured water until tender. Add the courgettes, optional chili pepper, raisins, and tinned chick-peas (if using them) to the lamb broth. Bring to the boil, reseal the two containers with cheesecloth, and steam the *couscous* another 20 minutes. Dot the *couscous* with the remaining butter during the last 5 minutes of steaming.

8 Dump the *couscous* onto the serving dish and toss with butter or *smen*. Use a fork to smooth out any lumps. Spread out and form a large well in the centre. With a perforated spoon, transfer the meat and vegetables into the well. Add the drained pumpkin slices. Taste the broth for seasoning and adjust, then strain. Moisten the grain with the strained broth. Serve Red Pepper Sauce (page 117) separately.

Note: I have heard that some Fassis use stewed quinces in place of raisins – an interesting idea.

Couscous in the Marrakesh Manner

Follow the instructions for Couscous with Seven Vegetables in the Fez Manner (page 117), but leave out the chick-peas and chicken and use any number (up to seven, for good luck) of the following vegetables: onions, broad beans, tomatoes, sweet potatoes, pumpkin, turnips, carrots, courgettes, sweet and hot peppers, cabbage.

Couscous with Dates and Seven Vegetables

Follow the instructions for Couscous with Seven Vegetables in the Fez Manner (page 117), but replace the chicken and lamb with 900 g (2 lbs) stewing beef cut into 5 cm (2") chunks, and the butter with 3 to 4 tablespoons beef dripping, and 30 minutes before serving place 225 g ($\frac{1}{2}$ lb) stoned dates in the steamer, pile the *couscous* grain on top and steam them together for 30 minutes. To serve, decorate the dish by arranging the dates around the *couscous*. This is a strong dish that warms the insides – it is usually made in winter.

Couscous with Lamb's Head and Seven Vegetables (Seksu Raseen Bahur)

In Fez this is a popular *couscous* on Friday, said to make the diner strong and clever. Prepare exactly the same as Couscous with Seven Vegetables in the Fez Manner (page 117) but substitute two lambs' heads – previously soaked in water, halved, well cleaned, and tied together – for the chicken and the lamb. The tongue is meaty and the brains are delicate and sweet. As for the eyes (everything but the pupils), they are considered the best part, and are plucked and handed to the guest of honour! *Chacun à son goût.*

Small Family Couscous

This recipe is not unlike those before and some that follow: what makes it unique is its size. Most *couscous* recipes are scaled to feed a mob and require some intricate preparation. This one is simple and geared to last-minute preparation: it was prepared to celebrate the surprise arrival in Tangier of my American editor, who came to help me finish this book.

On the opposite end of the *couscous* scale one hears of the *couscous* prepared in the Doubbala region of Morocco: up to sixteen people (and perhaps more) with arms spread out along the sides of a huge heavy cloth carry a *couscous* prepared for hundreds. This gigantic *couscous* is decorated with not only the ingredients listed below in enormous quantities, but with hard boiled sweets of all hues and boiled eggs dyed red, blue, yellow, green, and orange.

For 4–5 people

450 g (1 lb) *couscous*
4 tablespoons salad or peanut
   oil
2 tablespoons *smen*
1 small whole chicken, plus the
   giblets
salt
1¾ tablespoons freshly ground
   black pepper
½ teaspoon powdered ginger
3 pinches pulverised saffron
1 Spanish onion, sliced

a small bouquet of parsley, tied
   together with thread
115 g (4 oz) large black raisins
450 g (1 lb) sweet red onions
6 oz (2 oz) unsalted butter
1 tablespoon powdered
   cinnamon
2 tablespoons granulated sugar
2 tablespoons honey
115 g (4 oz) blanched almonds
Salad oil for frying

1 To prepare the *couscous*, follow step 1 (first washing and drying of *couscous*) in the master instructions (page 110).

2 To prepare the broth, place the oil, *smen*, chicken, 2 tablespoons salt, 1½ teaspoons black pepper, ¼ teaspoon ginger, 1 pinch of saffron, and the sliced Spanish onion in the bottom of a *couscoussier*. Cook gently, covered, over low heat, for 15 minutes, swirling the pot from time to time to avoid burning any of the ingredients. Pour in 450 ml (scant pint), add the parsley sprigs, cover again, and allow to simmer gently for 1 hour.

3 Soak the raisins in water to cover. Slice the red onions and place in a heavy-bottomed saucepan with a little salt and half the butter. Cook, covered, for 10 minutes, then add the remaining ginger and black pepper. Stir in the cinnamon, sugar, and another pinch of saffron. Continue to cook 15 minutes more, covered, then transfer 12 tablespoons of the chicken broth from the *couscoussier* to the onions. Uncover and cook until thickened.

4 Follow steps 2 and 3 (first steaming and second drying of the *couscous*) in the master instructions (page 111).

5 Drain the raisins and add to the onion sauce. Remove the chicken when tender and allow to drain.

6 Preheat the oven to 230° C/450° F/Gas 8.

7 Brush the chicken with the honey and set in the oven to glaze. Reduce the onion sauce to a syrupy glaze.

8 Meanwhile, wet your hands and break up the lumps in the *couscous* by working the grain lightly between your fingers. Reseal the steamer top and steam the *couscous* again for 15 to 20 minutes.

9 Fry the almonds in oil until golden brown and add to the onion glaze. Blend the remaining butter with another pinch of saffron and dot the steaming *couscous*, then dump the *couscous* out onto a large serving dish and toss well so that it becomes a pale yellow colour. Use a fork to smooth out any lumps. Spread out and form a well in the centre. Place the glazed chicken in the well and cover with the onion-almond-raisin glaze. Taste the broth for seasoning, then moisten the grain with it. Serve the *couscous* at once.

Couscous from Rabat and Sale
(Seksu Slaoui or Seksu Tafaya)

This sweet *couscous* is similar to the traditional *couscous* of Fez, and is excellent after a lemony chicken *tagine* or a spicy fish *tagine*. It is a classic dish in which the onions caramelise with sugar or honey, and the *couscous* grains are bright yellow from an additional touch of saffron just before serving.

For 10–12 people as part of a
   Moroccan dinner

1 kg (2¼ lbs) *couscous*
900 g (2 lb) lamb neck, cut into
   5 to 6 pieces
1 tablespoon salt
1½ teaspoons freshly ground
   black pepper
2 pinches pulverised saffron
1 teaspoon powdered turmeric
6 large Spanish onions,
   quartered

225 g (8 oz) unsalted butter
3 sprigs green coriander, tied
   together with a thread
   (optional)
2 cinnamon sticks
1½ teaspoons powdered
   cinnamon
225 ml (scant ½ pint) honey or
   granulated sugar
115 g (4 oz) black raisins

1 To prepare the *couscous*, follow step 1 (first washing and drying of *couscous*) in the master instructions (page 110).

2 To prepare the broth, place the lamb, 2 teaspoons of the salt, 1 teaspoon of the pepper, a pinch of pulverised saffron, the turmeric, 1 quartered onion, 3 tablespoons of the butter, the green coriander, and cinnamon sticks in the bottom of the *couscoussier*. Melt the butter over low heat, swirling the pan once or twice to let the spices and meat mix gently. Cover with 1·8 litres (3¼ pints) water and bring to the boil. Cover and simmer for 1 hour.

3 Meanwhile, slice the remaining quartered Spanish onions and place in the heavy-bottomed casserole with 550 ml (1 pint) water, cover tightly, and steam 5 minutes. Remove the cover and drain the onions well.

4 To prepare the glazed topping, when the lamb has cooked for 1 hour, transfer simmering broth to a heavy-bottomed casserole. (Add more water to the bottom of the *couscoussier* if necessary.) Put the drained onions, cinnamon, the remaining ½ teaspoon black pepper, the remaining teaspoon salt, 5 tablespoons of the butter, and

the honey or sugar in the casserole. Mix well to blend and cook, uncovered, for 5 minutes. Add the raisins, cover, and simmer for 30 minutes.

5 Follow steps 2 and 3 (first steaming and second drying of *couscous*) in the master instructions (page 111). (The broth has now cooked 1½ hours.) Continue cooking over very gentle heat for 30 minutes, adding water if necessary.

6 Meanwhile, remove the cover from the casserole and continue cooking until all the liquid has evaporated and the onions have reduced to a thick syrupy glaze. Set aside uncovered. [Up to this point the dish can be prepared in advance.]

7 Thirty minutes before serving, with wet hands break up the lumps of *couscous* by working the grains lightly between your fingers. Bring the broth to the boil, reseal the steamer top, and steam the *couscous* 20 minutes. Reheat the onion glaze. Blend the remaining butter with the remaining pinch of pulverised saffron and dot the *couscous* with the tinted butter during the last 5 minutes of steaming. Dump the *couscous* onto the serving dish and toss well so that the *couscous* becomes a lovely pale yellow. Use a fork to smooth out any lumps. Spread out and form a well in the centre of the *couscous*. Place the drained lamb in the well and cover with the glazed onions. Taste the broth for seasoning and readjust, then strain. Moisten the grain with the strained broth and serve at once.

Another Couscous from Rabat and Sale

Follow the instructions for the preceding recipe, but substitute 2 small pigeons (squabs) or 1 trussed chicken for the lamb. Just before serving remove the birds from the broth and glaze in a hot oven with a little honey or grape jelly. Serve under the onion glaze.

Traditional Fez Couscous

Follow the instructions for Couscous from Rabat and Sale (preceding receipe), but add 225 g (8 oz) chick-peas (prepared as instructed on page 161) to the broth.

Tangier Couscous
(Seksu Tanjaoui)

For 6–8 as part of a Moroccan
   dinner

120 g (4 oz) dried chick-peas or
  600 g (20 oz) tin of cooked
  chick-peas, drained
680 g (1½ lbs) *couscous* 680 g
  (1½ lbs) lamb neck or lamb
  shin
2 teaspoons salt
2 rounded teaspoons salt
2 rounded teaspoons freshly
  ground black pepper
1 rounded teaspoon powdered
  ginger

¼ teaspoon pulverised saffron
  mixed with turmeric
a pinch of cayenne
3 quartered medium onions
2 sprigs each parsley and green
  coriander, tied together with
  thread
225 g (8 oz) unsalted butter
1 large Spanish onion,
  quartered and thinly sliced
  lengthwise
115 g (4 oz) raisins

1 Soak the dried chick-peas overnight.

2 The next day, cover the chick-peas with fresh, cold water and cook, covered, 1 hour. Drain, cool, and remove the skins by submerging the chick-peas in a bowl of cold water and gently rubbing them between the fingers. The skins will rise to the top of the water. Discard the skins and set the chick-peas aside. (If you are using tinned chick-peas, peel and set aside.)

3 To prepare the *couscous*, follow step 1 in the master instructions (page 110).

4 To prepare the broth, place the lamb, the salt, pepper, ginger, saffron, turmeric, a pinch of cayenne, the quartered onions, herbs, and half the butter (or less, if desired) in the bottom of the *couscoussier*. Melt the butter over low heat, swirling the pan once or twice to let the spices and meat mix gently. Cover with 2·4 litres (4½ pints) water and bring to a boil. Add the drained chick-peas, cover, and simmer for 1 hour. (Tinned chick-peas should not be added until 30 minutes before serving.)

5 Follow steps 2 and 3 in the master instructions (page 111). (The broth has now simmered for 1½ hours.) [Up to this point the dish can be prepared in advance.]

6 Thirty minutes before serving, with wet hands break up the lumps of *couscous* by working the grains between your fingers. Remove the

lamb shin bone and discard, then cut the lamb into chunks. Add the thinly sliced onions, chick-peas, raisins, and the lamb cubes to the broth. Bring to a boil, reseal the two containers with cheesecloth, and steam the *couscous* another 20 minutes. During the last 5 minutes of steaming, dot the *couscous* with the remaining butter.

7 Dump the *couscous* onto a very large serving dish, tossing to distribute the butter. Smooth out any lumps with a fork. Spread out and form a well in the centre. Place the lamb in the well and cover with the onions, raisins, and chick-peas. Cover slightly with the *couscous* to give a pyramid effect. Taste the broth for seasoning and readjust, then strain. Moisten the grains with the strained broth and serve.

Tangier Couscous with Vegetables

Follow the directions for Tangier Couscous (above), but add a small bunch of quartered carrots and turnips 30 minutes after the lamb has begun cooking, then add 3 small quartered courgettes just before the last steaming.

Tangier Couscous with Chicken

To make this dish with chicken, follow the recipe for Tangier Couscous (above), excluding the chick-peas, doubling the amount of ginger and turmeric, tripling the amount of herbs, and substituting a 1·3 kg (3 lbs) to 1·5 kg ($3\frac{1}{2}$ lbs) chicken, quartered and with giblets, for the lamb shin.

Berber Couscous
(Seksu Bidaoui)

This is the kind of *couscous* you will find in small villages in the foothills of the Middle Atlas Mountains, and it is extraordinary. It is served in the spring, when everything that grows is fresh and young and tender, and it has a miraculous, clean taste. Everything in it should be as fresh as possible, except of course the *smen*, which, ideally, should be about a year old. But I think a month-old *smen* made with oregano water (Herbed Smen, page 34) makes an excellent substitution.

For 6–8 people as part of a
  Moroccan dinner

680 g (1½ lbs) *couscous*
1 small chicken, freshly killed
2 teaspoons salt
2 teaspoons freshly ground black pepper
115 g (4 oz) unsalted butter
1 good pinch pulverised saffron mixed with a little turmeric
2 large, ripe tomatoes, peeled and chopped
8 sprigs each parsley and green coriander, tied together with a thread
1 Spanish onion, quartered
1 cinnamon stick

8 white baby onions, peeled
450 g (1 lb) small, tender white turnips, cut into large chunks
300 g (¾ lb) small courgettes, quartered
2 cups baby peas, or broad beans
1 fresh green or red chili pepper (optional)
2 to 3 tablespoons Herbed Smen (page 34) or 4 to 5 tablespoons fresh butter
550 ml (1 pint) medium cream or fresh, creamy milk

1 To prepare the *couscous*, follow step 1 (first washing and drying of *couscous*) in the master instructions (page 110).

2 Wash the pullet or chicken well under running water, then drain. Remove all excess fat.

3 Melt the butter in the bottom of the *couscoussier* without browning. Add the salt, spices, half the chopped tomatoes, the herbs, quartered onion, and cinnamon stick. Take the pot in your hands and give it a good swirl. Add the pullet or chicken, cover the pan, and cook gently for 15 minutes. Pour in 900 ml (1½ pints) water, cover, and simmer for 30 minutes more. Then add the peeled white onions.

127

4 Follow steps 2 and 3 (first steaming and second drying of *couscous*) of the master instructions (page 111).

5 Add the turnips to the simmering broth and cook for 15 minutes. (The broth has now cooked for 1 hour 20 minutes – add more water if necessary.) [Up to this point the dish can be prepared in advance.]

6 Thirty minutes before serving, purée the remaining chopped tomato in an electric blender or food mill. Add the purée, courgettes, peas or beans, and optional chili pepper to the broth. Bring to the boil, reseal the two containers with cheesecloth, and steam another 20 minutes.

7 Dump the *couscous* out onto a large serving dish and mix in the *smen* with your fingertips, working it in gently. Smooth out any lumps with a fork. Make a well in the centre and place the pullet or chicken in the well. Cover with the vegetables. Meanwhile add the cream or milk to the broth and bring to the boil. Turn off the heat. Strain the broth and use some of it to moisten the *couscous*. (The remaining broth can be served to guests in small cups for additional moistening of individual portions, or as a soup.) Serve at once.

Note: To avoid burning the chicken and the vegetables, give the pot a swirl from time to time and add more water whenever necessary.

Berber Couscous with Cracked Barley
(Cheesha Belboula)

If you want to make *couscous* unlike any other, try this. It is precisely the same as the Berber *couscous* in the preceding recipe, except that instead of semolina it is made with barley: the flavour is nutty, rustic, and extraordinarily good. The first time I tasted this *couscous* it was served on a wooden tray – the vegetables looked very bright piled over the pearl-coloured grain, and there was one, a long pale green gourd called a *slaoui*, that I had never tasted before, which I later found in an Italian market in New York. This is all by way of introduction of special instructions on the steaming and handling of barley grits or kasha. The grain is different in texture from semolina, and requires three steamings. If you like this dish you can substitute cracked barley (available in all organic and health food stores) for semolina in any of the *couscous* recipes, using these notes on its handling. The most important thing is to remember that water must be added to this kind of grain *very slowly*, as described in step 3 below.

Same as preceding recipe, but
substitute 680 g (1½ lbs)
cracked barley for the *couscous*

1 Prepare the broth as in steps 2 and 3 on page 127.

2 Wash the grain in a large, shallow pan by pouring ample water over them, stirring and then draining off the excess water. Let stand 3 minutes. Meanwhile, butter the inside of the upper container of the *couscoussier*. Squeeze the grain to extract excess water and add slowly to the top container by rubbing them between your palms as you drop them in. Before sealing the top container with cheesecloth, makes sure there is plenty of liquid in the bottom of the *couscoussier*. Steam the grain 20 minutes.

3 Turn the grain out into a large roasting pan and break up the lumps with a fork. Add 1 tablespoon butter. *Slowly*, add water while raking and working the grains to help them swell and separate. It should take about 3 minutes to add 2 cups water. Do not let them become soggy. Rake and toss them, smooth them out, and let them dry for 10 minutes.

4 Pile the grains back into the top container, reseal with cheesecloth, then steam for 20 minutes.

5 Turn the grain back into the roasting pan again and break up any lumps. Allow to stand 15 minutes, working them from time to time to keep them separate and prevent them from becoming lumps. *Do not add water.*

6 Add the turnips as in step 5 on page 128. [Up to this point the dish can be prepared in advance.]

7 Thirty minutes before serving, add the vegetables as in step 6 of the preceding recipe, reseal the two containers, and steam the grain for 20 minutes.

8 To serve, pile the grain into a serving dish. Add the *smen* and work in lightly. Form a mound and then a well, pushing the grain away from the centre. With a perforated spoon transfer the vegetables and chicken to the well. Taste the sauce and, after adding the milk, readjust for seasoning. Strain the hot, creamy broth over the grain and vegetables to moisten well. Serve at once.

Cracked Barley and Broad Bean Couscous
(Cheesha Sikuk)

This simple recipe was given to me by Mr Abdeslam Bennis, president of a gastronomic society in Morocco. It is very Moroccan, very elegant, and should be made only in the spring, when the broad beans are tender and fresh. Here is my adaptation

For 4 people

115 g (4 oz) shelled fresh broad beans	salt and freshly ground black pepper
450 g (1 lb) cracked barley	115 g (4 oz) butter
2 spring onions, sliced	

Steam the barley three times, over plain boiling water, as directed in steps 2–5 of previous recipe. Boil the beans with the spring onions, a small amount of water, salt, and pepper. Drain and serve with the freshly steamed grain, which should then be buttered. Serve with an iced glass of buttermilk.

Note: Some people sprinkle a little sugar over the grains.

Berber Couscous with Barley Shoots
(Azenbu)

This *couscous*, a speciality of the nomadic tribes, is made with barley shoots or green barley. It is considered one of the most delicious in Morocco, though it is available only in the Rif and in the Souss. Admired for its purity and utter simplicity, it is *the* ultimate country dish. Unmatured barley is grilled in a pan with *za'atar*, then cracked and sieved. The smaller grains are used in soup, and the larger grains are steamed over boiling water, placed on a serving dish, buttered, and served with a bowl of cold milk or buttermilk in the Berber style.

Fish Couscous with Maize Meal
(Baddaz Bil Hut)

This is a speciality of the southern coastal city of Essaouira – a spicy *couscous* in which a *tagine* of fish, tomatoes, wild turnips with their tops, onions, fennel and carrots is used to steam hand-rolled pellets of stone-ground maize meal.

Rabat Couscous with Acorns

In the winter months in Rabat a *couscous* is made in which crushed and ground acorns are substituted for semolina, and steamed above various *tagines*.

Large-Grain Couscous
(Mhammsa)

A hand-rolled semolina *couscous* called *mhammsa*, which is twice the size of the regular packaged grain, is unfortunately not available outside the southern part of Morocco, where it is extremely popular, particularly in the Souss area, where it is prepared with chicken, onions, chick-peas and raisins as a holiday dish. More often it is served with the preserved meat, *khelea*. Since *mhammsa* is so large, it must be steamed 5 times before it becomes light and tender. With each steaming some *smen* is worked in, and during the final steaming it is garnished with chopped or quartered hard-boiled eggs. Even by Moroccan standards *mhammsa* is considered heavy fare, but for people who rise at five and dine on their first *tagine* by ten o'clock in the morning, it is a good and substantial dish.

Fine-grain Couscous with Chicken or Lamb (Seffa Merdurma)

Seffa is the opposite of *mhammsa*, an extremely fine *couscous* grain of great delicacy, which is also, unfortunately, not easily available. I suggest you perform this recipe with regular *couscous* and steam it an extra time to obtain extra lightness. If you use real saffron threads and chicken meat or lean pieces of lamb, you will just barely be able to get away with calling this dish *seffa* (or *sfaa*) *merdurma*, an expression suggesting a particularly fine dish that might be served at the palace. With giblets it runs under the plebeian title of *seffa miftoon*.

For 10 people as part of a
    Moroccan dinner or for 6
    people as a supper dish

900 g (2 lbs) *couscous* or *seffa*
butter
680 g (1½ lbs) chicken thighs,
    lean lamb cut into small
    pieces, or chicken giblets,
    wings, and necks
½ teaspoon freshly ground black
    pepper
½ teaspoon powdered ginger

pinch of pulverised saffron
¼ oz teaspoon turmeric
grated onion
3 cinnamon sticks 5 cm (2″)
115 g (4 oz) butter
675 g (1¼ pints) hot chicken
    stock
icing sugar
powdered cinnamon

1 If using *seffa*, dampen the grain very lightly with salted water, but if substituting *couscous* wash and dry it as directed in step 1 (first washing and drying of *couscous*) of the master instructions (page 110).
2 Fill the bottom of the *couscoussier* with water and bring it to a boil. Rub the steamer heavily with butter, seal to the bottom with cheesecloth, and steam as in step 2 (first steaming of the *couscous*) of the master instructions (page 112). (*Seffa* is covered loosely with a cloth while steaming.)
3 Meanwhile, cut up the poultry or lamb into 2·5 cm (1″) pieces, discarding skin, bones, excess fat, and gristle. Place the poultry or lamb pieces in a large casserole (*not* the *couscoussier* bottom) with some salt, spices, grated onion, cinnamon sticks and 3 tablespoons of the butter. Cook gently, covered, for 5 minutes, then add the hot chicken stock. Bring to the boil, cover again, and simmer for 45 minutes.

4 Dump the *seffa* or *couscous* into a large, shallow pan. Sprinkle with one cup water by quarter cupfuls and 'work' the grain for the maximum absorption, before adding more water. Add 2 tablespoons of butter and toss well. Return to the container top, reseal, and steam again for 20 minutes over boiling water.

5 (If using *seffa*, ignore this step.) If using *couscous*, turn it out and work it again, adding more water, but avoid making the *couscous* soggy. Dry for 10 minutes, then return the *couscous* to the container top and steam again for 10 minutes.

6 Remove the poultry or lamb and keep warm. By boiling rapidly, uncovered, reduce the broth to 12 tablespoons. Discard the cinnamon sticks.

7 To serve, place half of the *seffa* or *couscous* on a large serving dish. Dot with half the remaining butter and 4 tablespoons of the sauce, then toss. Spread out to make a flat cake. Arrange the pieces of poultry or lamb on the grain in one layer. Spoon over another 4 tablespoons sauce. Toss the remaining butter and sauce with the remaining *seffa* or *couscous* in the container and place over the poultry or meat. Making sure no meat is visible, form into a hemisphere, then sprinkle with a little icing sugar and decorate with lines of cinnamon. Serve with a bowl of icing sugar on the side.

Note: Homemade *seffa* can be made by moistening 450 g (1 lb) *rough-grained* semolina flour and a pinch of salt with 2 tablespoons saffron water. The semolina is rubbed into tiny pellets and then pressed through a fine wire sieve. It is then steamed 20 minutes, loosely covered with a kitchen cloth. The *seffa* is then returned to the *gsaa* and 'worked' with 8 tablespoons saffron water. A final sieving through a fine colander or coarse wire sieve prepares the grain for a second steaming just before serving. Homemade *seffa*, as opposed to commercial varieties, must be steamed twice.

—— •• ——

SHERIYA

Sheriya is a short noodle very similar to vermicelli, formed between the thumb and forefinger from pellets of dough. Moroccans use them in soups and in various other dishes, where they are treated precisely as if they were *couscous* grains. They are steamed at least three times for 20 minutes, and between each steaming they are 'worked' with cold water so that they will remain separate and soft.

Steamed Noodles with Meat
(Sheriya Miftoon)

You can make *sheriya miftoon* by breaking the thinnest spaghetti you can find (vermicelli, or use soup egg noodles) into 2·5 cm (1″) pieces and then treating them as if they were *seffa* or *couscous* by steaming them over boiling water three times. (Follow the master instructions on pages 110–12, but boil the egg noodles and drain well.) To serve, use the *sheriya* to cover and conceal various spicy bits of cooked lamb, pigeon, chicken or giblets, and then decorate with a sprinkling of cinnamon.

Steamed Noodles with Sugar and Cinnamon
(Sheriya Bahara)

Another *sheriya* dish that I first tasted in a home outside Rabat is simple to make. Again, steam 2·5 cm (1″) pieces of vermicelli or over boiling water three times. Then butter them heavily, pile them into a mound, criss-cross them with lines of powdered cinnamon, and serve with a bowl of loaf sugar powdered into dust. The dish is eaten with large spoons, washed down with cold milk and is delicious in the evening.

CHAPTER 8

Fish

ONE HEARS curious stories about the coastal region between Agadir and Tiznit. Here, near the estuary of the Massa River, the great seventh-century Arab warrior and proselytiser Ogba ben Nafi is said to have ridden his horse into the sea and proclaimed that there were no more lands to conquer or Berbers to convert. He is said, too, to have saluted 'the subjects of Jonah,' for it is here, a little north of the place where the Massa River meets the Atlantic, that Jonah is supposed to have been disgorged by the whale. Jonah is remembered in these parts as 'the fish man,' and if you ask a shepherd he may show you a stone, covered with meagre offerings (handfuls of grain, a few tufts of wool), where Jonah took his first step onto dry land.

The coast of the Souss, from Essaouira to a point south of Tiznit, is fishing country, and here, near the end of summer, people come to eat the *tassargal*, a large and tasty bluefish that rivals in popularity the alose caught in the Sebou River near Fez. Fish is popular on the Atlantic Coast of Morocco, in Casablanca, Safi, and Essaouira, and in the Rif Mountains that rise from the Mediterranean the *Riffian* people have a saying: 'If a man is with God he can put his arm into the water and by each of its hairs pull up a fish.'

When I first heard this proverb I thought, Yes, and if you are talking about the fish market in Tangier each of the fish hanging from your hairs will be different. In that wet, noisy place I used to find skate, whiting, alose, red mullet, John Dory, sardines, eels, anchovies, sea bream, turbot, sole, *changuetes* one inch long and a quarter inch wide, crabs, lobsters, angel-fish, shrimps, baby clams, mackerel, squid, swordfish, tuna, *loup*, weevers, gurnards, and God knows what else. Once I decided to cook a different fish in a different way each day, and actually went three weeks before my family rebelled and put an end to my marathon.

As everyone knows, the success of fish cookery depends in great part upon the freshness of the ingredients. In a land where refrigerators are an enormous luxury, absolutely fresh

135

fish is taken for granted.

There is no doubt in my mind that fish cooked in earthenware tastes better than fish cooked in ovenproof glass or enamelled cast iron. As for tin-lined copperware and aluminium, they definitely alter the flavour.

Of the many Moroccan fish recipes I have collected I offer here the ones I particularly like – such delights as *hut benoua* (Fish Baked with Almond Paste, page 138), a richly textured and delicately perfumed preparation that should be served at the precise moment that the crusty almonds are slipping off the fish into the onion sauce, and *hut tungera* (Fish Tagine with Tomatoes, Potatoes, and Green Peppers, page 140), a spicy robust *tagine* to which the tomatoes, potatoes, and green peppers give an Andalusian mood.

Fish Baked with Stuffed Fruit

This is my adaptation of a recipe originally published in *Fez vu par sa cuisine* by Z. Guinadeau. Madame Guinadeau calls this dish one of the 'great marvels of Moroccan cooking,' and she is absolutely right – it is delicious.

It is made with the alose (shad) that run the Sebou River near Fez in winter. The fish are stuffed with dates, which in turn have been stuffed with chopped almonds and spices. Lacking the large luscious fleshy dates of the Tafilalet region (and there are over thirty varieties, including the famous delicate and small-pitted *bu-et-tob*), you can substitute any large dates or large, fleshy prunes. If you can't get shad, use any freshwater fish; I particularly recommend carp, which can absorb a good deal of seasoning, or sea bass.

For 6 people

1 shad , carp, or sea bass 2 kg (4¼ lb), cleaned, scaled, back-bone removed, and undersection gutted and split, but with head and tail intact
salt and black pepper
2½ tablespoons granulated rice ('cream of rice')

140 g (5 oz) whole, blanched almonds
powdered ginger
granulated sugar
90 g (3 oz) butter
450 g (1 lb) stoned dates or stoned prunes
2 tablespoons chopped onion
powdered cinnamon

1 Wash the fish rapidly under running water. (Shad shouldn't be soaked, but carp must be – about 15 minutes.) Pat dry with kitchen paper, then rub with salt and pepper.

2 Bring 12 tablespoons water to boil in a small saucepan. Sprinkle with salt and quickly pour in the granulated rice. Boil for 30 seconds, beating well. Turn off the heat and allow to stand, covered, a few minutes, then cool before using.

3 Grind the almonds and mix with the cooled rice mixture, keeeping 2 tablespoons ground almonds for later use. Add a scant $\frac{1}{2}$ teaspoon ginger, 2 to 3 teaspoons sugar, $\frac{1}{4}$ teaspoon freshly ground black pepper, and 1 tablespoon of the butter to the almond–rice mixture. Blend well.

4 Open the dates or prunes and stuff each one with about $\frac{1}{2}$ teaspoon of the almond–rice mixture. If the dates are small, push two together to form a sandwich.

5 Sew the opening of the fish three-quarters of the way, then fill the stomach cavity with as many stuffed fruits as possible. Complete the sewing up.

6 Preheat the oven to $180°$ C/$350°$ F/Gas 4. Butter the ovenproof dish and place the stuffed fish on its side. Pour 8 tablespoons water over, then sprinkle with salt and pepper and a little ginger. Add the chopped onion and the remaining stuffed fruit and dot the fish with the remaining butter.

7 Bake for 45 minutes on the middle shelf of the oven, basting frequently.

8 Remove the fsh from the oven, then raise the oven heat to its highest setting. Untie the thread, pull out the stuffed fruit, and place it around the fish. Sprinkle both fish and fruit with $\frac{1}{2}$ to 1 teaspoon cinnamon and the remaining 2 tablespoons ground almonds. Set the baking dish on the highest rack of the oven and bake until golden brown and crusty, about 15 minutes. Serve at once.

Note: Cooked rice can be substituted for the granulated rice, but the creamy texture of the stuffing will be affected.

Fish Baked with Almond Paste
(Hut Benoua)

This dish, which comes from the fishing city of Safi, was served often at the New York home of a great Moroccan family, where its marvellous flavour never failed to create a sensation. My recipe was originally collected for *A Quintet of Cuisines*, one of the Time-Life 'Foods of the World' series.

For 4 people

1 bream or sea bass 1·36 kg (3 lbs), cleaned and scaled but with head and tail intact
4 tablespoons salad oil
225 g (8 oz) whole, blanched almonds
60–90 g (2–3 oz) unsalted butter, softened
1 tablespoon orange-flower water

1 tablespoon powdered cinnamon
80 g (2¾ oz) icing sugar, or more to taste
175 g (4 oz) chopped onion
1 tablespoon saffron water (page 20) or ⅛ teaspoon pulverised saffron
¼ teaspoon freshly ground black pepper

1 Rinse the fish under running water and rub it inside and out with 2 teaspoons salt. Let stand 10 minutes. Rinse again and pat dry with kitchen paper.

2 Heat the oil in a sauté pan and dry the almonds, stirring continuously with the spoon until just golden. Cool on kitchen paper.

3 Pulverise the almonds in an electric blender, then add 2 tablespoons of the softened butter, the orange-flower water, cinnamon, sugar, and 3 tablespoons (or more) water and blend to make a smooth paste. Set aside.

4 Preheat the oven to 190° C/375° F/Gas 5.

5 Stuff the belly of the fish with half the almond paste. Use 1 tablespoon of the butter to butter an ovenproof serving dish, then add the chopped onion, 4 tablespoons of water, and the saffron water and mix. Sprinkle with salt and ¼ teaspoon black pepper. Place the fish over the onion bed. Use a spatula to spread the remaining almond paste over the fish, forming a ripple design.

6 Melt the remaining 1 to 2 tablespoons butter and dribble it over the fish. Bake 45 minutes, or until the fish is completely cooked and

the almond paste is crusty yet soft – just beginning to fall into the onion sauce. Serve hot, with Moroccan Bread (page 44) or *pita*.

Eel with Raisins and Onions
(Tasira)

I learned this dish, a great Safi speciality, from an old cook reputed to be the best in her town. She was short and black, with a large growth on one of her cheeks, and unlike all the great Moroccan cooks I've met, she rarely cracked a smile. She worked in the steady, effortless manner of a natural-born chef, completing three perfect dishes with the simplest cooking equipment in a kitchen that had been converted from a garage one hour before.

For 6 people

0·9–1·3 kg (2–3 lbs) conger or
  sea eel, cut into 6 large pieces
450 g (1 lb) red onions, sliced
1–1·5 kg (2–3¼ lb) black or
  white raisins
1 good pinch pulverised saffron
1 heaped teaspoon ground
  cinnamon

$\frac{1}{2}$ teaspoon freshly ground black
  pepper
salt
8 tablespoons granulated sugar
8 tablespoons salad oil
2 tablespoons orange-flower
  water

1 Wash the fish and drop into boiling water. Remove after 2 minutes and scrape off the skin with a thin-bladed knife. Remove the large centre bone.

2 Spread the onions out in the baking dish. Sprinkle with the raisins. In the mixing bowl blend the spices, salt, and half the sugar with a little water. Coat each piece of fish with the mixture and place on the onion bed. Pour in the oil and a few tablespoons water. Bake in a preheated 200° C/400° F/Gas 6 oven, covered, for 1 hour. (Moroccans cook fish far beyond the moment the flesh 'flakes.' They prefer to let the spices penetrate the fish entirely and then let the fish crumble, thus making a richer-tasting sauce.)

3 Transfer to the top of the stove and boil down the sauce to a thick gravy, adding the remaining sugar and the orange-flower water at

the same time. Just before serving, put the fish and sauce under a hot grill to glaze.

Fish Tagine with Tomatoes, Potatoes, and Green Peppers
(Hut Tungera)

Except for stuffed fish dishes and certain regional specialities, Moroccans cook fish with a marinade called *charmoula*. *Charmoula* is used throughout Morocco and invariably contains paprika, garlic, cumin, and green coriander, as well as such things as ginger in Marrakesh and red pepper oil in Tangier and Tetuán. The *charmoula* for this dish is fairly standard and can be used in the variations that follow; if you want to make it stronger you can add a few pinches of powdered cayenne.

Any of the following firm white-fleshed fish can be used in this and the following *tagines*: sea bass; rascasse; bream; or steaks of halibut, cod, haddock, or pollack.

When the Moroccans make fish *tagines* they almost always first arrange pieces of bamboo cane (or carrots or celery sticks) in a crisscross pattern in the earthenware *tagine slaoui*. This becomes a sort of bed for the fish, keeping it from sticking to the bottom and ensuring that there is always sauce underneath to give it flavour and keep it moist.

For 6 people

1 bass, or bream, or any large, firm white fish (2·2 kg (4$\frac{1}{2}$– 5 lb), head and tail removed, scaled, and cleaned	3 large potatoes
	3 red, ripe tomatoes
	3 sweet green peppers
	1 to 2 cloves garlic, peeled
lemon juice (optional)	1$\frac{1}{2}$ tablespoons tomato paste
salt	6 tablespoons lemon juice
charmoula (next page)	6 tablespoons salad oil

1 Early in the day, wash the fish. (If it smells 'fishy,' rub it with lemon juice and rinse.) Rub with salt and let stand 10 minutes. Rinse again and drain. Pat dry with kitchen paper.

2 Slice the fish crossways into 5 or 6 large pieces. Rub in some of the *charmoula* and let stand for at least 30 minutes (the longer the better) so that the spices can penetrate the fish.

3 One and one-half hours before serving, peel the potatoes and slice thinly. Slice the tomatoes crosswise. Halve the green peppers and remove seeds.

4 Preheat oven to 200° C/400° F/Gas 6.

5 Make a lattice pattern in the bottom of a baking dish by criss-crossing 6 pieces of cane 15 cm (6″) long or 6 bamboo chopsticks. Arrange the fish slices over the cane. Dip the sliced potatoes in *charmoula* and spread over the fish. Repeat with the tomatoes and green peppers. Chop the garlic and sprinkle over the vegetables.

6 Mix the remaining *charmoula* with the tomato paste, lemon juice, oil, and 8 tablespoons water. Pour this sauce over the fish. Cover with aluminium foil and bake for 35 minutes. Remove cover. Raise the oven heat to the highest setting and move the baking dish to the uppermost shelf of the oven. Bake 20 minutes, or until the fish is cooked and a nice crust has formed over the vegetables. Serve warm, not hot.

Charmoula

3 large garlic cloves, crushed
  with 2 teaspoons salt in a
  blender or mortar
2 tablespoons powdered cumin
2 tablespoons sweet paprika
$\frac{1}{4}$ teaspoon crushed hot red
  pepper flakes, seeds removed

4 tablespoons coarsely chopped
  Italian flat-leaved parsley
4 tablespoons coarsely chopped
  fresh coriander leaves
5 tablespoons mild vinegar
$1\frac{1}{2}$ tablespoons fresh lemon juice
2 tablespoons fruity olive oil

In a blender combine garlic, spices, herbs and salt and hot pepper. Add the vinegar, lemon juice and olive oil and blend until smooth. Scrape into a small saucepan and heat slowly, stirring, until hot and aromatic, about 30 seconds; do not boil. Let cool before using. These quantities make enough to marinate a 2·25 kg (5 lb) fish, or enough sauce for 6 people.

Tagra

This Tangier variation, which is named after the casserole it is cooked in (see below), is cooked precisely the same as the preceding recipe. The only difference is in the preparation of the *charmoula* and in the absence of the canes. Instead of adding paprika powder directly to the marinade, the paprika is added in the refined form of paprika oil, which is made as follows:

Boil 4 tablespoons salad oil in a small frying pan; add 2 teaspoons paprika and 4 tablespoons water; boil for 10 minutes; allow to cool. The oil that rises is added to the *charmoula*; the paprika sediment is thrown away.

The *tagra* is an unglazed peaches-and-cream-coloured pottery bowl found in Tangier, Tetuán, Chaouen, and surrounding countryside. Before it can be used, it must be seasoned with grated onion, oil, and salt, then left to bake in a hot oven until the seasoning turns black. Then the pot is allowed to cool slowly in a turned-off oven. When cold, it is washed well and left to dry. The pot is then ready for fish cookery, either over charcoal or in the oven. They are never used over a gas flame or an electric range.

Fish Tagine with Olives
(Hut Bil Zeetoon)

For 6–8 people

450 g (1 lb) green, cracked olives (preferably Greek, packed in brine)

1 fish, preferably carp (1·8 kg) (4 lbs), sealed, cleaned, belly opened, head removed

charmoula (page 142)

2 lemons, peeled and sliced

4 tablespoons salad oil

3 to 4 tablespoons lemon juice

1 Boil the olives three times, changing the water each time, to rid them of their bitterness (see page 30).

2 Follow steps 1 and 2 on page 141, but do not slice the fish. Mix half the *charmoula* with the olives; rub the remaining *charmoula* into the fish. Let it stand for 30 minutes. Preheat the oven to 200° C/400° F/Gas 6.

3 Make a lattice pattern in the bottom of the baking dish by criss-crossing the canes, then arrange the whole fish over the cane. Spread the lemon slices over the fish and cover with the olives and *charmoula*, 6 tablespoons of water, and the oil. Cover with the aluminium foil and bake for 45 minutes, then remove the cover, raise the oven heat to the highest setting and bake for 15 minutes longer. Sprinkle with lemon juice and serve warm.

Fish Tagine with Celery in the Style of Safi
(Hut Bil Karfas)

For this fish *tagine* from Safi the bamboo canes in the bottom of the casserole are replaced by fresh celery stalks.

For 6–8 people

1 bass or other firm white fish (1·8 kg (4 lbs)), cleaned and scaled, head and tail left on

lemon juice

salt

6 tablespoons chopped mixed fresh herbs (parsley and green coriander)

$1\frac{1}{2}$ teaspoons powdered cumin

1 tablespoon sweet paprika

$\frac{1}{8}$ to $\frac{1}{4}$ teaspoon cayenne

pinch of pulverised saffron

3 cloves garlic, peeled

4 tablespoons salad oil

680 g ($1\frac{1}{2}$ lbs) celery

450 g (1 lb) tomatoes (fresh or tinned), peeled, seeded and chopped

$\frac{1}{2}$ preserved lemon

1 teaspoon chopped parsley

1 Early in the day, wash the fish. If it smells 'fishy,' rub the flesh with lemon juice and rinse off at once. Rub inside and out with some salt, then let stand 10 minutes. Rinse and pat dry with kitchen paper. Score the fish at 3·75 cm (1½″) intervals.

2 Blend the herbs, spices, 1 teaspoon salt, the garlic, oil, and lemon juice into a *charmoula*. Turn the fish in the *charmoula* to coat evenly, then rub it into the cavity. Let stand *at least* 30 minutes or longer, so that the spices penetrate the fish.

3 Meanwhile, separate the celery stalks, cut away the leaves, and wash well. With a sharp paring knife, scrape off the strings from the back of each rib. Cut lengthwise down the middle, then cut crosswise in 5 cm (2″) pieces. Set the celery pieces aside.

4 Preheat the oven to 200° C/400° F/Gas 6.

5 Arrange the celery pieces, in one layer, in the baking dish. Lay the fish over the celery and pour the *charmoula* over the fish. Add the chopped tomatoes. Wash the preserved lemon, remove the pulp, and chop the peel into dice. Sprinkle the lemon peel and chopped parsley over the fish. Cover with aluminium foil and bake for 40 minutes.

6 Remove the foil and spoon the sauce over the fish to moisten. Raise the oven heat to its highest setting and continue baking the fish, uncovered, on the upper shelf of the oven for 20 minutes. Taste for seasoning – the dish should be slightly peppery – and add salt, if necessary. Serve at once or cool, cover, refrigerate, and reheat before serving.

Fish Tagine with Carrots
(Hut Bil Kreezo)

For a variation in the Casablanca manner, prepare Fish Tagine with Celery in the Style of Safi (previous receipe) but substitute carrots for the celery and decorate with thrice-blanched green, cracked olives (page 30).

Fish Stuffed with Eggs, Onions, and Preserved Lemons

For 6–8 people

1 firm white, lean fish, 2 kg
 (4½ lbs) or 1·6 kg (3½ lbs) fish
 fillets
450 g (1 lb) chopped red onions
pinch of pulverised saffron
¼ teaspoon freshly ground black
 pepper

salt to taste
9 tablespoons salad oil
12 teaspoons chopped parsley
90 g (3 oz) unsalted butter
3 eggs
1½ preserved lemons

1 Wash the fish as directed in step 1 on page 144, slit open the belly and clean well. Dry fish with a damp cloth.
2 Rinse the onions well under running water (to rid them of sharpness), then drain. Mix the onions, saffron, salt, pepper, half the oil, parsley, and 2 tablespoons of the butter. Cook 15 minutes, until the onions are soft and transparent.
3 Meanwhile, fry 3 eggs in 2 tablespoons butter. When almost set scramble them until firm. Remove from the heat and stir into onion mixture. Rinse the preserved lemon and remove and discard the pulp. Sliver the peel and add to the onions. Stuff the fish with half the onion mixture. Place the fish in the oiled baking dish and cover with the remaining onion mixture.
4 Preheat the oven to 200° C/400° F/Gas 6.
5 Sprinkle the fish and onions with remaining oil and butter. Pour in 8 tablespoons water, cover, and bake 1 hour.
6 Just before serving, run the fish under a hot grill to glaze.

Baked Fish with Rice

A savoury fish dish from Safi.

For 6–8 people

225 g ($\frac{1}{2}$ lb) raw rice, well
   washed
3 tablespoons chopped parsley
salt to taste
freshly ground black pepper
2 pinches pulverised saffron
60 g (2 oz) unsalted butter
3 tablespoons lemon juice

1 medium onion, grated
2 hard-boiled eggs, shelled and
   chopped
8 tablespoons peanut oil
1 fish, 2·25 kg (5 lbs) washed
   and cleaned, belly slit, head
   and tail left on

1 Bring plenty of water to a rolling boil in the bottom of a *couscoussier*. Fasten the perforated top on securely, as described on page 113, and steam the rice in the top, covered with a cloth and lid, for 20 minutes. Remove, stir, and moisten the rice with 450 ml (scant pint) boiling water. Drain, then return the rice to steam again, *covered*, 20 minutes. Repeat the process, moistening, draining, and steaming a third time.
2 Mix the parsley, salt, $\frac{1}{4}$ teaspoon pepper, a pinch of saffron, the butter, and lemon juice. Stir in the 1 tablespoon grated onion and the eggs.
3 Preheat the oven to 200° C/400° F/Gas 6.
4 Wash the fish as directed in step 1 on page 144. Stuff with the egg-rice mixture. Rub the fish all over with a little saffron until brilliant yellow. Place the fish in the oiled baking dish. Sprinkle with the remaining grated onion, the oil, and a little salt and pepper. Cover with the foil and bake for $1\frac{1}{4}$ hours. Remove the cover and continue baking until the skin is crisp.

——— •••• ———

REGIONAL FISH SPECIALITIES

There are many regional fish dishes that taste better on Moroccan soil, and you should try them if you visit any of the following towns.

RABAT: Shad prepared whole in a *tagine*. The fish is stewed on a bed of finely minced onions, seasoned with saffron, sugar, and cinnamon, and surrounded by a layer of white raisins. It turns crusty and golden, the raisins caramelise, and the result is delicious. It is similar to the eel dish of Safi called *tasira* (Eel with Raisins and Onions, page 139).

SAFI: You will always find a certain *finesse* in Safi cookery. For example, the *smen* here is washed with herbs and spices, and not just *za'atar*; the *charmoula* for fish is more aromatic here than elsewhere, no doubt on account of the addition of pure saffron. Other Safi specialities not recorded in this book are fish with lemon and olives; fish with butter, cumin and onions; fish with tomatoes and fennel stalks; and fish stuffed with freshly chopped tomatoes, rice, and plenty of herbs.

FEZ: This is, of course, an inland city, where fish dishes tend to be built around the river Sebou shad and trout. In addition to Fish Baked with Stuffed Fruit (page 136) there are a number of shad *tagines* definitely worth looking for: shad with the wild artichokes called *coques*, shad with broad beans, shad with hot or sweet green peppers, and shad roe fried and served with *charmoula* sauce.

TANGIER: Two variations of *Hut tungera* (Fish Tagine with Tomatoes, Potatoes, and Green Peppers, page 140), one substituting chopped Swiss chard and the other the wild greens called *gurneen*.

TETUÁN: The fish specialities here have mostly to do with stuffings, though the *tagine* of anchovies in garlic sauce is not to be missed, and the Tetuanese are renowned for their skill in the making of fish omelettes.

Among the great stuffings for fish are: tomatoes, rice, onion, olives, and preserved lemons; onion and eggs flavoured with lemon and cinnamon; a thick, rich jam made of sweet green peppers and tomatoes cooked down with spices; and other 'Andalusian-type' mixtures.

ESSAOUIRA: This is the city where the word 'spicy' begins to have meaning. Here the cooks create a fish *couscous* that is extraordinary, as well as the esoteric *teegree* – sun-dried mussels cooked with olives and hot peppers and served as a first course in 'salad' form.

Here also you will find squid stuffed with rice, tomatoes, and *charmoula*, and such Jewish specialities as fish balls poached in tomato sauce or stuffed inside pastry leaves and fried, and whole fish baked after being coated with cumin paste. There is also a scrumptious sardine *tagine* made with *charmoula* and wild greens from the nearby hills.

IN ALL CITIES: *Hut makalli*, or 'fried fish,' is a sort of street food that varies slightly from place to place. Basically, the fish is dusted in semolina flour before being fried, which gives it a fine crust, and often it is served – hot, warm, or cold – with *charmoula* as an accompanying sauce.

CHAPTER 9

Poultry

MR MEHDI BENNOUNA, once chief of the Agence Mahgreb Arabe Presse in Rabat, told me a story about chicken that is absolutely true. During the period of struggle against the French, he and several friends who were members of the Istiqlal (Independence party) used to meet once a week in Tangier to discuss politics, play cards, and enjoy each others' company. Each would bring a *tagine* from home, and when it was time for lunch would share it with his friends.

One of the men, like Mr Bennouna, was from the city of Tetuán. One day he told the others that in Tetuán there were fifty ways to prepare chicken, each different and each delicious. Those who were not from Tetuán laughed, an argument broke out, and finally bets were laid.

Once a week, over the next year, the man brought a Tetuán chicken dish to the meetings. As each week passed he amazed and astounded his friends with increasingly interesting and delicious variations. Anticipation mounted, and a list of the dishes was compiled. On the fiftieth week they assembled, eager to taste the final *pièce de résistance*. The man arrived with the same pot that had offered up so many great chicken preparations, opened it, reached inside, and pulled out a whole uncooked chicken.

'What's this?' asked his friends.

'Chicken with feathers,' he answered, and then with a smile: 'Why not? It comes naturally that way.'

He won the bet.

After he told me this story I asked Mr Bennouna if he could remember any of the other dishes. In an incredible *tour de force* he rattled off all but two of them. Here is that list, in the order in which Mr Bennouna gave it to me:

1. Chicken braised and fried (*mahammer*)
2. Chicken in highly spiced sauce with lemon and olives (*emshmel*)
3. Chicken in ginger sauce with lemon and olives (*makalli*)

4. Chicken stuffed with rice and tomatoes, steamed
5. Chicken stuffed with sweet *couscous*, served with sweet sauce
6. Chicken stuffed with salted *couscous*, served with brown sauce
7. Chicken stuffed with *sheriya*, fried in oil or roasted
8. Chicken stuffed with ground almonds, fried in oil or roasted
9. Chicken stuffed with celery and onions, served with savoury sauce
10. Chicken stuffed with giblets
11. Chicken stuffed with *bakoola* (a wild herb) and garlic, steamed
12. Chicken stuffed with diced vegetables (artichokes, peas, carrots, and so on)
13. Steamed chicken with cumin and salt
14. Chicken with layers of onions and tomatoes (*kammamma*)
15. Chicken with coriander, onions, fried almonds, and eggs (*tafaya*)
16. Chicken, Fez style, with *smen*, parsley, and sliced hard-boiled eggs
17. Chicken smothered in sweet tomato jam (*matisha mesla*)
18. Chicken with green olives (*meslalla*)
19. Chicken with lemon and eggs (*masquid bil beid*)
20. Chicken, braised, fried, and coated with spicy eggs (*mefenned*)
21. Chicken with *smen*, chick-peas, and almonds (*kdra touimiya*)
22. Chicken with *smen*, rice, almonds, and parsley
23. Barbecued chicken (*mechoui*)
24. Boiled chicken (*mafooar*)
25. *Bisteeya* Tetuán style, with plenty of lemons
26. *Couscous* with chunks of chicken in a cinnamon-flavoured sauce (*seffa merdurma*)
27. Chicken *couscous* with vegetables
28. Chicken with pastry leaves (*trid*)
29. Chicken with quince, honey, *amber*, and aga wood
30. Chicken with quince and onions
31. Boned chicken wrapped in an omelette made with peas
32. Chicken in *tagine* with a vegetable (string beans, fennel, carrots, etc.)

33. Chicken simmered in *smen*
34. Chicken with prunes and almonds in honey sauce
35. Chicken with raisins
36. Chicken with fried aubergine (*derbel*)
37. Chicken with fried courgettes
38. Chicken with fried pumpkin, sweetened
39. Chicken cooked with spices (cumin and coriander seeds) to make *khelea* (preserved meat)
40. Sweet chicken *couscous* with onions, raisins, and chick-peas
41. Chicken served with giblet sauce, onions, chopped olives, and lemons
42. Chicken stuffed with mint
43. Chicken stuffed with *kefta* (chopped spiced lamb or beef)
44. Chicken cooked with the spices used for fish (the marinade *charmoula*)
45. Chicken with fried almonds
46. Roast chicken
47. Chicken with raisins, chick-peas, and onions
48. 'Can't remember.'
49. 'Can't remember.'
50. Chicken with feathers!

Tetuán is just one of the great gastronomic centres of Morocco. Think of the chicken dishes invented by the cooks of Fez, Marrakesh, and other cities and regions. Of all the poultry dishes I have learned, I have selected more than twenty recipes which I think are extraordinary.

Basic Method for Preparing Poultry

For most of the recipes in this chapter, prepare poultry as indicated below – the timings in the recipes include these steps:
1 Wash the chickens or other poultry in salted water and drain. Pound 4 cloves garlic and 2 tablespoons salt into a paste. Rub the paste into the cavity and flesh of the poultry, at the same time pulling out excess fat from under the skin and from the neck and rump ends. Pull out the thin translucent membrane from under the skin of the breast. Rinse the poultry well under running water until it no longer

smells of garlic. (The garlic is used to rid the poultry of any bitterness that might spoil a sauce; it also acts to bring out its flavour, much like monosodium glutamate.) Drain the poultry well.

2 If you suspect that your poultry is tasteless on account of 'scientific breeding,' use a method invented by Janet Jaidi to improve its taste: Rub it with the spices to be used in the recipe, a little butter or oil, and marinate it overnight. (If you do this, remember that you may have to readjust the spicing of your sauce at the end.)

3 If you are using whole poultry, it must be trussed. Trussing poultry is easy: clip off the wing tips and discard; slip the ends of the legs into a horizontal incision made just above the rump (turkeys often come this way), or slip the legs into incisions made on the lower sides of the breast.

Note: If the poultry is to be stuffed, do not wash it with garlic or salt.

——— •••• ———

FOUR DIFFERENT WAYS TO MAKE CHICKEN WITH LEMON AND OLIVES

Chicken with lemon and olives is one of the great combinations in Moroccan cookery, the dish that most often seduces foreigners and turns them into devotees of Moroccan *tagines*. There are numerous variations on this exquisite theme; I have included four, each one delicious, each one unique: *Djej masquid bil beid* – a glorious variation enriched by the addition of whipped and baked eggs; *Djej emshmel* – a multi-spiced classic served in a plentiful onion-based sauce; *Djej bil zeetoon meslalla* – a variation literally smothered with whole or cracked green olives; and *Djej makalli* – a more subtle though no less delicious variation, flavoured with ginger and saffron and served with a thick sauce enriched by additional mashed chicken livers. I recommend that you try them all.

Before the recipes, however, a few words about lemons and olives. I could barely contain my rage and scorn when I read the following paragraph in an American women's magazine: 'You needn't brine

152

your lemons in order to taste a close reproduction of the Moroccan lemon chicken; fresh lemons do very well as a substitute. What you miss by making it with fresh lemons is the "preserved flavour" (much like bottled lime juice).' This same writer then described the olives in her recipe as, simply, 'green.'

There is, and I cannot emphasize this enough, *no substitute* for preserved lemons in Moroccan food. (There is also not much similarity between the taste of preserved lemons and the taste of bottled lime juice, and, of course, no similarity as far as texture is concerned.) Not to use preserved lemons is to completely miss the point, and also to miss a whole dimension of culinary experience. Preserved lemons are easy to make (page 27), and if carefully stored they will keep almost a year.

As for olives, I have written about them at length on pages 29–30. One does use 'green olives' to smother *Djej bil zeetoon meslalla*, unripened ones cracked and soaked in brine. (If you cannot get Moroccan olives, buy Greek ones and prepare as directed on page 30).

For the other three recipes the classic olive to use is the ripe reddish-brown Moroccan *mchqouq* perfumed with citrus juice. When they are not available I have had excellent luck with Gaetas from Italy, Kalamatas from Greece, and also Greek Royal-Victorias that have been rinsed to rid them of bitterness.

Chicken with Eggs, Lemons, and Olives (Djej Masquid Bil Beid)

For 6 people

2 chickens, cut up and prepared
  as directed on pages 151–2
1 large handful parsley,
  chopped
3 cloves garlic, peeled and
  chopped
1 medium Spanish onion,
  grated
salt to taste
$\frac{1}{2}$ rounded teaspoon ground
  ginger
pinch of pulverised saffron

$\frac{3}{4}$ teaspoon freshly ground black
  pepper
60 g (2 oz) unsalted butter,
  melted
3 large or 6 small cinnamon
  sticks
10 eggs
2 preserved lemons
8 'red-brown' olives, such as
  Kalamatas, stoned and
  chopped
8 tablespoons lemon juice

1 Place the cleaned chicken in the casserole. Add two-thirds of the chopped parsley, the chopped garlic, grated onion, salt, spices, half the butter, and the cinnamon sticks. Add 2 cups water and bring to a boil. Simmer, covered about 1 hour or until the chickens are *very* tender and the flesh is almost falling off the bone. (During the cooking you may need to add more water.)

2 Preheat oven to 180°C/350°F/Gas 4.

3 Transfer the chickens (but not the sauce) to the serving dish. Remove any loose bones and cinnamon sticks from the sauce in the casserole and, by boiling rapidly, uncovered, reduce to 450 ml (scant pint) of thick, rich sauce. Pour over the chickens.

4 Beat the eggs to a froth with the remaining parsley. Rinse and dice the preserved lemons, using the pulp if desired. Stir the lemons and chopped olives into the eggs and pour the egg mixture over the chickens. Cover the dish with aluminium foil and bake on the middle shelf of the oven for 20 minutes. Raise the oven heat to its highest setting, remove the aluminium cover, and dot the eggs with the remaining melted butter. Transfer the dish to the upper shelf of the oven and bake 10 minutes more, or until the eggs are completely set and the chickens have browned slightly. Sprinkle with lemon juice and serve at once.

Note: Six Moroccan pigeons or 3 squabs – about 2.75 kg (6 lbs) may be substituted for the chickens, in which case the dish is called *Frach masquid bil beid*.

Chicken with Lemons and Olives Emshmel (Djej Emshmel)

I first ate this dish in the city of Meknes, sometimes called the City of Olives. *Djej emshmel* (pronounced *meshmel* or *emsharmel*) is a classic Moroccan dish – chicken served in an intricately spiced, creamy, lemony, and sublime sauce with a scattering of pale-hued olives.

For 8 people

2 to 3 chickens, whole or
    quartered, with their livers
6 cloves garlic, peeled
salt
1 teaspoon ground ginger
1 teaspoon sweet paprika
$\frac{1}{4}$ teaspoon powdered cumin
$\frac{1}{4}$ ground black pepper
4 tablespoons salad oil
900 g (2 lbs) grated onion

$\frac{1}{4}$ teaspoon pulverised saffron
    (mixed with turmeric, if
    desired)
4 tablespoons mixed, chopped
    fresh herbs (green coriander
    and parsley)
225 g (8 oz) ripe 'green-brown'
    olives
2 preserved lemons
2 to 3 fresh lemons

1 The day before, using 4 cloves of the garlic and 2 tablespoons salt prepare the chickens as directed on pages 151–2, then marinate both chickens and livers in 1 teaspoon salt, the remaining 2 cloves of garlic, sliced thin, the spices, and the oil. Refrigerate, covered.

2 The next day, place the chickens, livers, and marinade in a large lidded casserole. Add 4 tablespoons of the grated onion, the saffron, herbs, and 450 ml (scant pint) water. Bring to the boil, cover, and simmer 30 minutes, turning the chickens often in the sauce.

3 While the chickens are cooking, rinse and stone the olives. (If they seem a little bitter, cover with cold water, bring to the boil, and drain.) Set aside.

4 Remove the chicken livers from the casserole and mash them fine. Return to the casserole with the remaining grated, drained onions. (This will give a good deal of body to the sauce.) Add water, if necessary. Continue cooking 20 minutes, partially covered.

5 Rinse the preserved lemons (discarding the pulp, if desired) and quarter. Add the olives and preserved lemon quarters to the sauce when the chickens are very tender, and the flesh falls easily from the bone. Continue cooking for 5 to 10 minutes, uncovered.

6 Transfer the chickens to a serving dish and spoon the olives and lemons around them. Cover and keep warm. By boiling rapidly, uncovered, reduce the sauce to 360 ml ($\frac{2}{3}$ pint). Add the juice of 2 fresh lemons to the sauce in the pan. Add more salt (and more lemon juice, if desired) to taste. Pour the sauce over the chickens and serve at once.

Chicken with Green, Cracked Olives
(Djej Bil Zeetoon Meslalla)

For this recipe you can use the bitter green olives often sold 'cracked' and packed in brine by Greek grocers; to get rid of the bitterness boil them three times. When I first learned this dish in Morocco I wondered how the olives were going to be stoned, since they were already cracked on one side. The Moroccans had a solution – they put them on the stone floor of the kitchen, tapped each of them smartly with a smooth stone, and the stones popped right out. I have often served this dish with uncracked Moroccan green olives, with great success.

For 6–8 people

2 chickens, whole or cut up, with giblets, prepared as directed on pages 151–2
1 teaspoon ground ginger
1 teaspoon freshly ground black pepper
$\frac{1}{4}$ teaspoon pulverised saffron (mixed with turmeric, if desired)
1 tablespoon finely chopped garlic
170 g (6 oz) grated onion

1 large handful finely chopped mixed herbs (parsley and green coriander)
6 tablespoons salad oil
$\frac{1}{2}$ teaspoon powdered cumin
$\frac{1}{2}$ teaspoon sweet paprika
salt to taste
900 g (2 lb) green olives, preferably Greek
8 tablespoons lemon juice, or more to taste

1 Place the prepared chicken in a large lidded casserole with all the ingredients except the olives and lemon juice. Cover with water and bring to the boil, then reduce the heat, cover, and simmer for 30 minutes, turning the chickens often in the sauce.

156

2 Meanwhile, stone the olives, using a paring knife or just smashing each one with a smooth stone. Cover the olives with water, bring to the boil, and boil for 5 minutes. Drain, cover with fresh water, bring to the boil, and cook for 5 more minutes. Repeat the procedure one more time. Taste the olives – they should no longer be bitter: if they are, boil them again. Drain and add to the casserole after the chicken has cooked for 30 minutes.

3 Pour in the lemon juice and continue cooking until the chickens are very tender, and the sauce is thick. Transfer the chickens to an ovenproof serving platter and place in a hot oven to brown. Reduce the liquid in the casserole to a thick gravy and adjust salt and lemon juice to taste.

4 To serve, cover the chickens completely with olives. Pour the sauce over and serve at once.

Chicken with Lemons and Olives, Makalli (Djej Makalli)

For 4 people

1 chicken, cut in 6 pieces, with 2 chicken livers
6 to 7 cloves garlic, peeled
salt
1 teaspoon powdered ginger
$\frac{1}{4}$ teaspoon freshly ground black pepper
1 preserved lemon, rinsed
4 tablespoons salad oil

$\frac{1}{4}$ teaspoon pulverised saffron (mixed with turmeric)
225 g (8 oz) grated onion, drained
6 sprigs green coriander, tied together with a thread
225 g (8 oz) 'red-brown' olives, such as Kalamatas or Gaetas

1 The day before, using 4 cloves of the garlic and 2 tablespoons salt, prepare the chicken as directed on pages 151–2. (Be sure to rinse well after rubbing with the garlic and salt.) Using the blender, combine the ginger, a little salt, the pepper, 2 to 3 cloves garlic, the pulp only of the preserved lemon (reserving the peel), and the oil into a sauce. Rub the sauce over the pieces of chicken and the livers. Cover with cling film and refrigerate overnight.

2 The next day, place the chickens, livers, and sauce in the casserole. Add the saffron, onion, bundle of green coriander sprigs, and water.

Stir and bring to the boil. Partially cover and simmer gently for 30 minutes. Turn and baste the chickens often.

3 Remove the livers and mash, then return to the sauce. Rinse the olives and stone them, if desired. Add the quartered preserved lemon peel and olives for the final 15 minutes' cooking. Transfer the chicken to a hot oven to brown. By boiling rapidly, uncovered, reduce the sauce to a very thick gravy, about 12 tablespoons. Remove the coriander sprigs. Spoon the sauce over the chicken, decorate with the lemon peel and olives, and serve at once.

In *The Moors*, by the British adventurer Budgett Meakin, there is a recipe for chicken with olives that is fascinating and extremely esoteric. He describes a dish made with olives *and* raisins and flavoured with grated nutmeg and allspice! I wish he had mentioned where he found it; I can find no traces of such a style of seasoning, and suspect it has been lost in the last eighty-seven years.

———— ••• ————

CHICKEN KDRAS

A *kdra* is a certain type of *tagine*, cooked with the strong Moroccan butter called *smen*, a lot of onions reduced to butter softness, spiced with pepper and saffron, and usually 'cut' at the end with a dash of lemon juice. The stew of many *couscous* dishes are based on the principles of the *kdra* sauce, as are some of the most famous dishes in the Moroccan repertoire: *Djej bil hamus* (Chicken Tagine with Chick-Peas, page 163), *Djej kdra bil looz* (Chicken Kdra with Almonds, page 160), and Chicken Simmered in Smen (page 164).

Kdras are delicious and rich, and if they have a failing it is their somewhat unattractive, pale yellow look. To make them appear more appetising Moroccans sometimes add an extra pinch of saffron at the end to make a yellower sauce. You can brown the chickens in a hot oven while preparing the sauce, though this is not done in classic *kdra* cooking.

In Fez *kdras* are always made without ginger, but in Rabat and Marrakesh and in the north this strict view is usually ignored; use ginger if you wish, but, if you are entertaining Fassis, do so with the knowledge that they will smile behind your back.

Chicken Kdra with Almonds and Chick-Peas (Djej Kdra Touimiya)

In one of the most famous *kdras* the chicken is accompanied by almonds as well as chick-peas. You might think that crisp almonds would go well with chicken, but, in fact, the almonds should be soft. If they are old it can sometimes take as long as two hours to transform them to this state.

For 4–5 people

160 g (5½ oz) blanched whole almonds
160 g (2 oz) dried chick-peas, soaked overnight, or 300 g (10 oz) tin cooked chick-peas
¼ teaspoon pulverised saffron (mixed with a little turmeric)
salt to taste
1 teaspoon white pepper
½ teaspoon powdered ginger
1 large cinnamon stick
3 tablespoons butter or 2 tablespoons *smen* (Cooked and Salted Butter, page 35)

1 chicken (1.35–1.60 kg (3–3½ lbs)), quartered, or 2 sets of chicken legs and thighs, or 3 squabs, or 6 Moroccan pigeons, prepared as directed on pages 151–2
2 Spanish onions, quartered lengthwise and finely sliced
900 ml (1½ pints) chicken stock or water, more if necessary
4 tablespoons chopped parsley
juice of 1 lemon, or to taste

1 Cover the almonds with cold water and simmer, covered, for at least 2 hours. (The cooking time is approximate – it depends upon the freshness of the almonds.)
2 In a separate saucepan, cover the soaked and drained chick-peas with fresh cold water, bring to boil, reduce the heat, and simmer, covered, 1 hour. Drain and submerge in a bowl of cold water. Rub the chick-peas to remove their skins. The skins will rise to the surface. Discard them. (If you are using tinned chick-peas, rinse, drain, and skin them, and set them aside.)

159

3 In a large casserole combine half the saffron, salt, the spices, butter or *smen*, and the prepared poultry. Cook over low heat, without browning for 2 to 3 minutes. Chop 4 or 5 slices of onion finely and add to the casserole with the stock. Bring to the boil, add the drained, skinned chick-peas, and simmer for 30 minutes, covered. (Do not add the tinned chick-peas until the poultry has finished cooking.)

4 Add the remaining sliced onions and chopped parsley and continue cooking 30 minutes more, or until the poultry is very tender (the flesh almost falling off the bone). Transfer the poultry to a warm serving dish. Add the tinned chick-peas to the sauce. By boiling rapidly, reduce the sauce in the casserole to a thick gravy.

5 Drain the almonds and add to the sauce, along with remaining saffron. Cook together for 1 or 2 minutes and spoon over the poultry. Sprinkle with lemon juice to cut the richness of the sauce. Serve hot.

Chicken Kdra with Almonds
(Djej Kdra Bil Looz)

This is simply a variation on the preceding recipe. Make it precisely the same way but omit the chick-peas and double the amount of almonds.

Chicken Kdra with Almonds and Rice
(Djej Kdra Bil Looz Bil Roz)

For this *kdra* I advise you to use *smen* and not to substitute butter, because *smen* goes so beautifully with rice (as it does with *couscous*). If you haven't any *smen* on hand, I suggest that you make some (see Cooked and Salted Butter, page 35) and return to this recipe when the *smen* is ready. In the meantime, you might as well sew up a cheesecloth bag for the rice. The principle behind poaching a bag of rice in the sauce is quite ingenious: the rice captures the flavour of the sauce, stays intact, and does not stick to the bottom of the pan.

For 4–5 people

same as in *djej kdra touimiya*
(previous recipe), but omit
the cinnamon stick and
substitute 225 g ($\frac{1}{2}$ lb) of rice
for the chick-peas

1 Follow steps 1 and 3 in the previous recipe.
2 Fold a piece of cheesecloth in half and sew up two of the sides. Spoon in the dry rice and sew up the remaining opening. Make the bag large enough so the rice has room to expand six fold.
3 After the poultry has simmered for 30 minutes, add the remaining onions, parsley, the bag of rice, and more water if necessary. (Be sure there is enough liquid in the pan both for the rice and for the sauce.) Poach the rice for 20 to 25 minutes in the sauce, then remove the bag. Remove the poultry, when very tender, falling off the bones. Keep the rice and poultry warm.
4 Drain the almonds and add to the remaining sauce. Add the remaining saffron, and a little water if necessary. Cook together for 5 minutes.
5 Meanwhile, open the bag of rice and form a pyramid in the centre of the serving dish. Arrange the pieces of poultry around the rice. Add lemon juice to the sauce, then adjust for seasoning. Spoon the almonds and sauce over the chicken. Serve at once.

Chicken Kdra with Turnips and Chick-Peas

I will never forget making a soup of young turnips from a French recipe of Elizabeth David's and discovering how delicious this vegetable can be. The turnips in Morocco are especially tender, and when I first began to cook Moroccan food I discovered there was hardly a *couscous* that didn't contain them. For this *kdra* try to use turnips that are young and freshly picked and that still retain their stalks and leaves. It's the stalks that 'make' this dish. I have been told that fresh spinach leaves can be substituted if necessary.

For 4 people

60 g (2 oz) dried chick-peas, soaked overnight, or 300 g (10 oz) tinned cooked chick peas
2 onions, quartered and sliced lengthwise
1 teaspoon white pepper
$\frac{1}{4}$ teaspoon powdered ginger
pinch of pulverised saffron
$\frac{1}{2}$ teaspoon turmeric
salt
4 tablespoons unsalted butter or 2 tablespoons *smen* (page 35)

1 chicken 1.35–1.60 kg (3–$3\frac{1}{2}$ lbs), quartered and prepared as directed on page 151
1.35 litres ($2\frac{1}{2}$ pints) chicken stock or water
900 g (2 lbs) young turnips, in 3.75 cm ($1\frac{1}{2}$")
the tender turnip leaves, finely chopped and the turnip stalks, finely chopped
juice of $\frac{1}{2}$ to 1 lemon
chopped parsley

1 Cover the soaked and drained chick-peas with fresh cold water, bring to the boil, reduce the heat, and simmer, covered for 1 hour. Drain and submerge in a bowl of cold water. Rub the chick-peas to remove their skins. The skins will rise to the surface. Discard them. (If you are using tinned chick-peas, rinse, drain, and skin them, and set them aside.)

2 Combine the onions, the spices, a teaspoon of salt, and butter or *smen* with the prepared chicken in a casserole. Pour in the chicken stock or water and bring to the boil. Add the drained, skinned chick-peas, turnips, turnip leaves, and turnip stalks. Cover and cook for 40 minutes, then remove chicken and turnips and keep warm.

3 Continue cooking the sauce until it has reduced to a thick gravy and the chick-peas are soft. Add the juice of half a lemon, then taste

the sauce for seasoning and adjust with salt and more lemon juice, if desired.

4 Place chicken and turnips (and tinned chick-peas, if using them) in the sauce to reheat. Serve with a sprinkling of parsley.

Chicken Tagine with Chick-Peas
(Djej Bil Hamus)

A sweet and spicy-sharp ginger-flavoured chicken stew that comes to the table bright yellow and fragrant. Strictly speaking it is not a *kdra*, but a modern variation of a classic dish.

For 6–8 people

450 lb (1 lb) chick-peas or 1.15 kg (2½ lbs) tinned cooked chick-peas
2 chickens, whole or quartered
5 cloves garlic, peeled
salt
1 teaspoon powdered ginger
1 rounded teaspoon freshly ground black pepper
pinch of pulverised saffron
1 teaspoon turmeric

2 tablespoons finely chopped parsley
1 cinnamon stick
90 (3 oz) chopped spring onions, white part only
80 g (2½ oz) butter
1 Spanish onion, sliced very thin
80 g (2½ oz) black raisins (optional)

1 The day before, soak the dried chick-peas in water to cover. Using 4 cloves of the garlic and 2 tablespoons salt, prepare the chickens as directed on pages 151–2. Then blend 1 teaspoon salt, the ginger, pepper, and the remaining clove garlic, crushed, with 2 tablespoons water and rub into the flesh of the chickens. Place in a large glass or stainless steel bowl, cover and let stand overnight in the refrigerator.

2 The next day, drain the chick-peas, place in a saucepan, cover with fresh water, and cook, covered, for 1 hour. Drain and submerge in a bowl of cold water. Rub the chick-peas to remove their skins. The skins will rise to the surface. Discard them. (If you are using tinned chick-peas, rinse, drain, and skin them, and set them aside.)

3 Transfer the chickens and any juices in the bowl to a large casserole. Add a pinch of saffron, the turmeric, parsley, cinnamon stick, spring onions, and butter. Pour in 1.15 litres (2 pints) and bring to

the boil. Reduce the heat, cover, and simmer for 1 hour, turning the chickens frequently in the sauce. When the chickens are very tender, remove and keep warm.

4 Add the finely sliced onions, freshly cooked chick-peas, and raisins to the sauce and cook until the onions are very soft and the sauce has reduced to a thick gravy. Return the chickens to the sauce to reheat. (If you are using tinned chick-peas, add them now.) Taste the sauce for salt, and add a pinch of pulverised saffron for a good yellow colour.

5 To serve, place the chicken parts in a deep serving dish, forming them into a mould. Spoon over the onion-chick-pea-raisin sauce. Serve hot with plenty of Moroccan Bread (page 44) or *pita*.

Chicken Simmered in Smen

This classic dish of Fez is like a *kdra*, except that it calls for less than the usual amount of onions. Rich Fassis (people from Fez) put up pounds of butter in airtight earthenware jugs and store it for years. When they want to impress a visitor they bring out some of their treasured *smen* and allow him a few sniffs. If they are feeling particularly gracious they may serve him *smen* in a dish like this, which, even when made with my 'young' *smen*, is bound to make you feel as prosperous as Fassi with a cellarful of it.

For 4 people

1 chicken of 1.3 kg (3 lbs), quartered and prepared as directed on pages 151–2, with 2 livers	salt
	2 tablespoons roughly chopped parsley
170 g (6 oz) onion, finely chopped	2–3 tablespoons *smen* (Cooked and Salted Butter, page 35)
$\frac{1}{4}$ teaspoon pulverised saffron threads (mixed with turmeric)	2 tablespoons fresh unsalted butter
$\frac{1}{2}$ teaspoon ground black pepper	$\frac{1}{2}$ preserved lemon
	2 tablespoons fresh lemon juice

1 Place the prepared chicken in a casserole with the livers and minced onion. Sprinkle with the spices and 1 teaspoon salt. Toss to coat evenly.

2 Purée the parsley in the blender with a little water. Add half the 'parsley water' and all the *smen* to the casserole. Pour in 225 ml (scant $\frac{1}{2}$ pint) and bring to the boil;. Reduce the heat and simmer, covered, for 1 hour, adding more water if necessary. Remove the chicken to the colander when very tender and keep warm while the sauce simmers for 1 full hour.

3 Heat the 2 tablespoons butter in a frying pan and gently brown the drained chicken quarters. Transfer to the flameproof serving dish, cover, and keep warm.

4 Meanwhile, add the remaining 'parsley water' to the sauce in the casserole and, by boiling rapidly, uncovered, reduce to 340 ml ($\frac{1}{2}$ pint). Put the sauce, livers, and odd bits of skin and bits in the blender jar. Whirl until the sauce is smooth. Pour over the chicken and reheat.

5 Discard the pulp from the preserved lemon and dice the peel. Sprinkle the diced lemon peel over the chicken. Simmer 5 minutes, taste for seasoning and add additional salt if necessary. Sprinkle with lemon juice and serve at once.

—— •●• ——

THREE UNUSUAL CHICKEN TAGINES

In addition to the chicken with lemon and olives dishes, and the *kdras*, there are literally dozens of other chicken *tagines*. Here are three that have struck me as unusual: *djej matisha mesla*, an extraordinary delicious *tagine* of chicken cooked with a sweet tomato jam; *djej bisla*, a *tagine* of chicken smothered in small white onions and perfumed with gum arabic, and *djej bil babcock*, a robust *tagine* of chicken with prunes as prepared in the Rif Mountains.

Chicken Cooked with Sweet Tomato Jam (Djej Matisha Mesla)

One of the best combinations of Moroccan cookery is the use of honey to bring out the flavour of tomatoes. The tomatoes are slowly simmered, then their liquid is rapidly evaporated and are finally slow-fried with the honey in the released oil. You can cut corners by using sugar in place of honey, but you will lose some of the fineness. Although you can make this dish with tinned tomato paste, I don't recommend it – the glory of *djej matisha mesla* is in the incredible richness of the tomato jam made from a big bowl of raw, fat, red, vine-ripened tomatoes. Of course it's expensive to buy that many tomatoes, but in my opinion it's worth every penny.

For 6–8 people

2 chickens, 1·35–1·60 kg (3–3½ lbs), quartered
4 cloves garlic, peeled
salt
pinch of pulverised saffron
¼ teaspoon ground ginger
½ teaspoon freshly ground black pepper
1 teaspoon chopped garlic
4 tablespoons salad oil
2·25 kg (5 lbs) fresh red ripe tomatoes

115 g (4 oz) grated onion
4 tablespoons 'coriander water' (see page 25) (optional)
2 teaspoons powdered cinnamon
2 tablespoons tomato paste
4 tablespoons thick, dark honey such as Greek Mount Hymettus
2 tablespoons sesame seeds, toasted to golden brown in the oven

1 The day before, using the 4 cloves garlic and 2 tablespoons salt, prepare the chickens as directed on pages 151–2. Mix the spices, salt, chopped garlic, and oil and rub into the flesh of the chickens. Let stand, covered, in the refrigerator overnight.

2 Also the day before, peel, seed, and coarsely chop the tomatoes (see page 58) and refrigerate overnight.

3 The next day, place the chickens, with the marinade, in a casserole. Add 675 ml ($1\frac{1}{4}$ pints) water, the grated onion, coriander water, salt, and 1 teaspoon of the cinnamon. Bring to the boil, reduce the heat, and simmer, uncovered, for 20 minutes.

4 Add the tomatoes, tomato paste, and a little sprinkle of salt. Cook over brisk heat, turning the chicken often in the sauce, until very tender. Remove chicken and keep warm while preparing the sauce.

5 Let the tomatoes cook down rapidly until all the water is completely evaporated (about 1 hour over high heat), stirring occasionally to avoid scorching and continuously for the last 15 minutes. When all the water evaporates away the oil from the marinade will be released; the tomatoes will begin to fry in it, and will start to thicken considerably. Add the honey and the remaining teaspoon cinnamon and cook a few minutes to bring out their flavours. Reheat the chicken quarters in the sauce, rolling them around to coat them evenly. Transfer to the warm serving dish, sprinkle with the seasame seeds, and serve hot or warm.

Chicken with Smen, Tetuán Style

An inexpensive Tetuanese version of this dish is made with 2 chickens cooked in a broth made with $\frac{1}{2}$ teaspoon freshly ground black pepper and turmeric, salt, 115 g (4 oz) butter, and 450 ml (scant pint) water. After 15 minutes three-quarters of the broth is transferred to another pan while the chickens continue to cook and brown slowly in the remaining fat. Meanwhile, the poured-off broth is used to cook 900 g (2 lbs) peeled, seeded, and chopped tomatoes (see page 58) until no water is left in the pan. Then 90 g (3 oz) granulated sugar, 4 tablespoons orange-flower water, and 1 teaspoon cinnamon is added to the tomatoes and they are reduced again until they become a thick dark jam. 115 g (4 oz) toasted blanched almonds and 1 tablespoon toasted sesame seeds are used to decorate the dish just before serving.

Chicken with Onions
(Djej Bisla)

The aromatic gum arabic is most often used in Middle Eastern sweet desserts; here it gives a chicken *tagine* a mysterious flavour.

For 6–8 people

2 chickens, 1·35 kg (3 lbs), whole or quartered, prepared as directed on pages 151–2
$\frac{1}{4}$ teaspoon black peppercorns
$\frac{1}{2}$ rounded teaspoon powdered ginger
6 tablespoons butter
$\frac{1}{2}$ teaspoon pulverised saffron mixed with turmeric

1 or 2 grains gum arabic, pulverised
170 g (6 oz) grated onion
1 tablespoon whole cumin seeds wrapped in a cheesecloth bag
2 5 cm (2″) cinnamon sticks
900 g (2lbs) whole white onions, peeled

1 Place all ingredients except the whole white onions in a large casserole. Cover with 675 ml (1$\frac{1}{4}$ pints) water and bring to the boil. Cover and simmer for 1 hour, turning the chickens often in the cooking liquid, adding water whenever necessary. Remove chickens when very tender and, if desired, brown in a hot oven.
2 Meanwhile, add the onions to the casserole and boil quickly until they are tender and the sauce is well reduced. Serve all together, at once.

Chicken with Prunes, Rif Style
(Djej Bil Babcock)

I heard about this dish from many people in Tangier, who told me the Moroccan writer Mohammed Mrabet had cooked it for them. Despite all the descriptions, I couldn't figure out the recipe. On a trip to Morocco I went to Paul Bowles, who had discovered and translated Mrabet, and he recalled the measurements from memory. Back in New York I tested it, and it came out well. In the Rif Mountains, which rise from the Mediterranean coast, the people are individualistic and do things their own way – for example, they rub cumin into the flesh of chickens, which is unknown in other parts of the country.

For 4 people

1 chicken 1·60 kg (3½ lbs), prepared as described on pages 151–2, with giblets	2 to 3 teaspoons cinnamon powdered
salt to taste	2 large Spanish onions, sliced lengthwise
freshly ground black pepper	1 teaspoon turmeric
2 teaspoons ground cumin, or more to taste	1 teaspoon powdered ginger
340 g (12 oz) prunes, stoned	whole, blanched almonds
	vegetable oil for frying

1 Cut off the wings and legs from the prepared chicken, leaving the breast in one piece. Rub all the pieces with salt, pepper, and cumin. Let stand for 1 hour.

2 In a separate saucepan, cover the prunes with cold water and add the cinnamon. Bring to a boil, reduce the heat, and simmer for 30 minutes. (If the prunes are excessively dry, you will need to soak them for at least 1 hour and cook them a bit longer, until tender.)

3 Steam the sliced onions in the casserole with the turmeric, ginger, salt, pepper and 4 tablespoons water for 15 minutes.

4 Meanwhile, brown the almonds in the oil, remove with a perforated spoon, and drain on kitchen paper. Brown the chicken evenly on all sides in the same oil, then transfer to the steamed onions with 225 ml (scant half pint) water. Cover and simmer for 30 minutes.

5 Add the cooked prunes and some of the prune water to the casserole and continue cooking until the chicken and prunes are very tender.

6 To serve, arrange the chicken breast in the centre of the serving dish, place the legs and wings around, and cover all with prunes and sauce. Sprinkle with the almonds and serve at once.

One day, when all the birds had gathered to make their final arrangement before beginning a pilgrimage to Mecca, they passed a resolution: 'If God wills we will start tomorrow.' But the hens and chickens cried out: 'Even if God does not will it we will start tomorrow.' When the time came to start they were punished for these irreverent words – they could not fly. The other birds cursed them and cried: 'The traitors shall stay at home!' Ever since that time chickens have been confined to the poultry yard. (A folktale, as related by Dr Françoise Legey in *The Folklore of Morocco*)

——— •• ———

CHICKENS ROASTED, FRIED, OR STEAMED

Here are four marvellous ways to cook chicken, totally different from chicken *tagines*: *Djej mechoui*, chicken roasted in the style of Marrakesh; *djej mahammer*, braised and browned chicken (or turkey, or rabbit) prepared in a spicy sauce; *djej mefenned*, a variation on *djej mahammer*, in which the chicken is finally served in a coating of eggs – difficult to make but a *tour de force* – and *djej mafooar*, chicken steamed to a delectable silken texture.

Roasted Chicken
(Djej Mechoui)

In one of the palaces of the royal family in Marrakesh there is a huge room set aside for the spit-roasting of chickens. At least a dozen spits are slanted diagonally across piles of burning hot coals, each attended by two men – one to crank the spit, the other to paint the roasting chickens with spiced butter.

For 4 people

3 spring onions, white part only, chopped
1 clove garlic, peeled (optional)
2 tablespoons roughly chopped mixed herbs (green coriander and parsley)
1 teaspoon salt
1½ teaspoons sweet paprika

pinch of cayenne
1½ teaspoons powdered cumin
60 g (2 oz) softened unsalted butter
2 frying chickens 900 g (2 lbs), whole, split, or quartered, prepared as directed on pages 151–2

1 Pound the spring onions in a mortar with the garlic, herbs, salt, and spices. Blend with the butter to make a paste. Rub the paste over the prepared chickens and into its cavities. Let it stand for at least 1 hour.
2 Heat charcoal in an outdoor grill or heat up the grill.
3 Arrange the pieces of chicken skin side up over the coals or skin side down under the grill. After 5 minutes turn and baste with any extra paste or the juices in the roasting pan. Continue turning and basting every 5 minutes until the chickens are done – depending on the heat of the coals.

Chicken Braised and Browned
(Djej Mahammer)

This is a Rabat recipe for a dish that is cooked and served throughout Morocco. In Tangier some people add a little bit of hot red pepper to the sauce and eat the chicken with sautéed potatoes; in Fez they sprinkle it with buttered and browned almonds; and in Marrakesh, where it is served without accompaniment, the sauce is usually jazzed up with extra paprika, and sprigs of mint are added with the green coriander.

For 8 people

$\frac{1}{8}$ teaspoon pulverised saffron
   soaked in $\frac{1}{4}$ cup hot water
1 teaspoon mashed garlic
$\frac{1}{4}$ teaspoon powdered turmeric
2 teaspoons paprika
$\frac{1}{4}$ teaspoon powdered cumin
salt
2 chickens 1·35 kg (3 lbs),
   whole, prepared as directed
   on pages 151–2, with 3 livers

90 g (3 oz) grated onion
170 g (6 oz) unsalted butter
4 sprigs green coriander,
   pounded to a paste in a
   mortar

1 Mix the saffron water with the garlic, spices, and salt. Rub into the prepared chickens and lay them on their sides in a large casserole. Add the livers, onion, and half the butter. Pour in 725 ml ($1\frac{1}{4}$ pints) water and bring to a boil. Add the coriander and simmer, covered, over moderately low heat for 1 hour, turning the chickens from time to time.

2 Halfway, remove and mash the livers, then return them to the sauce.

3 When very tender, remove the chickens and keep warm. Heat the remaining butter in the frying pan and brown one chicken at a time until crusty all over. Transfer to a serving dish and put in a warm oven while browning the second chicken. (They can also be browned in a very hot oven.)

4 Meanwhile, by boiling rapidly, uncovered, reduce the sauce to make about 12 tablespoons thick gravy. Serve the chickens with the sauce poured over.

171

Turkey Braised and Browned
(Bibi Mahammer)

This is a simple variation of *djej mahammer*: substitute a 3·6 kg (8 lbs) turkey for the two chickens and increase the cooking time in step 1 by 1 hour. For the browning portion of this dish you will need a restaurant-size frying pan; in Morocco they either use a huge pot, about 9 litres (16 pints) capacity, or brown the turkey in a hot oven.

Rabbit Braised and Browned
(Lernib Mahammer)

Another variation of *djej mahammer* uses a 1·8 kg (4 lb) rabbit cut up into parts. Add 1 teaspoon *ras el hanout* (page 23) to the sauce, and, when the rabbit is browning (step 3), add 225 g ($\frac{1}{2}$ lb) soaked and drained raisins to the sauce. In Fez this dish is always served with a good sprinkling of browned almonds.

Chicken Braised and Browned and Coated with Eggs
(Djej Mefenned)

This is yet another variation of *djej mahammer*, and one of the most difficult of all Moroccan dishes to execute well. If the technique of twirling the whole chicken in sizzling butter while basting it with seasoned eggs seems too difficult, you can do it the Tetuanese way: quarter the chicken, coat the pieces separately, and then fry them in the usual way.

James Skelton, an expatriate Australian who lived in a restored palace in the *medina* in Marrakesh, told me about a version of this dish he ate years ago at the Maison Arabe restaurant: the egg-coated chicken had been boned and then stuffed with browned, chopped almonds and honey. Before so awesome a feat of culinary skill even the *tour de force* of *djej mefenned* begins to pale.

For 8 people

Same as for *djej mahammer* (Chicken Braised and Browned, page 171) plus	$\frac{1}{2}$ heaped teaspoon paprika
8 eggs	$\frac{1}{4}$ teaspoon powdered cumin
4 tablespoons finely chopped parsley	$\frac{1}{8}$ teaspoon salt
	115 g (4 oz) unsalted butter
	4 tablespoons lemon juice

1 Follow steps 1, 2, 3 and up to the point of serving in step 4 in the recipe on page 171. Strain the fat from step 3 and reserve. Tie the chickens' feet together with string.

2 Beat the eggs with the parsley, paprika, cumin, and salt to a good froth and transfer to a large shallow pan. Roll the first crusty chicken in the eggs until well coated.

3 Clean the frying pan and return the reserved fat plus the butter. Heat the fat and butter, then add the first egg-coated chicken. As the egg coating browns, start spooning additional beaten eggs from the pan over the chicken. The eggs will slip over the chicken into the hot butter and begin to congeal. Immediately lift the congealing eggs with a spoon and apply them again to the body of the chicken, pressing lightly. As you do this, more and more of the egg mixture will adhere. (Regulate the heat as you work. It takes about 4 minutes to 'do' each bird.) Continue to 'patch' pieces of egg on to empty spaces and slowly turn the bird so the egg crust browns in the butter. (At the same time you can apply more egg coating to the other side of the bird.) Remove the first chicken carefully to the serving platter and keep warm in a slow oven, then continue with the next chicken. When both are ready, sprinkle them with the lemon juice. Heat the sauce, pour over the chickens, and serve at once.

Steamed Chicken
(Djej Mafooar)

This dish is quite beautiful in its simplicity. The chicken is rubbed with saffron, butter, and salt, then steamed above boiling water until very tender. Its skin becomes silken, and the whole chicken acquires a delicate taste.

In Tangier small white onions are placed inside the chicken along with a few sprigs of parsley. In Tetuán the chicken is stuffed with wild greens or rice, tomatoes, olives, and pickled lemons and is spiced with cayenne. Some people gently brown the chicken in butter after removing it from the steamer, but I think this method interferes with the delicacy.

One thing you should know is that a steamed chicken must be served at once if you want to eat it hot. It does not reheat well, but it is excellent served cold, accompanied, in the Tetuán style, by sliced raw onions and chopped parsley.

For 4 people

2 good pinches pulverised saffron
1 teaspoon salt
60 g (2 oz) unsalted butter, softened

1 whole chicken 1·3 kg (3 lbs), prepared as directed on pages 151–2
ground cumin
cayenne pepper (optional)

1 Pound the saffon with the salt and blend with the softened butter. Rub into the skin of the prepared chicken.
2 Fill the bottom of the *couscoussiere* (or steamer) with water and bring to the boil. Seal on the perforated top as directed in step 2 in the *couscous* master instructions (page 111). Place the chicken in the top container and cover with a double layer of cheesecloth. Close the lid tightly and steam for 1 hour *without lifting the cover*. Serve at once, *as it is*, with accompanying bowls of ground cumin and coarse salt, or, if desired, mix cumin and salt with a sprinkling of cayenne pepper.

Note: You can substitute a 3 kg (6–7 lbs) turkey for the chicken, increasing the steaming time to 2 hours (and changing the name to *bibi mafooar*). Of course, you will need an enormous *couscoussier* to do the job!

174

STUFFED POULTRY

When Moroccans describe feasts given by past sultans and pashas their eyes grow large as they speak of platters piled high with 'mounds' of stuffed pigeons, each bird stuffed with a different substance. If these stories of boundless luxury are true (and they probably are), there are certainly enough stuffings and almonds; almond paste; and an unlimited number of vegetable stuffings made of everything from celery, onions, and parsley to the bitter wild herb *bakoola*.

Stuffed Turkey
(Bibi Ma'amrra)

I first had this dish at a luncheon in an orange grove outside Rabat. After we had consumed one one-hundredth of a delicious *bisteeya* that was 62 cm (25″) in diameter, a servant brought out two young turkeys that had been braised in a huge vat. The stuffing was heavenly – almonds, spices, raisins, and steamed rice – and the outside of the turkey was coated in thick thyme-flavoured country honey. Then came a forequarter of lamb heavily spiced with paprika and cumin, followed by a vegetable *couscous* and, last, two enormous trays of fresh fruits. After that feast I began to understand Moroccan hospitality. After all, we were only six for lunch!

For 6–8 people

225 g ($\frac{1}{2}$ lb) raw rice
115 g (4 oz) blanched, slivered almonds
170 g (6 oz) raisins
115 g (4 oz) almond meal
1 teaspoon powdered cinnamon
225 g (8 oz) unsalted butter
40 g ($1\frac{1}{2}$ oz) icing sugar
1 turkey of 3 kg (6–7 lbs)
1 lemon, halved
pinch pulverised saffron

2 rounded teaspoons powdered cinnamon
$\frac{1}{4}$ rounded teaspoon powdered ginger
$\frac{1}{4}$ rounded teaspoon freshly ground black pepper
190 g (6 oz) grated onion, drained
225 ml ($\frac{1}{3}$ pint) dark honey, such as the Greek Mount Hymettus

175

1 Bring plenty of water to a rolling boil in a large saucepan. Slowly sprinkle in the rice without losing the boil. Cook fast for 10 minutes, stirring once. Drain the rice in the oiled top container of the *couscoussiere*. Toss with forks to break up the rice and sprinkle with a little cold water. Toss again to separate the grains.

2 Bring plenty of water to a rolling boil in the bottom of the *couscoussiere*. Set the container with rice on top and add the slivered almonds. Cover the container tightly and steam for 10 minutes. Toss rice and almonds with two forks to separate the grains. Add the raisins, cover again, and steam another 10 minutes. Dump into a mixing bowl. Add the almond meal, salt, cinnamon, a quarter of the butter, and the sugar. Taste for seasoning and adjust. Set aside to cool.

3 Rub the turkey well with lemon and salt. Rinse, drain, and pat dry with kitchen paper.

4 Stuff the turkey at both ends with the rice-almond stuffing, packing it loosely. Sew the openings closed with strong thread. (Extra stuffing can be heated and served separately.) Tie the turkey's feet together and place the bird breast side up in a roasting pan.

5 Mix the saffron, cinnamon, ginger, and pepper with 5 tablespoons water and rub over the turkey. Add 675–900 ml ($1\frac{1}{4}$–$1\frac{1}{2}$ pints) water, the grated onion, a sprinkling of salt, and half the remaining butter to the pan. Cover and cook over moderately high heat, adding water when necessary and basting the turkey frequently.

6 At the end of the first hour of braising add the honey to the juices in the pan. Continue cooking and basting the turkey until tender (approximately 2 hours; internal temperature 85°C/185°F). Remove the cover, turn up the heat, and reduce the sauce until all the liquid in the pan has evaporated and the honey begins to caramelise, constantly turning the turkey in the glaze to coat evenly. Transfer the turkey to the warm serving dish and remove the string. Stir the remaining butter into honey in the pan to make a rich, thick sauce. Pour over the turkey and serve at once.

—— •••• ——

An Adventure in Marrakesh

Winter nights are cold in Marrakesh. I shivered as I moved through the narrow passageways of the *medina,* searching out the El Bahia Restaurant in the maze. Moorish restaurants are often built in old palaces with windows starting on the second floor – a type of architecture that reflects the Moroccan desire to shroud life in mystery and to hide secrets from prying eyes. My visit to the kitchen of a restaurant would be an unprecedented invasion into a world of jealousy and intrigue – a fact I did not know as I pounded on the wooden door.

An unveiled young girl wearing floppy pantaloons led me through the empty dining room, across an open courtyard, and into a white-tiled shed. This large, stark place was the kitchen. Four women, ranging in age from twenty-six to sixty, were waiting there, talking and laughing. When I came in they stopped and looked me up and down with a small measure of scorn. They had been informed of my request. They knew that a *nasrani* was coming, and, in fact, my list of requested dishes was posted on the wall.

Three of them gave me shy smiles, but one, who was huge, fat, and black, expressed her derision with an outraged sniff. It was she, the black Chleuh, who had the recipes, whispered the owner's wife – *she* who had once worked in the kitchens of El Glaoui, the pasha of Marrakesh. There was no doubt that *she* was the Queen Bee of the group. I gaped as she fluttered her elbows and batted her eyelids in a monologue in her native Berber dialect which neither I nor the owner's wife could understand.

Whatever she said seemed to embarrass the youngest of the cooks; she stole off to the far corner and began quietly to knead dough. The pastry cook, a short, fair Berber woman with enormous breasts, set to work frying almonds. She was helpful and answered all my questions, giving long descriptions of desserts she could make for me if I wished. From time to time she threw indecipherable cracks in Chleuh at the Queen Bee, who sat in the corner plunging a chicken, up and down like a yo-yo, in boiling water. I felt that I had at least one friend in that kitchen, but I was hoping for a change in alliances. I knew – I could *feel* – that the Queen Bee was the best cook, and I wanted her to like me so she would tell me some of her culinary secrets.

177

At this precise moment one of the almonds popped out of the pan on to the floor. Suddenly all kitchen work came to a stop and everyone stared. I looked first at the pastry cook, but she turned hastily and avoided my eyes. Then the young one turned back to her dough. But the Queen Bee leered at me, and at that moment I knew what I had to do.

I bent down, retrieved the almond, sniffed it, and tossed it back into the pan. When I glanced again at Queen Bee, she gave me a mischievous smile. I had moved too quickly for her – she'd intended to return the almond herself, to show defiance of my American 'hygiene.' But I'd beaten her to the punch, and in some strange way this won her over. In her enthusiasm she revealed some of her recipes, including the following one, for chicken stuffed with rice and raisins. Then she stopped, as if realising these secrets were *her* wealth. They say in Morocco, 'What the tongue refuses, the eyes and hands can say.' She smiled, squeezed my hand, and I knew the lesson was over.

Chicken Stuffed with Rice and Raisins, Marrakesh Style

For 6–8 people

225 g ($\frac{1}{2}$ lb) raw rice
170 g (6 oz) unsalted butter
140 g (5 oz) raisins
6 tablespoons granulated sugar
1 teaspoon powdered cinnamon
salt and freshly ground black pepper

$\frac{1}{2}$ teaspoon *ras el hanout* (pages 23–4) (optional)
2 chickens (1·3 kg (3 lbs)), ready to cook, with giblets and necks
2 pinches pulverised saffron

1 Follow directions for handling rice in step 1 on page 175.
2 Bring plenty of water to a rolling boil in the bottom of a *couscoussiere*. Set the container holding the rice on top and steam, covered, for 10 minutes.
3 Stir in a third of the butter and the raisins. Toss with the rice and steam another 10 minutes. Dump into a mixing bowl and add 3 tablespoons of the sugar, half the cinnamon, salt and pepper to taste, and *ras el hanout*, if desired. Set aside to cool.
4 Wash the chickens well under running water. Salt them. Remove and discard as much fat as possible, but avoid tearing the skin. Rinse

off the salt and drain. Pat dry with kitchen paper.

5 Stuff the chickens with the cooled rice, then close the openings at neck and rump, sewing securely with heavy thread. Blend a third of the butter with the saffon and a little salt. Rub over the chickens.

6 Boil 3 cups of water in a casserole and carefully slip in the two chickens. Add the remaining sugar, giblets, and necks, and simmer, covered, over moderately low heat for $1\frac{1}{2}$ hours, turning the chickens frequently in the sauce. When they are very tender, remove from the casserole and keep warm. Reduce the sauce over high heat until the sugar begins to caramelise. Stir the remaining third of the butter into the sauce and combine well. Return the chickens and brown carefully on all sides. Remove the thread and serve hot with the sauce.

Note: The chicken can be browned in a hot oven.

Pigeons Stuffed with Couscous
(Frach Ma'amrra)

In this luxurious variation on the preceding recipe, the chicken is replaced by 6 Moroccan pigeons or 3 squabs; *couscous* is substituted in the stuffing for rice.

For 4–6 people as part of a
   Moroccan dinner

6 pigeons, or 3 squabs, or 1
   chicken
salt and freshly ground black
   pepper
90 g (3 oz) uncooked *couscous*
60 g (2 oz) raisins
90 g (3 0z) whole, blanched
   almonds
115 g (4 oz) unsalted butter,
   more if necessary

powdered cinnamon
2 pinches pulverised saffron
3 tablespoons dark honey, such
   as the Greek Mount
   Hymettus
pinch to $\frac{1}{2}$ teaspoon *ras el hanout*
   (pages 23–4)
140 g (5 oz) grated onions
1 cinnamon stick

1 Wash the poultry under running cold water and pat dry with kitchen paper. Rub cavities with salt and pepper. Set aside.

179

2 Follow steps 1 and 2 of the master *couscous* instructions on page 110. Steam the *couscous* 10 minutes, then turn out and let dry, as directed in step 3 (page 112), for 20 minutes.

3 Meanwhile, soak the raisins in hot water. Brown the almonds in a 130°C/250°F/Gas $\frac{1}{2}$ oven until golden brown. When cool, chop coarsely.

4 Steam the *couscous* a second time for 15 minutes, adding 2 table-spoons of the unsalted butter to the grains. Toss lightly.

5 Dump the *couscous* into a mixing bowl and add the chopped almonds, drained raisins, $\frac{1}{4}$ teaspoon cinnamon, $\frac{1}{4}$ teaspoon black pepper and 1 pinch of the pulverised saffron. Mix well and add 1 tablespoon of the honey and *ras el hanout* to taste. Mix well with two forks.

6 Stuff the poultry and sew up securely with thread. Blend 2 table-spoons of the butter with a pinch of saffron and a little salt. Rub over the poultry, then place in a casserole, breast side up, on a bed of grated onion. Add the cinnamon stick, a little salt, the remaining butter, $\frac{3}{4}$ teaspoon pepper, and 2 cups water. Bring to the boil, reduce the heat, and simmer, covered, for 30 minutes, basting the squabs from time to time. Continue cooking, uncovered, until the birds are fully cooked (i.e., when juice run yellow at the piercing of the thighs). Turn the poultry often in the liquid and add water, if necessary, to avoid scorching.

7 Remove the poultry and, by boiling rapidly, reduce the cooking liquid to 225 ml (scant $\frac{1}{2}$ pint). Add the remaining honey and 1 scant teaspoon cinnamon to the sauce. Stir to blend well. Return the birds to the thick sauce and glaze them by turning gently as the sauce reduces. (It may be necessary to add more butter during the glazing period.)

8 Transfer the poultry to the warm serving dish. Remove the threads. With a wooden spoon, swirl the sauce to combine. Add a little butter, taste for salt, pepper, cinnamon, and sweetness, and readjust to taste. Pour the sauce around the birds and serve at once.

Note: One-half teaspoon powdered ginger is sometimes substituted for the $\frac{3}{4}$ teaspoon black pepper.

Chicken Stuffed with Almond Paste
(Djej Mashee Bil Looz)

This dish is a speciality of Safi, a town about a hundred miles down the coast from Casablanca famous for its glazed pottery. *Djej mashee bil looz* is extremely sweet: when I taught it some of my students were sceptical, but a Hungarian importer who eats *lekvar* (mashed sweet prunes) every morning of his life told me it was the most delicious chicken he had ever tasted.

For 6–8 people

2 chickens, ready to cook
salt and freshly ground pepper
2 pinches pulverised saffron
1¼ teaspoons powdered
   cinnamon
¼ teaspoon powdered ginger
450 g (1 lb) cups chopped
   onions

90 g (3 oz) unsalted butter
salad oil for frying
225 g (½ lb) whole, blanched
   almonds
80 g (2¾ oz) icing sugar
1 tablespoon orange-flower
   water

1 Prepare the chickens as directed on pages 151–2, but instead of garlic and salt, rub with salt and pepper.
2 Soak the saffron in 2 tablespoons hot water, mix with ¼ teaspoon of the cinnamon, the ginger, salt, and pepper. Rub over the chickens, then place the chickens in a casserole with the onions and 60 g (2 oz) of the butter. Pour in 225 ml (scant ½ pint) and bring to the boil. Reduce the heat and simmer for 30 minutes, basting the chickens from time to time and adding more water to the pan if necessary.
3 While the chickens are cooking, heat enough oil in a frying pan to cover the bottom of the pan. Brown the almonds evenly, then drain on kitchen paper. When cool, pulverise them in a blender or pass them through a nut grinder. Mix with the sugar, the remaining 1 teaspoon cinnamon, the orange-flower water, and just enough water to give the mixture the consistency of paste. Separate into two equal parts.
4 Preheat the oven to 200°C/400°F/Gas 6.
5 Remove the chickens from the casserole and let drain. By boiling rapidly, uncovered, reduce the sauce to 12 tablespoons. Spoon into serving dish. Using half of the paste, stuff the cavity of each bird, then arrange the chickens in the serving dish and spread the remain-

ing paste over the chickens, packing it gently against the contours of their bodies. Melt the remaining butter and use it to coat the chickens. Bake for 10–20 minutes, or until the almond paste is midway between forming a crust and melting into the sauce. Serve at once.

Chicken Stuffed with Eggs, Onions, and Parsley (Lema Ma'amrra)

This recipe is adapted from *Moorish Recipes*, collected and compiled by John, Fourth Marquis of Bute, K. T. Though Lord Bute (whose book is both charming and instructive) says that his recipes from the Mennebi Palace in Tangier 'follow more closely the Marrakesh taste,' this particular recipe is decidely Tetuanese, with a strong Andalusian influence indicated by its egg crust.

For 4 people

1 chicken, 1·3–1·6 kg (3–3½ lbs), with neck and giblets
4 cloves garlic, peeled
salt
½ teaspoon freshly ground black pepper
5 large eggs
2 tablespoons butter
170 g (6 oz) chopped onion

2 tablespoons chopped parsley
1½ teaspoons turmeric
pinch of pulverised saffron
½ teaspoon powdered ginger
3 tablespoons salad oil
450 ml (scant pint) chicken stock or water
2 cinnamon sticks

1 Prepare the chicken as described on pages 151–2, but do not truss. Sew up the neck opening securely. Rub the large cavity with salt and pepper.

2 Fry the eggs in the butter until almost set, then scramble. When firm, mix with the onion, salt, parsley, turmeric, saffron, black pepper, and ginger. Stuff the chicken with a little more than half this mixture, sew up the rump opening, and tie the feet together. Reserve the remaining egg mixture.

3 Place the chicken in a casserole, breast side up, with the neck, giblets, oil, and chicken stock. Bring to the boil. Add the cinnamon sticks and simmer, partially covered, for 1 hour, basting the chicken often and adding more stock or water if necessary. Remove the

chicken when it is very tender and place in an ovenproof serving dish. Reduce sauce to a thick gravy, about 12 tablespoons. Discard the cinnamon sticks.

4 Preheat the oven to the highest setting.

5 Spoon the remaining egg mixture over the chicken and surround with the gravy. Place in the oven long enough to brown nicely, and serve at once.

Chicken Stuffed with Kefta and Eggs

Another version of stuffed chicken from the Tetuanese can be made with minced beef and eggs. It's equally good as a stuffing for *briouats* (page 99) with a good sprinkling of ground cinnamon.

For 8–10 people

115 g (4 oz) grated onion	8 to 10 eggs
4 tablespoons chopped parsley	8 tablespoons lemon juice
$\frac{3}{4}$ teaspoon freshly ground black pepper, or more to taste	salt
$\frac{3}{4}$ teaspoon turmeric	3 whole chickens, prepared as directed on pages 151–2
140 g (5 oz) butter	8 tablespoons salad oil
450 g (1 lb) minced beef	

1 Cook the onion, parsley, $\frac{1}{2}$ teaspoon each of the black pepper and turmeric, butter, and beef in a large saucepan over moderate heat for 3 or 4 minutes, stirring, then add 225 ml (scant $\frac{1}{2}$ pint) of water and bring to the boil. Stir to separate the meat and cook until the water has evaporated and the meat is lightly browned.

2 Beat the eggs and lemon juice and pour over the meat. Cook over low heat, stirring continuously, until the eggs set. Taste and adjust seasoning and allow to cool.

3 Stuff the three chickens with equal amounts of the stuffing and sew up carefully. Place the chickens in a large casserole with the remaining spices, a sprinkling of salt, the oil, and 225 ml (scant $\frac{1}{2}$ pint) water. Bring to the boil, and cook for 1 hour or until the chickens are tender.

4 Place the chickens on a serving dish and brown in a hot oven. Meanwhile, reduce the cooking liquid to a rich gravy. Serve at once.

183

Chicken Stuffed with Mint

Still another Tetuanese dish, to be made with freshly chopped mint leaves and scrambled eggs. Unusual but pleasant.

For 8–10 people

3 whole chickens, prepared as directed on pages 151–2, but not trussed, with necks and giblets
salt to taste
$\frac{1}{4}$ teaspoon freshly ground black pepper

$\frac{1}{4}$ teaspoon powdered turmeric
170 g (5 oz) butter
140 g (5 oz) grated onion
1$\frac{1}{2}$ handfuls chopped mint leaves
2 teaspoons lemon juice
6 eggs

1 Sew up neck openings of the chickens, then rub with salt, pepper, and turmeric. Place the chickens in a casserole, breast side up, with the necks, giblets, butter, onion, and 225 ml (scant $\frac{1}{2}$ pint) water. Bring to the boil, reduce the heat, and simmer, partially covered, for $\frac{3}{4}$ hour, or until tender.

2 Put the mint in a small saucepan and pour the remaining chicken gravy over, add the lemon juice and reduce until all the liquid has evaporated. Fry one-third of this mint mixture in a pan with 2 of the eggs. When the eggs are almost set, break up the yolks and allow the mixture to 'fluff', then stuff one chicken and sew up securely. Repeat with the remaining chickens. Brown in a hot oven and serve immediately.

CHAPTER 10

Meats

MOUSSEMS, the festivals and pilgrimages of the various Berber tribes, are marvellous occasions, a combination of religious celebration and folk festival in which whole cities of tents sprout up for several days in the mountains near the tombs of revered saints. Tradesmen appear with muleloads of goods, and there is much dancing and singing, often by night by the light of torches – and, always, plenty of food.

At some *moussems* there are secret rites, various forms of trance dancing and even religious-ecstatic mutilations. But most *moussems* are not like that – they are open to all, and the Moroccan government encourages foreign tourists to attend. Probably the most famous of these is the Festival of the Betrothed, held in late September every year near the tiny town of Imilchil, high in the Middle Atlas Mountains. The last time I went it was still a fabulous sight, those thousands of wool tents, those herds of goats and lambs and sheep, revealed through the mists at dawn nestled between barren and stony peaks.

The people of the Ait Hiddous tribe are sheepherders, and their women, who go about unveiled, are known to be generous, strong, proud, dignified, and equal to their husbands in every way. In fact there is an old Moroccan proverb: 'A Berber woman is the ridgepole of the tent.' A girl of the Ait Hiddous marries whomever she likes, and brings no dowry. She will work side by side with her husband, help him gather wood and tend the flocks, bear the children, and cook the Berber specialities: *mrouzia, mechoui, begri, tutlin,* and so on.

One of the purposes of the *moussem* of Imilchil is to provide an opportunity for widowed or divorced Berber women to find new husbands. They call these women *twindals,* and you will see them, if you go to Imilchil in September, standing about in groups of six or seven, wearing necklaces of egg-sized ambers, heavy silver bracelets, dark blue coats striped in red and green and white, and pointed headdresses held in place by multi-coloured ropes studded with sequins. They are waiting around, of course, to inspect and be inspected by the men who have come to Imilchil to find a bride. There is much scouting for and mutual eyeing of available mates, various forms of dalliance and flirtation with the eyes, and then proposals and acceptances that are resolved, on the last day of the festival, in a number of mass weddings.

Despite the tourists, Imilchil is still great – there is singing and dancing, the charming courtship rituals of the handsome young Berbers and the incredibly flirtatious *twindals*, and you can wander about from tent to tent, inhaling the aromas of marvellous Berber *tagines*, and, best of all, that great Berber speciality, *mechoui*, roasted lamb.

The Berbers claim to be first (vying with the Turks) to have developed an excellent way of barbecuing lamb. Here they roast the animals on spits over pits of burning charcoal embers, basting them all the while with herbal butter, having rubbed the flesh first with garlic and spices. This way the whole animal becomes incredibly crisp on the outside while staying juicy and butter-tender underneath. It is so tender, in fact, that you can eat it with your fingers, which is how it is done – even though it burns.

I've had wonderful-tasting *mechouis*, not only at *moussems* in the Middle Atlas, but all through Morocco. Some of the best have been in the Moroccan Souss, where the lambs graze on wild herbs and acquire a strong flavour very much like the *pré salé* lamb of Brittany. But in the town of Tineghir in the Sahara on the famous 'Route of the Casbahs' near the beautiful Todra gorges, I ate a *mechoui* prepared in a totally different style.

The *caid* obtained the services of the 'master butcher' of the town one November Sunday following the day of Independence. Before slaughtering the lamb the butcher had prepared charcoal embers inside a huge earthen furnace built against a wall. The furnace was terrifically hot. After the lamb was killed and cleaned and prepared for roasting, he skewered it on a thick piece of green wood and then inserted it vertically into the furnace. No spices of any sort were rubbed into the flesh. His assistant slit the stomach of the lamb, which was filled with undigested grass. He mixed this with mud and used it to seal the iron cover on top of the oven. Three hours later the *mechoui* was completely done – meltingly tender, it was served with powdered cumin and coarse salt. This style of cooking *mechoui* is Saharan.

Another big lamb-eating occasion for everyone in Morocco is the annual holiday called Aid el Kebir, the Festival of the Sacrifice of the Lamb, which occurs on the tenth day of the twelfth month of the Muslim calendar year and commemorates the sacrifice of Abraham. Every Moroccan tries to get hold of a sheep for Aid el Kebir; if he cannot get one he may settle for a kid or, if he is very poor, a fowl. The point is to make a sacrifice and then enjoy it.

The trick, as I found out, is to choose the best time to buy your lamb. It will be more expensive if you buy it early, but this gives you time to fatten it up. On the other hand, if you buy it at the last minute it will be very cheap, but scrawny and not likely to taste very good. So you balance the resources of your purse against the needs of your stomach, get help for the bargaining from a Moroccan friend, and buy sometime in the middle.

When the lamb is properly fat, you arrange with a slaughterer who will kill the lamb according to religious law. The meat is then hung in two halves, after which comes the portioning, which, for better or for worse, I always did myself, following a drawing in an old *House and Gardens* book that showed me where everything was. Actually I had only moderate success as a meat cutter. The odds and ends, the pieces I didn't know what to do with, and the pieces I accidentally sliced wrong, went into what I used to call the '*kefta* pile,' to be used for Moroccan mince dishes. I confess that for the first couple of years my '*kefta* pile' was very large.

As soon as the slaughterer left the house I would rush the lamb's liver into my freezer, and as soon as it was cool would rub it with a marinade and grill it on skewers over charcoal for the dish called *kouah*. The next day I would marinate the kidneys and heart in freshly chopped green coriander, grated onion, cumin, and salt and then grill them, too – they were always delicious. The brains went for the salad called *mohk* (Brain Salads I and II, pages 69 and 70), the slaughterer took the trotters for a dish called *hergma* (simmered with chick-peas, red pepper, and onions), which I have never wanted to eat, and Moroccan friends made a *tagine* they liked very much of intestines and lungs. As for the head, minus the brains, it was steamed and served with cumin and salt. In Fez there is a special area where these steamed lambs' heads, called *raseem bahaar*, can be bought, and I am told they are a morning favourite of the *kif* smokers, who believe the head is the richest part of the body and will give them strength.

Aside from the meat dishes that are grilled and roasted, the dishes of lamb that are braised, browned or steamed, and all the delicious things you can do with *kefta*, most of the recipes in this chapter are for meat *tagines*, those marvellous, slowly simmered Moroccan stews in which the sauce is everything and the meat literally falls off the bones. A whole book could be written of recipes for meat *tagines*; there are endless variations, and, though the spicing may look the same, each dish has subtle differences and special proportions that make it unique. I have divided these *tagines* into 'fragrant *tagines*,' made with lemons and olives; 'robust *tagines*,' made with cumin and paprika; and '*tagines* of meat with fruit.' Make them all, they are glorious – and like the numerous chicken *tagines* they form the backbone of the Moroccan diet.

———— ••• ————

LAMB GRILLED AND ROASTED

Roasted Lamb (Mechoui)

I am not going to suggest you spit-roast a whole lamb; I realise that for most readers that is out of the question. Instead I recommend that you make *mechoui* with a ten-pound forequarter. Though it may taste a little better if you can dig a pit, fill it with charcoal, and set up a roasting spit in your back yard, I guarantee that with this adaptation you will obtain good results in the oven of your home, be it a country house or city flat.

In fact, the same problem confronts the Moroccan city-dweller. She knows that the best place to eat *mechoui* is in the *bled*, because if she cooks it in the city, where most people do not have a full-sized stove, she will have to send her meat to a community oven, and there the workers will be extremely casual about basting the lamb. The best Berber *mechoui*, you see, is swabbed down every ten minutes with butter and spices.

Fortunately, most modern houses have large stoves in which a forequarter can easily be roasted, and are therefore in a better position to cook *mechoui* than the average person in Rabat or Casablanca.

The paste used to flavour the meat in this recipe is in the style of Rabat.

For 8 people as part of a
   Moroccan dinner

1 forequarter lamb 4·5 kg
   (10 lbs)
1½ tablespoons powdered
   coriander seed
4 to 5 cloves garlic, peeled and
   mashed

2 teaspoons powdered cumin
1 teaspoon sweet paprika
90 g (3 oz) butter, softened
salt to taste

1 Carefully remove excess fat from the lamb, then make deep incisions under the foreleg bone along the breastbone. Blend all the other ingredients into a paste and rub into the meat. Let stand 10 minutes.

2 Preheat the oven to 240°C/475°F/Gas 9.

3 Place the lamb, fatty side up, in a large roasting pan. Place on the middle shelf of the oven and roast for 15 minutes. Reduce the heat to 180°C/350°F/Gas 4 and continue to roast for about 3 hours, or until the meat can easily be removed from the bones with your fingers. Baste every 15 minutes with the juices in the pan. Serve at once, while still burning hot. Eat with your fingers and have a bowl of powdered cumin and salt ready for those who like to dip their meat.

Note: The secret of a good *mechoui* is to obtain a crisp beautifully browned crust, while the meat inside is sweet, juicy, and meltingly tender. The lamb should not be pink, as the French like it, or tough and dried out, as it is so often served elsewhere.

Skewered and Grilled Lamb
(Quodban)

One of the most famous dishes of the Middle East and the Arab world is skewered lamb or beef, known variously as *shish kebab*, *shashlik*, brochettes, and so on. In some parts of Morocco these are eaten with a good sprinkling of hot spices, followed by a soothing glass of highly sweetened mint tea. On the road between Meknes and Rabat there is a small town called Khemisett, which specialises in serving spicy *quodban* to travellers. Here, the vendors at the many competing stalls grill the meat on skewers, then remove it and place the pieces within pieces of barley bread encrusted with salt crystals.

For 6 people

680 g (1½ lbs) boned leg of lamb, cut into 1.5 cm (¾″) cubes
225 g (8 oz) beef or mutton fat, cut into 5 mm (¼″) cubes
1 onion, grated

2 tablespoons finely chopped parsley
salt to taste
½ teaspoon freshly ground black pepper

1 Place the lamb in the shallow dish with the chunks of fat and all the other ingredients. Toss well and let stand for 2 hours.
2 Heat up the grill.
3 Threat the meat alternatively with the fat chunks, pressing the pieces together. (There should be 6 to 8 small pieces of meat and 4 pieces of fat on each skewer.) Grill the meat a few inches from the heat, then turn when well browned and grill the other side. (Moroccans usually grill the meat until well done.)
4 To serve, each guest slides the pieces of meat, one by one, into a wedge of Moroccan Bread (page 44), and then sprinkles on some cayenne, cumin, and salt, which are served in separate bowls, to taste.

Note: For a spicier *kebab*, add a scant teaspoon paprika and cumin. Also, 680 g (1½ lbs) beef fillet can be substituted for the lamb.

Skewered and Grilled Liver, Berber Style
(Kouah)

For 4–6 people as part of a
  Moroccan dinner

450 g (1 lb) lamb's liver, in one piece	$\frac{1}{2}$ teaspoon cumin
115 g (4 oz) mutton fat	$1\frac{1}{2}$ teaspoons paprika
salt	pinches of cayenne to taste

1 Firm the lamb's liver by lightly searing on both sides on a hot griddle or in a well-seasoned frying pan. Cut into smallish chunks. Cut the fat into smaller chunks.
2 Mix the liver and fat with salt and the spices and thread on skewers, beginning and ending with pieces of liver. Grill quickly on both sides and serve very hot, with Moroccan Bread (page 44). In Tangier thinned Harissa Sauce (page 118) is often served with *kouah*.

Skewered and Grilled Liver, Berber Style
(Tutlin)

Substitute sheep's caul for mutton fat. The caul should cover the threaded meat entirely.

Seared Lamb Kebabs Cooked in Butter
(Tagine Kebab Meghdor)

In Marrakesh, where this dish is most frequently served, it is known as the 'ABC of Moroccan cooking.' The A stands for the grilled *kebabs*, the aspect of Moroccan cooking usually first observed by a tourist in the Djemaa el Fna. The B is for the *tagine slaoui*, in which the seared lamb *kebabs* are next cooked. And the C is for the sauce, which, the tourist finally learns, is the whole point of Moroccan food. Therefore, if you eat *tagine kebab meghdor*, you will eat a dish that encompasses these ABCs, and you will then comprehend what Moroccan cooking is all about. (This not only tells you about *kebab*

191

meghdor, but also gives you a taste of the Moroccan sense of humour.)

The Moroccans first grill the *kebabs* over charcoal before adding them to the *tagine*, but you can grill them on aluminium foil under the grill as long as it is sufficiently well heated for the meat to sear fast. Though it is not obligatory, I like the traditional way of serving this dish, with eggs poached in the sauce with the meat in the final minutes of cooking. People sometimes have difficulty extracting the eggs neatly from a central serving dish-*tagine* pot, so if you like you can finish off *tagine kebab meghdor* in individual gratin dishes, adding an egg to each, covering, then poaching the eggs in a preheated oven. Or you can serve them as I do, to be devoured communally from the same dish.

For 4–6 people

680 g (1½ lbs) boned leg of lamb, trimmed of fat and cut into 2.5 cm (1″) cubes
340 g (12 oz) grated onion
salt and freshly ground black pepper to taste
3 cloves garlic, peeled and crushed
60 g (2 oz) unsalted butter
2 tablespoons chopped herbs (fresh parsley and green coriander)

1 teaspoon powdered cumin
1 rounded teaspoon sweet paprika
1 small cayenne pepper or ¼ teaspoon (or less) powdered cayenne
1 cinnamon stick
juice of 1 lemon
4 to 6 eggs

1 Toss the lamb with half the grated onion, salt, pepper, and the crushed garlic. Let 'ripen' for at least 1 hour.

2 Turn the oven grill on to the highest heat; arrange the lamb on aluminium foil, and when the grill is very hot sear quickly on both sides. Or thread on skewers and grill on charcoal. Remove the lamb when seared (it need not be fully cooked).

3 Melt the butter in a casserole. Add the meat, the remaining onion, the herbs, and spices. Cook briefly, then add enough water to almost cover the meat. Bring to a boil, reduce the heat, and simmer, partially covered, 45 minutes, stirring from time to time and adding water if necessary to maintain about 225 ml (scant half pint) sauce.

4 Transfer the meat and sauce to an ovenproof serving dish and sprinkle with the lemon juice. Break in the eggs carefully, cover the dish, and poach until the egs are set, either in a hot oven or on top

of the stove. (If using gratin dishes to poach the eggs, divide the *tagine* into equal portions, drop one egg into each dish, cover each dish with foil, and bake 10 minutes in a preheated 190°C/375°F/Gas 5 oven.) Serve at once, with plenty of Arab bread or Moroccan Bread (page 44) for mopping up the sauce.

———— •••• ————

TANGIA

On one trip I asked the Ministry of Tourism to find a woman who could teach me to prepare the great speciality of Marrakesh – *tangia*. When I arrived the tourist office was in a state of pandemonium. The local director was frantically telephoning all over town calling all the women he knew, sometimes using two phones at once. He was chain-smoking cigarettes, thrashing in his chair, buzzing his secretaries and giving embarrassed glances, because, as he finally explained, though everybody was quick to agree that *tangia* was *the* great Marrakesh dish, nobody was prepared to teach me how to make it.

Then, finally success! The director learned from one of his informants that *tangia* is a dish made by *men* – a dish of soldiers, shepherds and others separated from women. He pushed a button on his desk. His chauffeur appeared at the door.

'Do you know how to make *tangia*?'

'Of course I do, sir,' said the chauffeur.

'Then take this American woman and teach her how to make it!'

I was dumbfounded, but I was also desperate and grateful. I had come a long way to learn to make *tangia*, had only a day for the task, and the hour was late.

The driver, Ahmed Labkar, was eager but also stunned by the request. We drove first to a gate to the *medina* so he could retrieve his precious *tangia* pot from his house. As soon as I saw it my confidence was restored. It was shaped like a Grecian urn with a wide belly, narrow neck, and handles on both sides, and it bore the patina of heavy use. Ahmed handled it with great care – a well-seasoned *tangia* pot, he told me, was one of the keys to the success of good *tangia* – and he further informed me that the best pots for this Marrakesh speciality were to be bought in Rabat!

It was dark by the time we reached the Djemaa el Fna, parked the car and entered the *souks* to buy materials for the dish: shoulder of lamb, a small amount of saffron threads and powdered cumin, a head of garlic (he later used 8 cloves), a preserved lemon, a bottle of oil, salt and pepper.

Our next stop was the kitchen of the *maison d'accueil* directly beneath the Koutoubia Mosque, where Ahmed completed the entire preparation of the dish in less than 10 minutes. Aside from crushing the garlic and rinsing the lemon, his only chore was to stuff the ingredients into the pot and then cover the opening with parchment paper, tie it down with a string, and punch four holes in it with a pencil.

'Voilà, Madame! It is now ready to cook!'

We next drove to a *hammam* – a bath house – walked around to the back and entered the furnace room area, or *femachie*. Here a number of old men were lying around on piles of broken nut shells, smoking pipes and tending the furnace that heated the stones in the baths. In exchange for one dirham our *tangia* pot was buried in hot ashes. Here it would cook, Ahmed explained, for a minimum of 16 hours. As we parted for the evening, his final words were: 'I'm sorry we didn't make it with camel meat – it makes a better *tangia*.'

The next morning I received word that the Khalifa of Marrakesh was waiting for me in the hotel lobby. Somehow during the night word of my mission had reached him.

Ye, he confirmed, indeed, *tangia* could only be made by a man, and it was also a dish that *must* be eaten out of doors. He had come to offer me the use of a pavilion in the Menara gardens for the midday tasting.

Around noon Ahmed and I fetched the *tangia* pot from the *femachie*, took it to the gardens and ate it upon an old Moroccan carpet that had been sent over for our use.

How did it taste? Very good, very good indeed.

——— •••• ———

LAMB BRAISED, BROWNED, OR STEAMED

The trick in these dishes is to cook the lamb *beyond* the point of stringiness to the stage where the meat is butter-tender and very moist.

Lamb Braised and Browned
(El Lahm Mahammer)

In this classic dish the lamb is first braised in a spicy sauce and then browned in butter; when complete the dish should be a reddish colour (from the paprika) and so tender the meat falls easily off its bones. I have found that the browning part is difficult to do when dealing with a large cut such as a shoulder or a leg; instead of frying I put the meat, just before serving, in a hot oven, from which it emerges crusty brown and delicious.

El lahm mahammer is traditionally served either with fried almonds or fried potatoes. I serve it with almonds if it is to be followed by a *couscous* with lots of vegetables; otherwise I offer potatoes.

For 6 people as part of a
Moroccan dinner

1·8 kg (4 lbs) shoulder or rack of lamb, cut into 4 parts
2 cloves garlic, peeled
pinch pulverised saffron
$\frac{1}{4}$ teaspoon turmeric
$\frac{1}{2}$ teaspoon powdered ginger
$1\frac{1}{2}$ teaspoons paprika
1 teaspoon powdered cumin
$\frac{1}{8}$ to $\frac{1}{4}$ teaspoon cayenne (optional)

30 g (1 oz) unsalted butter
70 g ($2\frac{1}{2}$ oz) grated onion
salt to taste
5 sprigs green coriander, tied together with a thread
70 g ($2\frac{1}{2}$ oz) whole, unblanched almonds
vegetable oil for frying

1 Early in the day, trim the lamb of excess fat. Mash the garlic cloves with the spices and blend with the butter to make a paste. Rub well into the pieces of lamb and let stand 10 minutes or longer.
2 Place the meat in a casserole with onion, 450 ml (scant pint), and salt. Bring to a boil, reduce the heat, and simmer, covered, for 1

195

hour, turning and basting the lamb. Add the green coriander sprigs. Continue cooking the lamb, adding water if necessary, until the meat is very tender and almost falling off the bone. Cool, skim, and discard the fat (or save it to fry potatoes).

3 Thirty minutes before serving; preheat the oven to 230°C/450°F/ Gas 8. Transfer the lamb to an ovenproof serving dish. By boiling rapidly, reduce the sauce to a thick gravy in the casserole. Spoon the gravy over lamb and brown in the oven.

4 Meanwhile, sauté the almonds in the oil until golden brown. Drain on kitchen paper and chop coarsely or leave whole. Sprinkle over the meat just before serving.

Braised and Browned Leg of Lamb (Risla Mahammer)

Substitute a half leg of lamb for the shoulder or rack of lamb in the preceding recipe. Follow the directions exactly as given, or, if you wish to be traditional, in step 3 fry the meat in the fat skimmed in step 2 – although leg of lamb tends to be a bit dry when prepared this way.

Forequarter of Lamb Braised and Browned (Delah Mahammer)

In this variation of *el lahm mahammer*, substitute a 4·5 kg (10 lbs) forequarter of lamb for the shoulder or rack. One rarely finds a pot large enough to do this in a normal western home. However, in Morocco, where in a traditional household a huge number of relatives and servants must be fed, there will often be several pots sufficient to hold such an enormous piece of meat. When I helped make this dish in such a house it was cooked on a charcoal brazier, thank God, because otherwise it would have been very difficult to turn it over. As it was, it took three of us to brown it in an enormous pot: two to turn the meat and one to steady the brazier.

Steamed Lamb
(Baha)

If you really love the taste of lamb you will love this dish. It's a pity that people still know so little about steaming meats; just as steamed vegetables keep their original flavours, so do steamed chickens and lamb.

If you don't have a steamer, use a *couscoussiere* or a colander with a tight-fitting lid that fits snugly over a pan.

Some people think that steamed lamb looks unattractive (though no one denies that it is incredibly good). If you feel this way you may brown the meat quickly in butter or oil at the end, or roast it at high heat until it browns.

Steamed food should be eaten the moment it is ready, when it is at its peak: if left too long, it will dry out.

For 8 people as part of a
    Moroccan dinner

2.50 kg ($5\frac{1}{2}$ lbs) shoulder and
    part of the rib section of young
    spring lamb
pinch pulverised saffron
unsalted butter, softened
$1\frac{1}{2}$ teaspoons coarse salt

$\frac{1}{2}$ teaspoon freshly ground black
    pepper
1 bunch fresh parsley sprigs
4 to 5 whole baby onions
    (optional)
vegetable oil (optional)

1 Trim the lamb of excess fat: a thin layer can be left on. Blend the saffron with 60 g (2 oz) butter, salt, and pepper. Rub into the lamb flesh.

2 Bring plenty of water to the boil in the bottom of a steamer, pan, or *couscoussiere* (to borrow a trick from Diana Kennedy, author of *The Cuisines of Mexico*, toss in a small coin – when it stops clicking you need more water). Dampen a piece of cheesecloth and twist into a strip the length of the circumference of the kettle's rim. Use this strip to fasten the perforated top so that it fits snugly on top. Check all sides for effective sealing: steam should rise only through the holes. Make a bed of parsley over the holes and rest the shoulder of lamb on it. Surround it with onions, if used, and cover with a double layer of cheesecloth and then, tightly, with a lid. *Do not lift the lid during the first $1\frac{3}{4}$ hours* of steaming. Be very careful, and stand back

·when lifting the lid. If the lamb is tender and falling off the bone it is ready; if not, continue steaming for 15 to 30 minutes longer.

3 If desired, brown in oil and butter or rub again with butter and brown in a very hot oven (highest setting). Serve with bowls of powdered cumin and salt, to be used as a dip.

Lamb with Almonds and Hard-Boiled Eggs, Fez Style (Tafaya)

This dish, which is served throughout Morocco at weddings, circumcisions, and other important occasions, is made particularly well in Fez. It dates from the time of the Andaluz, when much cooking was done with oil.

Another way to prepare *tafaya* is to let all the liquid in the casserole evaporate, then add some oil, allow the meat to fry for a short time, add more water, let it evaporate again, and then fry again. If you do this the meat will be very crusty and brown and the only sauce will be oil. Not so with the following recipe which is updated and very good.

For 4–6 people as part of a
Moroccan dinner

1·3 kg (3 lbs) lamb shoulder, cut into 3·5 cm ($1\frac{1}{2}''$) chunks	$\frac{1}{4}$ teaspoon turmeric
pinch of pulverised saffron	8 sprigs green coriander, tied together
1 rounded teaspoon powdered ginger	4 two-inch cinnamon sticks
$\frac{1}{2}$ teaspoon freshly ground black pepper	6 tablespoons grated onion
salt	60 g (2 oz) unsalted butter
3 cloves garlic, peeled and cut up	4 tablespoons salad oil
	340 g (12 oz) whole, blanched almonds
	7 hard-boiled eggs

1 Place all the ingredients except the hard-boiled eggs in a large casserole, cover with 670 ml ($1\frac{1}{4}$ pints) water, and bring to a boil. Reduce the heat and simmer, covered, 2 hours, or until the meat is very tender and the sauce has reduced by half. (You may need to add water during the cooking.)

2 Decorate with halved hard-boiled eggs just before serving.

198

Note: The almonds can be fried separately and sprinkled over the just before serving. Also, in some parts of the country the eggs are rolled first in saffron water (page 20) to colour them bright yellow.

———— •• ————

KEFTA

Kefta is meat (lamb or beef) finely minced and liberally spiced. In traditional Moroccan homes I've seen it chopped by hand with a heavy steel knife and then kneaded with spices into a smooth paste. The Moroccans knead their minced meat with great effort so their meatballs will be smooth.

When I first lived in Morocco I bought ready-mixed *kefta* from my butcher. After a while I decided he used too much paprika, so I began to make my own. In America I buy minced beef and shoulder lamb chops, which I cube and then run through a mincer. Then I add herbs, spices, and grated onion in various proportions and combinations, depending on the dish, and sometimes a little *ras el hanout* when I want a particularly exotic flavour. The fact is that most Morocco cooks make a variant of this recipe for *kefta*, learned from their mothers or typical of their hometowns; there is no wrong formula except a *kefta* that doesn't taste good.

Kefta is best when it is freshly ground, and when the meat contains enough fat so that it comes out moist. Anything less than one part fat to ten parts of meat is too lean. After being spiced *kefta* should be left to 'ripen' for at least an hour.

Claudia Roden, in her excellent *A Book of Middle Eastern Food* describes a way to prepare the meat in an electric blender. She starts off with the onion, then adds the spices and herbs, and when that is all puréed she slowly adds the meat until she obtains a finely blended paste.

There are many things you can do with *kefta*. The easiest and most classic is to place the meat on skewers in sausage shapes and then grill the brochettes over charcoal or under a grill. They make a marvellous first course when eaten with Moroccan bread, which your guests should use to slip the meat off the skewers. If you are driving around Morocco, you will see stands offering *kefta* grilled this way; don't hesitate to stop if you feel like a snack.

One of the most delicious *kefta* dishes, and one that will very cheaply serve an entire family, is *kefta mkaouara* (Meatball, Tomato, and Egg Tagine, page 202), a stew of *kefta* balls served in rich cinnamon-flavoured tomato sauce, in which eggs, in the final few minutes before serving, are poached. The meat, the eggs, and the sauce should be served together in the shallow pot in which they were cooked, accompanied by real Moroccan bread. If you like, you can do this dish in an electric frying pan set on the table. *Tagine kefta emshmel* (Meatball Tagine with Spices and Lemon, page 203) and *kefta meghdor* are delicious variations on lamb dishes in which meatballs have been substituted for cubes of meat. *Kefta ma'ammra* (Stuffed Vegetable Tagine, page 204) is a marvellous *tagine* of tomatoes and courgettes stuffed with *kefta* and glazed over at the end with herbed eggs.

There are numerous other *kefta* dishes, including the Berber *bisteeya* called *tarkhdoult*, in which minced meat is substituted for chicken, and *kefta*-stuffed *briouats*, similar to the Turkish *burek* but garnished at the end with a sprinkling of cinnamon and sugar.

Kefta on Skewers

I've been making *kefta* this way for fourteen years, ever since I first read Z. Guinaudeau's *Fes vu par sa cuisine*. After trying numerous other formulae I've returned to this one, convinced it is the best. Actually I've slightly altered Mme Guinaudeau's proportions to my own taste, and when *ras el hanout* is not available I've made a simplified version of this exotic spice mixture out of pinches of allspice, cinnamon, ginger, nutmeg, powdered cardamom, pepper, and cloves.

This is not a typical *kefta* recipe. If you buy *kefta* meat in the *souks*, raw or cooked on skewers, it is more likely to contain cumin, paprika, grated onion, salt, pepper, parsley, cayenne, and sometimes some finely chopped green coriander.

For 6 people

670 g (1½ lbs) beef or lamb, or a
  mixture of the two, 10 per
  cent of it fat
1 small onion, grated
3 tablespoons finely chopped
  parsley, mixed with some
  chopped green coriander
2 large pinches dried mint or 4
  pinches freshly chopped
  mint

1 large pinch dried marjoram
  or 2 pinches fresh marjoram
salt and freshly ground black
  pepper
½ teaspoon powdered cumin
½ teaspoon *ras el hanout* (pages
  23–4, or see above)
  (optional)

1 Combine all the ingredients and knead well. Let ripen at least 1
hour.
2 With wet hands, separate the meat mixture into 24 sausage shapes,
packing them around the skewers, two on each one.
3 Grill rapidly on both sides, 5–7 cm (2–3″) from a grill flame or
over charcoal, until done to taste. (Moroccans prefer them well
cooked.) Serve, hot, at once, with Arab bread such as *pita* or Moroccan Bread (page 44).

Meatball, Tomato, and Egg Tagine
(Kefta Mkaouara)

One of the delights of Moroccan home cooking, a marvellous dish to serve with Moroccan Bread (page 44) or warmed-up *pita*.

For 5–6 people as part of a
    Moroccan dinner

For the kefta:

450 g (1 lb) finely minced lamb
    or beef
2 tablespoons chopped parsley
1 tablespoon chopped green
    coriander
$\frac{1}{2}$ teaspoon powdered cumin
1 small onion, grated
1 to 2 good pinches cayenne
salt
2 tablespoons vegetable oil

For the sauce:

2 medium onions, chopped
1 small bunch parsley, chopped
900 g (2 lbs) tomatoes, peeled,
    seeded, and chopped or
    900 g (2 lbs) tin tomatoes,
    drained and seeded
1 teaspoon powdered cumin
1 teaspoon freshly ground black
    pepper
2 cloves garlic, peeled and
    chopped
$\frac{1}{2}$ teaspoon powdered cinnamon
$\frac{1}{4}$ teaspoon cayenne pepper
6 eggs

1 Combine all the ingredients for the *kefta* except the oil. Form into 2·5 cm (1″) balls with wet hands and brown in the oil on all sides. Remove from the pan and set aside, covered.

2 Add the remaining ingredients, except for the eggs, to the pan. Cook, uncovered, 30 minutes, or until the sauce has reduced to a thick gravy.

3 Return the *kefta* to the sauce and continue cooking together 10 minutes. Carefully break the eggs into the sauce and poach them until set. Serve at once, directly from the pan.

Meatball Tagine with Spices and Lemon
(Tagine Kefta Emshmel)

For 4–5 people

For the kefta:

450 g (1 lb) minced lamb or beef
1 teaspoon salt
$\frac{1}{4}$ teaspoon freshly ground black
  pepper
2 tablespoons grated onion,
  drained
1 tablespoon chopped parsley
cumin to taste
2 teaspoons sweet paprika

For the sauce:

40 g (1$\frac{1}{2}$ oz) unsalted butter
140 g (5 oz) grated onion
$\frac{3}{4}$ teaspoon powdered ginger
$\frac{1}{4}$ teaspoon freshly ground black
  pepper
$\frac{1}{4}$ teaspoon pulverised saffron,
  mixed with some turmeric
cayenne to taste (see note)
salt to taste
$\frac{1}{4}$ teaspoon powdered cumin
1 teaspoon sweet paprika
4 tablespoons chopped green
  coriander or parsley
juice of 1 lemon, or to taste

1 Mix all the ingredients for the *kefta* and run twice through a mincer. Knead well to a smooth paste, then shape into 2.5 cm (1″) meatballs.

2 Put all the ingredients for the sauce in a frying pan except the lemon juice. Add 340 ml ($\frac{3}{4}$ pint) water and bring to the boil. Reduce the heat, cover, and simmer 15 minutes. Add the *kefta* and poach in the sauce for 30 minutes. Add the lemon juice and serve at once, on a heated platter, with plenty of Moroccan Bread (page 44) for mopping up the thick sauce.

Note: In some Moroccan homes where fiery dishes are appreciated a whole dried red pepper is added to the sauce.

Kefta Cooked in Butter
(Tagine Kefta Kebab)

Prepare the *kefta* meat as described above. Brown in a frying pan or under the grill, then substitute for the lamb pieces in recipe for *tagine kebab meghdor* (Seared Lamb Kebabs Cooked in Butter, page 191). Serve with or without eggs poached in the sauce.

Stuffed Vegetable Tagine
(Kefta Ma'ammra)

Stuffed vegetables are not often found in Morocco, though they are very popular in neighbouring Algeria, where Ottoman cooking exerted a greater influence. However, in the cities of Tetuán and Rabat I have come across two *tagines* of stuffed vegetables that are quite unique. The Tetuanese one was served in a beautifully arranged *tagine slaoui* filled with four large, juicy stuffed tomatoes surrounded, around the rim, by courgette shells, also stuffed. The whole was glazed with herbed eggs, and it was very good. In Rabat the dish was more robust in flavour, and looked more like an artist's palette. It consisted of hollowed-out carrots, potatoes, green peppers, Spanish onions, tomatoes, and courgettes, all stuffed with minced meat covered by a tomato sauce highly seasoned with paprika, cumin, and lemon juice. The Tetuán dish is presented here:

For 4–6 people

5 or 6 medium courgettes
4 or 5 large red, ripe tomatoes
salt
340 g (12 oz) beef or lamb
½ teaspoon black pepper
½ teaspoon powdered ginger
1 two-inch cinnamon stick
3 cloves garlic, crushed
2 tablespoons mixed chopped
   herbs (parsley and green
   coriander)

½ teaspoon dried mint
60 g (2 oz) raw rice
340 g (12 oz) grated onion
60 g (2 oz) unsalted butter
2 to 3 tablespoons lemon juice
additional black pepper
2 tablespoons salad oil
3 large eggs, well beaten

1 Wash, top, and tail the courgettes and cut into 2-inch lengths. (If you wish to stuff the courgettes whole, soften by salting for 30 minutes and rinsing well before removing the cores.) Peel and cut off a thin slice from the top of four of the tomatoes. Scoop out the cores of both vegetables (the pulp can be frozen to be used for soups) and hollow the courgettes to within 5 mm ($\frac{1}{4}''$) of the skin. Sprinkle both with salt and let drain for 30 minutes.

2 Meanwhile, prepare the stuffing. Place the meats, spices, garlic, three-quarters of the herbs, the rice, onion, butter and 340 ml ($\frac{2}{3}$ pint) water in a saucepan. Bring to the boil, reduce the heat, and simmer, uncovered, for 25 minutes, or until the rice is fully cooked and the mixture is thick but still juicy. Stir the lemon juice and more salt and pepper to taste. Remove the cinnamon stick and let cool. [Up to this point, the dish can be prepared in advance.]

3 Preheat the oven to 180°C/350°F/Gas 4.

4 Rinse, drain, and stuff the tomatoes and courgettes loosely. Oil a baking dish with the 2 tablespoons oil and arrange the vegetables attractively. Pile the remaining stuffing over the tomatoes, then cover the stuffing and tomatoes with the tomato tops and the remaining tomato, sliced. Sprinkle with salt and pepper. Cover with aluminium foil, pierced with 2 holes, and bake 30 minutes.

5 Remove the cover and transfer the dish to the upper shelf in the oven. Raise the oven heat to 200°C/400°F/Gas 6 and continue baking for 20 minutes.

6 Meanwhile, beat the eggs with remaining herbs, salt and pepper to taste. Pour the egg mixture over the stuffed vegetables and return to the upper shelf in the oven to bake for 10 minutes, or until the eggs are firm. Serve hot.

FRAGRANT MEAT TAGINES

These *tagines* of meat and vegetables with preserved lemons and olives are marvellous fragrant dishes, particularly if the vegetables are absolutely fresh and not ripened in crates. If you live near an organic food store I recommend you buy the vegetables there on their delivery day – it can make all the difference.

Though these dishes are extremely good. Moroccans do not normally serve them when they entertain. However, I have found that in Morocco, as in France and Italy, everyday family dishes are sometimes better than the more grandiose fare served to guests.

The first recipe, for lamb with carrots and celery, should be treated as a master recipe from which the *tagines* of lamb with fennel bulbs, *fresh* globe artichokes, cardoons, broad beans, and baby peas can be made with slight indicated variations. These are wild cardoons whose taste is similar to artichoke hearts; wild artichokes, called *coques*; and Moroccan white truffles (*terfas*), which can be bought tinned and which are used in a Jewish variation.

Lamb Tagine with Carrots and Celery
(Tagine Makalli Bil Karfas Bil Kreezoe)

This fresh-looking *tagine* is best made with tender celery hearts and fresh sweet carrots. However, winter carrots sliced small and stringy celery well scraped will do nicely.

For 6 people as part of a Moroccan dinner

1·1–1·3 kg (2½–3 lbs) lamb shoulder, cut into 3 cm (1½″) chunks
2 cloves garlic, peeled and crushed
salt to taste
½ teaspoon freshly ground black pepper
¾ teaspoon powdered ginger
pinch of pulverised saffron
¼ teaspoon turmeric
4 tablespoons vegetable oil, or less

2 tablespoons freshly chopped green coriander (optional)
170 g (6 oz) grated onion
2 bunches celery hearts (about 450 g (1 lb))
450 g (1 lb) carrots
1½ to 2 preserved lemons, rinsed
½ cup 'red' olives, such as Kalamatas or Gaetas (see pages 29–30 for notes on substitutitions for Moroccan olives)
4 tablespoons lemon juice

206

1 Trim excess fat from the lamb. In a large casserole toss the lamb chunks with the garlic, salt, spices, oil, herbs, and onion. Cover with 225 ml (scant $\frac{1}{2}$ pint) water and bring to the boil. Reduce the heat, cover, and simmer over moderate heat for $1\frac{1}{2}$ hours, turning the pieces of meat often in the sauce and adding water whenever necessary.

2 Separate the celery ribs, cut away the leaves, and wash well. With a sharp knife or vegetable peeler scrape off the strings from the back of each rib. Cut lengthwise down the middle (if uncommonly large), and then crosswise into 5 cm (2″) pieces. Set the celery pieces aside.

3 Scrape the carrots and cut into strips the same size as the celery.

4 When the meat is almost tender, add the vegetables and more water, if necessary. Cover and continue cooking until the lamb and vegetables are done. The meat must be butter-soft, nearly falling off the bones.

5 Meanwhile, quarter the preserved lemons and discard the pulp, if desired. (I don't.) Rinse and stone the olives. Add both to the casserole for the last 10 minutes of cooking. Stir in the lemon juice.

6 Place the lamb in the centre of the serving dish. Arrange the celery and carrots around the edges of the dish and decorate with lemon quarters and olives. By boiling rapidly, uncovered, reduce the sauce in the pan to a thick gravy, taste for salt, and pour over the lamb and vegetables. Serve at once.

Lamb Tagine with Fennel
(Tagine el Lahm Besbas)

In Morocco, wild fennel is sometimes used for this dish; it has a slightly bitter stalk that is removed – it is the inner core that is used. However, they also use sweet Florentine fennel bulbs and achieve delicious results.

For 4–6 people

Same as the preceeding recipe,
   but halve the amounts of
   garlic, preserved lemon, and
   lemon juice, and substitute 4
   fennel bulbs for the carrots
   and celery

1 Follow step 1 above.
2 Quarter the fennel bulbs lengthwise, scrape off the strings, and cut into 5 cm (2″) lengths. Split unusually wide strips in half. Add to the casserole after the lamb has cooked for $1\frac{1}{2}$ hours. Cover and cook 20 minutes, or until tender.
3 Follow steps 5 and 6 above.

Lamb Tagine with Artichokes, Lemon, and Olives

The small artichokes found in Italian markets in the spring are especially good in this *tagine*. Note that tinned artichoke bottoms or frozen artichoke hearts will *not* produce a good dish.

For 4–6 people

Same as for *tagine makalli bil karfas bil kreezoe* (Lamb Tagine with Carrots and Celery, page 206, but halve the amounts of black pepper, preserved lemons, lemon juice, and onions; double the ginger and turmeric; substitute 8 to 10 small artichokes (about 1·15 kg ($2\frac{1}{2}$ lbs) for the celery and carrots; and leave out the green coriander

1 Follow step 1 on page 206.

2 Prepare the artichokes by removing the outside leaves and trimming the bases. Halve each one and remove the hairy choke. Place in acidulated water (water with 2 tablespoons of vinegar added) to keep from blackening while trimming the rest. Rinse and drain before using.

3 Place the artichokes over the pieces of meat after the meat has cooked $1\frac{1}{2}$ hours. Place the rinsed preserved lemons, cut in quarters, on top. Cover tightly and cook 30 minutes. Sprinkle with lemon juice olives and cook a few minutes all together.

4 Place the lamb in centre of the serving dish. Arrange the artichokes, flat side up, facing in one direction around the rim. By boiling rapidly, uncovered, reduce the sauce to a thick gravy. Adjust the seasoning of the sauce. Swirl the pan once to combine and pour over the meat. Decorate with preserved lemons and olives and serve at once.

Note: An alternative sauce includes a peeled and seeded tomato cooked with the sauce.

Lamb Tagine with Cardoons

Cardoons are domesticated thistles found in the spring, which have a taste similar to artichokes and an appearance similar to celery when all the stalks are tied together in a bundle. They make marvellous eating and should definitely be searched out and tried. They are not difficult to grow if you have a vegetable garden and can be bought throughout the Mediterranean.

For 6 people

Same as for *tagine makalli bil karfas bil kreezoe* (Lamb Tagine with Carrots and Celery, page 206), but double the amount of lemon juice (cardoons need a great deal of lemon juice); substitute 3 bundles of cardoons, cut into pieces, for the carrots and celery; add 6 tablespoons chopped parsley, and omit the green coriander

1 Remove the outer stalks and tough parts from the cardoons, separating the stalks, and cutting away the leaves. Wash the inner

stem and bleached inner stalks well. With a paring knife, remove the strings and cut the stalks into 6 cm (3″) lengths. Keep the cardoons in acidulated water (vinegar or lemon juice) to avoid blackening them.

2 Follow step 1 on page 207. After the lamb has cooked 1 hour, add the rinsed and drained cardoons, with enough fresh water to cover them in the casserole. (For the first 15 to 20 minutes of cooking, the cardoons must be covered by liquid.) Continue cooking for 40 minutes.

3 Follow step 5 on page 207, adding the lemon juice by tablespoons and tasting. Simmer gently, uncovered, to allow the sauce to reduce and flavours to blend.

4 Place the lamb in the shallow serving dish and cover completely with the cardoons. Decorate with the lemon peel and olives. Reduce the sauce, if necessary, over high heat to 370 ml ($\frac{2}{3}$ pint) and taste again for seasoning – add more lemon juice, if desired. Pour the sauce over and serve at once, or keep warm in a 130°C/250°F/Gas $\frac{1}{2}$.

Lamb Tagine with Baby Peas

For 4–6 people

Same as for *tagine makalli bil karfas bil kreezoe* (Lamb Tagine with Carrots and Celery, page 206), but substitute 570 g (1$\frac{1}{4}$ lbs) shelled peas for the celery and carrots, and omit the lemon juice

1 Follow step 1 on page 207, but do not add the coriander now.
2 When the meat is almost tender, add the chopped green coriander, shelled peas, and preserved lemon. Cover and cook gently 10 minutes. Serve at once.

Lamb Tagine with Broad Beans

Fresh broad beans are sweeter and more delicious than many other members of the bean family.

For 6 people

Same as for *tagine makalli bil karfas bil kreezoe* (Lamb Tagine with Carrots and Celery, page 206), but halve the amounts of the preserved lemons and lemon juice, and substitute 1·3–1·7 kg (3–4 lbs) broad beans for the celery and carrots.

1 Follow step 1 on page 207.
2 Shell the beans. Thirty minutes before serving, add the beans to the casserole with the rinsed preserved lemon. Cover and cook until the meat and the beans are both tender. By boiling rapidly, uncovered, reduce sauce to a thick gravy. After adding 3 or 4 tablespoons lemon juice, taste carefully before adding more.
3 Arrange meat in the centre of the serving dish and pour the beans over. Decorate with the preserved lemon and olives. Give a good swirl to the sauce in the pan and pour over. Serve hot.

Lamb Tagine with Wild Cardoons

This is a Tangier speciality. The wild cardoons are gathered by women just outside the city, and sold just outside the cemetery wall leading up from the *socco grande*. Barefoot and garbed in red and white striped cloth and big straw hats with decorative pompons on top, the women are delightful to look at but difficult to bargain with, for they know the value of these bittersweet plants in the kitchen.

For 6 people

Same as for *tagine makalli bil karfas bil kreezoe* (Lamb Tagine with Carrots and Celery, page 206), but use half the amount of garlic, and substitute 7 or 8 wild cardoons for the celery and carrots

Prepare the same as Lamb Tagine with Cardoons (page 211). The cleaning will take a little longer, since there are many prickles to scrape off.

Lamb Tagine with White Truffles

Before you get too excited about the utter decadence and luxury of serving a stew in which the meat is smothered in white truffles, you should know that Moroccan white truffles look and taste a little like potatoes, lack the brilliance of Italian ones, and are not a fraction as expensive. You can buy them in large tins. This dish is a typical Moroccan Jewish speciality.

> Same as for *tagine makalli bil
> karfas bil kreezoe* (Lamb
> Tagine with Carrots and
> Celery, page 206), but halve
> the amounts of preserved
> lemon, lemon juice, and
> onions; substitute 1·3 kg
> (3 lbs) tinned white truffles
> (Aicha brand) for the carrots
> and celery; and omit the
> olives and garlic.

1 Follow step 1 on page 207.
2 Drain the tinned truffles, rinse under running water, and drain again.
3 Follow steps 5 and 6 on page 207, omitting the olives and adding the truffles 5 minutes before serving.

Lamb Tagine with Wild Artichokes

In Morocco this is one of the most popular of the fragrant meat *tagines*. Wild artichokes (*Cynara humilis*) are the same vegetables used to 'turn' milk for *raipe* (see page 35). *Coques* are very difficult to clean and can ruin the fingernails very fast. They are so well loved in Morocco that 2·75 kg (6 lbs) is considered usual for this dish.

Tagine of Lamb with Lemon and Olives
(Tagine el Lahm Emshmel)

Strictly speaking, this excellent dish is not a 'fragrant *tagine*,' since the sauce is *emshmel* rather than *makalli*. However, it is a *tagine* with lemon and olives, and one of the great classic Moroccan specialities, spicy with a thick lemony sauce and a perfect blending of many flavours. The best olives for an *emshmel* are the green-ripe olives of Morocco, which are flavoured with *cedrat*, a kind of thick-skinned and very fragrant lemon that grows throughout the Mediterranean region. However, you can use Greek Royal-Victorias or Kalamatas or Italian Gaetas or even ripe green olives marinated in a little lemon juice. (See page 155 for *djej emshmel*, the famous chicken with lemon and olives dish, a variant on the same recipe.)

For 4–6 people

1·3 kg (3 lb) lamb shoulder, cut into 3 cm (1½″) chunks
pinch of pulverised saffron
¼ teaspoon turmeric
1 teaspoon powdered ginger
1 teaspoon sharp paprika
½ teaspoon freshly ground black pepper
¼ teaspoon powdered cumin
salt to taste
4 tablespoons salad oil
140 g (5 oz) grated onion

3 tablespoons finely chopped mixed fresh herbs (parsley and green coriander)
575 g (20 oz) finely minced onion
225 g (½ lb) green-ripe olives or 'red-brown' olives (Greek Victoria-Royals or Kalamatas or Italian Gaetas)
2 preserved lemons, quartered and rinsed
juice of 1 lemon

213

1 Trim the lamb of excess fat and discard. Soak the crushed saffron in a little hot water in the bottom of a large casserole. Add the spices, salt, oil, and grated onion, then toss the pieces of lamb in the mixture. Sauté very gently to release the spices' aromas and *lightly* sear the meat. Add 225 ml (scant ½ pint) water and bring to the boil. Cover and cook over low heat for 1 hour, adding water whenever necessary to avoid scorching the meat.

2 After 1 hour add the herbs and the chopped onion. Re-cover and simmer until the meat is very tender – that is, almost falling off the bones – and the sauce is thick. (An alternative way to prepare the dish to this point is to cover the meat with water and all the herbs and onions and cook 2 hours altogether.)

3 While the lamb is cooking, rinse and stone the olives. Remove and discard the pulp from the preserved lemon, if desired, then rinse and set aside.

4 Add the lemon juice, olives, and lemon peel 10 minutes before serving. Transfer the meat to a deep serving dish and keep warm. By boiling rapidly, uncovered, reduce the sauce to about 370 ml (⅔ pint) and taste for seasoning. Spoon the sauce over the lamb, decorate with the lemon peel and olives, and serve at once.

ROBUST MEAT TAGINES

These robust, highly aromatic *tagines*, flavoured with paprika and cumin, are sturdy dishes, nourishing and thick, filling in winter and satisfying to weary travellers and men who have done hard physical work or have just come off the ski slopes that are an hour from Marrakesh. Though they are not among the most elegant of dishes, these hearty stews are absolutely delicious.

Beef Tagine with Cauliflower

Beef *tagines* can be very good indeed. After hours of slow simmering the meat comes out buttery and soft, and the sauce is full of spicy flavour. The spicing in this dish follows the Marrakesh style, while the browning of the meat is Tetuanese.

For 4–6 people

1·13 kg (2¼–3 lbs) stewing beef cut into 3 cm (1¼″) chunks	¼ teaspoon powdered ginger
¼ teaspoon turmeric	1 teaspoon powdered cumin
salt	1 pinch cayenne pepper
¼ teaspoon freshly ground black pepper	1 onion, finely chopped
4 tablespoons salad oil	3 tablespoons mixed chopped herbs (parsley and green coriander)
1½ teaspoons hot paprika (see note)	1·1 kg (2½ lbs) cauliflower florets
	juice of 1 lemon

1 Remove and discard the excess fat from the beef. Place the beef in a large casserole with the turmeric, salt, pepper, and oil. Fry, turning the meat often to lightly brown all sides. Cover the casserole tightly and cook for 15 minutes, *without lifting the cover*. The meat will cook in its own juices, drawn out by the salt over low heat.

2 Stir in the remaining spices, chopped onions, herbs, and very little water. Simmer, covered for, 1½ to 2 hours over gentle heat, until the meat is very tender (almost falling off the bones). Add water whenever necessary to keep the meat from scorching.

3 Meanwhile, in a separate saucepan, cook the cauliflower in salted water until nearly tender. Drain and set aside until needed.

4 Preheat the oven to 200°C/400°F/Gas 6.
5 Transfer the beef and gravy to the serving dish. Placed the drained cauliflower over the meat, cover with foil, and bake for 15 minutes. Raise the oven heat to the highest setting, remove the covering, and transfer the dish to the upper shelf in the oven. Bake until the cauliflower is lightly browned. Sprinkle with lemon juice and serve at once.

Note: In Marrakesh *felfla harra* is used instead of the paprika.
This recipe and its variation may be prepared with lamb or veal shin instead of beef.

Beef Tagine with Sweet Potatoes

For 4–5 people

Same as the preceding recipe,
   but decrease the amount of
   hot paprika to $\frac{1}{2}$ teaspoon and
   cumin to just a few *optional*
   pinches; increase the amount
   of onions to $1\frac{1}{2}$ medium onions,
   finely chopped; substitute 2
   ripe tomatoes and 450 g
   (1 lb) sweet potatoes for the
   cauliflower; and omit the
   lemon

1 Follow steps 1 and 2 in the previous recipes.
2 Peel the tomatoes, halve them crosswise and cut them into 1 cm ($\frac{1}{2}''$) thick slices.
3 Preheat the oven to 180°C/350°F/Gas 4. Transfer the meat and gravy to a serving dish. Place the sweet potatoes over the meat and the tomatoes on top of sweet potatoes. Cover with foil and bake 40 minutes, until the meat and potatoes are tender. Remove the foil cover, raise the oven heat to 230°C/450°F/Gas 8, and transfer the dish to the upper shelf of the oven. Bake until there is a brown spotted crust over the tomatoes. (If there is a great deal of gravy in the pan, pour off into a small saucepan and reduce over high heat to 225 ml (scant $\frac{1}{2}$ pint) before returning it to the dish.) Taste for seasoning and serve at once.

Beef Stew with Chick-Peas
(Sefrina)

A Jewish speciality of Essaouira, but made similarly in all Moroccan-Jewish communities, *sefrina* is almost the same as *adefina*, said to be the mother of the Spanish *olla podrida*, and first cousin to the European *cholent*.

The name and its cousins aside, the dish is left to cook at a low temperature for a whole night. The original idea was to prepare the dish on Friday, before sundown, and send it out to a community oven, where it would bake all night and be meltingly tender and delicious for Saturday lunch.

This recipe was given to me by a lady from Essaouira, who also had the following instructions, which I find overwhelming but authentic: 'Sew a cheesecloth bag large enough to hold 225 g ($\frac{1}{2}$ lb) rice, cooked. Boil the raw rice, separately, for 10 minutes and drain. Then mix with oil, salt and pepper, and a little parsley. Spoon into the bag and tie up. Remove the cover, push aside the whole eggs, potatoes, beans, and meat and drop in the bag. When the rice is swollen and tender, remove and serve with the *sefrina*.'

In Tangier a variation of this dish, called *orissa*, is made with white beans instead of chick-peas, sweet potatoes instead of regular potatoes, and small white onions browned in oil and honey instead of garlic. The whole is then flavoured with cinnamon.

Eggs cooked for so long a time come out creamy and golden. They really are very good.

For 4 people

115 g (1 oz) dried chick-peas, soaked overnight in plenty of water	2 cloves garlic, peeled and roughly chopped
1·8 kg (4 lbs) breast of beef, cut into 8 pieces, plus extra bones	salt to taste
	$\frac{1}{4}$ teaspoon freshly ground black pepper
4 potatoes, peeled but left whole	$\frac{1}{4}$ teaspoon turmeric or pulverised saffron threads or a mixture of both
4 raw eggs in their shells, well washed	$\frac{1}{4}$ teaspoon powdered ginger

1 Preheat the oven to 190°C/375°F/Gas 5.
2 Bring 6 cups of water to boil in a kettle. Place the ingredients in

a heavy casserole in this order: drained chick-peas, meat, bones, potatoes, and raw eggs (along the sides). Sprinkle with garlic, salt, and spices. Pour in the boiling water, cover the casserole tightly, and bake for 1 hour.

3 Lower the oven heat to lowest setting and bake for 5 hours, or until the meat is meltingly tender. Serve directly from the casserole.

Lamb Tagine with Fried Aubergine
(Brania)

I adore this dish, especially the tiny nuggets that are the peeled stems of small aubergines, and that taste like mushrooms when they are cooked in a *tagine*. Note that this dish is for people who don't mind fried foods.

For 6 people

For the lamb and sauce:

1·3 kg (3 lbs) rib or shoulder or lamb, cut into 3 cm (1½″) chunks
4 tablespoons chopped parsley
5 cloves garlic, peeled and chopped
400 g (14 oz) grated onion
4 tablespoons salad oil, or less
1 rounded teaspoon paprika
¼ teaspoon powdered cumin
¼ teaspoon freshly ground black pepper

pinch of pulverised saffron
salt to taste
2 to 3 tablespoons lemon juice

For the aubergine garnish:

1·8 kg (4 lbs) aubergines
salt
vegetable oil for frying
4 cloves garlic, peeled and chopped
2 teaspoons sweet paprika
¼ teaspoon powdered cumin
5 tablespoons lemon juice

1 Trim the lamb of excess fat. Place in a casserole with all the ingredients for the sauce except the lemon juice. Cover the 900 ml (1½ pint) water and bring to a boil. Reduce the heat and simmer, covered , for 1½ to 2 hours, or until the meat is very tender – that is, falling off the bones – and the sauce has reduced to a thick gravy. Add water, if necessary, during the cooking time. Add the lemon juice and taste for seasoning.

2 Meanwhile, cut off the stems of the small aubergines. Peel the stems and throw these little 'nuggets' into the casserole as soon as possible, to cook with the meat. Peel the aubergine in alternating stripes lengthwise. Cut into 5 mm (¼″) thick slices, sprinkle heavily with salt, and drain in a colander for 30 minutes to draw off bitterness. Rinse the slices well and pat dry with kitchen paper.

3 Heat the oil in a frying pan and fry the aubergine slices in batches until they are well browned and crisp on both sides. Drain, reserving the oil.

4 Mash the fried aubergine with the garlic, spices, and salt to taste.

219

Reheat the reserved oil and fry the mashed aubergine until crisp and 'firm' (about 20 minutes), turning the purée over and over in the oil so that all the water evaporates, and only the oil is left to fry the aubergine, which will become very thick and rich in texture. Drain again and fold in the lemon juice.

5 Arrange the lamb and sauce in the serving dish. Spread the aubergine over the meat and serve hot or warm.

Tagine of Lamb with Green Peppers and Tomatoes

For 5–6 people

1·3 kg (3 lbs) shoulder of lamb, cut into 3 cm (1½″) chunks
2 cloves garlic, peeled and chopped
pinch of pulverised saffron
salt to taste
1 teaspoon powdered ginger
1 tablespoon sweet paprika
3 tablespoons chopped parsley

2 tablespoons salad oil or less
1·1 kg (2½ lbs) fresh, ripe tomatoes, peeled, seeded, and chopped (see page 58)
450 g (1 lb) green peppers, grilled, peeled, seeded, and chopped (see page 58)
juice of 1 lemon

Trim the lamb of excess fat. Place in a heavy casserole, along with a mixture of garlic, saffron, salt, spices, and parsley pounded to a paste in a mortar. Pour in the oil to make a sauce and toss with the meat. Add 450 ml (scant pint) water, bring to the boil, then reduce the heat and simmer 30 minutes. Add the tomatoes and continue simmering for 2 more hours, stirring from time to time while the tomatoes cook down to a thick purée. Add the green peppers 10 minutes before serving. Sprinkle with the lemon juice and serve hot or warm.

Tagine of Lamb with Green Beans Smothered in Sweet Tomato Jam

For 4–6 people

1·3 kg (3 lbs) lamb shoulder, cut into 3 cm ($1\frac{1}{2}''$) chunks, with bones

pinch of pulverised saffron

$\frac{1}{2}$ teaspoon freshly ground black pepper

$\frac{3}{4}$ teaspoon powdered ginger

salt to taste

2 cloves garlic, peeled and chopped

2 to 3 tablespoons salad oil

225 g (8 oz) grated onion

12 to 14 red, ripe tomatoes, preferably fresh, peeled, seeded, chopped and drained, 225 ml (scant $\frac{1}{2}$ pint) of the juice

340 g (12 oz) fresh green beans

3 tablespoons chopped fresh green coriander or chopped parsley

1 teaspoon sugar, or to taste

$\frac{1}{4}$ powdered cinnamon, or to taste

1 Trim and discard the excess fat from the lamb. In a heavy casserole, mix the spices, salt, garlic, and oil. Toss with the lamb to coat each piece. Stir in the grated onion and the fresh tomato juice. Bring to a boil, reduce the heat, and simmer, covered, $1\frac{1}{2}$ hours. Add water or any leftover tomato juice when necessary to keep the meat moist and avoid scorching.

2 Meanwhile, top and tail the green beans. Transfer 225 ml (scant $\frac{1}{2}$ pint) of the sauce to a saucepan and simmer the beans until tender, along with 1 tablespoon of the herbs. Cover the pan and keep warm.

3 When the meat is very tender – that is, when it falls easily off the bones – remove and keep warm. Add the chopped tomatoes to the sauce in the casserole and cook down quickly over very high heat, mashing the tomatoes to a purée and constantly turning them so they do not scorch as they reduce. Cook down to about 370 ml ($\frac{2}{3}$ pint), adding sugar and cinnamon to taste. Return the lamb to the sauce to reheat, and reheat the green beans separately.

4 To serve, arrange the green beans around the rim of the serving dish. Spoon lamb and tomatoes into the centre and sprinkle with the remaining chopped coriander or parsley. Serve hot or warm.

Lamb Tagine with Courgettes and Za'atar

The recipe for this delicious *tagine* was collected by an American Peace Corps girl, who liked it so much she made copies and handed them around to all her friends.

For 4–5 people

1·3 kg (3 lbs) lamb shoulder, cut into 3 cm (1½″) chunks
3 tablespoons salad oil or butter
300 g (10 oz) grated onion
pinch of pulverised saffron
½ teaspoon turmeric
1 teaspoon freshly ground black pepper
salt to taste

2 small cloves, garlic, peeled and chopped
4 tablespoons chopped fresh parsley
1·1 kg (2½ lbs) courgettes, preferably small ones
1½ to 2 teaspoons *za'atar*, or one or a combination of thyme, marjoram, oregano

1 Trim and discard the excess fat from the lamb, then gently brown on all sides in oil or butter. Add the grated onion, spices, salt, garlic, and parsley, tossing to coat the meat. Pour in 450 ml (scant pint) water and bring to a boil. Reduce the heat and simmer, covered, for 1½ hours, or until the meat is almost falling off the bones. Add small amounts of water whenever necessary.

2 Meanwhile, wash, top, and tail the courgettes and cut into 2 cm (¾″) slices. Salt lightly and drain for 20 minutes, then rinse and drain again. Spinkle with the *za'atar*, finely crushed between the fingers. Set aside.

3 When the meat is fully cooked, remove it from the casserole, arrange in one layer in an ovenproof serving dish, and cover with foil to keep warm. Add the courgettes to the sauce in the casserole and cook 10 minutes. Remove the partially cooked courgette slices and, removing the foil, cover the meat attractively with them.

4 Preheat the oven to 180°C/350°F/Gas 4.

5 By boiling rapidly, reduce the sauce to a thick gravy (about 225 ml (scant ½ pint)), pour over meat and courgettes and replace the foil, and bake for 20 minutes. Serve at once, with a small sprinkling of extra herbs.

Lamb with Okra, 'Roof Tile' Style

This Tetuán dish is called 'roof tile' style because the okra is arranged like the green roof tiles of many Moroccan buildings. It steams above a sauce so thick a spoon can stand in it, a prominent feature of Tetuanese cooking.

For 4–6 people

1·6 kg (3½ lbs) shoulder of lamb,
    cut into 3 cm (1½″) chunks
3 tablespoons vegetable oil
salt and freshly ground black
    pepper to taste
½ teaspoon chopped garlic
1 large onion, finely chopped
¼ teaspoon pulverised saffron,
    mixed with turmeric
3 tablespoons chopped parsley
640 g (1½ lb) fresh okra (assorted
    sizes)

1 Remove the excess fat from the lamb. Brown the meat gently in the oil in a casserole. Sprinkle with salt, pepper, garlic, onion, saffron, half the parsley, and 225 ml (scant ½ pint) water. Cover tightly and cook gently 1½ hours, adding more water if necessary.

2 Meanwhile, wash, top and tail the okra. Thread them together to form a necklace as described on page 73. Preheat the oven to 180°C/350°F/Gas 4.

3 Transfer the meat to a serving dish. Add the okra and remaining parsley to the sauce in the casserole. Poach the okra for 10 minutes, then remove, discarding the thread. Meanwhile, reduce the sauce over high heat to 275 ml (½ pint) and pour over the meat.

4 Arrange the okra in a pyramid fashion over the meat. Make a 'tepee' of aluminium foil over the okra, then bake for 30 minutes. Serve at once.

Lamb Tagine Layered with Okra and Tomatoes (Tagine Macfool Bil Melokhias)

Okra is known through the Middle East as *bamia*, but in Morocco it is confusingly called *melokhia*.

Melokhia, elsewhere, is a dark leafy plant (*Cochorus olitorius*), cultivated especially for use in sauces, or for drying and grinding into powder for soups. Fresh, it has a taste somewhere between watercress and sorrel. The only connection I can see between okra and *melokhia* is that they both can be dried in the sun, pulverised, put away for the winter, and then used to make gelatinous soups.

Okra is served often in *tagines* of lamb, where it is a good accompaniment to tomatoes, quinces, small sweet apples, pears, courgettes, and a vegetable very similar to yellow squash called *slaoui*. This is a long, smooth-skinned gourd shaped something like a cucumber but usually four times as long, with one end thin and the other bulbous. It is called *poo gwa* in Chinese markets and *doohi* in Pakistani and Indian markets. One rarely finds okra served alone, though I have heard of a dish prepared in Fez made of puréed okra cooked with onions, green coriander, and parsley.

For 4–6 people

1·1–1·3 kg (2½ to 3 lbs) lamb shoulder, cut into chunks or 5 or 6 thick chops
2 tablespoons salad oil
2 tablespoons butter
1 large onion, finely chopped
4 cloves garlic, chopped
salt to taste
freshly ground black pepper
2 cinnamon sticks
½ teaspoon turmeric

3 tablespoons chopped parsley
1 teaspoon chopped fresh green coriander (optional)
500 g (1¼ lbs) fresh okra or two 300 g (10½ oz) packages of frozen whole okra
6 ripe tomatoes, peeled, seeded and chopped, or a 225 g (8 oz) tin of Italian tomatoes, drained, seeded, and chopped

1 Lightly brown the lamb on all sides in the oil and butter. Add the onion, garlic, salt, ½ teaspoon pepper, and the other spices. Pour over enough water to almost cover the meat and bring to a boil. Reduce the heat, cover, and simmer for 1 hour. Remove the cinnamon sticks.
2 Add the herbs and continue cooking the *tagine* for 15 minutes. [Up to this point, the dish can be prepared in advance.]

224

3 Forty minutes before serving, preheat oven to 180°C/350°F/Gas 4.
4 Transfer the lamb to a shallow ovenproof dish. By boiling rapidly, uncovered, reduce the sauce to 225 ml (scant $\frac{1}{2}$ pint) in the casserole.
5 Wash, top, and tail the okra. Cut very large okra pods in half. Put them in the saucepan and boil, with a few tablespoons sauce, salt, and 8 tablespoons water, for 5 minutes, covered. Drain.
6 Arrange the okra over the meat and cover with sauce and the chopped tomatoes. Sprinkle with salt and pepper. Cover with foil, piercing once or twice so that steam can escape. Bake in the preheated oven for about 40 minutes. Serve at once, with plenty of Moroccan Bread (page 44).

MEAT TAGINES WITH FRUIT

No matter what the month, there is a tree somewhere in Morocco bearing fruit for the *tagine* pot. The combinations may seem unlikely at times, but I guarantee you will find them delicious: lamb with quinces, apples, pears, raisins, prunes or dates, with or without honey, with or without a complexity of spices.

In the spring, apples. In the summer, try fresh apricots, or the type of hard, fuzzy, green crabapples called, in Morocco, *lehmenn*. In winter, I recommend what may be best of all, the heavy and rich *tagines* made with prunes or dates, and, in the autumn, small Seckel pears – and quinces.

Quinces, I think, are a delightful fruit; With honey and lamb, lots of pepper and/or ginger, the quince *tagines* are wonderful.

Quinces can be found in most parts of Europe. There is a rumour that Eve really offered a quince to Adam in the Garden of Eden; it seems unlikely, since quinces shouldn't be eaten unless cooked, but then maybe Adam suffered the additional punishment of a bellyache.

Lamb with Quinces

For 4–6 people

1·3–1·6 kg (3 to 3½ lbs) lamb shoulder, cut into 3 cm (1½″) chunks
salt to taste
pinch of pulverised saffron
1 scant teaspoon powdered ginger
1 scant teaspoon freshly ground black pepper
1 to 2 pinches cayenne
70 g (2½ oz) grated onion, drained

30 g (1 oz) unsalted butter, or more
2 tablespoons chopped fresh herbs (parsley and/or green coriander)
340 g (12 oz) chopped onion
450 g (1 lb) quinces or 420 g (15 oz) tinned sliced quinces, drained
1 cinnamon stick (optional)
granulated sugar
ground cinnamon

1 Trim and discard the excess fat from the chunks of lamb. Mix the salt, spices, grated onion, butter, and herbs with the lamb in a heavy casserole. Toss together over low heat to release the aromas of the spices, but do not brown the meat. Pour in approximately 450 ml

(scant pint) and bring to a boil. Lower the heat and simmer, covered, for $1\frac{1}{2}$ hours, adding more water if necessary and turning the meat occasionally in the sauce.

2 After 1 hour, add the chopped onions and continue simmering over gentle heat another 45 minutes, or until the meat is very tender and the sauce has become thick.

3 Meanwhile, wash, quarter, and core but do not peel the fresh quinces. As you work, place pieces in acidulated water to keep them from blackening. Rinse and poach the quinces in mildly sugared water to cover (with the optional cinnamon stick) for 15 minutes, or until barely tender. Remove the quinces and let drain. (If using tinned quinces, simply drain.)

4 Preheat the oven to 190°C/375°F/Gas 5.

5 Transfer the lamb to a serving dish. Arrange the quince pieces attractively among the chunks of lamb, cut side down. (If using tinned, sliced quinces, arrange in clusters of slices.) Dust the quines very lightly with ground cinnamon and sugar. Swirl the sauce in the casserole and taste for seasoning (the taste of ginger and pepper should just be perceptible). Pour the sauce over and bake for 15 minutes on the upper shelf of the preheated oven to glaze. Serve hot, directly from the baking dish.

Tagine of Lamb with Pears or Green Apples

Follow the directions in the preceding recipe; do not poach apples or pears (except Seckel pears). Instead, gently sauté them in a little unsalted butter (with a sprinkling of cinnamon and sugar) until lightly caramelised before placing them among the pieces of meat in the baking dish.

Note: Though it is not traditional, I like to mix apples and quinces (using 340 g (12 oz) of each) or pears and quinces with the meat and sauce. Even medlars or crabapples could make a good *tagine*, though I have not experimented as yet.

227

Tagine with Lamb with Raisins and Almonds, Tiznit Style

Tiznit is a strange, flat city in the southern Souss famous for the silverwork of its jewellers and its red-brown crenellated walls. It was one of the main stopping places for caravans that crossed the Sahara, and its food shows a strong Senegalese and Guinean influence (as does the architecture of its most famous mosque).

This dish is lovingly referred to by Moroccans as 'the *tagine* that leaves nothing out.' At the end it is sprinkled with a thin film of ground black pepper (a Senegalese touch?), but even without this last fillip it is delicious, and makes a marvellous opening to a dinner with *couscous* of chicken and vegetables.

This *tagine* plays the game of sweet against spicy that I have come to love in southern Moroccan cooking.

For 5–6 people

1·3–1·6 kg (3 to 3½ lbs) lamb shoulder, cut into 3 cm (1½") chunks
salad oil
30 g (1 oz) unsalted butter, melted
300 g (10 oz) chopped Spanish onions
3 cloves garlic, peeled and finely chopped
salt to taste
freshly ground black pepper
1 teaspoon turmeric
¼ teaspoon powdered ginger
¼ teaspoon cayenne

225 g (8 oz) fresh, ripe tomatoes, peeled, seeded, and chopped (see page 58), or 225 g (8 oz) tinned imported Italian tomatoes, drained
1 tablespoon mixed fresh herbs (chopped parsley and green coriander)
170 g (6 oz) raisins, soaked in water
salad oil for frying
70 g (2½ oz) whole, blanched almonds
black pepper (optional – and not recommended)

1 Remove and discard the excess fat from the lamb. Place in a heavy casserole with 2 tablespoons oil, the butter, chopped onion, garlic, salt, 1 teaspoon pepper, and other spices. Toss to coat evenly. Add the chopped tomatoes and 225 ml (scant ½ pint) water. Bring to the boil, reduce the heat, cover, and simmer for 1 hour, turning the meat often in the sauce.

2 After 1 hour add the herbs and drained raisins. Continue cooking

all together for another 30 minutes, or until the meat is tender and the sauce has reduced to a thick gravy.

3 Preheat the oven to 180°C/350°F/Gas 4.

4 Transfer the meat and sauce to the serving dish. Bake, uncovered, until the meat is glazed.

5 Meanwhile, heat salad oil, enough to cover the bottom of a frying pan and fry the almonds on both sides. Drain on kitchen paper, then sprinkle over the lamb just before serving.

6 The black pepper is traditionally sprinkled over everything at the table – but I don't recommend it.

Tagine of Lamb or Beef with Prunes and Apples

One of the most unusual and lucious Moroccan combinations, this dish is also very good without the apples and with or without the sliced onions. If you leave out the sliced onions and the apples, sprinkle with 225 ml (scant ½ pint) browned almonds just before serving.

For 6 people

1·3–1·6 kg (3–3½ lbs) shoulder of lamb or stewing beef, cut into 3 cm (1½″) chunks
40 g (1½ oz) unsalted butter
2 tablespoons vegetable oil
pinch of pulverised saffron
salt to taste
½ teaspoon freshly ground pepper
1 scant teaspoon powdered ginger
powdered cinnamon

3 tablespoons grated onion
4 to 5 sprigs green coriander, tied together with thread (optional)
450 g (1 lb) stoned prunes
200 g (7 oz) finely sliced onion
4 tablespoons honey or granulated sugar
4 medium tart apples
1 tablespoon toasted sesame seeds, preferably in their shells

1 Trim the meat of excess fat. Melt 2 tablespoons of the butter, then mix with the oil, saffron, salt, pepper, ginger, ¼ teaspoon cinnamon, onion, and coriander. Dip each chunk of meat into the mixture and place in a heavy casserole. Over gentle heat turn the pieces of meat, being careful not to burn them, but allowing the aromas of the spices to be released. Add water to almost cover the meat. Bring to a boil, then lower the heat, cover, and simmer gently for 1 hour.

2 Meanwhile, soak the prunes in 450 ml (scant pint) cold water.

3 After the *tagine* has cooked 1 hour, add the sliced onions to the casserole and cook 30 minutes longer.

4 Drain the prunes and add to the meat. Stir in $\frac{1}{2}$ teaspoon cinnamon and 3 tablespoons honey or sugar. Simmer, uncovered, until the prunes swell and the sauce has reduced to 225 ml (scant $\frac{1}{2}$ pint).

5 Meanwhile, quarter and core the apples. Sauté in a frying pan, flesh side down, with the remaining tablespoon of honey, a pinch of cinnamon, and the remaining tablespoon of butter, until soft and glazed.

6 To serve, arrange the lamb on the serving dish, pour the onion-prune sauce over, decorate with the apples, and sprinkle with the sesame seeds. Serve at once.

Tagine of Lamb with Apricots and Honey

Follow the directions in the preceding recipe, substituting 2 pounds fresh stoned apricots for the apples and prunes. Don't fry or cook the apricots; just heat them in the sauce at the last minute.

Tagine of Lamb with Quinces and Honey

Follow the directions in *tagine bil* (Tagine of Lamb with Prunes and Apples, page 229), substituting 680 g (1$\frac{1}{2}$ lbs) fresh quinces (prepared as directed in step 3 on page 227) for the apples and prunes. Poach the quinces in sugared water with 2 cinnamon sticks until tender. For a richer taste, caramelise the drained quinces before adding to the casserole.

230

Tagine of Lamb with Dates

For this unusual *tagine* use the fleshy Tafilalet dates if in Morocco, or the best quality fresh dates you can find elsewhere. In Morocco no one bothers to stone the dates for date *tagines*; serve with or without their stones as you wish.

For 6 people

1·6 kg (3½ lbs) lamb shoulder, cut into 3 cm (1½″) chunks
salt to taste
pinch of pulverised saffron
1 teaspoon freshly ground black pepper
½ teaspoon powdered ginger
1 pinch cayenne
2 cloves garlic, peeled and chopped

30 g (1 oz) unsalted butter or vegetable oil
300 g (10½ oz) finely chopped onion
2 tablespoons 'coriander water' (see page 25)
225 g (8 oz) dates
powdered cinnamon

1 Trim and discard the excess fat from the meat. In a heavy casserole mix the salt, spices, and garlic. Stir in the butter or oil to make a sauce. Toss with the meat and cook over low heat to release the aroma of the spices. Stir in half the onions, the 'coriander water,' and 670 ml (1¼ pints) water. Bring to a boil and simmer 1 hour.

2 After 1 hour, add the remaining onions. Simmer, uncovered, for another 45 minutes, or until the meat is very tender and the sauce has reduced to a thick gravy. (You may have to add water during cooking time to avoid scorching the meat.

3 Preheat the oven to highest setting.

4 Transfer the meat and gravy to a serving dish and place the dates around or among the chunks of meat. Sprinkle each date or cluster of dates with pinches of cinnamon. Bake for 15 minutes on the upper shelf of the oven, uncovered, until the dates become a little crusty. Serve at once.

Lamb Tagine with Raisins, Almonds, and Honey (Mrouzia)

Mrouzia, though it is a combination of lamb and fruits, is different from the preceding *tagines*. It is a special and extremely sweet dish made after the celebration of the Aid el Kebir – the Feast of the Slaughter of the Lamb. On these occasions a family suddenly finds itself in possession of a great amount of meat. Since refrigeration is a luxury, and home freezing virtually unknown, a solution is to preserve the meat in some way – and that is what *mrouzia* is, a form of preserved lamb. If properly done, the meat will keep fresh and edible for as long as a month.

Mrouzia is famous in both Arab and Berber communities through-out North Africa. It is made with the infamous *ras el hanout* spice mixture (see page 23). This same recipe may be followed for rabbit.

Mrouzia is never eaten as a one-dish meal: it is so incredibly rich in sweetness and spices that it can only be consumed in small quantities as part of a large *diffa* of many courses.

This is a shortened version.

For 8 people as part of a
    Moroccan dinner

1·3 kg (3 lbs) lamb neck, cut into about 10 pieces, each with some bone left on
salt to taste
1½ teaspoons *ras el hanout* (pages 22–4)
¼ teaspoon powdered ginger
¼ teaspoon freshly ground black pepper
pinch of pulverised saffron
300 g (10 oz) blanched, whole almonds

2 cloves garlic, peeled and cut up
3 small cinnamon sticks
115 g (4 oz) unsalted butter or salad oil (see note)
450 g (1 lb) raisins
12 tablespoons dark, heavy honey, such as Greek Mount Hymettus
1 tablespoon powdered cinnamon

1 Place the lamb in a heavy casserole. Mix the salt, *ras el hanout*, ginger, pepper, and saffron with 225 ml (scant ½ pint) water and rub into each piece of meat. Add the almonds, garlic, cinnamon sticks, butter or oil, and 450 ml (scant pint) water. Bring to the boil, lower the heat, and simmer for 1½ hours. Add more water, when necessary, to avoid burning the meat.

2 Add the raisins, honey, and ground cinnamon and continue cooking for 30 minutes.

3 Uncover the casserole and, over high heat, reduce the sauce, turning the meat and fruit often to avoid scorching, until there is only a thick honey glaze, coating the meat, left in the pan. Serve warm or hot.

Note: You may reduce the amount of oil, but if you are planning to keep the preserved lamb a long time you will need the full amount. Obviously, it should be stored in the refrigerator, covered.

Tagine of Lamb, Quinces, Amber and Aga Wood

This extraordinary dish is a speciality of Tetuán, and in fact is made the same way as the chickens with quinces, honey, amber, and aga wood (twenty-ninth of the fifty Tetuanese chicken dishes mentioned in Chapter 9). It is usually made without the aga wood and ambergris unless the dish is to be served for a special occasion, since these two exotic ingredients are considered extremely fine and enormously luxurious. A fingernail scraping of ambergris dissolved in water, then added to the sauce, is credited with aphrodisiacal powers – which might help explain its price. A piece of aga wood the length of your upper thumb pulverised in a brass mortar with some sugar and then added to the sauce, imparts a rich and musky aroma somewhat reminiscent of the inside of a Gothic chuch.

For 6–8 people

1·6–1·8 kg (3½ to 4 lbs) lamb shoulder, in 5 cm (2″) pieces
salt to taste
black pepper to taste
pinch pulverised saffron
½ teaspoon turmeric
8 tablespoons salad oil, or less
60 g (2 oz) chopped Spanish or sweet onion
1·3 kg (3 lbs) quinces, washed, quartered, cored, and skin scored twice

8 tablespoons orange-flower water
1 teaspoon ground cinnamon
$\frac{1}{16}$ teaspoon scraped ambergris (optional)
3 cm (1¼″) piece of aga wood (optional)
340 g (12 oz) granulated sugar
2 tablespoons toasted sesame seeds

1 In a large casserole mix the lamb, salt, pepper, saffron, turmeric, oil, and onions. Brown the lamb and onions, turning several times, then cook over low heat for 30 minutes. Add 670 ml (1¼ pints) water, cover, and let it simmer for 1½ hours, adding water when necessary.
2 After 1½ hours, arrange the quinces, cut side down, in a smaller casserole. Sprinkle the scored skin with orange-flower water, 8 tablespoons water, the cinnamon, and 670 ml (1¼ pints) of the lamb gravy. Bring to the boil and let simmer 30 minutes *without stirring the fruit.* (The quinces will not hold together if they are stirred.)
3 Continue cooking the lamb until soft and almost falling off the bone. Remove to a warmed platter and reduce the gravy until very thick by boiling rapidly, uncovered. Scrape a fingernail-sized piece of ambergris into a small cup. Moisten with 2 tablespoons lamb gravy. Crush with a spoon, then pour into the remaining gravy. Reheat just before serving.
4 Meanwhile, pulverise the aga wood in a mortar or spice grinder with 1 tablespoon of the sugar. Sprinkle the quinces with the aga-wood mixture and the remaining sugar. Continue cooking over moderate heat until the liquid begins to evaporate and the sugar begins to caramelise. Swirl the pan (don't stir) to avoid burning the sugar and fruit. When nicely browned, remove from the heat and keep warm.
5 Spoon the lamb gravy over the lamb. Cover with the caramelised quinces and syrup. Sprinkle with the sesame seeds and serve at once.

Note: Aga wood can sometimes be found in Middle Eastern grocery stores or, in Morocco, in Tetuanese *parfumeries*. It is called *oud kameira*. *Amber*, or ambergris, is generally unavailable; a substitute called by the same name can be purchased in Marrakesh spice shops but it has no potent side effects.

CHAPTER 11

Desserts

I WAS staying with the Jaidi family outside Rabat for the final phase of field work for this book. I have forgotten to bring my alarm clock, which annoyed me, since so much of the important kitchen work is done early in the morning and I never want to miss a thing. But I needn't have worried. The first sounds from the kitchen, which was in a separate building in the orange grove that is the Jaidi compound, were loud enough to wake me up, no matter how late I had gone to bed the night before. These were the clinking sounds of brass pestles against brass mortars as various ingredients were steadily, meticulously crushed.

In the courtyard I would find Fatima sitting true Moroccan style, the way many Moroccans seem to do when they are working or relaxing, resting on their heels with their toes as high as two inches off the ground. And usually when I found her she would be pounding the spices for the dishes to be cooked that day, or else almonds for almond paste – the necessary ingredient for several of the greatest Moroccan desserts.

My orange crate was soon set up and covered with Moroccan rugs, and here I would sit with pen and notebook, scales and measuring cups and spoons, for five hours at a time, noting down all I saw, moving only to look into various pots on various braziers or to practise some piece of kitchen work that I knew I would have to learn. This included all work (without benefit of electrical appliances) including the killing, plucking, and purifying of chickens. In a western kitchen the work involved in preparing a series of Moroccan dishes is considerably less.

Madame Jaidi had her crate, too, and would sit there in great regal style (she was a marvellous, masterful woman whose father was the pasha of Mogodor) while huge slabs of meat were brought to her for hacking, or vast pots into which she would throw, always with precision, the various spices that had been ground at dawn.

It went on like this day after day, taking five hours always to prepare the midday meal, which in a traditional Moroccan home is the major meal of the day. I sat on my rug-covered orange crate for weeks, learning and writing and tasting and nibbling, always looking forward to my reward for so much hard work, the midday lunch, at which there were never less than a dozen guests.

It is best to be honest and say that, though this chapter is entitled 'desserts,' most of the things in it are not actually eaten at the end of a meal. The traditional way to end a Moroccan dinner, and the traditional 'dessert' also of most North Africans, is a bowl or tray of fruits and nuts. Usually an enormous platter is offered of carefully arranged plums, apricots, bananas, oranges, and figs, as well as, on a separate platter, cubed melon. In winter a bowl of raisins, dates, dried figs, almonds, and walnuts may replace the fresh fruits. Other fruit dishes, including Orange Salad with Rosewater (page 67) or a dessert of pomegranate seeds mixed with almonds, sugar, and orange-flower water, may also be offered – and, of course, there is always the simple but soothing glass of tea.

But the Moroccans are great connoisseurs of sweets, even if they do not usually eat them at the end of their meals. Two of their most famous (and two of my favourites) are the *Kab el ghzad* ('Gazelles' Horns,' page 239), those divine, sugar-coated crescent-shaped pastries stuffed with almond paste, and *m'hanncha* ('The Snake,' page 237), that sublime coil of browned almond-stuffed pastry. These, like the many cakes and cookies and pastries in Moroccan confectionery shops, are usually eaten with tea – which can be at any time. In fact, Moroccans will sometimes fill themselves with sweet cakes *before* sitting down to a special-occasion feast, such as a wedding.

There is another category of sweet dishes that I have included in this chapter: the sweet supper dishes, or pre-fruit dishes, such things as the sweet desert *couscous* on page 259, *roz mafooar* (Sweet Steamed Rice, page 260). Moroccan Rice Pudding (page 261), and *keneffa* (sweet Bisteeya with Milk and Almonds, page 264). All of these are incredible confections that follow a rich and nourishing soup or a series of *tagines*, which in turn are followed by fruit and nuts and sweet mint tea.

But in Morocccan food, as in all Moroccan things, there is always a great exception. There are times when sweet confections are eaten at the important meal of the day, and one of these times occurs during the fasting month of Ramadan, when everything is topsy-turvy, and sweet, fried, honeyed cakes are devoured along with the famous and hunger-quenching hot spicy *harira* soup. But these cakes, called *mahalkra* or *shebbakia* (Free-Form Honey Cake, page 245), are eaten *with* the soup, and not *after* the soup.

—————— ••• ——————

ALMOND PASTE CONFECTIONS

'The Snake' (M'hanncha)

'The Snake' is one of the glories of Moroccan confectionery, a treat not to be missed.

For 8 people

For the almond paste:

6 oz (2 oz) unsalted butter, melted and cooled
225 g (8 oz) blanched almonds, finely ground
$\frac{1}{2}$ teaspoon almond extract
$\frac{1}{8}$ teaspoon gum arabic (optional)
70 g ($2\frac{1}{2}$ oz) icing sugar, or to taste
4 tablespoons rosewater or orange-flower water, or to taste

For the pastry:

6 oz (2 oz) phyllo pastry or strudel leaves or 8 large *warka* leaves (page 81)
5 tablespoons melted unsalted butter
1 egg, beaten
icing sugar
powdered cinnamon

1 Mix the cooled melted butter with the ground blanched almonds and almond flavouring. Pound the gum arabic in a mortar until finely ground and add to the almond mixture. Add the sugar and fragrant water, then mix well and knead to a solid, well-blended mass. Chill.

237

2 Separate the chilled almond paste into 10 balls and roll each ball into a 12·5 cm (5″) cylinder. Chill.

3 Preheat the oven to 180° C/350° F/Gas 4.

4 Spread out 1 strudel or phyllo pastry leaf. Brush with some of the melted butter. Cover with a second layer of pastry and brush with butter again. (If using *warka*, spread out 2 warka leaves and overlap them slightly. Do not butter them.)

5 Place 5 cylinders of almond paste along the lower edge, 5 cm (2″) from the bottom of each leaf, and roll up the pastry tightly, tucking in the ends. Shape into a loose coil.

6 Brush a cake tin lightly with butter and place the coil in the centre. Repeat with the remaining pastry leaves and cylinders of almond paste, extending the coil in the shape of a coiled snake, to fill the pan.

8 Beat the egg and add $\frac{1}{2}$ teaspoon cinnamon. Brush the pastry top with the cinnamon-egg mixture and bake for 30 minutes, or until golden brown. Turn out on to the baking sheet and return to the oven for ten minutes. Invert again, or to a serving plate, and dust with icing sugar. Dribble cinnamon in straight lines to form a lattice pattern. Serve warm.

Note: This cake will keep several days in a cool place. Reheat before serving.

'Gazelles' Horns'
(Kab el Ghzal)

You will see these pastries everywhere in Morocco, in all sweet shops and bakeries, and they will be of varying quality – sometimes too hard or brittle, sometimes too thick. My suggestion is to try one first before buying a whole bag; the best are those made from the thinnest pastry – they break in half practically at a touch.

Makes 3–4 dozen

For the almond paste:

Same as the previous recipe, but
   omit gum arabic and
   rosewater (see note below)

For the pastry:

225 g (8 oz) plain unbleached
   flour
3 teaspoons unsalted butter,
   melted
pinch or salt
orange-flower water (optional)
icing sugar (optional)

1 Prepare the almond paste as described in step 1 of the previous recipe, but divide into 4 equal parts before chilling.

2 Make a firm dough with the flour, 2 tablespoons melted butter, and about 225 ml (scant $\frac{1}{2}$ pint) lukewarm water. (In very rich Moroccan homes orange-flower water is used.) Add a pinch of salt. Knead for at least 20 minutes, until silky and elastic. (If you have a mixing machine with a dough hook attachment, knead on slow speed 12 minutes.)

3 Preheat the oven to 170° C/325° F/Gas 3.

4 Separate the dough into 4 equal parts. Grease 3 of the parts with a little melted butter and cover with a slightly damp cloth. Roll out the remaining dough, on a lightly buttered surface with a lightly buttered rolling pin, into a long strip, pushing with the rolling pin to stretch the dough. Make half turns with the dough, rolling in both directions. Dust with flour if the dough seems too sticky, but only very lightly. As you roll, wrap the dough around the wooden rolling pin to help stretching, being very careful not to break the dough. Roll and stretch until you have the thinness of cardboard.

5 Place the long strip horizontally in front of you. Using one part of the chilled almond paste, roll $1\frac{1}{4}$ teaspoons of it at a time between

your palms to make sausage shapes 4 cm ($1\frac{3}{4}''$) long – thicker in the centre and tapered at the ends. Place the almond paste cylinders in a row, 2·5 cm (1″) up from the lower edge of the dough and about 5 cm (2″) apart. *Stretch* the sheet of dough below the almond paste as thin as possible and fold over the paste to cover it completely. Press the dough together to seal it. Cut with the pastry wheel around each mould to form a crescent horn shape. Repeat with the remaining dough.

6 Pick up each 'horn,' and, pressing lightly with the second and third finger and thumb of each hand, shape it into a crescent. Prick each horn with a needle twice, to prevent puffing and splitting. Place them on a baking sheet, and bake 10 to 15 minutes, or until only very pale gold in colour. Do not allow the crescents to brown or they will harden. The crusts should be rather soft but will crisp slightly upon cooking. Sprinkle at once with orange-flower water and roll in icing sugar if desired. Serve piled high on a serving plate.

Note: Another excellent almond paste, more work but much lighter in texture, can be made with 300 g ($10\frac{1}{2}$ oz) *freshly* blanched and peeled almonds *pounded in a mortar*. These are then mixed with 70 g ($2\frac{1}{2}$ oz) granulated sugar, orange-flower water, and $\frac{1}{4}$ teaspoon almond extract.

Shredded Pastry with Almonds
(Ktaif)

This Tetuanese pastry dessert was no doubt adapted from the Turkish *cadaif* (a honey-walnut pastry made with a type of pastry similar to *warka* but differently prepared) learned when the Turks occupied Algeria in the sixteenth century. This recipe is adapted from Lord Bute's *Moorish Recipes*.

Ktaif is indeed very similar to *cadaif*. In the Middle East the dough is pushed through a sieve onto a hot pan and then removed before it is fully cooked. In Tetuán there is a special instrument for making *ktaif*, a tin cup with two fine, protruding, open nozzles. The soft pastry dough is pushed through this gadget into a lattice pattern on a flat metal tray. The lattice is then removed and another made until all the batter is used up. The 'lattices,' which look like shredded wheat, are piled on top of each other and moistened with melted butter. In the Middle East the 'lattices' are baken in even layers and look very attractive, while in Tetuán they are, in the words of Lord Bute, 'by no means the most attractive to the eye.'

You can buy the dough already prepared in Middle Eastern pastry shops, where it is called '*cadaif* pastry.' (If frozen, defrost thoroughly.)

This pastry will keep about four days, and, if broken up and piled onto a serving dish, it will look *somewhat* attractive.

For 8 people

450 g (1 lb) sugar	butter for frying
1 cinnamon stick	2 to 3 teaspoons powdered
1 tablespoon lemon juice	cinnamon
12 tablespoons orange-flower	450 g (1 lb) '*cadaif* pastry'
water	threads
34 g (12 oz) whole, blanched	225 g (8 oz) butter, melted
almonds	

1 Prepare a syrup by boiling 37 g (12 oz) of the sugar with 540 ml (scant pint) 900 ml (1½ pints) water, the cinnamon stick, and lemon juice, uncovered, until it thickens (about 105° C/220° F on a sugar thermometer). Stir in 4 tablespoons of the orange-flower water and continue cooking a few minutes longer. Set aside to cool.

2 Meanwhile, prepare the filling. Fry the almonds in butter until lightly browned. Drain on kitchen paper. Pulverise in the blender, then mix with the cinnamon, remaining icing sugar, and enough orange-flower water to moisten to a paste.

3 Place half the pastry strands in a large frying pans and pour over half the melted butter. Cook together *without browning*, by regulating the heat. After 10 minutes there should only be a light golden crust on the bottom of the pastry. Turn the pastry over and gently fry the other side very lightly. (The strands will tend to stick together in one or two big pieces.) Transfer the strands to a plate and, using the remaining butter, repeat with the second batch of pastry. Pour off any excess butter and spread the almond mixture over the pastry in the pan. Cover with the first batch of pastry. Pour the syrup over and cook the whole thing together for about 15 minutes, basting the pastry with the syrup until well absorbed, and turning the pastry from the bottom to the top as it crisps. Continue until all the strands are crisp and well moistened, and the 'whole is one shapeless mass.' Leave in the pan to cool. Break up into 3 cm (1½″) nuggets and serve at room temperature.

241

Pastry Stuffed with Almond Paste and Dipped in Honey
(Briouats)

These are extremely rich pastries, and no more than one or two are likely to be consumed by each person. It's not that they're not delicious; they are incredibly sweet. Happily these sweet *briouats* keep a long time when put up in airtight containers.

This is the traditional recipe as prepared in Fez, but you can make them a number of different ways – that is, you can use plain almond paste, made according to the directions in the *m'hanncha* recipe ('The Snake,' page 237), or you can blend 115 g (4 oz) almond paste with 225 g (8 oz) dried, stoned dates that have been pounded and mixed with a little orange-flower water and butter. I have heard that some people make the filling with dried figs, too.

Makes 2 dozen pastries

225 g (8 oz) blanched whole
    almonds
salad oil for drying
unsalted butter, melted and
    cooked (optional)
1½ teaspoons powdered
    cinnamon
scant ½ teaspoon almond extract
2 to 3 tablespoons icing sugar

orange-flower water
115 g (4 oz) phyllo pastry or
    strudel leaves or 24 small
    (20 cm (8″)) *warka* leaves
    (page 81)
450 ml (scant pint) dark, heavy
    honey, such as Greek Mount
    Hymettus

1 Fry the almonds in the oil until golden. Drain on kitchen paper and grind in blender until smooth and pasty – if you have drained them too well you will need to add a few tablespoons cooled melted butter. Transfer to the mixing bowl and flavour with the cinnamon, almond extract, sugar, and 1½ tablespoons orange-flower water. Knead to a solid mass.

2 If using phyllo or strudel pastry leaves, unroll one sheet at a time, keeping the others under a damp towel. Brush the entire sheet sparingly with melted butter (you will need about 7 tablespoons altogether). Cut lengthwise into 3 equal parts and place a nugget of almond paste at the bottom of each strip. Fold according to *Klandt* directions into triangles, as explained on page 95. (If using *warka*

leaves there is no need to brush with butter; otherwise follow the procedure for strudel or phyllo dough.)
3 Preheat the oven to 180° C/350° F/Gas 4.
4 Heat the honey with 2 or 3 tablespoons orange-flower water. (Avoid burning by continually controlling the heat.)
5 Bake the rolls in the oven for 30 minutes, or until puffed and golden brown on both sides, or dry in not-too-hot oil until golden, turning once. Transfer at once to the simmering honey, allowing the hot honey to penetrate the pastries for 2 to 3 minutes. Remove to a flat dish to dry. Store when cool.

Sesame Seed, Almond, and Honey Cone
(Sfuf)

A charming Tetuanese confection considered a great fortifier – to be served at weddings.

For 6 people

450 g (1 lb) plain flour	1 teaspoon powdered cinnamon
90 g (3 oz) sesame seeds	a pinch of grated nutmeg
30 g (1 oz) butter, softened to room temperature	1 to 2 tablespoons liquid honey icing sugar
45 g (1½ oz) granulated sugar	
60 g (2 oz) almonds, blanched and ground fine in a blender	

1 Toast the flour in a frying pan, turning it constantly until it turns a lovely light brown. Add the sesame seeds and butter and continue stirring over moderate heat until the sesame seeds turn golden and are well mixed with the flour. Then add the sugar, almonds, and spices and cook together for 2 or 3 minutes, stirring all the while.
2 Put the honey in a mixing bowl and gradually, with the aid of a wooden spatula, beat in the almond–sesame seed–flour mixture. Place on a serving plate, form into a cone, decorate with crisscrossing lines of icing sugar (or coat completely with sugar), and serve with Moroccan tea.

Note: Sfuf is eaten communally with small coffee spoons.

243

Zomita

Substitute ginger for the cinnamon and nutmeg, in the previous recipe, toast the almonds before grinding, and mix the butter when hot with 225 ml (scant half pint) honey. Combine the mixture of almonds, sesame seeds, spices, and flour with the butter and honey, then roll into fingers and serve as a sweetmeat.

Note: In some parts of the north barley flour is used in place of ordinary white flour.

FRIED CAKES

Free-Form Honey Cake
(Mahalkra or Shebbakia)

This is one of the famous honey cakes served with spicy *harira* soup for Ramadan, but it is also good on the dessert tray. These cakes are very sweet – when you bite into *mahalkra* you are biting into pure honey.

This somewhat difficult recipe has been vastly scaled down for this book. In a Moroccan home it wouldn't make sense to make less than five hundred cakes. Friends and neighbours help, and then everyone goes home with a large batch. Ramadan lasts a whole month, and the culinary frenzy at sundown is truly incredible.

For 35 cakes

340 g (12 oz) unsalted butter
1 package 8 g ($\frac{1}{4}$ oz) active dry
    yeast
3 large eggs
$\frac{3}{4}$ teaspoon salt
$\frac{1}{2}$ teaspoon double-acting
    baking powder
2 to 3 tablespoons orange-
    flower water

1 tablespoon vanilla extract
$2\frac{1}{2}$ tablespoons white wine
    vinegar
900 g (2 lbs) plain flour
pinch of pulverised saffron
salad oil for deep frying
1·1 litres (2 pints) dark honey
4 tablespoons sesame seeds,
    oven toasted

1 Melt and cool the butter. Sprinkle the yeast over 4 tablespoons lukewarm water, stir to dissolve, and set in a warm place until bubbly.

2 In a mixing bowl beat the eggs with the salt, baking powder, orange-flower water, and vanilla. Then add the vinegar and melted butter.

3 Place the flour in large mixing bowl and make a well in the centre. Slowly pour the egg mixture into the flour, stirring constantly with a wooden spoon until well combined. Then add the bubbling yeast. Work into a stiff dough, adding only as much water as you need. Knead well by pressing down and pushing forward with the heel of your hand and folding the dough over onto itself. Knead until smooth and elastic.

245

4 Blend 1 tablespoon butter with the pulverised saffron until bright yellow. Then blend into the dough. Separate the dough into 4 equal parts. Cover and let stand for 10 minutes.

5 Take one ball of dough and slap it around to flatten it out. Butter the rolling pin and start rolling the dough out until it is as thin as thick cardboard, about 25 cm (10″) round. Make 5 parallel incisions to form 6 strips *within* each piece. Loop every other strip in your fingers and then bring the lower opposite points together so that a plaited bread stick shape is formed. Place them on a buttered baking sheet covered while preparing the others. (The shape is really unimportant as long as they look more or less right.)

6 Heat the honey in a large, deep saucepan. (Honey tends to boil up rather high.) Heat the oil in a frying pan to a depth of at least 2·75 cm ($1\frac{1}{4}$″). Fry 6 or 7 cakes on both sides until brown (not light but not too dark). Immediately drop the cakes into the hot honey. As soon as the honey boils up, remove the cakes to the colander to drain. Sprinkle at once with sesame seeds. Serve cool.

Note: Another type, also called *shebbakia*, is made by pressing leavened batter through a forcing tube (or flower pot), in the shape of rosettes, into boiling oil.

Fried Pastry from Sefrou

Sefrou is a charming town near Fez with a large Sephardic community. These cakes no doubt come from Spain, brought by the Jews in 1492.

Makes $2\frac{1}{2}$ dozen pastries

300 g ($10\frac{1}{2}$ oz) plain flour
icing sugar
$\frac{1}{8}$ teaspoon salt
2 whole eggs, plus 1 egg yolk

2 tablespoons orange-flower
  water
salad oil
450 ml (scant pint) honey

1 Mix the flour, 30 g (1 oz) sugar, and salt in a bowl. Add the eggs, egg yolk, and enough orange-flower water to make a rather soft dough. Turn out on to a board and knead well until both smooth and elastic. Separate into 6 equal balls, coat with oil, and let stand for 30 minutes.
2 Heat oil in a sauté pan or deep fryer to a depth of 5 cm (2″). Have a colander or draining rack ready.
3 Roll out one ball of dough by first flattening with oiled hands and then rolling to stretch into a large rectangle. Repeat with a second ball, place the rectangles on top of one another, and roll them together. Cut into 5 cm (2″) strips lengthwise.
4 Place one end of the strip in the oil, and as it swells and fries *slowly* start to wrap the *fried end* around a long, pronged fork, while at the same time feeding more of the uncooked strip into the oil. Keep on turning and folding the strip until the strip is finished. The oil should be maintained at a constant temperature so that the pastry does not brown too much, but comes out a pale beige. Remove to drain and continue until all pastries have been rolled, fried, and drained well.
5 Dribble the honey over the pastries and sprinkle with sugar. Serve at room temperature.

Note: These pastries will keep a few days in a cool place.

Sponge Doughnuts
(Sfinges)

Sfinges are commonly eaten in the morning, along with a glass of mint tea or a cup of coffee. Their name derives from the Greek σπονγος, which is the word for 'sponge.'

Just outside Tangier, in the village of Hayani, there are some light-blue coloured stalls (light blue being a symbol of good luck in Morocco) where *sfinges* are prepared. I would often stop by these stalls to fetch some for my children. I used to watch, fascinated, as the *sfinge* maker squeezed dough in his oiled hand, and then allowed a round 'crown' the size of a plum to emerge from between his forefinger and thumb. He would pierce a hole through the centre, twirl the dough into a ring, and then toss it into boiling oil, where it immediately puffed up into a large, crisp golden crown. He then fished it out with an iron hook and strung it with others on a wire coat-hanger to drain. I would choose a particularly well-formed lot, pay for them by weight, and rush home while they were warm, to sprinkle them with icing sugar and serve them to my children along with hot chocolate.

Makes 2–2½ dozen

8 g (¼ oz) active dry yeast	1 teaspoon salt
½ teaspoon granulated sugar	salad oil for frying
400 g (14 oz) plain flour	icing sugar (optional)

1 Sprinkle the yeast and sugar over 4 tablespoons lukewarm water. Stir to dissolve, cover, and set in a warm place until the yeast is bubbling and has doubled in volume.

2 Combine the flour and salt. Make a well in the centre and pour in yeast and enough lukewarm water to make a stiff dough. Knead well by vigorously pushing parts of the dough outwards and folding it back on to itself until it is smooth and elastic.

3 Place a bowl of lukewarm water by your side. Gradually add water to the dough by sprinkling 2 to 3 tablespoons water on the work surface and covering it with dough. Punch down with your fists, making squishy noises as you work the dough, until it absorbs the water. Turn the dough over and repeat. Wet your hands as you work and continue adding water in this fashion until the dough looks

spongy and is very sticky. Pick the dough up and begin to slap it down many times to loosen it up. Continue adding water by tablespoons at intervals, until the dough is so elastic that it moves with the movement of your hand en masse as you raise it and slap it down again. Place the dough to rest in a bowl that has been rinsed out with warm water, then cover with a clean towel and leave to rise in a warm place for 1 hour, or until it has doubled in volume. To test the dough, twist off a piece and flip it in your hands; it should become a smooth ball. If it is not ready, leave another 10 minutes before forming rings.

4 Pour oil into the skillet or deep fryer to a depth of 6 cm ($2\frac{1}{2}''$). Heat to 200° C/400° F.

5 Oil your hands lightly and squeeze out a small amount of dough between thumb and forefinger to form a smal ball. Break it off with your other hand and punch a hole in the centre with your thumb. Let it fall loose to form a 'bracelet,' and then slip it into the hot oil. Repeat with the remaining dough. Fry 4 or 5 doughnuts at a time until golden, swollen, and crisp, turning them over once with a skewer. Drain on kitchen paper. Serve with a sprinkling of icing sugar if desired, though in Morocco they are usually eaten plain to be dipped in coffee.

Pancakes

The dough used for *sfinges* can be thinned to make a pancake batter. These pancakes are best cooked on a flat earthenware pan or on a soapstone griddle. In Morocco soft soap or beaten egg yolk is first rubbed on the surface of the pan make it smooth. When it is well heated a spoonful of batter is dropped on and cooked on both sides until lightly browned. These pancakes, a type of *rghuif*, puff up considerably, and go well with butter and honey.

Note: Another pancake popular in Morocco is the *beghrir*, which is a pale yellow yeast-semolina pancake cooked only on one side. It looks like a honeycomb with many little holes. To be good it must be very light; unfortunately this isn't always the case in Moroccan homes.

Stamp Pastries
(Taba)

This Tetuanese dessert is made with eggs, flour or cornflour, and a special iron usually patterned in the form of an eight-petalled rose. (A 'Sokurstuvor rosette' iron from Scandinavia produces the right effect.) The iron in first heated up by being dipped in fat, then slid over the batter and returned to the fat, where the picked-up batter cooks. The resulting pastry, light and golden yellow, is then immediately dipped into an orange-flower water syrup called *knelba*. Piled high and decorated with almonds, *tabas* are a lovely sight.

Makes 18 *tabas*

185 g (6¾ oz) granulated sugar
1 tablespoon lemon juice
2 tablespoons orange-flower
   water
2 eggs, plus 1 egg yolk
pinch of salt

100 g (3½ oz) plain flour
225 ml (scant ½ pint) milk,
   approximately
salad oil for frying
handful of slivered almonds,
   previously toasted in the oven

1 Make a syrup by boiling 1 cup sugar with 280 ml (½ pint) water and the lemon juice 5 minutes, or until it has thickened. Add the orange-flower water and set aside to cool.
2 Beat the eggs and extra egg yolk, with a pinch of salt and the teaspoon of sugar, until creamy. Stir in the flour and enough milk to form a smooth batter. Let it stand for 2 hours, covered.
3 Pour oil to a depth of 6·25 cm (2½″) into a frying pan or deep fryer. Heat to 190° C/375° F.
4 Plunge the iron into the fat and immediately lift, drain, and dip into the batter. (Do not let batter run over top of rim; it will be difficult to remove from the rosette iron.) Immediately dip the batter-coated iron into the hot fat and fry until the butter turns golden. (When cooked the *taba* will just start to slip off the iron.) Spoon out, drain on kitchen paper, dip into the cooled syrup, and place on the serving dish. Reheat the iron in the fat and repeat until all the batter is used.
5 Sprinkle the pastry with the slivered almonds and serve at room temperature.

————— •••• —————

MOROCCAN BISCUITS

Though the Moroccans make many types of biscuits, only the *ghoribas* and *fekkas* seem unusual and good to me, hence the brevity of this section.

Semolina Biscuits
(Ghoriba)

These biscuits are somewhat different from the traditional Middle Eastern and North African *ghoriba* in that they are based on semolina flour (hard wheat), which has its own marvellous taste and texture. These are lovely light buscuits, sugar-dipped, the size of a medium coin.

When I was learning to make these biscuits I was a good student, following the lead of all the ladies in the kitchen. Whatever they did I followed, but when it came time to making *ghoriba* mounds, with their perfectly shaped domes, I couldn't seem to get them right. No matter what I did I couldn't achieve the domes because the dough kept sticking to my palms. The other ladies, however, used a complicated rolling, clutching, squeezing, and back-and-forth motion that produced perfectly smooth balls and left their hands clean of dough. They then transferred the dough to their other palm, tapped the balls lightly, and produced discs with slightly raised domes that were smoother and much more celestial than mine.

I was glad, however, that when the time finally came to eat them our biscuits tasted the same.

Makes $3\frac{1}{2}$ dozen biscuits

unsalted butter	1 teaspoon double-acting
4 tablespoons salad oil	baking powder
2 large eggs	$\frac{1}{8}$ teaspoon salt
210 g ($7\frac{1}{3}$ oz) icing sugar	$\frac{1}{2}$ teaspoon vanilla extract
450 g (1 lb) semolina flour	

1 Heat $\frac{1}{4}$ cup of butter in the oil. When melted, remove from the heat and set aside.

2 Use an electric beater to beat the eggs and all but 30 g (1 oz) icing sugar together until soft and fluffy. Add the butter-oil mixture and beat a few seconds longer. Using the spatula, fold in the semolina flour, baking powder, salt, and vanilla. Blend well.

3 Preheat the oven to 180° C/350° F/Gas 4.

4 Prepare the baking sheets by smearing with dabs of butter. Place the remaining icing sugar in a flat dish. Form the biscuits by pinching off walnut-sized balls of dough and rolling between your palms until a perfect sphere is formed. (Since the dough is very sticky, it's a good idea to moisten your hands from time to time.) Flatten the sphere slightly, dip one side into powdered sugar, and arrange on a buttered baking sheet.

5 Bake on the middle shelf of the preheated oven for 15 to 18 minutes. When they are done, the biscuits will have expanded and crisscross breaks will appear on their tops. Allow to cool and crisp before storing.

Note: They will keep at least a month in an airtight tin container.

Anise-Flavoured Melba Toast Rounds (Fekkas)

These little biscuits must get their name from the 'runner' chickens also called *fekkas*, for they are tough little things with a good taste. They are very popular for dipping in tea, doubtless because they can stand the heat!

There are two ways to make them, the traditional way and the way that produces *krislettes*. *Krislettes* are not as popular as *fekkas*, possibly because it's hard to dunk diced biscuits into tea, but they are good for exercising the teeth.

The traditional *fekkas* require two bakings, which in Morocco means sending trays of biscuits twice to the community ovens. If you live far away, this can make life difficult. In fact, when I made these biscuits I had to cross town to the house of a friend who had an oven nearby. The dough is rolled into 30 cm (12″) long cylinders and left to rise for an hour or two. These cylinders are then pricked all over and sent at once to the oven to be only partially baked. They are next returned to the house and left to harden all night. By the following morning they are very heavy. A thin-bladed knife is used to cut very fine slices, which are then sent back to the oven for a final baking. When the biscuits are cool they are packed in tin boxes to be brought out for days afterwards for afternoon tea.

Makes enough to fill a good-
  sized cake tin

8 g (($\frac{1}{4}$ oz) active dry yeast
325 g (11$\frac{1}{2}$ oz) plain flour
$\frac{1}{4}$ teaspoon salt
100 g (3$\frac{1}{2}$ oz) icing sugar plus
  more for handling the dough
115 g (4 oz) unsalted butter,
  melted and cooled

1 scant tablespoon aniseed
1 scant tablespoon sesame seeds
  (toasted, optional)
4 tablespoons orange-flower
  water

1 The day before, soak the yeast in 4 tablespoons lukewarm water until bubbly.

2 Combine the flour, salt, 1$\frac{1}{4}$ cups sugar, the bubbling yeast, cooled melted butter and spices in the large mixing bowl. Stir in the orange-flower water and then enough lukewarm water to form a firm dough. Knead well until smooth, then turn out on to a board dusted with more icing sugar. Break into 4 portions. Roll each into a ball and cover.

3 Take one of the balls and shape the dough into a 2·5 cm (1″) thick cylinder by rolling back and forth with some force. The dough will be sticky at first, but after some strong, firm rolling with palms down it will start to stretch as you slide your palms toward the ends to lengthen the mass. Stretch and roll the dough until you have a 25–30 cm (10–12″) cylinder of even thickness. Repeat with the remaining balls. Place on the baking sheets, cover with towels, and let rise in a warm place until doubled in volume. When doubled, prick each tube with a fork to deflate.

4 Preheat the oven to 190° C/375°F/Gas 5.

5 Bake the tubes for 20 minutes, or until barely golden. (They should not be cooked through.) Remove from the oven and let cool on racks overnight.

6 The following day, slice the cylinders crosswise into very thin biscuits and arrange flat on ungreased baking sheets. Bake in a 180° C/350° F/Gas 4 oven until pale golden brown and dry, about 10 minutes. When cool, store in airtight tins.

—— •••——

SWEET SUPPER DISHES or PRE-DESSERTS

I would love to say something romantic about these sweet supper dishes, often served after a rich and nourishing soup or a succession of meat or chicken *tagines*, though not strictly speaking as desserts. However, good-tasting and substantial as they are, I cannot think of them without beginning to laugh, recalling some experiences in Moroccan homes when there were no guests for dinner and the evenings were devoted to watching television.

It seemed almost absurd to me to sit at a table with a Moroccan family, devouring these sublime sweet dishes with large tablespoons from a communal platter while we watched the tube, where third-rate Saudi-Arabian love stories were being enacted with much feverish movements of the eyes. However, since centuries of invasions, the rise and fall of mighty dynasties, and forty-three years of being a 'protectorate' of France have not destroyed this culture, it will probably survive the horrors of the television age.

Sweet Dessert Couscous

A palace dish – very rich and good, though its sweetness can be overwhelming, even when followed by ice-cold milk. A good after-theatre dish to be served following the scrambled eggs and *harira* described on page 49.

Correctly this should be made with *seffa*, a type of *couscous* that is finely rolled semolina and water with other flour omitted. As I've noted, this finer form of *couscous* is not yet available easily, but you can simulate its lightness and texture by steaming ordinary *couscous* for an extra time.

For 12 people as part of a
    Moroccan dinner

900 g (2 lbs) *couscous* or *seffa*
160 g (5½ oz) unsalted butter
160 g (5½ oz) whole, blanched
    almonds
160 g (5½ oz) shelled and peeled
    walnuts

5 tablespoons granulated sugar
salt
225 g (8 oz) dates, stoned and
    chopped
powdered cinnamon
icing sugar

1 Follow step 1 (first washing and drying of *couscous*) in the master instructions, page 110). (If for some reason you are able to obtain real *smeeda*, used to make *seffa*, ignore this step. Simply dampen before steaming.)

2 Melt 5 tablespoons of the butter. Chop the nuts coarsely, then pulverise them with the granulated sugar in the blender. Knead with 3 tablespoons of the melted butter to make a paste.

3 Fill the bottom of the *couscoussier* with plenty of water and bring to a boil. Then rub inside of the top container with butter. Follow steps 2 and 3 (first steaming and second drying of the *couscous*) in the master instructions (page 111). Steam the *couscous* 30 minutes.

4 Toss the drying *couscous* with the remaining 2 tablespoons butter.

5 Return the grain to top container and continue steaming 20 minutes, fastening the top to the bottom as instructed on page 112. Dump out again and slowly work in about 450 ml (scant pint) and 1 tablespoon salt. (If you continuously work the grains and *then* add 3 or 4 tablespoons of water at a time, the *couscous* will easily absorb the water. If, on the other hand, you add water too quickly and the grains do not absorb it, simply spread them out and let them

dry for a while.) Rub the nut paste between your fingers and toss with the dried *couscous* grains.

6 Steam the dates alone for 15 minutes in the top part of the *couscoussier*. Remove the dates and pile the *couscous* back for a final steaming of 10 minutes. Mix with the dates and remaining butter. Arrange in an elongated mound and decorate with lines of cinnamon shooting from the top like rays of sunlight. Serve with spoons and ice-cold milk, and with icing sugar separately in a bowl.

Note: A handful of raisins or fried almonds can be substituted for the nut paste and dates. In this case the dish is called *msfouf*.

Sweet Steamed Rice
(Roz Mafooar)

Rice can be steamed like *couscous*, decorated with cinnamon and sugar, and served with a cold glass of milk as an evening dish. It is delicious when preceded by a bowl of soup or a *tagine kebab meghdor* (Seared Lamb Kebabs Cooked in Butter, page 191).

Of course you can prepare steamed rice the French way, which is easier and will give you an excellent result, but if you handle rice just as you do *couscous* you will get absolutely separate grains, and that is a fine point that can *make* this dish. It will come out light and airy and will look splendid piled high on a silver dish streaked with icing sugar and powdered cinnamon.

For 12 people

Vegetable oil	
680 g (1½ lbs) raw rice,	salt to taste
preferably long grain	icing sugar
60 g (2 oz) unsalted butter	powdered cinnamon

1 Toss the dry rice with oiled fingers until all the grains are lightly coated. Bring plenty of water to the boil in the bottom of a *couscoussier*. Pile the rice into the lightly oiled top container. Fit one top on to one bottom as for making *couscous* (page 113), *cover* the top container tightly, and steam 20 minutes.

2 Dump the rice into the shallow pan and sprinkle with water. Press the rice down with the spoon to break up lumps and enable the rice

to absorb the water, then stir up and smooth out again. Sprinkle with a little more water and let it stand for 5 minutes. Pile back into the top part of the *couscoussier*.

3 Steam for 20 minutes, *tightly* covered, being certain no steam escapes from the sides.

4 Dump out again and sprinkle with salted water, working it in as you would with *couscous* and raking it to keep it fluffy. Spread out to dry for 5 to 10 minutes, then pile back into the top container.

5 Steam again for 10 minutes, then turn out and break up the lumps. Stir in the butter and some salt to taste. Form a huge mound on a serving plate and dust with icing sugar and streaks of cinnamon, as described in step 6 of the previous receipe.

Moroccan Rice Pudding
(Roz Bil Hleeb)

In Morocco, where the electric blender is virtually unknown, the execution of this recipe is a long and arduous task. The pounding of the almonds alone is a labour of love, and they are only used as a base for milk, orange-flower water, and other ingredients that will overwhelm them. It also takes a long time to knead the almond paste in water and then extract all the resulting juices. The cooking is long, but requires little attention if the burners of your stove can be set at a very low heat; otherwise you will have to stir often to avoid burning the rice.

The decoration of this dish is very simple: the rice is presented in an enormous bowl spotted with 4 dabs of unsalted butter just on the verge of melting. Each guest is given a large spoon and the pudding is eaten in communal style.

Roz bil hleeb is good cold and will keep a few days in the refrigerator.

For 12 people

50 g ($1\frac{3}{4}$ oz) whole, blanched almonds
970 g (2 lb 2 oz) medium- or small-grain rice
40 g ($1\frac{1}{3}$ oz) icing sugar
2 7·5 cm (3″) cinnamon sticks
115 g (4 oz) butter
$\frac{1}{2}$ teaspoon salt

$\frac{1}{2}$ teaspoon almond extract
900 ml ($1\frac{1}{2}$ pints) milk (approximately) (may be half fresh and half condensed milk)
5 tablespoons orange-flower water

257

1 Chop the almonds coarsely, then liquify in the blender with 8 tablespoons very hot water. Press through the sieve into the sauce-pan. Return the almond pulp to the blender and add another 8 tablespoons hot water. Whirl in the blender again, then sieve into the saucepan once more.

2 Add 450 ml (scant pint) water to the almond milk and bring to the boil. Sprinkle in the rice, sugar, and cinnamon, then add half the butter, $\frac{1}{2}$ teaspoon salt, the almond extract, and half the milk. Bring to a boil, then reduce the heat, cover, and simmer 30 minutes, adding more milk if necessary.

3 Continue cooking the rice, adding more milk and stirring often until the whole is thick and velvety, but loose. As the milk becomes absorbed add more. Add the orange-flower water and taste for sweetness. (The dish should be barely sweet; add more sugar if desired.)

4 Continue cooking for 15 to 20 minutes, stirring continuously to prevent the rice from burning.

5 Pour into the serving bowl and decorate with the remaining butter, in 4 dabs.

Pudding
(Mulhalabya)

This Tetuanese dish comes from the Middle East. The recipe was given to me by a young Tetuanese girl who told me the modern way to serve *mulhalabya* is with a fruit cocktail underneath. However, I prefer it 'straight' and find its slightly shimmery, not-quite-firm texture soothing.

For 6 people

5 tablespoons cornflour
675 ml (1¼ pints) cold milk
90 g (3¼ oz) granulated sugar
  (or to taste)
2 tablespoons orange-flower
  water

½ teaspoon grated lemon peel
  (optional)
50 g (1¾ oz) whole, blanched
  almonds
salad oil for frying
½ teaspoon ground cinnamon

1 Mix the flour with 8 tablespoons of the cold milk to a smooth paste. Heat the remaining milk to a boil, then lower the heat and mix in cornflour mixture, all but 2 tablespoons of the sugar, and stir constantly with a wooden spoon until thickened – that is, when a thick coating appears on the back of the spoon. Stir in the orange-flower water and optional lemon peel. Remove from the heat, and pour into individual serving dishes.
2 Brown the almonds in the oil, drain on kitchen paper, and crush well. Mix with the remaining 2 tablespoons sugar and the cinnamon. When a skin begins to appear on the surface of the pudding – and not before – sprinkle with the almond mixture. Chill.

Moroccan Cream of Wheat
(Herbel)

This is a favourite dish of Berbers, and is eaten on New Year's Day.

The new wheat is soaked in hot water for over 24 hours and then drained and pounded in a wooden mortar, after which it is sieved, to remove the husks, and cooked a long time (5 to 6 hours) over a charcoal brazier. It is then seasoned with salt and made creamy with fresh milk and butter.

259

To make it, simmer 1 part whole wheat grains to 4 parts water for 3 hours, adding a little sugar and milk at the end. Dab with butter.

Maizemeal Porridge
(Asidah)

Someone called this dish 'the hamburger of the Souss.' *Asidah* is made from white cracked maize (hominy grits), boiled in water to cover for hours until it is like a creamy pudding, thick and pale yellow, salty and buttery from the addition of a good dollop of *Smen*. The first three fingers of the right hand are used to pluck some *asidah* from the communal plate, dip it into liquid *smen* and then convey it to the mouth. The men of the Souss say that *asidah* makes them virile and strong.

Sweet Bisteeya with Milk and Almonds
(Keneffa)

This speciality of Marrakesh is considered a regal ending to an important meal, when you feel fruit would not be enough. Actually, it is and it isn't, depending on how you feel about watching a delicate creation destroyed before your eyes. The *warka* leaves (you can substitute phyllo or strudel dough) are fried, two at a time, until golden crisp, then drained and piled high (sometimes as high as 40 cm (16″) with browned almonds and thickened almond-milk sauce spooned between layers. It looks splendid, until you are forced to serve it by cutting it with a knife. Immediately the frail tender leaves break into a million pieces, become soggy in the sauce, and 5 minutes later you are facing a badly crumbled mass.

There is however another way: you can put just a tiny bit of milk sauce between the layers and serve the major part in small bowls as 'dips' for each guest. By this method *keneffa* more or less maintains its dignity while being consumed.

For 6 people

5 phyllo or strudel leaves or 20
   warka leaves (page 81)
salad oil for frying
160 g (5½ oz) whole, blanched
   almonds
2 tablespoons icing sugar
powdered cinnamon
3½ tablespoons cornflour

975 ml (1⅔ pint) cup milk
90 g (3¼ oz) fine granulated
   sugar
pinch of salt
2 to 4 tablespoons ground
   blanched almonds
2 tablespoons rosewater or
   orange-flower water

1 Early in the day, separate the leaves of pastry and cut into uniform 20 cm (8″) circles. (When working with phyllo or strudel dough remember to keep the leaves you are not actually handling under a towel so they do not dry out.)

2 Put the oil in a frying pan to a depth of 1 cm (½″) and heat. Fry the pastry leaves (2 pressed together at a time) on both sides until pale golden and crisp, adjusting the heat to avoid browning. Drain on kitchen paper. Make 10 sets. (Fry the *warka* the same way.) Leave the oil in the frying pan.

3 Brown the whole almonds in the oil. Drain and, when cool, chop coarsely or crush with a rolling pin. Mix with icing sugar and cinnamon to taste.

4 Blend the cornflour in the cold milk to a paste. Heat the remaining milk to boiling with the fine sugar and pinch of salt. Stirring constantly with a wooden spoon, add the paste and cook until thick or until the sauce coats the back of the spoon. Add the ground almonds and perfumed water. Whisk until very smooth and continue cooking 1 minute. Remove from the heat and let cool in the pan. Chill, if desired.

5 Later in the day, just before serving, assemble the *bisteeya*, or *keneffa*. Place 2 sets of leaves on a large plate and sprinkle with half the chopped browned almonds. Cover with 3 sets of leaves and spoon over 2 spoonfuls of milk sauce. Cover with another 2 sets of leaves and sprinkle with the remaining almonds. Cover with the remaining leaves and spoon over 1 or 2 spoonfuls of sauce. Serve the remaining milk sauce as described in the introduction or pour around the *keneffa*.

CHAPTER 12

Beverages

YOU WILL SEE water-sellers in *souks* throughout Morocco, portioning out their penny's worth of liquid after elaborate exercises designed to convince the buyer that his cup has been hygienically rinsed. While the poor buy water by the cup, however, the rich drink water that has been perfumed with gum arabic or the essence of orange blossoms. In Fez I once had a deliciously refreshing drink served between the spicy courses of a lengthy meal. I was told the method for making the perfumed water: some grains of gum arabic are thrown into a charcoal brazier and then an empty water-jug is inverted over the fumes. Afterwards the jug is filled with water, which catches the aromatic scent.

Fruit juices are popular in this country, where Islam forbids the consumption of alcohol. One often drinks orange juice and lemonade flavoured with orange-flower water, and sometimes, too, concoctions of pomegranate and lemon juice, and grape juice flavoured with cinnamon.

Sharbat (a fruit or nut milk drink) is particularly rich, cool, and satisfying served in the late afternoon on hot days when dinner will be late and members of the household need sustenance.

Apple Milk Drink
(Sharbat)

For 2–4 people

2 red eating apples	orange-flower water
2 scant teaspoons rosewater or	450 ml (scant pint) cold milk
2 tablespoons granulated sugar	shaved ice (optional)

Peel and cube the apples. Place in the blender jar with the sugar, perfumed water, and milk. Whirl at high speed for 15 seconds. Serve, with shaved ice, if desired, in small glasses.

Almond Milk Drink
(Sharbat Bil Looz)

For four people

225 g (8 oz) whole blanched
    almonds
90 g (3¼ oz) orange-blossom
    water or rosewater
225 ml (scant ½ pint) milk

Blend the almonds with the sugar, a dash of perfumed water, and
225 ml (scant ½ pint) water until smooth. Pour through a strainer,
pressing down hard with the back of a wooden spoon to extract as
much liquid as possible. Stir in another 225 ml (scant ½ pint) water
and the milk. Chill and serve in small glasses.

Note: if the flavour is bland, add a dash of almond extract.

Coffee Ras el Hanout
(Maure Kaoua)

For those who love to play with spices, coffee with *ras el hanout* has got to be some kind of *ne plus ultra*. The mixture of peppery and sweet spices give it a flavour that is both sweet and warm, mysterious and indefinable.

I have met Moroccans who dismiss this kind of coffee as 'low class,' but I also know others who drink it regularly, and even one family from Rabat whose members add grilled ground chick-peas to give the coffee an additionally strange and smoky flavour.

Makes 6 tablespoons

2 whole nutmegs (about 4 teaspoons powdered nutmeg)
4 blades cinnamon (about 1 teaspoon powdered cinnamon)
6 to 8 dried rosebuds
12 whole cloves (about $\frac{1}{2}$ teaspoon powdered cloves)
$\frac{1}{8}$ teaspoon gum arabic
1 tablespoon powdered ginger
2 pieces of galingale (laos) (about $\frac{1}{2}$ teaspoon powdered galingale)

2 allspice berries (about $\frac{1}{8}$ teaspoon powdered allspice)
$\frac{3}{4}$ teaspoon ground white pepper
3 blades mace (about $\frac{1}{2}$ teaspoon powdered mace)
15 white or green cardamon pods
1 teaspoon fennel seeds
1 teaspoon aniseed
1 tablespoons sesame seeds

1 Combine the spices in an electric spice grinder or blender. Sieve and bottle carefully to preserve the freshness.
2 When making coffee, add $\frac{1}{4}$ teaspoon to every 30 g (1 oz) ground coffee before making coffee in your usual fashion. (It makes no difference whether you are using black Turkish-style coffee or ordinary roast.)

—— •••• ——

MOROCCAN TEA

Moroccans, along with the Chinese, the Japanese, and the British, are a people who make an enormous fuss over tea. Tea is often served before and always after every meal, is sipped for endless hours in Moorish cafés, and is prepared at any hour of the day or night that a friend or stranger enters a Moroccan home.

One of the most interesting articles I have ever read about Morocco was published some years ago by Paul Bowles. He wrote of the ambience and meaning of Moorish cafés, and in so doing explored much of the meaning of Moroccan life in sensual terms.

Tea first came to Morocco in the 1800s, brought from the Far East by British traders who quickly found a limitless market. It is always served in small glasses decorated with coloured rings, arranged on a tray (usually silver) etched in elaborate concentric circles. It is poured from a high-held, silver-plated pot of the so-called 'Manchester' shape.

I loved Moroccan tea from the first moment I drank it – loved its excessive sweetness and its strong minty taste. (Spearmint is considered the best for tea, but other kinds of mint will do.) The seasonal addition of fresh white orange blossoms will perfume tea even further, and I have been informed that some Moroccans also add scraped ambergris.

There is something sublime about sitting in a familiar Moorish café. My favourite is perched high on rocks in the Marshan of Tangier, overlooking the Straits of Gibraltar, where hawks hang in mid-air and then drop suddenly down. I've spent hours there holding a glass, thumb on its bottom and forefinger on its rim, inhaling its sweet essence, then slowly sipping.

Everyone, of course, makes tea his own way, but there is a basic formula. First you should use green tea, preferably the type known as Gunpowder or Chun Mee. Secondly, the spearmint should be fresh – dried mint from bottles simply won't do. Thirdly, and very important, the pot should be absolutely clean.

To make a 3-cup pot (enough for 6 small glasses) rinse the pot with boiling water and then throw this water away. Put in 1 tablespoon tea, 25 g (1 oz) sugar, and a handful of fresh spearmint. Cover with boiling water and allow the tea to brew for *at least* 3 minutes, stirring a little at the end, but not too much. Then pour out a glass,

265

look at it, taste it, and correct the sweetness if necessary before serving.

Traditionally you drink three glasses (whether at a reception, at teatime, or after dinner) before taking your leave. Today this rule is rarely observed, and in a Moorish café all rules are meaningless; you sip for hours, you talk, you read, and you enjoy.

——— ••• ———

WINES AND LIQUEURS

The Koran, of course, forbids the use of alcohol, but Moroccan Jews have for many years distilled liquers from such things as pomegranates, grapes, raisins, dates, and honeycombs. There is a famous colourless aniseed flavoured fig brandy called *mahya* that is brewed by the Jews of Telouet in the High Atlas Mountains.

When the French took over Morocco they immediately planted vineyards, just as they had in Algeria and Tunisia. Today the three countries of the Maghreb produce nearly 10 per cent of the world's wine, some of it very good and very inexpensive. The principal Moroccan vineyards are around Rabat and between Meknes and Fez, but to me the most interesting Moroccan wine, and one that is quite good and unique, is the Gris de Boulaouane – the so-called 'grey' rosé made from grapes grown south of Casablanca.

Red wines of note are Cabernet, Vieux Papes and Sidi Larbi. The white wines are Chaudsoleil, l'Oustalet, and Valpierre.

Appendixes

RAS EL HANOUT

1	Allspice	14	Cubebe pepper
2	Ash berries	15	Earth almonds
3	Belladonna leaves	16	Galingale
4	Black cumin seeds	17	Ginger
5	Black peppercorns	18	*Gouza el asnab*
6	Cantharides	19	Grains of paradise
7	Cardamom pods	20	Long pepper
8	Wild cardamom pods	21	Lavender
9	Cayenne	22	Mace
10	Cassia cinnamon	23	Monk's pepper
11	Ceylon cinnamon	24	Nutmeg
12	Cloves	25	Orris root
13	Coriander seed	26	Turmeric

2 HOLARRHEN, called *lissan ettir* in Morocco. A tan, elongated spice that looks like a bird's tongue and is alleged to have strong medicinal and aphrodisiacal properties.

3 ATROPA BELLADONNA, called *zbibet el laidour* in Morocco, sometimes known as 'deadly nightshade.' Collected in the Rif Mountain area and often used as an antispasmodic.

4 NIGELLA ARVENSIS SATIVA, called *habet el soudane* in Morocco. These seeds, which have nothing to do with cumin, have a very sharp, acid taste.

6 LYTTA VESICATORIA, called *debbal el hand* in Morocco. The very sight of these green, metallic beetles, called 'Spanish fly,' terrifies me.

7 ELETTARIA CARDOMOMUM, called *qaqula* in Morocco. This green pod is one of the most expensive spices in Morocco. Inside are roughly a dozen seeds, which are aromatic, clean tasting, sweet, peppery, and bitter. Sometimes used to flavour coffee.

8 ELETTARIA CARDOMOMUM, VAR. MAJOR, called *abachi* in Morocco, and popularly known as 'bitter black cardamom.' Similar to the green cardomom pods but with a completely different appearance, sort of a brown root with a beard at one end that smells to me like old shoes.

14 PIPER CUBEBA, called *kabbaba* in Morocco. Bitter, sharp-tasting berries with a slightly elongated shape. Sometimes called 'tailed pepper,' this comes from Java.

15 CYPERUS ESCULENTUS, called *tara soudania* in Morocco. They look like small elongated nutmegs, and have a perfumed chestnut taste. In Tangier there is a small Spanish ice-cream parlour that sells *horchata* – a very good iced drink made from earth almonds.

16 ALPINIA GALANGA, called *kedilsham* in Morocco. A highly aromatic spice that tastes like a cross between ginger and cardamom. In Indonesia it is frequently used, and is called *laos*.

18 GOUZA EL'ASNAB. This is a kind of nut about an inch in diameter, that is really a spherical cluster of pin-sized white balls. I have not been able to identify its botanical name and am indebted to the Fez cook-book of Mme. Z. Guinaudeau for being able to idenfity it at all.

19 AFRAMOMUM MELEGUETA, called *gooza sahraweea* in Morocco. These grains, also called 'malagueta pepper,' are about half the size of black peppercorns, reddish-brown, and are used as a stimulant and an aphrodisiac. They were called 'grains of paradise' in old books which described how they were found along the pepper coast of Africa in Guinea and Sierra Leone. They came to Morocco in caravans from Senegal and Mauretania, and were first used by southern Berbers to spice meat and flavour breads.

20 PIPER LONGUM, called *dar felfel* in Morocco. They look like elongated and pock-marked black peppercorns.

21 LAVANDULA VERA, called *khzama* in Morocco. These small purple flowers have a sweet, lemony aroma, and must be used with care because they are very strong. Sometimes added to tea.

22 MYRISTICA FRAGRANS, called *bsibsa* in Morocc. Made from the outer covering of the nutmeg shell, it is an indispensable ingredient in *ras el hanout*.

23 AGNUS CASTUS, called *kheroua* in Morocco. Another potent aphrodisiac.

24 MYRISTICA FRAGRANS, called *gouza* in Morocco. This, of course, is the inner kernel of the nut of which mace is the outer covering; thus the two spices have the same botanical name. Also indispensable in *ras el hanout*.

SUGGESTED MENUS

DINNER FOR 8 (I)

Bisteeya
Chicken with Lemon and Olives
Omar's Couscous
Moroccan Bread
Fruit

DINNER FOR 8 (II)

Five Salads:
Orange, Lettuce, and Walnut Salad
A Tomato and Green Pepper Salad
Carrot Salad
Zeilook
Mohk (Brain Salad I or II)
Djej Mechoui (Roasted Chicken)
Seksu dar Marhzin (Pumpkin Couscous)
Moroccan Bread
Fruit

DINNER FOR 8 (III)

Fish (Shad) Baked with Stuffed Fruit
Lamb Tagine with Courgettes and Za'atar
Seksu Tanjaoui (Tangier Couscous)
Moroccan Bread
Fruit

BERBER DINNER FOR 8 TO 10

Kouah (Skewered and Grilled Liver)
Byesar (Puree of Dried Beans)
Mechoui (Roasted Lamb), Served on Lemon Leaves
Cheesha Belboula (Berber Couscous)
Hot Miklee, with Butter and Honey
Moroccan Bread

269

TETUÁN DINNER FOR 8 TO 10
Balakia (Bisteeya, Tetuán Style)
Marak Silk (Tagine of Swiss Chard)
Lamb with Okra, 'Roof Tile' Style
Moroccan Bread
Mulhalabya

FEZ DINNER FOR 8 TO 10
Four Assorted Salads
Djej bil Hamus (Chicken with Chick Peas)
Tagine bil Babcock (Tagine of Lamb with Prunes and Apples)
Moroccan Bread
Melon

MARRAKESH DINNER FOR 8

Djej Emshmel (Chicken with Lemons and Olives Emshmel)
Tagine Kebab Meghdor (Seared Lamb Kebabs Cooked in Butter)
Moroccan Bread
Keneffa (Sweet Bisteeya with Milk and Almonds)

RAMADAN DINNER FOR 8
Harira I or II
Scrambled Eggs
Dates
Shebbakia (Free-Form Honey Cake)
A Fragrant Lamb Tagine
Moroccan Bread

FAMILY DINNER FOR 6
Kefta Mkaouara (Meatball, Tomato, and Egg Tagine)
Djej Mafooar (Steamed Chicken)
Moroccan Bread Fruit

FAMILY DINNER FOR 6
Marak Matisha bil Melokhias (Tagine of Okra and Tomatoes)
Beef Tagine with Cauliflower
Couscous with Seven Vegetables in the Fez Manner
Moroccan Bread Fruit

270

Glossary

Agadir	A Southern port town on the Atlantic coast, in the heart of the Souss.
Aid el Kebir	The Festival of the Sacrifice of the Lamb, occurring on the tenth day of the twelfth month of the Muslim calendar and commemorating the sacrifice of Abraham.
Atlas	Any one of three mountain ranges (the Middle Atlas, the High Atlas, or the Anti-Atlas) that run roughly east to west across Morocco.
Baqqula	A wild Moroccan herb combining the tastes of watercress, arugula, and sorrel.
Baraka	A special kind of God-given luck, often associated with leadership.
Berber	The original inhabitants of North Africa, now constituting about 80 per cent of the Moroccan population. By religion they are Muslim, but their ethnic origin is not Arab.
Bled	The countryside.
Bisteeya	Perhaps the greatest of all Moroccan dishes, a pie of fine pastry stuffed with chicken, eggs, almonds, spices, and covered with cinnamon and sugar. Also, the generic term for a variety of pastry dishes.
Caid	A governor or chief. Usually appointed.
Casablanca	The largest city in Morocco, as well as the principal port and centre of business and commerce. Not especially known for its cuisine.
Casbah	A fort or fortified castle.
Charmoula	Marinade for fish.
Coque	A small wild artichoke.
Couscous	Two meanings: (1) the national dish of Morocco, prepared in numerous variations; (2) the tiny balls of rolled semolina flour with which the dish is made.
Couscoussier	The utensil in which couscous is cooked.
Dar Mahkzen	Palace.

271

Diffa   Moroccan banquet.

Djej   Chicken

Djemaa el Fna   The great square of Marrakesh.

Erfoud   An oasis famous for its many varieties of dates.

Essaouira   A port town on the Atlantic coast, due west of Marrakesh. Essaouira had a large Jewish population, and is something of a gastronomic centre.

Fassi   A person from Fez. Sometimes used to refer to the powerful and wealthy élite of that city.

Fez   A great inland city, the oldest of the four royal capitals. One of the three great gastronomic centres of Morocco.

Gdra del Trid   An enamelled earthenware dome used for stretching the dough for the classic Arab dish, *trid*.

Gsaa   A large, shallow wooden or clay basin used for kneading dough.

Imilchil   A tiny town in the Middle Atlas, the site of the famous Berber *moussem* called The Festival of the Betrothed.

Istiqlal   Name of the Independence party, whose original members were instrumental in ending the French Protectorate.

Kefta   Minced meat.

Kif   Marijuana.

Kimia   A kind of magic that gives its possessor the power to multiply food.

Kissaria   The portion of a *medina* devoted to commerce.

Kliir   A kind of preserved meat, similar to *basturma*.

Koutoubia Mosque   The largest and most famous building in Marrakesh.

Ksra   Moroccan bread from the *bled* (countryside).

Maghreb   That portion of North Africa encompassing Morocco, Algeria, and Tunisia.

Marrakesh   A great city in southern Morocco, one of the four royal capitals and one of the three gastronomic centres.

Mechoui   Berber-style spit-roasted lamb. Can also be used to describe a form of roasting chicken.

Medina   The old quarter of a Moroccan city, usually a place of closely built homes with few windows, and narrow, maze-like streets.

Meknes   Somewhat west of Fez, one of the four royal capitals and a city of gastronomic importance. Built, like Versailles, as a royal enclave.

Mhamnsa   Large semolina pellets.

Moussem   A Berber festival, usually with some religious significance, at which Berber folk-dancing and singing may be observed and Berber food tasted.

Nasrani   Literally, a Nazarene – that is, a Christian. Used by Moroccans to describe non-Muslim foreigners such as Europeans and Americans.

Pasha   Similar to the major of a large city.

Ramadan   The Muslim month of fasting.

Rif   The most northern range of mountains in Morocco, running parallel to the Mediterranean.

Safi   An important city, south of Casablanca and north of Essaouira on the Atlantic coast, known for certain fish and seafood specialities.

Sebou   An important river that runs from the Middle Atlas, through Fez, to the Atlantic. Famous for its delicious trout and shad.

Sefrou   A town south of Fez with a large Jewish population. Known for some delicacies.

Seffa   Fine rolled semolina flour containing no additions of other flours.

Shaban   Total satisfaction, as at the end of a Moroccan *diffa*.

Smeeda   Semolina flour.

Smen   Preserved butter.

Souk   Shop, store, or stall.

Souss   Southwestern region of Morocco.

Sultan   The king of Morocco.

Tagine   A slowly simmered Moroccan stew, the basic Moroccan dish – there are literally hundreds of recipes for *tagines*.

Tagine slaoui The shallow earthenware pot in which a *tagine* is cooked and also served.

Tangier Important Moroccan city, situated on the Straits of Gibraltar, known for its cosmopolitan atmosphere. Perhaps the most Europeanised Moroccan town.

Tetuán One of the three great gastronomic cities of Morocco, where the cuisine shows a strong Andalusian influence.

Tobsil del bisteeya The pan in which *bisteeya* is cooked.

Tobsil del warka The pan upon which *warka* leaves are cooked.

Warka Fine pastry leaves, used in *bisteeya* and other dishes.

Za'atar A herb, close to oregano, marjoram, and thyme, found only in the Mediterranean region.

——— •••• ———

Some Books on Morocco and Moroccan Cookery

Barbour, Nevill, *Morocco* (London, 1965).

Bowles, Paul, *Their Heads are Green and Their Hands are Blue* (New York, 1963).

Bute, John. Fourth Marquis of, *Moorish Recipes* (London, 1954).

Cowan, George, D., and Johnston, L. N. *Moorish Lotus Leaves* (London, 1883).

Field, Michael and Frances, *A Quintet of Cuisines* (New York, 1970).

Guinaudeau, Z., *Fes vu par sa cuisine* (Rabat, 1958).

Harris, Walter, *The Land of an African Sultan* (New York, 1889).

Landry, Robert, *Les soleils de la cuisine* (Paris, 1966).

Laoust, E., *Mots et choses berbères dialetes de Maroc* (Paris, 1920).

Legey, Françoise, *The Folklore of Morocco* (London, 1935).

Maxwell, Gavin, *Lords of the Atlas* (London, 1966).

Meakin, Budgett, *The Moors* (London, 1902).

Oppenheim, Monah, *Contributions to the Culinary Art: A Collection of Family Recipes and Cookery Clues* (New York, 1961).

Perrier, Amelia, *A Winter in Morocco* (London, 1873).

Roden, Claudia, *A Book of Middle Eastern Food* (New York, 1972).

Sefroui, Ahmed, *The Moussem at Imilchil* (Rabat, 1967).

Smires, Latifa Bennani, *La cuisine marocaine* (Paris, 1971).

Westermarch, Edward, *Wit and Wisdom of Morocco* (New York, 1931).

Index

277

CONTENTS

1

A VERY SHORT HISTORY OF THE BICYCLE

The Leonardo Museum in Vinci, Italy, has on display a supposed fifteenth-century sketch of a bicycle, invented by the master. It is accompanied by a wooden reimagining of the machine. Unfortunately, the sketch is a fake, perpetrated during the restoration of the Leonardo Codex in the late 1960s by monks of the Grottaferrata near Rome. The reproduction model is a travesty of history.

Without question Karl von Drais of Karlsruhe in Badenia invented the first two-wheeler in 1817. It became known in Germany as the *draisine*, in France as the *draisienne* and in England as the hobby-horse and, while making a stir in fashionable society, it was very soon abandoned. Little happened until the French pedal velocipede appeared in 1869. This craze, although bigger and much more widespread, was similarly brief and in turn the machine became quickly derided as a 'boneshaker'.

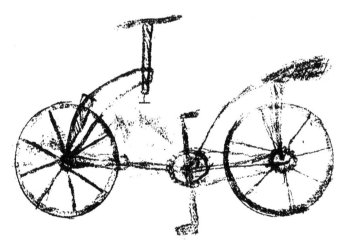

The hoax drawing of 'Leonardo bicycle', perpetrated during restoration of the codex in the 1970s.

Happily, the arrival of the suspension wire wheel saved the day and the ordinary bicycle, later to be called a penny-farthing, immediately took its place. The ordinary blossomed for fifteen years and only surrendered to the hard-tyred safety bicycle in 1886. Four years later, the final solution evolved. This was the diamond-framed, pneumatic safety of 1890 that ushered in cycling's golden era during the *belle époque*. Equipped with a free wheel, rim-brakes and multiple gears, and with new materials following over time, racing success and fashion have kept the bicycle modern and exciting to the present day.

Karl Drais velocipede, 1817.

French pedal velocipede or boneshaker, 1868.

Grout Tension ordinary
bicycle, 1872.

Hillman Kangaroo dwarf
front-driver, 1884.

Humber rear-driving dwarf
safety, 1885.

Diamond-framed
pneumatic safety 1891.

NOMENCLATURE

Karl von Drais (rhymes with 'ice') named his 1817 invention a velocipede (swift foot), while in England Denis Johnson called his copy of von Drais's machine a pedestrian curricle. It became known to the public as a hobby-horse or dandy-horse.

Over the next fifty years, human-powered machines were rare but they were still known as velocipedes and, confusingly, this same name was then used for the Michaux pedal bicycle when it arrived from France in 1869. The French, however, had coined the word 'bicycle' and this was quickly adopted into English. It was then applied to the high bicycle, which succeeded it in 1870.

By 1878, safer, lever-driven, high bicycles began to be introduced so that, while they were termed safeties, the ordinary high bicycle became simply the ordinary. It is a name still fondly used by the cognoscenti today.

Hillman's 1884 Kangaroo was called a dwarf front-driver and was then overtaken by 1886 by the dwarf rear-drivers of the Rover pattern. Rudge exported their 1886 Bicyclette rear-drive model to France where it supplied an alternative name to *le petite reine*. Rear-drivers were initially of two types: the Rover style, open-diamond frame and the cheaper Hillman cross-frame. By the end of the 1880s the safety bicycle had ousted the ordinary to become the bicycle, while the ordinary was nostalgically referred to by devotees as the Grand Old Ordinary. Street urchins called it a penny-farthing.

The 1890s saw enthusiasm for crypto-geared front-drivers and bicycles with shaft-drive replacing the chain. From 1903, three-speed hub gears became popular in England while derailleur gears were refined during the 1920s in France. Hand-built lightweights of the 1930s–1960s are often referred to in the UK as classic bicycles, while Americans reserve the term for balloon-tyred models from roughly the same era. The 1930s saw a growth in recumbents that were quickly banned from competition by the ICF, but which have remained popular among enthusiasts.

The cross-frame design was reinvented in the 1960s by Alex Moulton with small wheels, high-pressure tyres and rubber suspension. This led to a rash of shopper bicycles with lower specification that gave the small wheelers a poor reputation.

Mountain bikes were introduced in California in the 1970s and are now known as MTBs or ATBs – all-terrain bicycles – while fixed-wheel, low-riding bikes, beloved of cycle couriers, are familiarly called fixies.

2
HISTORIOGRAPHY

Since the days of the boneshaker, cycle magazines and bicycle histories have been the natural accompaniment to peaks in bicycle sales. Many small booklets were published in 1869 explaining the history of human-powered machines to those who might be contemplating purchasing a velocipede. These were often anonymous, under-researched tracts, recycling old myths and giving them new legs. The misinformation spread and with every new cycling wave the stories became entrenched in the cannon. New names have regularly emerged over the years to be hailed as the inventor of the bicycle, and it was only well after the end of the Second World War that the subject became considered worthy of proper academic scrutiny.

During the great bicycle boom of the *belle époque*, Baudry de Saunier, H. H. Griffin, Archibald Sharp, Henry Sturmey and others wrote books on the history of this important new invention, as well

Favre, A. – *Le Velocipede*, 1868.

Anonymous early guide to the
Michaux bicycle.

as articles for the regular cycling periodicals of the period. It was a
time when there was great competition between France, Germany
and England to claim the inventor of the bicycle as one of their
own. The French built a monument to Pierre and Ernest Michaux
in answer to the statue the Germans had raised to Karl von Drais,
while England had earlier built its own memorial to James Starley
in Coventry.

Unsurprisingly the authors tended to be old cyclists rather than
academic historians, and they unconsciously stoked up nationalistic

The cover image from
H. H. Griffins' invaluable
review of 1877.

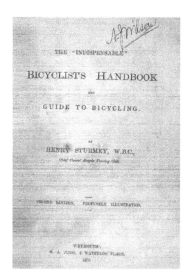

Sturmey's indispensable guide, 1879.

The cover image of Sharp's impenetrable
Bicycles & Tricycles, 1896.

Michaux Monument at Bar le Duc, erected 1894.

bias. Baudry de Saunier promoted a fictitious French inventor, the Compte de Sivrac with his celerifere, while the Scottish tricyclist James Johnson promoted blacksmith Kirkpatrick Macmillan as the maker of 'The First Bicycle'.

Between the wars, *Bartleet's Bicycle Book* and Louis Bonneville's *Le Velo, fils de France* were more reliable but still retained many of the earlier errors as well as some of the nationalism of the previous generation. Following the Second World War, with petrol still rationed, cycling bounced back and Philip Sumner, Keeper of Transport at the London Science Museum, produced several scholarly monographs based on the collection. In England, the Southern Veteran-Cycle Club was formed in 1954 with the twin aims of research and restoration. The club's journal, *The Boneshaker*, assumed the mantle of investigative historian and sixty years on the V-CC still thrives, having spawned the annual International Cycling History Conference (ICHC) in 1990. The Wheelmen was founded in the United States in 1967, recapturing the ethos of the League of American Wheelmen in the high bicycle days and Andrew Ritchie's

The Boneshaker, Journal of the Veteran-Cycle Club. 1954 to date.

1976 *King of the Road* remains a reliable and vibrant academic study of the whole subject.

The International Veteran Cycle Association was formed in 1981 to encourage enthusiasts to ride old bicycles at its annual meets in different countries around the world and, with cycling currently enjoying everywhere a huge renaissance, the study of its history has never been more vibrant.

Collectors of old bicycles and cycling memorabilia are not always keen historians but they frequently instigate breakthroughs in understanding the past simply by discovering and preserving rare items. Tracing the development of ordinary domestic appliances must be much harder than for sewing machines and bicycles, which both have an aesthetic appeal and often a practical modern use.

Fresh historical information still occasionally turns up on the web, while falsehoods disposed of thirty years ago can also be recycled. Below are listed some of the exploded myths that will not be appearing here, the consensus being they had little or nothing to do with bicycle development. Nor will this account much concern itself with the social construction of technology. In a different age or different culture things would have happened differently but what happened, happened and it seems enough to record when, where and by whom. The names we remember today are those who, from ability or serendipity, added something to the story. The bicycle was effectively weaned in a Darwinian age when people were expecting technology to change things annually for the better. Good ideas born before their time sometimes fail to take root, and there is no space for the might-have-beens who required the American Patent Office to construct a second building in the 1890s simply to house bicycle patents. Instead, we will try to follow the thread of successful innovation that has produced 100 million bicycles to date and today provides pleasure and utility to cyclists across the world.

There will also be no apology for the many dates. In any fast-moving technology priority is king, and to understand the story one has to know who first did what and when.

Exploded myths (exploder and date in brackets)

Leonardo da Vinci bicycle, 1492 (Lessing, 1998).
Stoke Poges church bicycle window, 1642 (Bowerman, 1988).
Le Comte de Sivrac and the celerifere, 1791 (Seray, 1976).
E. M. Artomov, grand bi., 1801 (Street, 1992).
Nicephore Niepce, two-wheel hobby-horse, 1816 (Roberts, 1962).
Kirkpatrick Macmillan and Gavin Dalzell bicycles, *c.* 1839 (Dodds, 1999).
Philipp Moritz Fischer velocipede, *c.* 1852/3 (Lessing, 1991).
Mr. Magee of Paris, 1868 (Kobayashi/Clayton, 1996).
Lawson's Sussex Dwarf, 1873 (Roberts, 1969).
George Larkin's Bowden cable, 1902 (Clayton, 2014).

THE DRAISINE AKA THE HOBBY-HORSE

Every cyclist must wonder, from time to time, who it was that first enjoyed the breathtaking abandon of coasting downhill on a bicycle, and when. Since that first occasion, millions have delighted in, and frequently put into words or even rhyme, the feeling of euphoria still awaiting every novice cyclist. With some confidence it can now be said that the very first bicyclist was the prolific inventor Karl von Drais (rhymes with 'ice') from Karlsruhe in Badenia, and the date was Thursday 12 June 1817. On that day Drais rode his newly invented *laufmaschine* some 9 miles from Mannheim to the relay station on the road to Schwetzingen. He constructed his two-wheel *laufmaschine* (running machine) some four years after his four-wheeled crank-driven *fahrmaschine* (driving machine) had proved to be a failure.

Karl von Drais, publicity for the *draisine* 1817.

In Europe, 1816 was known as the 'year without a summer' when the aftereffects of a volcanic eruption in Indonesia had led to a poor harvest, increasing the cost of horse fodder. Drais claimed that his new mode of transport obviated the need for horses, but unhappily the *laufmaschine* never threatened to replace them. He managed to patent it in France where it became known as the *draisine* and it was demonstrated in the Luxembourg gardens in Paris. His brochure offered to license local makers, supplying, on payment of one Carolin, a badge bearing his family coat of arms to be attached to each machine sold. However, his success in licensing it around Europe was patchy because pirated copies robbed him of his privilege, most notably in England.

In London, Denis Johnson (1760–1833), a Covent Garden coach maker, having in his own weasel words 'procured one of these very useful machines from abroad' applied for and was granted British patent No.4321 on 22 December 1818. He referred to it as a Pedestrian Curricle although the public soon preferred the popular names hobby-horse, dandy-horse, or even velocipede (swift foot). This name had been coined by Drais or maybe by his French agent Louis Dineur. Propulsion was achieved by the rider's feet pushing on the ground, with the chest and forearms resting on a padded balance board.

Johnson's steering mechanism was undoubtedly an improvement on the *draisine*, which essentially used carriage or farm-cart technology with the front wheel mounted in a bogey steadied by

Johnson's Pedestrian hobby-horse, announced in the *Ladies Magazine*, May 1819.

Johnson's riding school,
1818.

a wooden quadrant and steered with a tiller. Johnson chose to use iron forks, with the steering post passing vertically up through the beam. His first model was steered with a rather cumbersome handle, attaching to the front axle and looping back towards the rider, but this was quickly replaced by a plain straight handlebar fixed to the steering post that could be directed while still resting the elbows on the breast board.

Johnson hobbyhorse No. 25, courtesy of
Roger Street (1998).

Body movement greatly assisted in the steering. The forward-leaning position was hardly ergonomic but there can be no doubt that, when coasting downhill with the feet on rests or held off the ground, the true joy of cycling would unquestionably have been experienced. The *Analectic Magazine*, Philadelphia, 1819, cautioned: 'It is only after having acquired dexterity in the equilibrium and direction of the velocipede that an attempt to increase the motion of the feet, or to keep them elevated while it is in rapid motion, should be attempted.'

Denis Johnson promoted his machine widely during the spring of 1819 and ironically received useful publicity from the political cartoonists of the day, including Robert and George Cruikshank, whose aim was to ridicule the royal princes and the dandies who were prominent among Johnson's customers. The swift-walker featured in over eighty socio-political cartoons, widely displayed in the print shops of London. As original Johnson machines are now rarer than hen's teeth, the prints provide some small consolation for the dedicated hobby-horse collector.

Sales of the pedestrian hobby-horse began in March 1819, priced at £6–£10, and Johnson was soon turning out some twenty-five machines a week. He opened two riding schools in London and demonstrated the machine in Manchester, Birmingham, Liverpool and Leeds. In July he even took it to New York. He soon added a dropped-frame model for ladies, perhaps inspiring Hancock & Co. of Pall Mall to produce the Pilentum; a ladies' tricycle propelled by foot-boards and hand levers driving the front wheel via cranks.

The Prince Regent and Lady Hartford in a political print from 1819.

London coachmaker Charles Lucas Birch joined the fray with his Velocimanipede, a machine for two riders and a lady passenger, while a range of manumotive tricycles for men – Manivelociter, Bivector and Trivector – employed a variety of rowing-action mechanisms to turn the rear axle.

Surprisingly, around a dozen of Johnson's machines survive today, mainly having been originally bought by the upper classes who, equipped with ample stabling, tended not to throw things away. The wooden beam is usually branded beneath the saddle with a serial number in Roman numerals, the highest number discovered so far being 320; one of two bought by Radical Jack the Earl of Durham and made no later than July 1819. The small output and the short season of popularity underlines that, had it not been for the publicity provided by the cartoonists, very little of the brief hobby-horse craze would be remembered today. Figures for other UK makers are unknown and, although some quality pieces survive, Johnson unquestionably had the lion's share of this restricted market.

Street (1998) attributes the swift demise of the *draisine* partly to its association with the ridiculed dandies and partly to a reputation for causing injury through rupture or hernia. Another factor was undoubtedly the by-laws restricting their use in London, where many of the buyers had town houses. New York, Calcutta and other towns introduced similar restrictions, accelerating the decline. Caricaturist Robert Cruikshank collided with his publisher

Ladies' Pilentum,
1818.

Local-made hobby-horse by William Plenty of North Wooton. (Author's Collection)

French zoomorphic *draisine*. (Claude Reynaud Collection)

Sidebetham when descending Highgate Hill in the winter of 1819 and thereafter both devoted themselves to turning the sport to ridicule.

Fundamental to the machine's abandonment was undoubtedly its limited utility. No riding clubs were formed and few social groups rode together for pleasure. Distance travel was fatiguing and, while the occasional solo tour is recorded, the two-wheeled horse, although not needing fodder, failed to multiply. Crucially, there were no technical improvements to encourage buyers to update or replace their machines and, after its demise, sightings during the next fifty years were only of the odd eccentric in country districts.

Drais' invention was vaguely remembered half a century later when the Michaux bicycle arrived from France, while his neologism, velocipede, had meantime become adopted into the English language. Two generations had failed to address the challenge of powering a two-wheel velocipede and public interest in it effectively died.

THE DRAISINE IN AMERICA

The hobby-horse arrived in America only a few months after it had captivated England, the first sighting being an advertisement in Baltimore for the TRACENA – 'this curious, useful and simple machine, was invented in Germany, by Trace.' [sic.]

One J. Stewart claimed to have patented several improvements to it and was ready to execute orders, while William C. Clarkson filed a patent in June 1819. Unfortunately Clarkson's patent was destroyed in the US patent office fire of 1836 and so remains tantalisingly unknown. The painter Norman Vincent Peale had a draisine made locally and his children became enthusiastic velocipedists but, as in the old world, after the early fervour, interest in the machine died out, probably before the oil had dried up in the bearings.

4

THE QUADRICYCLE YEARS
1820–1868

The seventeenth and eighteenth centuries saw reports of several machines in which one could travel on the road without horses. These usually involved the owner seated and steering the vehicle, while a servant or even two servants, provided mechanical power to the rear axle via a treadmill or by using cranks. Dr Richard of La Rochelle (1696), John Vevers (1769), Ovenden (1774) and Jean-Pierre Blanchard (1779) were all reported as constructing garden phaetons along these lines. Because the accounts are rare it would seem safe to conclude they had little or no influence on later

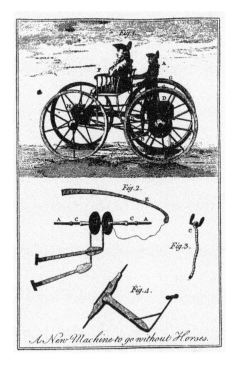

Ovenden's 1671 horseless carriage.

developments, although it is possible that Karl von Drais might have seen the Jackman of London park phaeton at Schwetzingen prior to making his four-wheeled *fahrmaschine*.

The hobby-horse craze certainly showed that in 1919 there was an enthusiasm for cheap personal transport but, in the end, it proved only a brief summer diversion for the rich in their pleasure-grounds. Over the next half-century velocipedes, as they were now called, were occasionally reported as having been sighted, but more often than not these were three- or four-wheelers rather than bicycles. After 1830, the new railway provided the means for mass transport and, in direct consequence, road maintenance deteriorated and would not improve until the high-bicyclists of the 1870s began to lobby local government for better roads.

Jackman's gartenwagon, *c.* 1770/75.

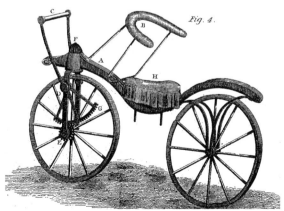

Gompertz 1821 patent for an improved velocipede.

Louis Gompertz, a founder of the RSPCA and friend of the horse, filed a patent in 1822 for a *draisine* with the front wheel driven by a toothed quadrant, operated by the handlebar, but it must have been impractical for it never reached production. In the same era, power-loom inventor Dr Edmund Cartwright designed what he called his locomotive carriage or Centaur, capable of carrying a 16-cwt load 27 miles in a day, but he was eighty by the time he felt satisfied with it and the project died with him.

Only Willard Sawyer, a Dover carpenter who began making quadricycles around 1830, had any success. He was awarded a medal at the 1851 Great Exhibition and supplied his elegant vehicles to several crowned heads, including the Prince of Wales and the young Prince Imperial of France. They were expensive machines and Sawyer had to supplement the infrequent sales by supplying machines for holiday hire at the Crystal Palace and south-coast seaside resorts. Over a forty-year career one sees little technical improvement in his machines, probably on account of him receiving little feedback from customers. Only a handful of Sawyer machines have survived, although a particularly graceful example is now in the care of the London Science Museum.

Around 1840, there was a flickering of interest around Dumfries for lever-driven hobby-horses, possibly beginning with James Charteris and involving Gavin Dalzell and Kirkpatrick Macmillan, but their productions went unnoticed elsewhere and it is unrealistic to claim them as having had any influence on bicycle development. Thomas McCall

Dr. Cartwright's Centaur

Cartwright's Centaur, 1823.

claimed to have copied what he remembered of Macmillan's machine and he sold a few in Glasgow, but this was only after the Michaux machine had arrived there and his rear-wheel propulsion was less effective than front-wheel pedals. A lone McCall survivor from 1869 is in the London Science Museum, while a copy made by him much later is in Dumfries Observatory. Because of James Johnson's public championing of Macmillan in the chauvinistic 1890s, and the persistence of the myth, most bicycle museums around the world sadly find it necessary to display a suitably distressed reproduction.

During the 1860s, in the satellite industrial towns around Manchester, amateur velocipede builders exchanged ideas through *The Mechanics' Magazine* and *The English Mechanic*, building their own three- and four-wheeled machines. Mr Goddard of Stalybridge journeyed 200 miles (320 km) to the 1862 London International Exhibition on a two-man, back-to-back, lever-driven velocipede, and by 1868 a few enthusiasts had formed England's first cycling club – The High Peak Velocipede Club. In 1863 Joseph Goodman

Sawyer quadricycle. (Ned Passey Collection)

Thomas McCall's 1869 Kilmarnock velocipede.

patented the Rantoone tricycle, propelled by hand and foot levers. Its brief run was crowned by winning a race at the Crystal Palace against the new two-wheel velocipedes in 1869. The Edinburgh tricycle made by Mathew Brown was similar, but had a single rear driving wheel and front steering.

All these experiments indicate a desire to substitute human power for horsepower and yet none really achieved take-up. All were to be swept away after Rowley Turner brought a Michaux pedal velocipede from Paris to Coventry in November 1868.

Above left: J. Hastings on his homemade velocipede, 1868.

Above right: Rantoone, photo courtesy of Lorne Shields.

Left: Mathew Brown's Edinburgh tricycle, *c.* 1865.

THE VELOCIPEDE BICYCLE OR BONESHAKER

THE INVENTION CLAIMANTS

The two-wheeled pedal velocipede was certainly being made in Paris by 1864 and after a short meteoric career it was virtually abandoned everywhere by 1871. It led down what proved to be the wrong road of front-wheel propulsion and might therefore be seen as flawed; yet it was a defining step forward and was known in many countries across the world. Henceforward, invention and improvement was to be continuous and bicycles have developed steadily to the present day.

Surprisingly, the name of the person who first fitted pedal cranks to the front wheel still remains unresolved and it now provides the liveliest debating topic for cycle historians. As Tom Rolt maintained, 'the reason why the question of priority is so often the subject of heated debate is that an historic invention is never wholly original.' Recent research has suggested that tricycles with a crank-driven front wheel, rather than rear axle, originated around 1855–60 and that it is possible that the pedal bicycle was created from one of these in around 1862. The conjecture competes with nineteenth-century claims that Pierre and Ernest Michaux modified a hobby-horse in 1861 or that Pierre Lallement did likewise in 1863.

A recently discovered memoir of Raymond Raddison, a cousin of the Oliver brothers, claimed that after seeing children racing on hobby-horses in Switzerland he made a machine with pedals in 1855 with another for his cousin Marius Olivier. Whatever turns out to be the truth, by the time of the 1867 Paris International Exposition the boulevards and parks were buzzing with velocipedes. The World

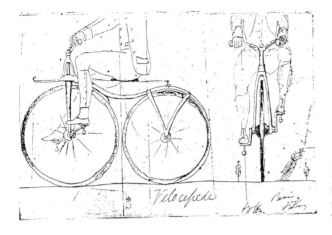

Michaux's
serpentine-framed bicycle,
sketched by Townsend
Trench in 1864.

Bill Haylor with
his 1867 Michaux
serpentine model.

Fair attracted international visitors, many of whom returned home with tales to tell, some even taking a bicycle back with them.

In 1828, a three-wheeled omnibus in Paris had been known as a tricycle and one early use of the word is in a French patent of 1867: 'un vélocipède tricycle', i.e. a three-wheeled velocipede. The word 'bicycle' followed from this, 'un vélocipède bicycle', i.e. a two-wheeled velocipede, and America and England adopted the name at the same time as they adopted the machine. The nickname 'boneshaker' was coined in 1871 when the velocipede had become outdated.

At the 1862 London International Exhibition, a small London firm, Laroche & Mehew, had exhibited a front-driving, three-wheeled velocipede. Unfortunately there is no picture extant but it was later identified by cycling journalists as 'a distinct improvement on all its predecessors, inasmuch as it had the germ of the true principle, a rotating axle worked by crank action.'

A similar style of tricycle may have existed at the time in France. Hat-maker Auguste-Arsène Brunel used a tricycle for delivering his hats around Paris, and Pierre Michaux, a maker of carriage ironwork in Avenue Montaigne, maintained it for him. In 1869, René Olivier, the new owner of the Michaux company, gave his account of the origins of the pedal:

> Ernest Michaux, eldest son of Pierre, having in his hands a tricycle – a velocipede with three wheels – on which the front wheel was fitted with cranks, took it to pieces and transformed it into a bicycle. This took place around the year 1854 or 1855.
>
> [Author's translation]

The date seems early and there is no contemporary confirmation, but Michaux's machine undoubtedly had a slow start with few or none sold before 1864. Much later, Henry Michaux, youngest son of Pierre, who would have been fifteen in 1861, supplied a contrasting tale claiming that Brunel had a *draisine*, not a tricycle, and that the transformation took place in March 1861 not 1855. In 1895, a German priority myth that musical-instrument maker Philipp Moritz Fischer had added cranks to a *draisine* as early as 1855 became known in France and to counteract it the French press supported Henry's version.

What remains undisputed is that, in August 1865, engineering students René and Aimé Olivier, with their college friend Georges de la Bouglise, made a 500-mile velocipede trip from Paris to Lyons, evaluating the performance of Michaux's machines and in October de la Bouglise applied to the World Fair office to exhibit a velocipede at the coming 1867 exposition. Although the application was declined, René lent 10,000 FF to Michaux in 1867 to be used on the velocipede project, and the brothers promoted the bicycle among their friends. It was their enthusiasm that primed the explosion in demand.

Late in 1867, a race was held from Paris to Versailles, beginning a two-and-a-half year craze for racing. Over 150 makers started up across France and the velocipede was suddenly everywhere but, by the end of 1869, enthusiasm was waning and *Le Vélocipède Illustré*, the country's first cycling periodical, was suggesting the future might lie with tricycles rather than bicycles. Another factor was that local ordinances began restricting and prohibiting velocipede riding. The more social roller-skating rinks, with their get-together events like masked balls, stole the show from the 'bachelor machine' velocipede but, before the matter could be resolved, in August 1870, the Franco-Prussian War erupted.

Bicycle racing ceased, Paris bicycle factories were requisitioned and the centre of cycle development moved to England, particularly to Coventry. This was a big blow to French engineering pride as for five years they had led this exciting new industry. The Societe Pratique du Velocipede had been formed in Paris in 1868 to regulate the sport and races were a regular event in many provincial towns. The brief but violent war, followed by the Commune, effectively snuffed out

Vélocipède Illustré, the leading cyclist's paper, from March 1869.

the French flame and it was twenty years before parity was restored. By this time both the ordinary and tricycle eras were over and the pneumatic safety had transformed the bicycle and the sport.

BONESHAKER DESIGN

The Michaux machine of 1867 was similar to a *draisine* but with the important addition of cranks and pedals to the front axle. The serpentine frame was made from D-section malleable cast iron, rather than wood. This was *fonte malléable*, the material Michaux used for his carriage fittings, being stronger than wood and less brittle than cast iron. Castings were heated in boxes packed with hematite for five to twelve days, reducing the carbon content to the equivalent of wrought iron, even though the fibrous structure and consequent strength was somewhat lacking.

In April 1868, Michaux filed a patent based on the Olivier brothers' ideas. It included a cord-operated brake, self-righting pedals and, most significantly, a diagonal frame incorporating the rear forks. The germ of this design seems to date from the wooden velocipede made by a mechanic named Gabert, who worked for the Olivier family chemical concern and made velocipedes used for part of their 1865 trip. One survives in the museum at Compiegne. The design

Compagnie Parisienne advert.

Surviving Gabert diagonal-frame
bicycle, *c.* 1865.

was suitable for forging and the Pastré family, into which René and
Aimé had both recently married, owned large forges in Marseilles.
Pierre Michaux was then fifty-five and, though the Oliviers liked and
respected him, they considered his marketing and manufacturing
methods outdated. His persistence in the use of *fonte malléable* was
just one of the reasons for their decision to sever the partnership.

Front-wheel bearings needed to be easy running, yet tight enough
to resist the twisting effect of the pedals. Michaux at first used plain
bushes but, on the Olivier model, which became the archetype,
they had bronze shell bearings, held in tuning-fork ends by a
wedge-shaped key. This enabled riders to take up any play resulting
from wear. The rear wheel ran loose on a bushed fixed axle.

Early road races in France led makers to experiment with front-wheel
ball bearings and James Moore famously won the first long-distance
road race, from Paris to Rouen in November 1869, on a machine
equipped with balls ground by hand. It was made by Jules-Pierre
Suriray but, as the bearings could not be adjusted for wear, the idea
did not progress. Rudge and Bown separately introduced adjustable
bearing cases for the English ordinary bicycle in 1878.

The wooden wheels were initially iron hooped, in the tradition of
carriage wheels, making them noisy on metalled roads and subject to
sideslipping. By 1869, makers were offering rubber or leather coverings
over the iron rims, some even using a channel to hold a solid rubber
tire, but the iron tyre remained the norm until the wire wheel arrived.

The Michaux brake was a long double lever, hinged midway on the frame and lifted via a strap to press down on the rear tire. The Olivier's 1868 patent introduced a neat lever brake, operated from the handle by a cord, and practically all manufacturers adopted this arrangement. These brakes were generally suitable for purpose and there are few reports of accidents due to failure to stop.

At first, mounting was by a flying leap. Manchester manufacturer Andrew Muir advised,

> Take hold of the cross bar guide handle, and run alongside the machine till you have a moderate speed, and then spring into the saddle, placing your feet in the treadle and then propelling yourself as before described. When the rider is very proficient, and can vault into the saddle, he can use a larger velocipede, although his feet do not touch the ground, but there is always a little danger in so doing.

In 1869 Alfred Berruyer offered a *jambe-étrière*, or retractable stand/step, allowing the rider to mount when stationary but, before the end of 1869, a mounting step fixed on the rear fork or hub was provided, making it easier to throw the leg over the bicycle when starting off. This idea was credited to James Starley of the Coventry Machinists Co. Ltd, although French manufacturer Cadot may have had a step on the front fork the year before.

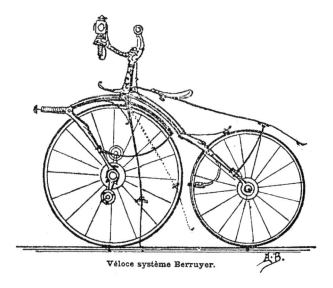

Berruyer marche pied or mounting step.

Véloce système Berruyer.

With its solid metal body and painted wooden wheels, le vélocipède bicycle was a handsome vehicle, but weighed 80 to 100 pounds, twice as heavy as a draisine. The handling can be compared to that of a modern motorcycle. Mounting was especially fraught although dismounting was easier: one simply stopped and let the machine tilt sideways onto one foot. On bends, the front wheel tended to clean itself on the rider's trousers so a wire trouser-guard was fitted to the forks, turning with the wheel. Difficulties in learning led to a rash of riding schools springing up in cities across Europe and America with smaller towns being accommodated by traveling schools. The social milieu closely paralleled the contemporary roller-skating scene. Some courageous women, like actress Sarah Bernhard in Paris, tried the machine and there were ladies' lessons in Vienna although they were not noted in England.

William John Macquorn Rankine, Professor of Engineering at Glasgow University, wrote a series of articles on cycling theory in *The Engineer* in August 1869, arriving at what had already been stated by Drais, i.e., that for balancing one has to steer towards the side to which the velocipede begins to skip. He added the observation that this also serves to manoeuvre the line where the wheel contacts the ground back underneath the centre of gravity again. Moreover he arrived at the conclusion that the velocipede does not roll in a straight line but in a wavy one.

There were several hundred velocipede makers worldwide, usually associated with the carriage-making trade or sometimes small iron workers. Another category would be young enthusiasts like the Oliviers, who enjoyed the sport and could buy the necessary parts from sub-contractors. Typically, production was small and even the Compagnie Parisienne at peak only managed fifteen machines a day. Manufacture was on the European system even in America – that is to say all parts required filing, fitting and numbering before being disassembled for paint and then final assembly. There was no pretence to interchangeability of parts. While no reliable estimate of total production exists, if we allow Michaux, the biggest company, about 8,000, it is unlikely that worldwide production exceeded 50,000 bicycles.

6

AMERICA AND GERMANY

International visitors to the 1867 Paris Exhibition took home reports, as well as a few velocipedes, and the craze rapidly spread around the world. It was more widespread than the *draisine* fashion had been fifty years before, not least because populations and towns had grown in that time. New York was one of the first cities to be infected and in the spring and summer of 1868 velocipede riding schools mushroomed. Local manufacturers saw the opportunity and fifty patents for improvement were registered within two years, encouraged by *Scientific American*, which had its own patent agency. New York entrepreneur Conrad Witty snapped up the 1866 American patent of French immigrant Pierre Lallement and applied a stranglehold on the trade, demanding a $5 royalty from manufacturers and importers. Michaux had never patented his velocipede and Lallement had carried a machine with him from Paris in 1865, filing US patent No.59,915 with James Carol, for a new 'Improvement in Velocipedes' in 1866. This patent, the world's earliest for a pedal bicycle, together with Lallement's later claim to have personally invented the machine in July 1863, has led to schism among cycle historians. All that can be said is that Lallement's patent and Michaux's first machines seem so similar as to demand a common parentage. Who copied who is the question.

   Under different ownerships, the Lallement patent controlled the American bicycle trade for a decade after the boneshaker had died out. As in 1820, city ordinances of 1869 forbade velocipeding on the sidewalks of New York and, it being impractical on the streets, velocipedists had to go indoors or to skating rinks.

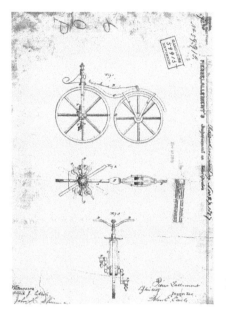

Lallement, 1866. The earliest bicycle patent, but maybe not the earliest bicycle.

Two officials from the Grand Duchy of Baden ordered velocipedes while in Paris for the World Exhibition and encouraged local tradesmen to manufacture them. Carl Friedrich Müller was the first of about thirty German manufacturers, starting in 1868 in Stuttgart, but all had closed down before the beginning of the Franco-Prussian war. Automobile pioneer Karl Benz of Mannheim taught himself riding within two weeks on a Stuttgart velocipede and later stated that his exhilarating experience on the velocipede changed his plans for making a steam street-locomotive to that of a motor vehicle for personal transport.

THE VELOCIPEDE IN ENGLAND

At the close of 1868, the bicycle crossed the Channel. While the odd bicycle had been purchased privately at the time of the 1867 exhibition, and at least two were bought previously by Irishmen, John Townsend Trench and Dr Austin Meldon, when in Paris in 1864 and 1865, the first the wider British public knew was when on 19 February 1869 *The Times* reported a ride by three young men from London to Brighton. It was subsequently syndicated in

300 local papers. One of the three riders, Rowley Turner, was nephew to Josiah Turner, manager of the Coventry Sewing Machine Co. Ltd and the Paris agent for their sewing machines. His proposal led the company into making velocipedes, effectively starting Coventry's long involvement with bicycles and subsequently motorcars.

Turner had learnt to ride at Pascaud's Paris gymnasium and planned to use Coventry's idle engineering capacity to supply velocipedes for his new agency Turner & Cie. He marketed them as Vélocipèdes Américains. In the event, demand soon blossomed in England and new companies came in. The exemplar was the second Michaux pattern, with the Olivier diagonal frame that Turner brought to England in November 1868, and this became the pattern for English copyists.

The first English velocipede patent of 1869 was taken out on 2 January and over a hundred were filed by September.

Above left: 1870 Turner advert for CMC bicycles. Note the single rear fork.

Above right: Rowley Turner with CMC machine.

Unfortunately, none of them did much to make the machine more rider friendly – it remained a recreational toy for young, athletic, middle-class males. On the poorly surfaced roads of the day, it was hardly the mount for happy relaxation, weighing 80 lbs. Although over 120 suppliers jumped into the market, by the end of the first year the new craze was already on the wane. The *Manchester Evening News* carried no velocipede advertisements in the spring of 1870, compared with over 200 the previous spring. All this was despite England not being involved in the Continental war nor banning velocipede riding. It was to be the improvements stemming from bicycle racing that saved the day.

THE SUSPENSION WHEEL

If the wire wheel had not appeared when it did, the velocipede craze would surely have died out just as the *draisine* had done under the widespread bans of fifty years before. The boneshaker, although pedal-driven, was little faster and it became clear that only by gearing it up or enlarging the driving wheel could speed be improved. This desideratum was quickly acknowledged and several patents were taken out for geared bicycles. The famous 1870 Ariel patent of James Starley and William Hillman included an option for spur gears on the front forks, giving a 2:1 advantage. At least one race was won on it but Starley's engineering methods were agricultural and the necessary precision was lacking.

In France, another iconic machine was made, probably that same year. Watchmaker André Guilmet, using Meyer parts, constructed a machine with a chain drive to the rear wheel. The plan now appears to be spot on, but the execution was flawed. The simple pin-chain of the time was not up to the strain of driving a bicycle and it had no arrangement for chain adjustment. The machine survives in the Arts et Metiers Museum in Paris and has been the subject of much debate since being discovered in a loft in 1906. However there seems no reason to doubt its velocipede origins or suggest that it is a fake.

Another experimenter in France around this time was the Italian consul to Nantes, Émile Viarengo de Forville. He described in his 1871 patent six safety designs, three for men and three for women. Henry Michaux was given one to demonstrate in England, but De Forville heard nothing further, possibly because the drive to the rear wheel used connecting rods rather than chain and would therefore have had a top dead centre problem. Four other French patents in 1868/9 show that the idea of gearing-up was being addressed, but none of these ideas ever reached the market.

A far simpler alternative to gearing-up was to increase the diameter of the driving wheel and some large-wheeled boneshakers have survived. In New York, A. T. Demarest & Co. offered machines with wheels of up to 45 inches in diameter and a 50-inch Demarest was reported racing at Union Course, Long Island. In London, Snoxell & Spencer advertised 48-inch machines made by the Coventry Machinists' Co. but wooden-wheeled machines of this size were cumbersome and, as late as the spring of 1870, racing men in England, even where wheel diameters were unrestricted, rarely chose machines over 38 inches in diameter. The velocipede had been led down a technologically blind alley. Bicycling could not advance without a solution being found.

In fact a Frenchman had actually solved the problem in the early months of 1870, but the war intervened and the fact that it had been solved somehow escaped the English until August. Many cycle histories, particularly those written by British historians, claim that Starley's Ariel was the first penny-farthing. James Starley, widely acknowledged as 'the father of the cycle trade', must have been the inventor, but Starley, like other English makers in mid-1870, was only following the lead established in France.

It was a twenty-five-year-old Parisian, Eugène Meyer, who made the first successful wire-wheeled bicycle and he patented it in August 1869. The following month he formed Meyer & Cie., and in November showed 'elegant polished veloces' at the Pré-Catalan exhibition.

Like many patentees before and since, Meyer gained little profit from his idea. He failed to defend the patent in 1870 against a breach by the powerful Compagnie Parisienne and, following bad advice, failed in court against another transgressor in 1878.

The eye-opener for the English trade came when James Moore, the expatriate cycle racer, fled Paris at the onset of war and competed in the Champion Bicycle Contest at Molineux Park, Wolverhampton, on 6–8 August 1870. He was riding a 43-inch Meyer tension-wheel bicycle, equipped with toe pedals, while his competitors were still pedalling with the instep on small wooden or Phantom type wheels. By October, English racing men were all using wire wheels of 41–46-inch diameter and within two years the champion John Keen was regularly riding a 57 inch.

The velocipede era was effectively over and wooden-wheeled machines were retained only as learning devices for the new, high-wheel ordinary bicycle.

Meyer wire-wheeled machine, 1870.

Meyer-patented spoking system.

7

THE PENNY-FARTHING OR ORDINARY BICYCLE

With the wire-suspension wheel successfully overcoming the speed problem, bicycling in Britain recovered from its temporary setback and began a steady growth that would last twenty-five years. By 1874 there were eight bicycle clubs in London and twelve in the provinces, while two years later the number had tripled, including nine in Ireland where the Michaux boneshaker had received an early welcome. The machines the new clubmen rode were pioneering makes like the CMC Spider, Keen's Eclipse, Starley's Ariel, and Grout's Tension, although in some towns a local maker had a monopoly on supply.

Ixion was the earliest UK journal aimed at bicyclists.

The CMC Coventry Roadster, 1872.

Keen racing machine, 1872.

Grout Tension, 1872.

Starley Ariel 1872.

Typical 1880s
cycling-club outing.

1876 saw the launch of *Bicycling News*, *The Bicycle* and *The Bicycle Journal*. The new sport soon developed its own customs, clubs and dress codes. In every town or district, cyclists established clubrooms and adopted rules modelled on the Amateur Athletic Association or the longer-established rowing and cricket clubs. Membership invariably required a uniform, cap and badge, usually of semi-military style, along with a wealth of accessories like bells, lamps, multum in parvo luggage bags, oil cans, toolkits, cyclometers and dog pistols. The last item was essential to avoid close contact with sheltered canines that had not yet seen a bicycle.

Fewer than 10 per cent of velocipede makers remained in the trade, which now required the skills of the engineer rather than carriage builder or iron founder. Companies began to specialise and sub-contractors set up to supply bearings, saddles, hubs and even frames. Many makers, like Keen, Hillman and Warman, were themselves enthusiastic cyclists, so the time from prototype to production would often be short.

The name boneshaker arose in 1871, coined by cyclists who were glad to be rid of the now-outdated velocipede. The term ordinary bicycle arose in 1878 to differentiate it from the new high-wheel safety bicycles. After 1891, ordinary became used nostalgically, as in 'grand old ordinary', while street urchins derided the outdated high bicycle as a penny-farthing. Both terms survive today.

The late 1870s saw the ordinary bicycle blossom into a splendid, lightweight, recreational mount and by 1885 a quarter of a million had been sold in Britain by some 350 makers. The bicycle of 1870 had been transformed and by the end of the decade was considered to be the consummate artifact. Henry Sturmey, in his 1879 *Indispensable Bicyclist's Handbook*, maintained 'last Season, one would almost have thought the bicycle a perfect article, so strong, swift, handsome and almost lifelike it had become,' while Harry Griffin, in *Bicycles of the Year 1883*, speculated 'Roadsters have reached so great a pitch of structural perfection, that it is difficult to find room for further improvement'. J. S. Whatton, one of the stars of the Cambridge University Bicycling Club wrote,

> The early part of this year saw the completion of 20,000 miles of cycling, the work of eight years pleasure – pleasures such as no other exercise, unless it be rackets – can in my opinion approach: and of course, this lacks the great glory of cycling, the multitudinous opportunities it adds for an intellectual and one may add – a spiritual appreciation of life.

Hundreds of patents had been filed during the seventies, including ideas that would become standard in the bicycle and motor trades for generations. To list just a few: Roller Bearings, 1871 (John Keen); Tubular Frames, 1872, (Ariel); Hollow Forks, 1874 (Jules Truffault);

The last lap.

Detachable Cranks, 1876 (J. K. Starley); Rat-trap pedals, 1876 (John Keen); Adjustable Ball Bearings, 1877 (Hughes and Rudge); Hollow rims, 1878 (Coventry Machinists' Company); Detachable Handlebars, 1878, and Drop Bars, 1879.

The bicycle of 1880 was indeed King of the Road and those that were young, fit, and rich enough to afford one were indeed blessed. The motion of the ordinary was more exhilarating than that of its predecessor, or indeed that of its immediate successor. As Luther Porter said in 1898,

> The position, so nicely balanced, nearly on one wheel; the absence of a wheel to be pushed in front, wheelbarrow fashion; the free, billowy, rolling motion that ensued, gave to riding and coasting on it a peculiar charm that was wholly its own, and afforded sensations which those who have enjoyed them count as among the most beautiful of their lives.

One particular joy was coasting. The approved method for enjoying a descent, where the road could be seen to be clear, was to swing both legs over the handlebars and let rip. Barring mechanical failure, such as the tyre leaving the rim, or misadventure like a dog running out, the practice was less dangerous than it might seem. In the event of misfortune the rider was at least propelled clear of the bicycle, rather than being centrifugally smashed into the roadway.

Legs over, the best way to enjoy a descent.

The Bicycle Union and then the National Cyclists Union erected over 4,500 'DANGER' boards on steep or dangerous hills during the last decades of the century, and those not riddled with grape shot or saved by collectors may still occasionally be met with today. This was a red-blooded sport and riders were not unaware that speed had been bought at a price. For ten years a safety bicycle was talked about without any acceptable solution being found while danger added piquancy to the sport. The cycling press happily printed letters from mavericks who had experienced falls and lived.

SELECTION FROM *ICYCLES CHRISTMAS ANNUAL 1880*

'A rider was thrown on to some iron spikes, one of which ran through his jaw, cheek and eye. He happily recovered.'

'Mr. H. A. Venables sustained frightful injuries from a fall, while racing down Handcross Hill; he fractured his skull and dislocated his jaw, which together with concussion of the brain, served to make his an almost hopeless case.

Danger board,
somewhere in Cheshire.

He was taken to Guy's Hospital, and, with the vigorous vitality of a bicyclist, came round, and is, we are glad to say, happily recovered.'

'A younger brother of the well-known P. G. Hebblethwaite, of Dewsbury and the L.A.C., met with a tremendous cropper down Garrowby Hill, in Yorkshire, through attempting to descend it on a brakeless 64-inch Carver; he sustained serious injuries, but is progressing favourably.'

'Fred Crampton had a serious smash, through the breaking of a hub lamp. Harry Swindley had a bad fall over a gutter riding up from Ripley; T. Cowell Barrington, a cropper over a dog, with as result a very serious injury to the muscles of his arm; and many more minor injuries might be chronicled.'

BRAKES

The problem of headers, croppers or Imperial crowners, as they were cheerfully called, put urgency into the search for a satisfactory brake. Both the *draisine* and the boneshaker had used a robust brake shoe, pressing onto the face of the rear iron tyre. Considerable force could be applied without danger of upset, but the new wire suspension wheel, and new riding position, overturned this equilibrium. Firstly, a large front wheel meant that, to reach the pedals, the rider had to sit further forward, nearly over the front axle. Secondly, the almost redundant rear wheel became smaller, shortening the wheelbase, lightening the machine and diminishing its braking potential. The 34-inch rear wheel of 1869 was down to 18–20 inches by 1876, so the little wheel skipped along behind, ineffective as a restraint. Better brakes became an urgent desideratum.

One bonus of sitting up near the head was that backpedalling became more effective. A rider could apply his full weight behind the front axle with little risk of a header. For this reason many preferred to dispense with a brake altogether and rely on backpedalling. It worked well as long as the bicycle was kept in hand. Much ingenuity was expended in designing new brakes. 1875 saw Carter's trailing brake, where a hardened lever, pivoted on the rear forks, was dragged down against the roadway. It was more effective than the roller, but it did not act as a fail safe if the cord snapped. Even ground brakes that did act as a fail safe had limited success because road surfaces varied and the clattering against the roadway could annoy fellow clubmen.

Surprisingly, it was a front brake that finally won out. The London maker Stassen, on his Nonpareil of 1875, had a handsome bronze eccentric on the straight handlebar, which pushed a roller down onto the front tyre with controlled precision. Others followed this lead and the Surrey Machinists Company in 1876 introduced a hinged spoon, worked by a simple lever on the handlebar. It was not patented and became adopted as the standard for the remaining years of the ordinary. It even carried over to safeties, both hard-tyred and pneumatic. If the brake lever on an ordinary was gripped in

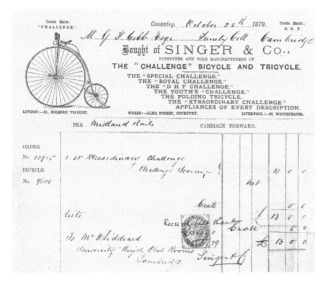

Singer Challenge invoice showing Carter trailing brake.

Stassen Nonpareil brake, 1875.

panic, a header might result, but the circumspect rider, sitting well back in the saddle, could hope to restrain his machine on most of hills he was likely to encounter. Brakes were usually omitted on racing machines to save weight, as were seat-springs. Even the small mounting step might be left off, in which case a mounting stool and assistant would be provided at the start.

BALL BEARINGS

The flanged shell bearings of the boneshaker continued in use on the early ordinaries, but a large wheel demanded firmer restraint so cones or roller bearings were adopted. Bown's adjustable bearing of 1877 had a single row of ball bearings held in a coned case, threaded so that it could be adjusted to a nicety for wear. This, and the similar Rudge bearing, remained standard until the much later use of sealed bearings. A large ball-bearing industry arose and, where balls had previously been turned individually on lathes, the American Simonds rolling machine of the mid-1880s allowed precision spheres to be run off at around 18,000 a day. The machines were installed in British factories with Premier of Coventry supplying balls to much of the trade.

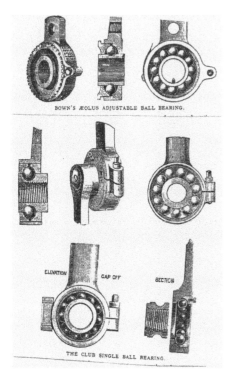

Rudge and Bown ball bearings from 1885.

TUBING

Tubing in 1869 was mainly used for gas or hydraulic piping and was expensive. Pickering & Davis of New York were first to make boneshaker frames from gas tube, brazed into handsome brass lugs. In 1872, a few ordinary makers started to lighten their machines with hollow backbones. Jules Truffault of Tours first made hollow front forks in 1874 out of scabbards, and the Coventry Machinists' Co. Ltd extended the hollow craze to include rear forks, handlebars, axles and even hollow wheel-rims. James Carver of Nottingham took it to the ultimate with his New Hollow Spoke bicycle of 1877.

Most makers in the 1880s fitted their premium models with tubular frames and forks and reserved the solid frame for the cheaper lines. The bicycle thus created a new demand for cold-drawn tube and the Mannesmann process of 1887 produced seamless tube from solid within seconds. By the 1890s the bicycle trade had given birth to a huge cold-drawn steel tube industry, large enough to provoke a tariff war with America during the bicycle boom.

Pickering & Davis, early use
of tubing, 1869.

Carver Hollow Spoke
bicycle, 1886.

SPOKING SYSTEMS

We have noted Eugène Meyer's 1869 patent that described
individually adjustable tension spokes secured by nuts within the
hub flange. In 1870, The Coventry Machinists' Co. Ltd copied
the Compagnie Parisienne's variation of Meyer's patent, where the
spokes were screwed directly into the hub and secured with lock
nuts. These spokes were radial, i.e., running directly from the rim
to the centre of the hub, and therefore stressed and unstressed on
each pedal stroke. Even when made from best Low Moor iron,

frequent breakage would still result and it took fifteen years to find a satisfactory solution to the problem.

The first British wire-spoked bicycle wheel had been Reynolds and Mays Phantom of April 1869. This had hairpin spokes fed through staples at the rim with the two ends clamped at the hub. The hub flanges were then forced apart to tension the spokes. For a season the Phantom was a favourite on the track but, while its spokes did not break, they could not be individually tensioned. The fact that the frame hinged midway between the wheels made steering an art, giving it a unique and terminal disadvantage. Grout's tension

Owner Bob Jones with his 1870 Phantom.

Coventry Spider bicycle, August 1870.

Starley's Tangent
wheel, 1875.

wheel of 1870 overcame the breakage problem with the spokes
headed at both ends and tightened by turnbuckles at the rim but the
most successful of the early designs was Starley's Ariel. Starley and
Hillman had copied a set of Compagnie Parisienne wheels in August
1870 for the successful Coventry Spider and that same month they
took out a patent for the Ariel. Starley left CMC soon after to start
on his own. The Ariel also used hairpin spokes passing through
staples at the rim, but the ends were bent at 90 degrees and slotted
into holes in the hub flanges. They were tensioned by two screwed
rods attached to the ends of stout levers welded across the hub. All
the spokes were thus tightened simultaneously and in achieving
full tension the rim would revolve slightly so the spokes became
somewhat tangential. It was the first step towards a tangent-spoked
wheel where the driving force from the hub is transmitted to the
rim in a direct line without bending the spokes. The system worked
well when pedalling forwards, although backpedalling slackened the
wheel, sometimes with unhappy consequences. The spokes could not
be trued individually and yet the Ariel lasted ten years, becoming the
object of much happy nostalgia among early riders. Starley's next
wheel design, the Tangent of 1874, used threaded spokes screwed into
studs passing transversely through the hub flanges. This produced a
tangent wheel, rigid in both directions, although the hub could only
accommodate a limited number of studs and hence spokes.

A plethora of spoking systems provided selling features during the 1870s. This was often an aesthetic rather than a technical judgment and 1878 saw a spoke explosion, culminating in the Surrey Machinists' Invincible model with 300 spokes. This proved difficult to clean and impossible to pass a hub-lamp between the spokes, or to light it when in place, so by 1880 makers settled on direct butted spokes with a count of 'spokes for inches' – that is to say fifty-four

Surrey Machinist Co. Invincible, 1881.

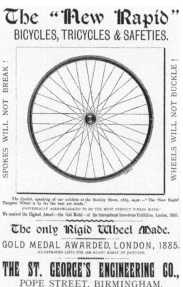

Palmer's New Rapid true tangent wheel, 1885.

spokes in a 54-inch wheel. The annual scramble for improvement and weight reduction abated during the 1880s and after a brief popularity of laced, piano-wire spokes the final solution appeared at the 1885 Stanley Show.

This was the New Rapid true tangent wheel of the St. George's Eng. Co. Ltd. It used headed spokes in light hub flanges, running at 90 degrees, with five crossings, to nipples at the rim; apart from Humber, who continued to use direct spokes, the trade fell into line, but it was all of little consequence. At the same 1885 Stanley Show, seven rear-driving safeties, including John Kemp Starley's Rover, were unveiled and the countdown had begun for the end of the ordinary era.

THE STEP

The step is a small device but essential for mounting an ordinary. One can conceivably mount by other methods, i.e., spectacularly via the pedal or the backbone, but the standard precept was, and is, to place the left foot on the step, take a few hops, stand up and, while the bicycle is moving, slide neatly into the saddle. This could not be done on the early boneshakers because they were without a step, but the problem was resolved by a corpulent man of thirty-nine – the inventive James Starley. The French vélocipède he copied at the end of 1868 lacked a step and boneshakers continued without them through most of 1869. Starley fitted CMC boneshakers with a mounting step, supposedly to overcome his own mounting difficulties, and his 1870 Coventry model was named in his obituary as the 'C-Spring and step model'. The idea quickly caught on and steps became universal.

During the ordinary years, the design of the bicycle step could sustain a discussion in a pub or promote an argument among friends. There were mushroom steps, saw-tooth steps, rubber-clothed, safety, skeleton, and many patent adjustable steps. By 1887, Henry Sturmey described the saw-tooth as the 'most universal' but nevertheless found it necessary to describe eight other styles.

THE PEDAL

The pedal was also perfected during the ordinary years. The rider of a velocipede sat well back, placing the instep on the pedal, which had flanges to hold the shoe, often surprisingly narrow to modern eyes. Michaux pedals had an acorn plumb bob keeping the flat side upwards, while other makers used triangular blocks or bobbins.

The riding style for the ordinary was different. James Moore, at Molyneux Park in 1870, used neat, two-faced bronze pedals of the style Meyer was still making ten years later. Grout patented a rubber-clothed flat pedal, but the most important improvement came in 1881 when ball pedals were 'very much in vogue'. Both Bown and Rudge supplied adjustable pedal bearings to the trade, although by 1887 many makers had their own designs. Lightweight rat-trap pedals were introduced for racing machines by John Keen in 1876 but widely condemned for road work as being 'prone to wear out the boots.' Professionals would use toe-clips for racing, although the risk of falling while still attached to one's machine was an additional hazard.

THE HANDLEBAR

The annual Stanley show encouraged annual change, meaning that surviving machines can today often be pinpointed to a precise year. *The Cyclist* noted in 1880,

> Perhaps no single portion of the bicycle marks the general improvement of the age so much as the handle-bar, for by looking at this alone the experienced eye is almost enabled to give the year in which the machine to which it is attached was turned out.

Boneshakers typically had straight handlebars 2 feet wide, necessary for controlling the heavy wooden wheel, but the lightweight ordinary could be ridden hands off and there was a brief period where bars were reduced to barely 18 inches wide, supposedly allowing the rider to avoid being trapped in the event of a header. Sanity returned and, by 1880, they were back to 24 inches wide, very often with dropped handles or a moustache profile giving clearance for the knees. They peaked at 29 inches and settled down between 26 and 28 inches during the final years.

Handle grips too were slaves to fashion. Boneshakers usually had turned, tapered wooden or bone grips, occasionally enhanced with brass or silver inlay. Ordinaries tended to favour a rounded, pear-shaped grip, often turned from Indian water-buffalo horn. This was claimed to be cooler to the hands and also would not split like wood in the inevitable fall. Riders using fancy handle-grips like ivory or ebony were advised to protect them by keeping their hands over the ends before hitting the deck. Some riders preferred the T-shaped American spade-handle grips that later became available, but comfort could be best assured by having handle grips that could be held in different ways, undergrip, overgrip or at the ends, depending on the road conditions and on the rider's whim.

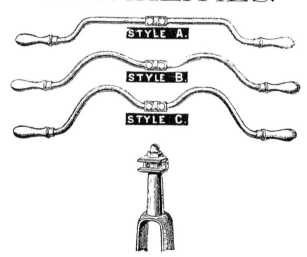

Andrews handlebars, 1887.

8
TRICYCLES 1876–1886

By the late 1870s the ordinary bicycle had become part of British life. Few villages would have not seen bicyclists passing through and yet cycling still remained untried by women and less athletic men. Clearly there were many who would have liked to ride if only a safe mount had been available.

In France at the start of 1870, when the velocipede craze was starting to wane, press speculation suggested that the velocipede of the future would have three wheels rather than two and indeed races were staged just for tricycles and quadricycles. William Jackson, an Englishman living in Paris, had competed in the Paris–Rouen race on a tricycle of his own make, fitted with Meyer wire wheels. During 1870 he advertised

Wooden tricycle velocipede (and rider), c. 1869.

several tricycle models along with an impressive monocycle, which he also claimed as being a faster alternative to the bicycle. Temporarily fleeing the war, he challenged John Keen, the English champion bicyclist, to a 50-mile handicap race but lost due to understating the weight of his tricycle to the handicapper. He returned to Paris yet England, which had seized initiative in the bicycle trade, failed to produce any three-wheelers for the next six years. Wooden-wheeled tricycles were too heavy for recreational use and it was 1876 before two inventors patented tricycles with wire wheels – Dublin's William Blood on 3 November and Coventry's James Starley fifteen days later.

Blood's tricycle was passed around five different makers during the next nine years and was never a match for Starley's Coventry

Jackson tricycle with Meyer wire wheels, 1869.

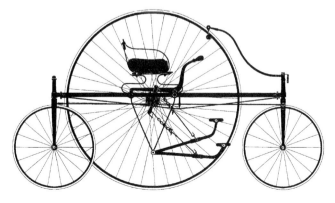

James Starley's 1876 Coventry lever-driven tricycle.

Rudge rotary
Coventry tricycle,
1880–92.

CMC Club tandem
tricycle, 1885.

model nor for the Singer No. 1 of 1877. The Coventry tricycle was initially lever-driven, with a big driving wheel positioned alongside the rider and two small wheels in line on the other flank, steered with one hand. In 1880 it was fitted with chain drive, becoming the highly popular Rudge Coventry Rotary, and it eventually enjoyed a sixteen-year run. For a few years, tandem (in-line) and sociable (side-by-side) tricycles were the rage. They allowed a man and wife, or even two ladies, to explore the countryside together, thus greatly extending the potential market for the machines.

Tricyclists were encouraged to join the Bicycle Touring Club but, with princes, dukes and earls among their number, they saw themselves as superior to the common herd of bicyclists and in 1882 formed the Tricycle Union with *The Tricyclist* and *The Tricycling Journal* providing for their prejudices.

By 1880, the Coventry tricycle, now with rotary drive, could be geared up or down to suit the rider, an option not available on the ordinary, and with tricycling also now attracting club men and record-breakers, tricycle champions enjoyed publicity comparable to that of bicyclists. G. P. Mills of the Anfield Bicycle Club, in abominable weather, took the Lands End to John o'Groats tricycle record in 6 days, 15 hours and 22 minutes shortly after completing the same ride on an ordinary bicycle in 5 days, 1 hour and 45 minutes.

During this brief tricycle interregnum, invention moved fast. H. H. Griffin described sixteen different wheel configurations possible for the tricycle of 1880 and, because of their size and complication, they could demand twice the price of a bicycle. James Starley's final *pièce de résistance* was the 1878 Salvoquadricycle (safe four wheeler). It was justly famous for its balance gear that solved the long-term problem of cornering on a machine with two wheels driving. The trade quickly adopted this ingenious solution, which later became familiar as the differential when applied to motorized vehicles. The Salvo was renamed the Royal Salvo after two were ordered for the Royal Household at Osborne, although it is not thought that Queen Victoria ever actually rode one. Front-wheel steerers soon replaced rear-steerers, inherently being safer, particularly on hills, while the fast Humber pattern tricycle – essentially an ordinary with two large front wheels – provided a record-breaker for the suicidal.

Most major makers added tricycles to their catalogues and Sturmey could list fifty manufacturers by 1884, twenty in Coventry alone, offering 120 different models. At the 1883 Stanley Show, tricycles outnumbered bicycles for the first time and, as things turned out, also for the last time. The Humber Cripper of 1884, named after their 'maker's amateur' Robert Cripps, became the definitive

Above left: The 1878 Salvo with Starley's balance gear provided his lasting memorial.

Above right: The 1886 Humber-style tricycles broke many records and a few bones as well.

Below: The Humber Cripper direct steerer eventually became the style of choice.

Young Jackson in the
monocycle, 1870.

design having a small front steering wheel and two slightly larger
driving wheels, coupled by a balance gear. The plan remains with us
today. Reaching a peak in popularity, tricycles began to be ousted
over the next three years by rear-driven safety bicycles but, like the
ordinary, the tricycle, though never again to have such allure, did
not die out. It retained a following from clubmen who enjoyed its
stability, serenity and unique cornering requirements. This involves
moving the rider's weight across the frame rather than banking
over. Three-wheelers are still alive and well today. The Tricycle
Association continues to thrive and the Road Records Association
still supports town-to-town and fixed-distance record-breaking, as
it has done since the 1880s.

MONOCYCLES

Jackson's 1870 monocycle was certainly not the first, nor was it to
be the last. At a time when the long-term possibility of two or three
wheels was being debated, logic suggested that one wheel would

incur less friction than two. It was proposed that a large diameter wheel would reduce rolling resistance and that manoeuvring would be easier with only one point of contact with the road. Jackson announced a demonstration run from Paris to Versailles on 18 July 1870. Unfortunately, he had wounded his knee and his son had to stand in. 'Sitting like a squirrel in a cage', the fourteen-year-old bravely completed the 7-km journey in a creditable half an hour, but war was declared that same week and Jackson and his son fled the country. The machine ended up in a Birmingham café, grinding coffee, but it was not the end for monocycles. They have regularly appeared in the patent record almost every decade since and Jackson replicas, with whirling lights, thrilled the crowds at the opening ceremony of the 2008 Beijing Olympics. The monocycle may be the future, but for the present two-wheels are still preferred by the majority.

9

THE SAFETY BICYCLE

The transition from the boneshaker to the ordinary bicycle was effected in barely two seasons, so why did it then take nearly fifteen years to make a safe bicycle? The reason was simple; it was all due to the enormous success of the high-wheel design. By the 1880s, the *draisine* had been virtually forgotten, the boneshaker was just a distant memory and bicyclists knew only the high-wheelers, either with two wheels or three. There was certainly no shortage of inventors or of ideas during the 1870s.

In America, during the velocipede craze, four patents had been filed for lever-operated rear-driving bicycles and in France there were three for chain drivers. Most surprising, because it resembles the eventually successful safety and demonstrates how minds were thinking, is a prototype attributed to Meyer and Guilmet that is still to be seen in the Musée Des Arts et Metiers in Paris. It was discovered in an attic in Saint-Étienne and shown at the Paris Retrospective Exhibition of 1906. There have been many allegations since then that it must be a fake but the construction of the frame clearly announces it as an unsuccessful prototype from the boneshaker era. The crude pin chain and rough-cut sprockets were most probably not up to the job of propelling it and it also lacked provision for chain tensioning. As the chain wheel and rear sprocket are of similar size, the initial aim must obviously have been safety rather than speed enhancement, suggesting that it was conceived after the first large wire wheels had demonstrated the coming dangers of cycling in early 1870. Guilmet was killed in the brief war, declared on 19 July 1870, and the machine suggests the scenario that in other circumstances

Meyer-Guilmet prototype *c.* 1870, now in the Musée des Arts et Metiers, Paris.

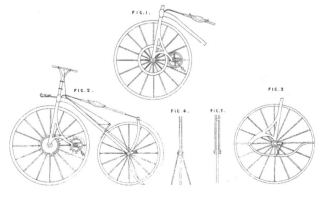

Newton Wilson chain-geared front driver. 1869.

he might have perfected the design and that bicycle evolution would have been short circuited, leaving out the high-wheel era altogether.

There had also been patent applications in England during 1869 for belt and lever-drive machines and in August 1870 Starley and Hillman filed their Ariel patent, which was a high-wheel design, but also described a small-wheeled version with spur gears fixed to the front forks giving a 2:1 ratio. They called this a speed gear. As with the Meyer-Guilmet, it was probably the crudeness of the construction that prevented success. While the Ariel wheel survived for ten years, its geared version was soon abandoned.

All these early experiments were overwhelmed when the wire wheel was adopted in mid-1870. While a 48-inch wooden wheel could possibly make a boneshaker faster on the track, it was irksome as a recreational mount, but a 50-inch or even 60-inch wire wheel was not only manageable but also liberating. Almost overnight the speed problem was solved and the bicycle reborn but, simultaneously, a new problem was created. From being slow and safe the bicycle overnight had become fast and dangerous and the next fifteen years saw many attempts to break this bind. Two early

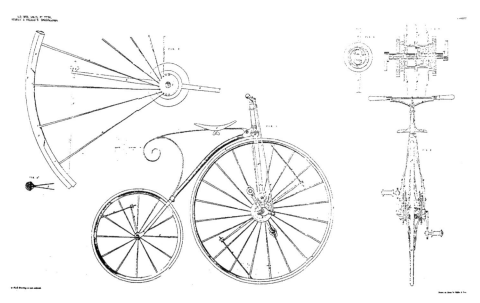

Starley & Hillman Ariel patent 1870 with speed gear.

designs stand out, both launched by major bicycle companies and both devised by the same man – Harry J. Lawson.

Lawson, having first registered the name Safety, licensed manufacture of his new invention, named the Sussex Giant, to the recently established George Singer & Co., Singer having previously worked under James Starley at CMC. The Singer Safety had a 54-inch or 56-inch rear wheel with small front steering wheel and it caused a stir on its launch in 1877, but only fifty were sold in the first year and Singer decided to drop it. Lawson attempted improvements but in 1879 he returned to Coventry as manager for George Woodcock who was amalgamating three bicycle businesses to form D. Rudge & Co. Here he patented a second safety, which he named the Bicyclette, and which, although derided by many, appears today as much more practical. The catalogue promised that it would 'become the most comfortable and tempting to ride of steel steeds'. This time, despite being well advertised, only a dozen or so were sold and the Bicyclette was withdrawn too. The new boss, Woodcock, apparently fell off when testing it and the explanation for its failure later offered by the company in their house magazine was simply that the steering

THE PATENT "SAFETY" BICYCLE.

NO DANGER.	NO RISK.
NO LOSS OF POWER.	NO LOSS OF SPEED.
NO DIFFICULTY IN MOUNTING.	NO DIFFICULTY IN DISMOUNTING.
NO DIFFICULTY IN STARTING.	NO DIFFICULTY IN STOPPING.
NO DIFFICULTY IN BALANCING.	NO ASSISTANCE IN LEARNING.

ANY SIZE. MAY BE USED BY RIDERS OF ANY HEIGHT.
We venture to anticipate objections by remarking that the driving wheel
DOES *NOT* SPLASH THE RIDER WITH MUD.
DOES *NOT* OSCILLATE OR "WOBBLE."
And that all the details have been well considered and thoroughly tested.

Sole Manufacturers—SINGER AND CO., COVENTRY.
MANUFACTURERS ALSO OF THE WELL-KNOWN
"CHALLENGE" BICYCLE.
Price Lists, one stamp. Cabinet Photo., six stamps.
London Agents—MOIR, HUTCHINS, and HICKLING; 30, Queen Victoria-street, E.C.
Dublin Agents—BOOTH BROTHERS, 64, Upper Stephen-street.

THE "SAFETY."

THE "SAFETY" SEMI-RACER.
Is now completed. The Inventor's first idea, introduced by SINGER & Co. at
the beginning of the year, has resulted in a most splendid success.
Send Stamped Envelope to H. LAWSON, Sole Inventor and Patentee, at
Regent Works, North Road, Brighton, where numbers are now being made.
Every test welcomed.

Lawson's failed 'Safety' model, made by Singer in 1876.

was 'queer'. Clearly with bridle-rod steering and no fork offset this might have been expected. Unfortunately it has never been possible to test-ride the only surviving Bicyclette in the London Science Museum, but reproductions indicate that this was the problem.

Meanwhile Singer remodelled the unsuccessful Safety as the Challenge tricycle, making two small front steering wheels collapsible to fit through a doorway, and it then had a successful run. Additionally,

Lawson's Bicyclette
made by Rudge
in 1879, another
failure.

THE "BICYCLETTE".

For particulars see Page 7.

Singer Challenge tricycle,
1878.

with his Challenge range of ordinaries being strongly admired, he devised and patented what can be seen as the first successful safety. The lifelong bicyclist and ex-Home Secretary, Sir Robert Lowell, thought

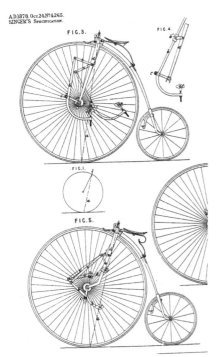

Singer 1878 'Xtarordinary, a great hill-climber lasting ten years.

'Xtraordinary patent drawings.

it so good it should be named the *ne plus ultra* but Singer chose the name 'Xtraordinary Challenge (note the apostrophe) and the key to its design was spelt out in his patent: 'The fork of the driving-wheel is raked backwards, the head being arranged so that its axis, if extended, would meet the ground at the point of contact with the wheel.'

If only Lawson had managed to figure out this fundamental requirement for a raked fork, his Bicyclette might well have had a better fate, might even have 'set the fashion to the world'. As it was the 'Xtraordinary, or Xtra as it was called by its many devotees, gained recognition for its great safety and, despite the added weight of the levers, a reputation for being a fine hill climber. It remained in the catalogue for eight years and the number of surviving machines today bears witness to its popularity.

Beale & Straw of Greenwich patented the second successful safety, the Facile, in 1878 but production remained small until 1881 when I. W. Boothroyd, returning with a fortune made in America, purchased Ellis & Co. and devoted his energies to promoting the Facile. It had shorter levers than the Xtra, hinged on extensions of the forks below the hub. The maximum wheel size was only 48 inches but it won

The sturdy Facile made by
Ellis & Co., 1878–1888.

THE "FACILE" SAFETY BICYCLE.

many prizes on the road particularly in distance events, including one for an incredible record of 266 miles in one day.

The Facile's success prompted William Hillman to design and patent the Kangaroo in March 1884. This revived the idea of a chain-geared front-driver, which had several times previously proved unsuccessful. The stub axles for the pedals were fixed to the forks while the wheel was held in brackets, sliding up or down the forks to tension the chain. It was advertised as the 'Kangaroo Safety Bicycle', although Sturmey noted that 'very little safety is induced by its use, a cropper being quite as easy of occurrence as on an ordinary bicycle – the inevitable fall over the handles simply occurring from a lower altitude'. Nevertheless, speed was the zeitgeist and, when the Kangaroo took eight minutes off the 100-mile road record, fifty competitors set about producing clones in time for the following season. To avoid contravening Hillman's patent, their sprockets had to be adjustable and the wheel centre fixed. The 1885 Stanley Show is remembered for the launch of J. K. Starley' Rover bicycle, perhaps the most iconic bicycle design of all time, although like many others it was launched before it had been perfected. Lots of makers had been working the previous year on the safety problem, Coventry was a relatively small

LE " KANGAROO "

Hillman's Kangaroo was a big success from 1884 to 1886.

THE ROVER SAFETY
BICYCLE (PATENTED).

The Rover, January
1885.

town and manufacturers had many intertwined connections. Apart
from the Xtra, the Facile and the fifty odd Kangaroo copies, which
Sturmey saw as being on the 'now general lines', there were seven
geared rear-drivers at the show. These were the Humber, Pioneer,
Swing Frame, National, B.S.A., Antelope and Rover. The Rover had a
36-inch front wheel while the rest were around 20 inches in diameter,
which without suspension on the rough roads of the day made them
hard to steer and uncomfortable. The Rover and the Antelope both
had the bridle-rod steering that had been one of the bugbears of the
Bicyclette six years before.

The small handful of surviving 1885 rear-drivers today, including
no original Rover, confirms the lack of impact that they made on the
herd of Kangaroos. Although John Kemp Starley became lauded as
the inventor of the safety bicycle, he later confessed that the reception
at the show was unflattering and that 'business in the first year was
nothing to speak of'. *The Tricyclist* suggested that the Rover might
be better named the Camel, while ordinary riders coined the term
Beetle for what they considered to be low-life machines.

J. K. Starley began his working life with his Uncle James before
moving to the associated firm of Haynes & Jefferies and, when
they folded in 1879 he started on his own, funded by draper
William Sutton, to make tricycles. His first tricycle, the Meteor,
was well received and in 1883 was modified to the popular

Rear-drivers at the 1885 Stanley Show.

J. K. Starley Rover tricycle, 1883.

Humber style and renamed the Rover. The rider sat between two large leading wheels in an upright position as on an ordinary with the small rear wheel steering. This was also successful and in 1884 he designed the Rover bicycle with the deliberate intention of challenging the supremacy of the ordinary. His aim was to place the rider at the proper distance from the ground, arrange gearing that could be varied to suit the owner, place the seat in the correct relation to the pedals and make the handlebars easily adjustable. The 36-inch front wheel marked out the Rover from its six competitors, although the bridle-rod steering did not compare with Lawson's third safety, the National, launched at the same show. This time Lawson had not protected it by patent and Starley's 'maker's amateur', a polite term for professional rider, having ridden the National, suggested to Starley that he reshape the front end of the Rover, sloping the forks back towards the rider and doing away with the bridle-rods. This was done and at the same time the chain was put on the right hand side rather than the left. In a special 100-mile race for Rovers that Starley organized in September, the Kangaroo record of the previous year was broken. Hillman immediately retaliated with the Kangaroo regaining the title but, in a famous 1885 cartoon in *Cycling*, the Rover is shown half a wheel in front. The following two years saw Rover-style copies being made by practically all the major companies and the kangaroo type became practically extinct.

The Rover as modified during 1885.

T. LAWSON & CO.,

LONDON AND COVENTRY,

The Original Patentees of SAFETY BICYCLE, and Sole Manufacturers of "LAWSON'S BICYCLETTE," and all the most popular patterns of Bicycles and Tricycles, including Two-Track, with Spiral Steering, and the Direct Action Tricycle, which has *no Chains or Cogs*, and is celebrated above all others for Hill-climbing.

"LAWSON'S BICYCLETTE."

Stationary   Stand

for   is brought

Mounting   down

and   by turning

Dismounting.   Handle.

The only Safe Safety.

ADDRESS:

LONDON SHOW ROOMS, 22, COLEMAN ST., CITY.

Above: Lawson 1885 National.

Left: G. E. Moore drawing, Rover *v*. Kangaroo 1885.

Harry Griffin noted in 1887,

The revolution in dwarf machines, and the adoption of rear drivers – generally recognized as the Rover type – is a marked feature. Owing to the shape, great liberties can be taken in varying the constructive detail – denied to the builder of ordinary bicycles and a remarkable variation is to be found in the framing. One thing is certain – bicyclists can now enjoy their sport under safer conditions than at any previous date.

The 1881 Star was an American success and had some followers in England.

He complained that in brake power and rigidity some of the models showed room for improvement, but the most serious criticism concerned comfort. The safety did not deal with the exigencies of the roadway as well as the ordinary. A 50-inch wheel absorbed the road shock while a 30-inch wheel transmitted every bump directly to the rider. In consequence, 1888 saw a rash of spring-framed machines with springs inserted into all parts of the frame, allowing the wheels to react to the roadway without the shock being transferred to the saddle or handlebars.

EARLY BICYCLES IN AMERICA

America came late to the ordinary, taking up the high machine only after several English makers exhibited at the 1867 Philadelphia Centennial Exhibition. Colonel Albert E. Pope saw them there and first began importing bicycles before arranging local manufacture with the Weed Sewing Machine Co., which had mastered the American system of interchangeable parts. This gave Pope's Columbia an advantage over the craftsman-made imports and by 1882 he had two-thirds of the US market.

Early safeties were imported from England, with the Facile 'Xtraordinary and Kangaroo being favourites. In 1886, Pope produced a Kangaroo clone – the Columbia safety and others made high-wheel safeties based on English patterns, but the Star (1881) and the Eagle (1889) were distinctly American, having the large wheel at the rear. On these, headers over the front were exchanged for difficulties in mounting, particularly with the Eagle, while an involuntary backward dismount might also occasionally be enjoyed.

10

THE BRACED DIAMOND FRAME

What we today call a diamond frame has the seat tube as a diagonal brace but, in the mid-1880s, when the rear-driving safety was developing and the Rover pattern was being widely copied by the trade, a diamond frame was an open four-sided construction that shared the market with the alternative pattern, the cross-frame. The late Sheldon Brown used to maintain that 'it is unlikely that the diamond frame will ever be surpassed as a way to build a rigid framed bicycle, using joined tubes as a construction medium'. Today, bicycles frames are of carbon, resin or composite – steel, aluminium or alloy – so joined tubes might be seen to be losing ground, but the braced diamond configuration still endures.

A typical open diamond frame from 1886.

Hillman's patented
cross-frame design
in 1886.

During the 1890s, after the debate had been resolved, cyclists were keen to honour the inventor of the design that they saw as having transformed their pastime and yet no prize was ever awarded nor monument raised. Back in 1878, choice had been restricted to either the ordinary bicycle or the high-wheel tricycle, but then the pioneering 'Xtraordinary and the Facile, swiftly followed in turn by the Kangaroo, Rover, cross-frame, spring-frame, cushion-tyre and pneumatic, all changed the mix, until by 1889 a passable likeness to the modern bicycle had evolved.

Of the big companies in 1886, Rover, CMC and Centaur all chose an open diamond configuration, while Bayliss Thomas, Rudge and Singer copied Hillman's 1886 cross-frame design. *Bicycling News* complained of 'an exasperating lack of originality' and declared that Dearlove's Rational ordinary made a more comfortable mount. Dearlove threw in this late lifebuoy, a safer ordinary with a raked fork and larger rear wheel, giving hope to aficionados that their beloved ordinary might still somehow survive. The following year, makers were obliged to add Rationals to the kaleidoscope of new patterns in their catalogues but by then the safety had already become established.

Improvement will often create fresh weakness, and the Rover, while famously solving the danger problem, had introduced torque

Dearlove's 1887 Rational (slightly safer) ordinary.

into the bicycle frame that was virtually absent in the ordinary and Kangaroo. In use, the frame flexed and exaggerated every bump in the road, disrupting the steering. The machine also sideslipped so that tyros had to be taught balance on an outdated ordinary. Happily, the problem had been resolved by the time that *Bicycling News* reported on the February 1889 Stanley Show:

> A great number of makers are copying the Humber No 1 diamond frame, in some cases a diagonal or perpendicular strut being fitted, thus making a frame of the utmost strength and rigidity. Makers generally seem to have passed the experimental stage in safety machines, and have reached a point at which radical improvement seems almost impossible, and only detail can be dealt with.

Humber declared their 1889 Light Roadster to be 'the lightest, strongest and most rigid form of framework yet invented', 'one of Mr. Humber's greatest achievements' and, apart from its solid tyres, it was, indeed, effectively a modern bicycle, but this same solution had actually been launched the year before, at the 1888 show.

This was the Referee; it was the work of a young London firm of which the chief partners were barely in their twenties. G. L. Morris, Wilson and Co. produced the Referee with the frame braced by a curved seat tube that followed the line of the rear wheel. Mr. Humber's 'great achievement' of 1889 was merely to substitute

The first braced diamond frame – George Morris's Referee of 1887.

The influential Humber diamond frame, 1889 catalogue.

a straight, rather than curved seat tube by slightly increasing the distance between the rear axle and the bottom bracket, a move that did incidentally improve the handling. As Rover and Humber had never patented their frame designs and Referee only registered their pattern after it had appeared in public, the diamond frame was free for everyone to copy, and copy it they did.

Referee noted this with some resentment in their 1891 catalogue, complaining,

> Every improvement we invent in cycles is outrageously copied by unscrupulous makers, who barefacedly foist infringements upon the public as their own inventions. Our Original Diamond Frame invented in 1887, has been most shamefully treated in this respect, nearly every maker in the world offering to the public inferior imitations.

But if Referee had not invented the braced diamond frame, then almost certainly somebody else would have done so within months.

G. L. MORRIS, WILSON & CO.,   3

With Hearty Thanks for Past Patronage.

February, 1891.

WE are including several minor improvements in our cycles for 1891, which we feel confident will meet with our customers' approval. We have built up a sound commercial business in a few years by good, honest manufacture and originality, and have secured a reputation second to none for our cycles. They are acknowledged to be the finest machines extant, hence their great popularity with the hardest riders in the cycling world. We use only the best obtainable material and workmanship in the construction of our machines. We are nothing if not original, and should despise ourselves were we to resort to the mean practice (so prevalent, we are sorry to say, in the cycle trade) of stealing other people's ideas. We do not believe there has been a firm more badly treated in this respect than ourselves. Every improvement we invent in cycles is outrageously copied by unscrupulous makers, who barefacedly foist infringements upon the public as their own inventions. Our "Original Diamond Frame," invented in 1887, has been most shamefully treated in this respect, nearly every maker in the world offering to the public inferior imitations. However, this is positive proof that our design cannot be improved upon.

Extract from " THE CYCLIST," January 14th, 1891.

"It will, we think, be found that there is a strong tendency throughout the Trade to adopt the diamond form of frame, and more especially that design better recognised perhaps as the 'Referee' pattern, in which the diagonal stay across the frame follows the curve of the back wheel from the crank-bracket upwards."

In 1889 we fitted an entirely new and original Ball Socket Head to all our cycles. Our readers have only to look at the illustrations of the various machines in the cycling papers, to see how this and also several of our other improvements have been copied by nearly the entire Trade.

66, TURNMILL St., FARRINGDON Rd., LONDON, E.C.

Reference Catalogue, 1891.
(Les Bowerman Collection)

Change was happening at breakneck speed, although nobody could know that the final outcome would be the chain-driven rear-driver. It might well have been a lever drive or a geared front-driver or, again, even the tricycle. All these options, and many more, had to be tried out by many thousands on the road and track until the final solution was resolved.

J. K. Starley is remembered for his 1885 Rover bicycle that 'set the fashion to the world', but it certainly didn't do that at its first showing. Had Starley not listened to Steve Golder's advice to change the steering from indirect to direct, he could well have been just another also-ran. Somebody else would have claimed the glory, although we can now say that the result would still have been much the same. One feels that the perfected machine was waiting to be discovered.

What remains surprising is that, five years after the Rover's arrival, manufacturers were still attempting to solve the vibration problems by fitting springs throughout the frame, as witnessed by the £22 Whippet of 1886–89. Cushion tyres provided the only alternative amelioration and of these there were very many types. Over half the 1,053 cycles at the January 1891 show were fitted with cushions. These expensive, patented alternatives all proved transitory and it fell to a complete outsider to come up with the perfect answer.

JAMES STARLEY (1831–81) AND THE COVENTRY MACHINISTS CO. LTD

At the time of James Starley's early death in 1881, his peers already referred to him as the 'father of the English cycle trade' and his inventions quickly became legendary. Starley's modest nature and lack of schooling meant that he gave few interviews during his life, while his only biography is the unreliable *Life and Inventions of James Starley* written by his son William in 1902. His role at CMC was managing the shop floor and working on his inventions; he was never a director or a shareholder of the company or of any of its precursors. With his late-flowering career it is unsurprising that misunderstandings have grown up among collectors and old bicycle enthusiasts. He is still frequently confused with his nephew, John Kemp Starley, and mistakenly credited with having invented the penny-farthing, rather than Eugene Meyer, who contemporary English writers vaguely referred to as M. Magee. Many collectors confidently explain that their prized ordinary is a 'Starley'.

Starley was born of farming stock in Sussex. He left school at nine and then left home at sixteen to work as a gardener in Lewisham before joining the sewing-machine maker Newton Wilson and Co. in Holborn. The work there suited his inventive cast of mind and he contrived improvements to the sewing machine including one that allowed the circular sewing of cuffs and trouser bottoms. In his home workshop he devised a completely new sewing machine, the Europa, and his friend and fellow employee, Josiah Turner, persuaded him in May 1861 to move to Coventry where the traditional industries of ribbon weaving and watchmaking were in decline due to foreign competition. Money was apparently available from local entrepreneurs for new industries including that of sewing-machine manufacture.

It turned out to be not quite that easy for, despite Starley's mechanical prowess, the European Sewing Machine Company soon failed. It was re-founded by local capitalists as the Coventry Sewing Machine Co. Ltd with Turner as manager and Starley works foreman. In November 1868, Turner's nephew, Rowley, brought one of the new French two-wheel velocipedes (boneshakers) from Paris, suggesting it would make an additional line. The directors agreed and on 7 May 1869 the company became The Coventry Machinists' Co. Ltd. As managing foreman, Starley found himself by chance at the centre of the new bicycle trade and over the next decade he cemented a reputation as the most creative of the English cycle pioneers.

He was the first to fit a mounting step in 1869, reputedly due to his own mounting difficulties, and his Coventry, C-Spring and

An early 1869 CMC boneshaker, without step. (Ron Callan Collection)

Step design was launched in early 1870. Here the two wheels were of markedly different size with a distinctive saddle spring fixed to the backbone rather than supported by rear stays as in the French pattern. It also had a single rear fork but, as there was little necessity to remove a rear wheel, this idea was dropped when Starley fitted 40-inch and 26-inch rubber-tyred, wire wheels sent from Paris. Transformed, it became the Coventry Spider. This development sparked his interest in wire spoking and on 11 August 1870, while still at CMC, he and Hillman patented their Ariel bicycle. The patent described an arrangement for tensioning all the spokes simultaneously with two levers fixed across the hub, carrying

1870 Coventry No. 1 model. (Author's Collection)

Coventry 'Spider' model, mid-1870. (Nash Collection, Brooklands)

threaded rods connecting to the rim. The patent also proposed spur-gears on the front fork to allow the wheel to be geared up. The spoking system was a ten-year success while the speed gear, incapable of being engaged on the move, was soon dropped.

Starley left CMC on 26 November 1870, taking his sewing machine and bicycle patents with him and set up in St John's Street, with the first Ariel being made by Christmas suggesting the move was well planned. For a year the Ariel had a boneshaker-type socket-head before he invented his well-known open head late in 1871. This was cannily protected by a registered design costing just a shilling rather than £275 for a patent. Most surviving Ariels have the open head with the diamond-shaped, registered design mark stamped on the forks. The expense of taper boring the socket was saved, it was lighter and the need for frequent lubrication was reduced. By April the Ariel backbone was being made of hollow tube, another first. Hillman had left CMC to join him in February 1871

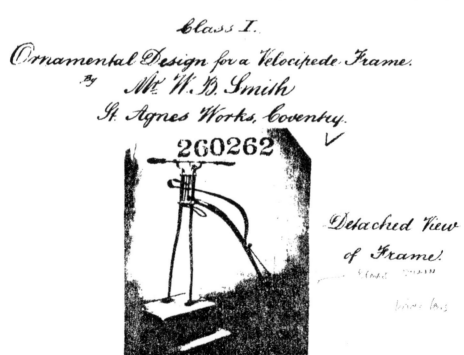

Registered design for the Ariel Open Head, February 1872.

but the partnership struggled. William Borthwich Smith, a wholesale watchmaker was brought in within the year to help with funding and Hillman left the partnership in December 1872.

In 1874, Starley patented his Tangent wheel, allowing the spokes to be individually tensioned thus truing the wheel. It was an important step although being protected by patent had little influence on the trade and cycles did not generally adopt tangent spoking until four years after Starley's death. Despite the progress made since boneshaker days, it was still unclear whether the bicycle was more than a passing phase and in 1874 Smith and Starley decided to concentrate on sewing machines and license out Ariel

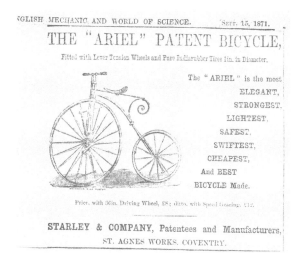

First Ariel advertisement showing the new open head.

1874 84-inch Tangent demonstrating the strength of the new wheel design.

manufacture to Haynes and Jefferis, two of their employees, In May 1876, Starley signed an agreement with them whereby he supplied them with tangent wheels, which he made at his home, receiving 15s for each bicycle sold. Meanwhile the sewing machine trade continued in decline and Smith's partnership in the watch trade was also dissolved. By January 1877 Smith and Starley was in liquidation and the assets were bought by the entrepreneurial solicitor George Woodcock to combine with the similarly failed Haynes and Jefferis. The following year Woodcock bought the respected business of the late Daniel Rudge of Wolverhampton, amalgamating it all under the name of D. Rudge & Co.

Starley's 1874 Tangent patent had also included the idea of a high bicycle for ladies with the rider sitting side-saddle and the rear wheel offset to provide balance. It proved totally impractical but, with another small wheel similarly offset at the front, it serendipitously formed the prototype for his highly successful Coventry tricycle. This arrived too late to save Haynes and Jefferis but became a regular moneymaker for Rudge over the next ten years.

The first Coventry tricycle with lever drive and tiller steering.

What little money Starley had salvaged from the partnership with Smith, he now used to finance Starley Brothers where, with his three sons, James Jnr, John Marshall, and William, he made his newly invented Salvo tricycle. This proved the most notable of all his cycling inventions. It was the final development of the Coventry tricycle with a second driving wheel added, coupled through what he called a balance gear to allow both large wheels to be driven. Here at last was a double-driving tricycle that could be geared up to suit the rider. The balance gear revolutionized not just the tricycle, but also much later the motorcar, where it became known as the differential.

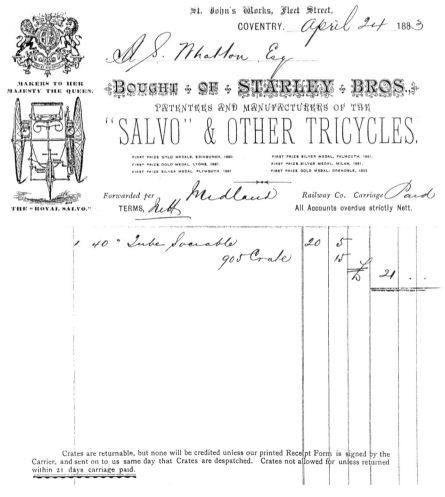

Starley's influential 1989 Salvo design that crowned his career.

The royal household at Osborne ordered two Salvos and later another two, although not, as sometimes reported, for the Queen. After receiving the Royal Warrant, it was renamed the Royal Salvo. Unhappily, soon after delivering the first machine to Osborne, James Starley succumbed to cancer of the liver and died aged fifty-one.

The principal cycle makers of Coventry closed their factories on the day of his funeral, while all who knew him stressed his unassuming manner and quiet persistence in tackling mechanical difficulty. He had experienced many setbacks in life including the accidental loss of his youngest son Joseph, aged five, and his commercial life had been punctuated by bankruptcies and failed inventions. His cycles never had the style or polish of the competition and yet he invented mechanical ideas that nurtured the infant bicycle and tricycle trades for a decade.

It might appear unkind to say that his death was perfectly timed but Coventry was booming, owing to the huge success of its tricycle trade. A committee was formed and a 20-foot memorial unveiled by the mayor on 8 November 1884. On one side was depicted a Coventry Rotary and on the other a Royal Salvo but, within a year the Rover bicycle of his nephew, J. K. Starley, would be the talk of the town and within five years Griffin would be reporting the demand for tricycles as 'having greatly fallen off'.

THE COVENTRY MACHINISTS COMPANY LTD

If Starley was the father of the cycle trade, then the Coventry Machinists Co. Ltd was its nursery. As well as Starley, Turner and Hillman, other employees of 'the old firm' included George Singer, John Warman, John Thomas, Thomas Bayliss, and Nahum Salamon, all later founding successful cycle companies. CMC remained influential with their Club models throughout the ordinary, tricycle, and hard-tyred safety years becoming The Swift Cycle Co. Ltd in 1897 and later making motorbikes and cars. The firm lasted until

1931 when Alfred Herbert took over the assets, later becoming part of Tube Investments. James Starley should not be confused with his equally famous nephew, John Kemp Starley of Rover fame. His third son William who helped his father with his early inventions later became a noted inventor himself.

HANS RENOLD AND THE BUSH ROLLER CHAIN

Hans Renold patented the bush roller chain in 1880 and it remains a design classic still in use today. For the first few years it shared the cycle market with other chains such as block chain. This was preferred by track racers until after the Second World War because of its instant response, but the versatility and low maintenance requirements of bush roller chain in harsh conditions allowed for its general adoption on cycles.

Motorcycles, motorcars and machinery all benefited from the cycling experience and, while the Industrial Revolution had managed power transmission without chains, relying on ropes or belts, Renold, in 1893, drove the line-shafts of his six-storey Manchester factory entirely by chain.

Portrait of Hans Renold by
T. C. Dugdale R. A.

The son of a Swiss baker, Hans Renold was born in 1852 and, after engineering studies and military service in Zurich, went to Paris to help with reconstruction work after the siege. From there he took a job in Manchester with machine exporter Felber-Jucker and in 1879 bought the small bankrupt business of James Slater in Salford, which made chains for mills and quarries and held patents for both bowl and bush chain dating from 1864. Renold could hardly have foreseen the coming of the cycle age but his timing was perfect. Lever-driven tricycles were just starting to be converted to chain drive and James Starley, not knowing where he could buy chains for his Salvo, first made them himself before discovering Slater. The bowl chain proved unsatisfactory for cycles because the pins quickly stretched the holes in the side plates and Renold's 1880 patent was the neat and effective solution.

Hans Renold's son Charles succeeded as M.D. in 1919 and through merger and acquisition the company has maintained its place in the international chain and transmission market. Hans Renold had at first considered that roller chain could not be made in short pitch and he left it to his competitors to produce half-inch pitch chain when his patent expired in 1894. The flexibility required for operating early derailleurs was developed in the 1920s when ¼-inch pitch chain gave way to ³⁄₁₆-inch and then ⅛-inch. This allowed for multiple gearing combinations and the pioneer bushingless Sedisport chain of the 1980s has since led to a variety of lightweight, flexible alternatives.

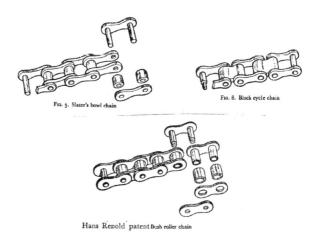

Fig. 5. Slater's bowl chain

Fig. 8. Block cycle chain

The Bush roller chain
patented by Renold
in 1880.

Hans Renold patent Bush roller chain

13

HARRY JOHN LAWSON
1852–1925

Lawson was jailed in 1904 for his part in Terrah Hooley's fraudulent company flotations, so he comes painted with a black brush, but in his early career he did as much as anyone to promote the safety bicycle so his place in the story deserves to be remembered.

Following an engineering apprenticeship, he opened a cycle agency in Brighton and patented his first safety bicycle in 1876, licensing it to Singer of Coventry. It was safe but the wallowing rear wheel and awkward riding position failed to attract customers. Even when he redesigned it back in Brighton it remained unsaleable, so he returned to Coventry as works manager for the newly reorganised Rudge Company, where he devised and patented a totally new design, the 1879 Bicyclette, which, due to its difficult steering, again failed to

Singer Safety, 1876.

sell. Lawson departed Rudge in 1881 to start his own National Bicycle & Tricycle Mfg. Co. in Coventry where his third safety, the National – unpatented as money was tight – was launched at the 1885 Stanley Show. Despite being well reviewed and recognised as 'the only bicycle on the market suitable for a woman', it proved yet another disappointment.

Lawson had reached the end of his safety bicycle ambitions and moved on to a new career. When assisting with the 1885 flotation of D. Rudge & Co. Ltd he discovered a taste for high finance and later, as an early motorist, he recognised the opportunity for creating a British automobile industry. He teamed up with financier Ernest Terrah Hooley, buying up patents and promoting a series of bicycle and motor company flotations during the cycling boom years of the 1890s.

Although his contribution to the successful safety is usually overlooked, he is still remembered by veteran motorists for organising the first London to Brighton motorcar run in 1896, celebrating the relaxation of the Red Flag Act. French cyclists still use his name Bicyclette, unaware of its origin. It has provided them with a lasting alternative name for *le velo*. Lawson allowed Rudge

Bicyclette 1879

Lawson's 1879 Bicyclette.

T. LAWSON & CO.,

LONDON AND COVENTRY,

The Original Patentees of SAFETY BICYCLE, and Sole Manufacturers of "LAWSON'S BICYCLETTE," and all the most popular patterns of Bicycles and Tricycles, including Two-Track, with Spiral Steering, and the Direct Action Tricycle, which has *no Chains or Cogs*, and is celebrated above all others for Hill-climbing.

"LAWSON'S BICYCLETTE."

Stationary		Stand
for		is brought
Mounting		down
and		by turning
Dismounting.		Handle.

The only Safe Safety.

ADDRESS:

LONDON SHOW ROOMS, 22, COLEMAN ST., CITY.

National safety, 1885.

Rudge 1886 Bicyclette.

98

to use the name for their first successful safety of 1886, exported and sold through their Paris agency. They could thus claim that it was simply an updated version of their 1878 Bicyclette rather than a blatant copy of the Rover and that Rudge, therefore, were the true inventors of the safety.

France had, by then, made up the lost ground in bicycle production and design and makers like Meyer, Truffault, Renard and Clement were producing ordinaries and tricycles of equal or better quality than English makers. In November 1885, George Juzan of Bordeaux took the 100-km record on a safety of his own design, but whether or not this was secretly modelled on the Rover, as alleged at the time, is and was of little moment. The safety was already on its way.

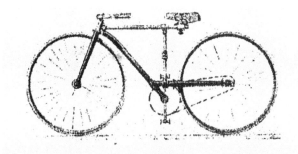

Fig. 28. — 15 Novembre 1885. Record du Monde.
G. Juzan (100 k., 4 h. 40).
La première Bicyclette moderne.

George Juzan
safety, 1885.

14

LADIES' BICYCLES

Gender historians frequently remark on the fact that the development of the bicycle accelerated the fight for women's liberation. Much ink has been used in pinpointing the first ladies' bicycles of the safety era, while ignoring the Ladies' Pilentum and Johnson's Ladies' hobby-horse of over sixty years before, but it is certainly true that few ladies regularly cycled before tricycles arrived in the late 1870s. While a handful of women rode velocipedes in the USA and in France, it was not so in England, and no ladies rode ordinaries outside the circus or on the stage. S. W. Thomas patented a side-saddle velocipede in 1870 and James Starley a high bicycle of similar design but, along with Sparrow's 1880 Amazon, they were all quite impractical. In France, Viarengo De Forville included a ladies' model in his 1871 patent but this again came to nothing.

A suitable safety was eventually produced in 1884, the work of Harry Lawson, tireless promoter of safety for over a decade. Henry Sturmey described Lawson's National as 'the only bicycle on the market that is rideable by a lady'. Unhappily, Lawson was always pressed for cash and neither his ladies' safety nor his company reappeared the following year. Ladies had to remain tricyclists until the trade risked making dedicated bicycles in 1887. Dan Albone offered an Ivel Lady's Tricycle, which by loosening a couple of nuts allowed the machine to be converted into a safety. The tubing was shaped 'so that a lady can ride in the ordinary costume and can mount and dismount either in front or behind.'

The following year Singer and Andrews joined in, helpfully suggesting that 'with a little knack mounting may be accomplished

Smiling Dan Albone designed this early ladies' convertible bi-tricycle in 1886.

without help, but it is advisable to have assistance'. Not until 1889 did major companies like CMC and Rover decide there was a sufficient market. George Singer, when asked whether ladies' safeties would become really popular, averred,

> That is impossible to say, but so far very few are used in this country. In America, however, they have a big run, and we have now a considerable number of orders on hand for ladies' safeties in that country.

The adoption of pneumatic tires was the key to unlocking demand and in the 1895/6 boom women's bicycles provided about a third of the market. They were almost all loop frames with a full chain guard, while decorative dress guards, similar to those seen today in Holland, protected the rear wheel. During the twentieth century, women generally were happy to adopt the traditional man's bicycle although mixte frames and small-wheeled shopper bicycles have often been promoted to attract the lady cyclist.

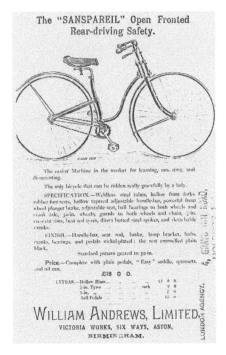

The "SANSPAREIL" Open Fronted
Rear-driving Safety.

The *easiest* Machine in the market for learning, mounting, and dismounting.

The only bicycle that can be ridden really gracefully by a lady.

SPECIFICATION.—Weldless steel tubes, hollow front forks, rubber foot-rests, hollow tapered adjustable handle-bar, powerful front wheel plunger brake, adjustable seat, ball bearings to both wheels and crank axle, 30-in. wheels, guards to both wheels and chain, ⅜-in. crescent rims, best red tyres, direct butted steel spokes, and detachable cranks.

FINISH.—Handle-bar, seat rod, brake, lamp bracket, hubs, cranks, bearings, and pedals nickel-plated ; the rest enamelled plain black.

Standard pattern geared to 50-in.

Price.—Complete with plain pedals, " Easy " saddle, spanners, and oil can.
£18 0 0.

EXTRAS.—Hollow Rims...

WILLIAM ANDREWS, LIMITED,
VICTORIA WORKS, SIX WAYS, ASTON,
BIRMINGHAM.

Left: William Andrews was one of the first to make a lady's drop-frame in 1887.

Below: CMC Lady's Swift 1889.

The
Lady's "Swift" Safety.

"Royal Psycho"

CYCLES.

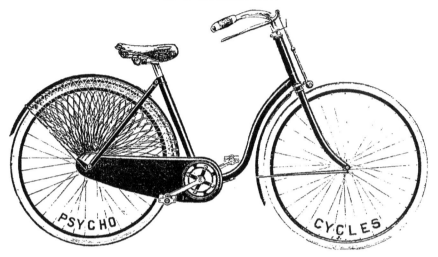

The original and registered design which cannot be improved upon.

A typical drop-frame lady's bicycle of 1897 with chain guard and dress guard.

15

DUNLOP AND THE PNEUMATIC SAFETY

John Boyd Dunlop (1840–1921) is the most unlikely inventor in our story. In 1885, John Kemp Starley, by then well steeped in the trade, and particularly familiar with tricycles, had revolutionised the concept of the bicycle with his Rover safety. When widely copied, the safety became subject to criticism for its unpleasant vibration and tendency to sideslip, compared with the comfortable stability of the trusted ordinary.

By this date the cycle trade was no longer a cottage industry there were half a million cyclists in the UK and 20,000 in America. Thousands were employed in their manufacture and hundreds of firms were attempting to find a solution to the problem. Over 270 British patents were filed in the years 1886/7, for spring saddles, spring frames, cushion tyres and spring wheels, yet all of them missed the jackpot – the air tyre.

Back in 1845, R. W. Thomson had patented an air tyre for use on the railways, which was ultimately unsuccessful and had been

Linley & Biggs
Whippet of 1888
with springs all over
had a three-year run
before the pneumatic
tyre took over.

forgotten. Dunlop produced his first pneumatic tyre with no help from outside and no inkling of Thompson's priority. He was a vet, boasting 'the most extensive practice in Ireland', but neither an engineer, nor at that time a cyclist, just an inveterate tinkerer. He often constructed rubber appliances for his veterinary work and by his own account had 'long taken an interest in locomotion'. He entertained the idea that spring wheels would run lightly on the road and he tested his homemade tyres on his son Johnny's tricycle. Johnny had complained that riding home from school over the setts between the tram rails made his tricycle so slow.

After his prototype proved successful – secretly tested by Johnny during an eclipse of the moon – a friend drew up a simple patent application and Dunlop arranged for the Belfast cycle agents Edlin & Sinclair to fit up a batch of tricycles and bicycles with 'pneumatics', a neologism he coined himself.

At the Belfast Queen's College Sports on 18 May 1889, William Hume of the Cruisers Cycle Club, an undistinguished athlete, but the only one on pneumatics, swept the board, while at the same event Dunlop met the Dubliner William Harvey du Cros and his cycle-racing sons. Not being a man of the world, Dunlop agreed that

Johnny Dunlop
with the prototype
pneumatic-tyred
bicycle in 1888.

WILLIAM HARVEY DU CROS.

Above left: William Harvey du Cros who made Dunlop's idea a commercial success.

Above right: J. B. Dunlop at an Old Timers' meet in 1917.

du Cros should take the lead in manufacturing and promoting the pneumatic tyre. While Dunlop lent his name to the new company, he never became a company man and found no comfort in his role as technical director. Until 1896, Du Cros, an entrepreneur of great vitality, remained the sole executive director.

The late discovery of Thomson's earlier invention rather dramatically invalidated the Dunlop patent but did not deflate du Cros. By then he had purchased most of the competing and compatible patents – C. K. Welch's wire bead, Wood's cycle valve, Bartlett's beaded-edge tyre and Westwood's tubular-edged rim. The Dunlop Company spent the rest of the decade defending its golden egg in the courts with their Q.C. John Fletcher Moulton MP receiving 'virtually a fresh case every working day' while the Dunlop flotation of 1896, masterminded by E. Terrah Hooley, who collected a million pounds out of the deal, was the largest of the nineteenth century.

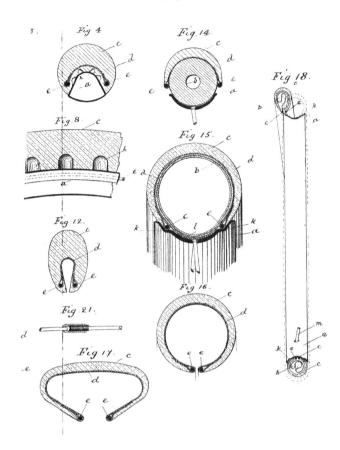

Welch's wire bead patent.

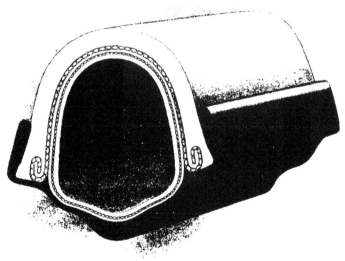

W. E. BARTLETT'S PNEUMATIC TYRE, 1890.
THE FIRST "DETACHABLE" PNEUMATIC TYRE.

Like the beetle – the derisory name given by ordinary riders to the safety – it was only the aesthetics of the 'pudding tyre' that held it back. There were jeers when it first appeared on the track but, in 1890, six racers of the Irish Brigade, came to England and swept the board on pneumatics wherever they competed. William Harvey's son, Arthur du Cros, later said,

> When I first rode it (the pneumatic tire) over the streets of Dublin it took me just one turn around Nelson's pillar to be convinced that granite setts and rough surfaces had lost their terror for good and all. I was on velvet for once in my life.

Naturally, not everyone shared this rosy view. Early Dunlops were handmade, bandaged to the rim and known as mummy tyres. On puncturing, customers were encouraged to return them to Dublin for repair. Nevertheless cushion tyres and spring frames soon succumbed to the perfected pneumatic in its wired-on or clincher forms, particularly when fitted with Wood's valves from 1891. By 1900, Dunlop wired-ons had a near monopoly of the UK market.

A myriad of makes of tyre competed during the decade, most notably Michelin in France from 1892, while other oddball ideas were promoted involving thin strips of steel or unvulcanized rubber to prevent or close punctures. In America, the Tillinghast single-tube tire, effectively an inflated garden hose glued to the rim, was virtually responsible for killing off adult bicycle use for forty years. When Schwinn revived detachable balloon tyres in 1933, the national perception of the bicycle was that it was for kids, a view that surprisingly persisted well into the 1970s.

Henry Sturmey, doyen of cycling pundits, asserted in 1887 that the youth of England and other active nations would ever select the ordinary in preference to its safer rival but by 1891, when shod with Dunlop pneumatics, the safety had eclipsed all records on road and track and silenced such objections. With its adjustable handlebars and seat posts, in contrast with the fixed geometry of the ordinary, bicycle dealers now needed to keep less stock in order to satisfy different-sized customers and the number of new dealers and new makers multiplied. They could now sell to the whole of the population rather than to a small elite, and bicycling was set to explode.

16

THE BICYCLE BOOM

Cycling had reached its nineteenth-century popularity peak in the spring of 1896, after the pneumatic safety had opened the gate to the wider field, particularly women and older men, who would never have contemplated an ordinary or a hard-tyred safety. Pneumatic tyres increased the cost of the already expensive safety bicycle by some 25 per cent, so newcomers came mainly from the moneyed classes, enticed by accounts of the aristocracy cycling in the royal parks. Like lawn tennis, which had been invented in 1874, cycling was the thing to do. Cycling gymkhanas and tennis parties were the way to meet new people.

A mid-1890s cycling gymkhana.

The *Salford Reporter* noted,

It is only a couple of years since bicycling was still regarded by English society as essentially a 'common' pastime, and as such it was condemned by everyone with the slightest pretensions to style or position. Even after bicycling had become fashionable in Paris and New York the British swells still looked askance at it, and only took it up tentatively to be practised in the seclusion of their country estates. But when it became known that the young princesses of Wales were ardent devotees of the wheel smart society plunged madly into the amusement … Mr Balfour, the leader of the House of Commons, rides to Downing Street to his duties on a safety.

Balfour was not the only celebrity bicyclist; the list included many famous authors. Shaw, Wells, Conan Doyle and Hardy all rode bicycles and indeed included bicycles and bicyclists in their writings. C. P. Scott, the renowned editor of the *Manchester Guardian* was a keen cyclist, riding home every night in the dark from the centre of Manchester to the suburbs until he was in his eighties. His paper carried a regular cycling column suggesting places to visit and noting the weekend plans of around fifty local clubs. The paper reported that the total number or regular cyclists in the country exceeded one and a half million.

Lady's Swift roadster, 1894.

At this date most of these bicycles and tricycles would be British made with the bulk made in Coventry so, unsurprisingly, from 1895, bicycle company shares replaced Australian gold mine stock as the hottest ticket during the late-Victorian economic depression. Amalgamations and flotations fuelled a speculative frenzy. £50 million capital was invested in the industry and 250,000 workers depended on it. Most dealers stocked up during the winter of 1895 and had sold out by May. Cycling did not die with the summer, as was the usual. There were over 2,600 machines on display at the Stanley Show, one third of them ladies' models, and prices reached new heights. With stocks again replenished, the trade expected 1897 to provide yet another bonanza but it was not to be. In July, the American cycle makers' compact collapsed and cheap American imports were dumped into the already overheated British market. The party was over and prices crashed. Membership of the Cyclist's Touring Club dropped from 60,000 to 15,000 by 1914 and by 1904 Rudge was offering their cheapest roadster for £6.

New ideas had been introduced during the years of boom. Geared front-drivers like the Crypto had some success as did shaft-drive bicycles, particularly on the Continent and in America. An enclosed shaft, carrying bevel gears or spin rollers, replaced the chain and

Crypto front driver, 1896.

1899 Columbia shaft drive, particularly popular in America.

when accurately made they could be as efficient as chain, but production was never large and they always remained expensive.

From boneshaker days, a fixed wheel had assisted braking and when pneumatic tyres proved incompatible with a plunger brake, hub and coaster brakes were developed, particularly in America, while in England rim brakes like E. M. Bowden's 1897 horseshoe brake were generally preferred. The Bowden cable was utilised from 1903 for operating hub gears and then later for derailleurs, while the new reliable brakes allowed for a free wheel. This was an old device that could now be easily incorporated with hub gears and at the turn of the century proved highly popular. In turn it facilitated mounting from a standing start or via the pedal. The mounting step on the rear axle was therefore no longer required. James Starley's first bicycle-related invention, which had lasted thirty years and never been patented, was finally discarded until it returned on trick bikes a century later.

Towards the end of the century, Continental and British road racing practice diverged. Club riders had at first invaded the countryside at weekends with scorchers tearing through villages, scattering chickens and children, and engaging in place-to-place record-breaking that involved teams of pacemakers, essential for high speeds, menacing the rural population. Restrictions were demanded and the cycling authorities sensibly promoted time trials as an alternative to mass racing. This became and remains the British way while in France, with more space, mass races like Paris–Bordeaux, Paris–Brest–Paris and in 1903 the Tour de France have become the national sport.

Riding in groups had begun tentatively during boneshaker days and the ordinary years saw a big rise in bicycle clubs organised on quasi-military lines with uniforms, captain, sub-captain and club bugler sounding the riding instructions. Clubs have remained popular ever since, partly through comradeship and partly because drafting helps riders in groups to maintain higher average speeds. The lone cyclist was never forced to join in and indeed the joys of solo cycling have been the subject of a thousand books. Thomas Stevens rode around the world on a 50-inch Columbia high wheel during 1884–86 and his journey has been reprised many times since. Multitudes have discovered in bicycling an opportunity for testing their mental and physical reserves or simply for just enjoying the scenery and reflecting on life.

17

GEARS

Gears are now seen as an essential for the modern bicycle but, from 1870, when the big wheel was first crowned king and for the next thirty years, through to the bicycle boom, a fixed wheel remained the norm. Tricyclists might be able stop to engage a suitable gear for speed or for hill climbing, but bicycles required different chain wheels to be fitted and the chain suitably adjusted. Shaw & Sydenham's Crypto Dynamic gear became available on tricycles from 1882 and in the 1890s it was adapted for use on bicycles. In 1899 Charles Linley's New Protean gear gave two speeds, selected by a swinging fork.

British and French practice diverged at this time, both the New Protean and Gradiant gears being further developed in France while the British abandoned chain shifting in favour of epicyclic hub gears. In 1902, James Archer patented William Reilly's ingenious three-speed gear and together with journalist Henry Sturmey, formed the Three-Speed Gear Syndicate. From 1910, Sturmey-Archer

Gradient gear, 1900.

wide-ratio hubs, made by BSA, became standard for club cyclists and record-breakers alike, until after the Second World War.

In France, chiefly in Saint-Étienne, the French Coventry and home of Velocio and his mountain-touring friends, the derailleur was seen as being the future. Chain shifting, at first using a stick or a gloved hand, was steadily improved. The retro-direct had two gears, although bizarrely one involved pedalling backwards. Narrow, more flexible chains allowed faster, more positive shifting with an increased number of sprockets. For three-speed hub gears, indexing was fairly simple to achieve, needing only one detent for middle gear, but it took longer to devise changers for the derailleur. Not until 1984 did the Shimano SIS system, utilising the SunTour, out of patent, slant parallelogram, fully solve the problem. Paradoxically, despite the great enthusiasm in France for the derailleur, its use was prohibited in the Tour de France until 1937. Competitors in

SIMPLICITY

is another feature of the B.S.A. Three-Speed Hub. This hub possesses no complicated mechanism to get out of order ; no superfluous parts to add weight. Each detail is constructed to perform its definite mission, and the whole hub is assembled with the utmost care, the result of which is a Three-Speed Hub upon which the cyclist can place the utmost reliance—a Three-Speed Hub the trader can recommend with every confidence. The

B.S.A. THREE-SPEED HUB

is the only Three-Speed Hub which **runs on ball bearings through-out**, including the **planet pinions.** You know, and every cyclist knows too, that for free running and easy cycling a hub with any moving parts running on plain bearings cannot be compared with one running on ball bearings throughout, therefore, it is to your own and your customers' interest that you should have the B.S.A. Three-Speed.

Write us now for full particulars and advertising matter.

THE BIRMINGHAM SMALL ARMS CO., LTD., SMALL HEATH, BIRMINGHAM.

THIS IS THE B.S.A. THREE-SPEED HUB.

Above left: BSA three-speed hub gear, 1900.

Above right: The legendary Velocio.

Retro-direct gear.

the early years had to stop and reverse the rear wheel to use the sprocket on the opposite side.

The patent record is bursting with bicycle gearing arrangements that offered variable speed continuous ratios, as achieved by a Croft pulley on a lawn mower, as well as automatic gear-changing systems activated by the force being applied. These always looked good on paper and in some cases actually worked, but a weight penalty was frequently incurred and it seems that most cyclists prefer to change gear at a time of their own choosing, depending on road conditions and their own state of wellbeing. In the end, gear selection by the rider will probably continue to prevail.

Another oft-patented device has been the oval or asymmetric chain ring, claimed to alleviate or eliminate the top dead centre effect. Riders of both ordinaries and safeties were advised to copy a monkey, employing the technique of 'ankling' or clawing the pedal around its circular path, not merely pressing up and down. An asymmetric chain ring theoretically helps to overcome the top dead centre problem but, despite Bradley Wiggins and Chris Froome winning the TdF using one, and the late Sheldon Brown extolling the more technical Biopace ring of the 1980s, the jury persistently remains out. It would appear to be a princess-and-the-pea situation and as there should theoretically be no cost difference between circular and odd-shaped rings anyone should be able to make their own decision.

18

THE LIGHTWEIGHT BICYCLE

The question of weight was never a concern for the hobby-horse or boneshaker maker, but it is rare to find any manufacturers from the ordinary era that were not keen to reduce the weight of their machines. By 1889, Harry James had squeezed the weight of his 52-inch racing ordinary down to an extraordinary 11 lbs, but the safety, with chainguard, mudguards, lamps, etc., ballooned in weight. In 1892, Jelly's Light Racer was advertised as under 25 lbs but, by the turn of the century, companies saw low price and high specification as a more important selling point than weight.

Rover's Light Roadster of 1900 weighed 33 lbs and only small companies like Lovelace could make a living specializing in light machines. Centaur, whose Edmund Mushing was considered

The 11-lb, 54-inch James racing bicycle of 1889.

'The Apostle of the Lightweight Bicycle', went into liquidation in 1909, but fashions change and the lightweight eventually made a comeback.

The catalyst for the twentieth-century Lightweight movement was Bastide, a small Parisian maker whose frames with BSA fittings were shown by Leon Meredith in 1912. Small firms began copying his designs and by the early 1920s many unorthodox frames were being offered. Taper tubes arrived in 1926 and double-tapered – like Bates Cantiflex – in 1932. Specialist components such as Endrick rims and Bowden caliper brakes catered for lightweight enthusiasts but were too expensive for the mass market.

Cycle builders making fewer than 300 machines per year were denied membership of the so-called Cycle Trade Union, the manufacturers' association that dominated the UK trade and set prices during the first half of the twentieth century. They therefore formed the Lightweight Association and activist Jack Holdsworth

The "Centaur Featherweight" Roadster.

The "Centaur Featherweight" Ladies'.

Above: By 1900, 33lbs was considered a light machine.

Right: The Meredith's Bastide-inspired lightweight.

launched the Lightweight Show in 1932, aiming to attract the elite club cyclist. This showcased new ideas about gearing and touring products. Lightweight Association members also attempted to improve the forty-year-old basic diamond frame to achieve greater riding efficiency. They debated more upright head and down-tube angles, handle positions, handlebar stems, crank lengths, wheelbase and how to position the rider over the pedals to allow fuller use of ankling. Significantly, the Association pioneered lowering the bottom bracket and reducing wheel diameters from 28 inches to 26 inches, producing the low-built roadster.

The 1930s through to the 1950s saw a plethora of new frame designs. The cycling authorities frowned on commercial advertising in amateur competition, even banning frame transfers, but distinctive frame profiles like Baines Flying Gate, Paris Galibier, Thanet Silverlight, Bates BAR and Hetchins curly stays ensured identification by the cognoscenti, even from the black and white photographs in *Cycling*. Gimmicks, such as vibrant triangles, diadrant forks and cantiflex tubing, helped to sell bikes, although

A Curly Hetchins Classic lightweight frame, 1947.

the speed advantages were slight and now mainly excite only the collector. Perhaps the only lasting legacy from this period has been tighter frame angles, lower build and the smaller wheels used on competition machines today.

New frame materials have long been sought out for weight reduction. Premier made a feature of helical tubing in the 1890s using lighter gauge, higher tensile, carbon steel, spiral-rolled and brazed along the joint. In the twentieth century, Renold 531 and 753 steel alloy tubing triumphed over aluminium for lightweight high-end frames. Since its introduction in the 1980s, carbon fibre has become mainstream and today is standard for professional cycle racing and quality road bikes. Dedicated cyclists have always enjoyed their frames custom made, like bespoke suits or shirts, and, while the practice lives on, it is still in its infancy for moulded carbon fibre frames. Perhaps one day we will be able to design and print our own bicycle frames at home on the computer.

From early days, riders have sought out lighter machines in the expectation of gaining greater speed with less effort, and while professional racers have found some slight advantage here, much more important is the effect of hill-climbing and the drag from rolling friction and air resistance. Modern gearing systems enable the average rider to surmount most hills without walking, and tyre and gear-chain friction are small enough to be discounted. Only wind resistance remains to be overcome. The answer to this is drafting, which was discovered very early on. Riding close behind another rider, or riders, has always been a major strategy in massed start and track racing. Early champions like James Moore were frequently criticised in the press for trailing their opponents in order to reserve their powers for the last lap. Moore had studied horse-racing, where the practice was born, and cyclists on club runs build comradeship by riding in echelon against a cross-wind and taking turns at breaking the wind at the front. It remains one of the tactical joys of a day out.

19

MOUNTAIN BIKES

The sixteenth International Cycling History Conference in 2005 was held in Davis, California – cycling capital of the USA. At one memorable evening session in the Cantina del Carbo, eight pioneers of the Marin County mountain-bike craze – Joe Breeze, Gary Fisher, Charlie Kelly Jacquie Phelan, Tom Ritchey, Alan Bonds, Otis Guy and John Finley Scott – talked to the assembled notetaking historians on the birth of dirt in 1970. Perhaps unsurprisingly, there was little agreement as to who first did what and when. If

Joe Breeze's Breezer from 1976, the prototype for an idea that swept the world.

you could remember the 1970s in San Francisco you weren't there. Ten-speed racers had begun to be imported and Americans had at last discovered that in Europe adults rode bicycles, not just children.

The bikers at first raced down trails on Mount Tamalpais on modified forty-year-old Schwinn clunkers with frames made for balloon tyres, but then they soon began designing their own customised frames. Limited batch production followed and the MTB craze spread around the world.

The UK's Rough Stuff Fellowship had been founded in 1955, so off-road cycling was not new, but 1970s California was its time and place and the influence on bicycle design and usage is still being felt today. MTBs have developed specialised hardware and the town bike hybrid, while paying tribute to its origins, has spawned a myriad of different models. The most lasting benefit is that, instead of having to inelegantly ride drop-handlebar pseudo racers, tyros can now safely ride comfortable roadsters in an upright position with straight handlebars.

20

THE FUTURE

'In proportion as history removes from first witnesses, it may also recede from truth, as in passing thro' the prejudices, or mistakes of subsequent compilers, it will be apt to imbibe what tincture they may chance to give it. The later Historian's only way, therefore, to prevent the ill effects of that decrease of evidence which the lapse of years necessarily brings with it, must be, by punctually referring to the springhead from whence the stream of his narration flows; which at once will cut off all appearance of partiality, or misrepresentation. As in law, the rectitude of a person's character is not alone sufficient to establish the truth of a fact, so in history, not merely the Writer's testimony, be our opinion of his veracity ever so great, but collateral evidence also is required, to determine every thing of questionable nature'. Monthly Review, 1757

The origins of the bicycle are less than 200 years old and little happened during the first fifty, yet the story is replete with myth, fiction and downright falsehoods. Late nineteenth-century distortions often carried a chauvinistic taint, although lack of documents and the misreading of foreign texts were equally responsible for egregious error. The internet now enables bike shop hucksters and bike-mad students to produce lengthy and attractively illustrated histories. Unfortunately, being compiled from secondary sources, they also frequently recycle many of the falsehoods that have been debunked at the International Cycle History Conferences since 1990, giving them new legs. I make no apology in restating work that has been done in demolishing these myths and hope that those interested in the bicycle might themselves be encouraged to enquire into the genuine questions where consensus has not yet been reached.

The hot spots of invention and manufacture have moved around the world, depending the accidents of war and the costs of production. Bicycle history, in its turn, has also been influenced by the nationality of the historian and even today writers have difficulty disentangling the machine's history from their own life experience. Such is the thrall of the machine. From Germany in 1817 to France in the 1860s, then Britain in the 1870s joined by America in the 1880s and 1890s. Japan became important between the two world wars and Taiwan, India and China in more recent years. Many, many countries have made their contribution to the bicycle's present success.

We have identified here the earliest pneumatic safety as dating from 1891 and certainly some from that year perform not unlike a fixed-wheel bicycle of today. The ordinary of 1880 was certainly considered a perfected bicycle by its many devotees although the riding technique, particularly mounting and dismounting, are different from those of the safety. The boneshaker had a similarly enthusiastic following but most cyclists today would rate the riding position as uncomfortable and its propulsion laborious. We have also noted that without the wire wheel it would have been the end of the line. The hobby-horse was similarly lauded across the world, but, although today it makes for a fun carnival attraction, few owners, even of cheaper reproductions, would use them for daily recreation or popping down to the shops.

Karl von Drais was rightly proud of riding 10 miles in one hour on his newly invented velocipede, and children on balance bikes experience the same joy today when, without trying, they somehow acquire the counterintuitive knack of steering into the fall rather than away from it. Every child remembers their first bicycle with affection. It is an attachment coming from sharing adventures with it, admiring its finer details and attending to its simple needs. The most unromantic of cycle tourists have invariably given sentimental names to their trusty mounts.

Bicycle makers understand this bond and mechanical efficiency has from day one been embellished with artistic style and flourish. For 200 years, a handsome profile, slender stays, stylish accoutrements and an elegant paint job have all been designed to capture the cyclist's heart. That is why the youth of today can still spend hours looking at bike shop displays.

As we have noted, the geometrical layout of the bicycle was effectively resolved by 1890 and tomorrow's machines will surely continue to have a similar arrangement. It is a perfected artefact that does not require radical change, excepting perhaps the wider adoption of battery-powered assistance, particularly for those who do not actively seek too much exercise or who perhaps may have reached a stage where assistance is a necessity.

Today's cyclist needs only to select the machine that fits his or her size, aesthetic tastes, pocket book and cycling objectives but, if it is not in the shiny new bike shop, it may well be found in the past. The vast cyclorama from two centuries is still around to choose from. A penny-farthing from 1880, a scorcher from the 1890s, perhaps a turn of the century Dursley Pederson or classic lightweight from the nineteen fifties – none of these will need to cost more than one of today's top brands. They were built to last and there are enough of them for all. Bicycling has never been more popular and it clearly has a secure future. Fashion and cycle racing has led design from the beginning and the bicycle has come into its own as the ideal vehicle for saving the planet and helping to combat global warming. 120 million bicycles are today made annually, twice the number of cars, and the buyers, more than ever, are keen to get out riding them rather than just hanging them up in the garage.

When looking back, there can be no question. In 1817, Charles Frederic Christian Louis Baron Drais von Sauerbronn undoubtedly started something big.

FURTHER READING

Bartleet, H. W., *Bartleet's Bicycle Book* (1932, reprinted 1983).
Berto, Shepherd and Henry, *The Dancing Chain* (2005).
Dodds, Alastair, *Scottish Bicycles and Tricycles* (1999).
Griffin, Brian, *Cycling in Victorian Ireland* (2006).
Hadland, Tony and Hans-Erhard Lessing, *Bicycle Design* (2014).
Herlihy, David, *Bicycle, the History* (2004).
Hillier, G. Lacy & Viscount Bury, *Cycling* (1887).
Norcliffe, Glen, *The Ride to Modernity* (2001).
Reid, Carlton, *Roads Were Not Built for Cars* (2014).
Ritchie, Andrew, *King of the Road* (1975).
Street, Roger, *The Pedestrian Hobby-Horse* (1998).
Wilson, David Gordon, *Bicycling Science* (2004).
Guroff, Margaret, *The Mechanical Horse* (2016).

WHERE TO SEE BICYCLES

National Cycle Museum, Llandindrod Wells.
Coventry Museum of Road Transport.
Brooklands Museum.
Velorama, Nijmegen, Netherlands.
Musee du Velo, Domazan, France.
Musee d'Art et d'Industrie, Saint-Étienne, France.

The format of this book does not allow for detailed notes but where possible the author will supply sources and welcomes any corrections via email at claytonnicholas@hotmail.com.